Final Report on City Services for Fiscal Year 2020-2021

PERFORMANCE AND COST DATA

MARCH 2022

COSPONSORED BY:

THE CITIES OF APEX, CHAPEL HILL, CHARLOTTE, CONCORD, GOLDSBORO, GREENSBORO, GREENVILLE, HICKORY, RALEIGH, WILSON, AND WINSTON-SALEM

SCHOOL OF GOVERNMENT

NORTH CAROLINA LOCAL GOVERNMENT BUDGET ASSOCIATION

The School of Government at the University of North Carolina at Chapel Hill works to improve the lives of North Carolinians by engaging in practical scholarship that helps public officials and citizens understand and improve state and local government. Established in 1931 as the Institute of Government, the School provides educational, advisory, and research services for state and local governments. The School of Government is also home to a nationally ranked Master of Public Administration program, the North Carolina Judicial College, and specialized centers focused on community and economic development, information technology, and environmental finance.

As the largest university-based local government training, advisory, and research organization in the United States, the School of Government offers up to 200 courses, webinars, and specialized conferences for more than 12,000 public officials each year. In addition, faculty members annually publish approximately 50 books, manuals, reports, articles, bulletins, and other print and online content related to state and local government. The School also produces the *Daily Bulletin Online* each day the General Assembly is in session, reporting on activities for members of the legislature and others who need to follow the course of legislation.

Operating support for the School of Government's programs and activities comes from many sources, including state appropriations, local government membership dues, private contributions, publication sales, course fees, and service contracts.

Visit sog.unc.edu or call 919.966.5381 for more information on the School's courses, publications, programs, and services.

Michael R. Smith, DEAN
Aimee N. Wall, SENIOR ASSOCIATE DEAN
Maurice A. Ferrell, ASSOCIATE DEAN FOR INFORMATION MANAGEMENT
Lauren G. Partin, ASSOCIATE DEAN FOR FINANCE AND OPERATIONS
Jennifer Willis, ASSOCIATE DEAN FOR DEVELOPMENT

FACULTY

Whitney Afonso
Trey Allen (on leave)
Gregory S. Allison
Lydian Altman
David N. Ammons
Maureen Berner
Frayda S. Bluestein
Kirk Boone
Mark F. Botts
Anita R. Brown-Graham
Peg Carlson
Connor Crews
Leisha DeHart-Davis
Shea Riggsbee Denning
Sara DePasquale
Kimalee Cottrell Dickerson
Jacquelyn Greene
Margaret F. Henderson

Norma Houston (on leave)
Cheryl Daniels Howell
Willow S. Jacobson
James L. Joyce
Robert P. Joyce
Diane M. Juffras
Dona G. Lewandowski
Adam Lovelady
James M. Markham
Christopher B. McLaughlin
Kara A. Millonzi
Jill D. Moore
Jonathan Q. Morgan
Ricardo S. Morse
C. Tyler Mulligan
Kimberly L. Nelson
Kristi A. Nickodem
David W. Owens

Obed Pasha
William C. Rivenbark
Dale J. Roenigk
John Rubin
Jessica Smith
Meredith Smith
Carl W. Stenberg III
John B. Stephens
Charles Szypszak
Thomas H. Thornburg
Shannon H. Tufts
Emily Turner
Jeffrey B. Welty
Richard B. Whisnant
Brittany L. Williams
Teshanee T. Williams
Kristina M. Wilson

© 2022
School of Government
CB# 3330 Knapp Building,
The University of North Carolina at Chapel Hill,
Chapel Hill, NC 27599-3330

Preparation and printing of this report were made possible
by funding from the participating cities.

This report is published by the School of Government.
Public agencies and officials may photocopy portions of the report,
if it is copied solely for distribution within a public agency or to officials or
employees thereof and if copies are not sold or used for commercial purposes.

Printed in the United States of America

26 25 24 23 22   1 2 3 4 5

ISBN 978-1-64238-050-7

CONTENTS

PREFACE

North Carolina municipalities are continually looking for ways to improve the efficiency and effectiveness of service delivery. As part of this effort, a group of municipalities joined together with the School of Government at the University of North Carolina at Chapel Hill and the North Carolina Local Government Budget Association to create an ongoing project to compare performance and cost data for selected governmental services. This joint undertaking is known as the North Carolina Local Government Performance Measurement Project or, more commonly, the North Carolina Benchmarking Project. This report presents performance and cost data for the fiscal year ending June 30, 2021, for the eleven North Carolina municipalities participating in the benchmarking project: Apex, Chapel Hill, Charlotte, Concord, Goldsboro, Greensboro, Greenville, Hickory, Raleigh, Wilson, and Winston-Salem. Twenty-five previous reports regarding municipal services have been published.

The benchmarking project is a collaborative effort. Officials from the participating local governments, including budget and finance staff, program and service staff, and city and town managers, have made vital contributions to the success of the project. Special thanks are owed to the members of the steering committee, who provide the necessary leadership demanded by such a project: Amanda Grogan, Budget and Performance Manager, and Paul Broussard, Systems and Performance Analyst of Apex; Brian Murphy, Budget and Management Analyst of Chapel Hill; Jordan Paschal, Budget Analyst of Charlotte; Lesley Reder, Budget and Performance Manager, Amanda Newton, Senior Budget Analyst, and Brandon Edwards, Senior Budget Analysis of Concord; Octavius Murphy, Assistant to the City Manager of Goldsboro; Tracy Nash, Budget Analyst of Greensboro; Johnathan Rosales, Budget Analyst of Hickory; Toy Beeninga, Budget Analyst and Greg Reger, Budget Analyst of Raleigh; Teresa Holland, Budget Analyst of Wilson; and Scott Tesh, Budget and Performance Management Director of Winston-Salem.

The Benchmarking Project receives contributions from other individuals who strongly support benchmarking and performance measurement. William C. Rivenbark and David N. Ammons, faculty members of the School of Government, serve as project advisors. Special thanks go to Michael R. Smith, Dean of the School of Government, and Aimee Wall, Senior Associate Dean of the School of Government, for their leadership and support of the Benchmarking Project. The author wishes to acknowledge other School of Government staff who have contributed many hours to the Benchmarking Project, including Kevin Justice and Hana Haidar in Publications.

Dale J. Roenigk
March 2022

SCHOOL OF GOVERNMENT
North Carolina Benchmarking Project

Performance and Cost Data

INTRODUCTION

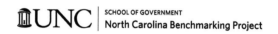

INTRODUCTION

Can local governments measure their performance and cost in a meaningful way? Can performance measures in one local government be legitimately compared to the those of another? In the fall of 1995, fourteen large municipalities and counties in North Carolina agreed to participate in a collaborative project to answer these and other questions relating to benchmarking. Seven of the jurisdictions were municipalities, forming Phase I of what is now known as the North Carolina Local Government Performance Measurement Project or, more commonly, the North Carolina Benchmarking Project. The other seven jurisdictions were counties, constituting Phase II of the Benchmarking Project. A third phase of the Benchmarking Project began in January 1997, consisting of fourteen municipal and county, small- and medium-sized North Carolina jurisdictions. These phases represented the pilot stage of the Benchmarking Project.

Since the beginning, the Benchmarking Project has proceeded with an ongoing agreement to collect, clean, and report comparative performance and cost data from the participating municipalities. Listed below are the eleven municipalities that participated in the Benchmarking Project and whose data for fiscal year 2020-2021 appear in this report:

- Apex
- Chapel Hill
- Charlotte
- Concord
- Goldsboro
- Greensboro
- Greenville
- Hickory
- Raleigh
- Wilson
- Winston-Salem

This project was the result of a joint undertaking of the participating municipalities, the School of Government, and the North Carolina Local Government Budget Association. The North Carolina League of Municipalities and the Local Government Commission also contributed to the development of this project. The goals of the benchmarking project are:

1. to develop/expand the use of performance measurement in local government,
2. to produce reliable performance and cost data for comparison, and
3. to facilitate the use of performance and cost data for service improvement.

SERVICES

This report presents performance and cost data and accompanying explanatory information for the following service areas:

- Residential Refuse Collection
- Household Recycling
- Yard Waste/Leaf Collection
- Police Services
- Emergency Communications
- Asphalt Maintenance and Repair
- Fire Services
- Building Inspections
- Fleet Maintenance
- Central Human Resources
- Water Services
- Wastewater Services
- Core Parks and Recreation

The participating units did not agree to continue the Benchmarking Project to endure the challenges of data collection and data cleaning simply to produce a report. They continue with the belief that performance measurement and benchmarking are catalysts for service improvement. No jurisdiction can be the best in every service that it provides, highlighting the notion that even outstanding performers can learn from the practices of others. Performance measurement and benchmarking are about tracking performance and cost data and making changes based on both internal and external comparisons over time.

This report is the twenty-sixth publication representing municipal services. The previous twenty-five reports and their publication dates are listed below.

- *Performance and Cost Data: Phase I City Services* (October 1997)
- *Performance and Cost Data: Phase III City Services* (March 1999)
- *Final Report on City Services for Fiscal Year 1997–98* (March 1999)
- *Final Report on City Services for Fiscal Year 1998–99* (February 2000)
- *Final Report on City Services for Fiscal Year 1999–2000* (February 2001)
- *Final Report on City Services for Fiscal Year 2000–2001* (February 2002)
- *Final Report on City Services for Fiscal Year 2001–2002* (February 2003)
- *Final Report on City Services for Fiscal Year 2002–2003* (February 2004)
- *Final Report on City Services for Fiscal Year 2003–2004* (February 2005)
- *Final Report on City Services for Fiscal Year 2004–2005* (February 2006)
- *Final Report on City Services for Fiscal Year 2005–2006* (February 2007)
- *Final Report on City Services for Fiscal Year 2006–2007* (February 2008)
- *Final Report on City Services for Fiscal Year 2007–2008* (February 2009)
- *Final Report on City Services for Fiscal Year 2008–2009* (February 2010)
- *Final Report on City Services for Fiscal Year 2009–2010* (February 2011)
- *Final Report on City Services for Fiscal Year 2010–2011* (February 2012)
- *Final Report on City Services for Fiscal Year 2011–2012* (February 2013)

- *Final Report on City Services for Fiscal Year 2012–2013* (February 2014)
- *Final Report on City Services for Fiscal Year 2013–2014* (February 2015)
- *Final Report on City Services for Fiscal Year 2014–2015* (February 2016)
- *Final Report on City Services for Fiscal Year 2015–2016* (May 2017)
- *Final Report on City Services for Fiscal Year 2016–2017* (May 2018)
- *Final Report on City Services for Fiscal Year 2017–2018* (April 2019)
- *Final Report on City Services for Fiscal Year 2018–2019* (June 2020)
- *Final Report on City Services for Fiscal Year 2019–2020* (August 2021)

REPORTING FORMAT

This is primarily a data report. It incorporates graphs, summary tables, and explanatory information to present the performance and cost results for each service area under study. The results of each service area by municipality are displayed in a standard, two-page format. The following information is contained in this report:

1. **Explanatory Information.** This segment of the report describes how the service is provided and identifies the conditions or dimensions that affect the performance and cost data of service delivery.
2. **Municipal Profile.** This section includes a limited number of characteristics of each municipality, such as population density which may affect service performance and cost. Some of the general characteristics, such as population, appear in the municipal profiles for all of the service areas. Others, such as weather and estimated tax base in the service area, appear only in selected profiles.
3. **Service Profile.** This area provides input and output data and identifies important dimensions of service delivery.
4. **Full Cost Profile.** A cost accounting model is used to calculate the full or total cost of providing each service area under study. Although the cost data were collected in detail, using a collection instrument with more than seventy specific line items, the reporting format aggregates the detailed cost data into three general categories for the purpose of presentation: personal services for the direct expenses of salaries, wages, and related fringe benefits; operating costs which include direct operating expenses and indirect cost allocations; and capital costs which represent depreciation of equipment and facilities.
5. **Resource Measures.** These measures gauge the amount of resources or inputs municipalities allocate for the provision of a given service.
6. **Performance Measures.** Three types of performance measures are used and reported: workload, efficiency, and effectiveness. A municipality's performance is compared to the performance average, noting that the average is based on services with numerous variations and should be viewed with caution. The measures used in this report do not assess total service performance. They gauge certain service dimensions and should be approached with an understanding of the service being provided.

SUMMARY OF OVERALL RESULTS

What the project has achieved

1. The project's methodology, consisting of service profiles, performance measures, cost accounting, and an explanation of results, works extremely well for data consistency and comparability. The project's accounting model is especially effective in producing reliable and materially accurate cost data.
2. The performance data have been used in numerous jurisdictions for service improvement, especially in the areas of residential refuse collection, household recycling, police services, and fleet maintenance.
3. The project's success directly correlates with consensus among numerous local government officials from the participating municipalities regarding service definitions and measurement formulas.

What we have learned

1. Local governments can produce accurate, reliable, and comparable performance and cost data, which can then be used for service improvement.
2. Highly specific service definitions are vital to accurate performance measurement.
3. Data availability and quality are very important for performance measurement.
4. Performance measurement and cost accounting are time consuming. However, performance measures provide valuable feedback when the goal is to deliver quality services at a reasonable cost.

READING THE REPORT

This report presents the performance and cost data for the eleven North Carolina municipalities participating in the Benchmarking Project for the fiscal year ending June 30, 2021. It also presents multiyear data for participants based on the number of fiscal years each municipality has participated in the Benchmarking Project.

The municipal profile, full cost profile, service profile, and explanatory information for each municipality are based solely on performance and cost data for the fiscal year ending June 30, 2021. Readers should be extremely careful when interpreting the performance and cost data of municipalities with multi-year data. Changes may have occurred in operations or program offerings. Municipal profiles, full cost profiles, service profiles, and explanatory information that support performance measures for the fiscal years ending June 30, 2017, through June 30, 2020, are located in previous performance and cost data reports and can be obtained from the School of Government.

The Benchmarking Project considers new service areas and service changes on an annual basis under the guidance of the steering committee. Asphalt Maintenance and Repair represented a new service area for the fiscal year ending June 30, 2000. This service was previously reported as Street Pavement Maintenance. Police Services represented a new service area for the fiscal year ending June 30, 2001. This service was presented as Police Patrol and Police Investigations in prior reports. Fleet Maintenance represented a new service area for the fiscal year ending June 30,

2002. Central Human Resources represented a new service area for the fiscal year ending June 30, 2004. Water Services represented a new service area added in the fiscal year ending June 30, 2007. Wastewater Services was added in the fiscal year ending June 30, 2012. Finally, Core Parks and Recreation was added in the fiscal year ending June 30, 2013.

Municipalities do not participate in every service area for a variety of reasons. Certain municipalities do not participate in Emergency Communications and Building Inspections because those services are county functions. In some cases, a municipality may not participate due to organizational structures or other issues. The following table provides the jurisdictions participating in each service area contained in this report.

Service Area	Jurisdictions
Residential Refuse Collection	Apex, Chapel Hill, Charlotte, Concord, Goldsboro, Greensboro, Greenville, Hickory, Raleigh, Wilson, and Winston-Salem
Household Recycling	Apex, Charlotte, Concord, Goldsboro, Greensboro, Greenville, Hickory, Raleigh, Wilson, and Winston-Salem
Yard Waste/Leaf Collection	Apex, Chapel Hill, Charlotte, Concord, Goldsboro, Greensboro, Greenville, Hickory, Raleigh, Wilson, and Winston-Salem
Police Services	Apex, Chapel Hill, Concord, Goldsboro, Greensboro, Greenville, Hickory, Raleigh, Wilson, and Winston-Salem
Emergency Communications	Apex, Concord, Greensboro, Greenville, Hickory, Raleigh, and Winston-Salem
Asphalt Maintenance and Repair	Apex, Chapel Hill, Charlotte, Concord, Goldsboro, Greensboro, Greenville, Hickory, Raleigh, Wilson, and Winston-Salem
Fire Services	Apex, Chapel Hill, Charlotte, Concord, Goldsboro, Greensboro, Greenville, Hickory, Raleigh, Wilson, and Winston-Salem
Building Inspections	Apex, Chapel Hill, Goldsboro, Greensboro, Greenville, Raleigh, Wilson, and Winston-Salem
Fleet Maintenance	Apex, Chapel Hill, Concord, Goldsboro, Greensboro, Greenville, Hickory, Raleigh, Wilson, and Winston-Salem
Central Human Resources	Apex, Chapel Hill, Concord, Goldsboro, Greensboro, Greenville, Hickory, Raleigh, Wilson, and Winston-Salem
Water Services	Apex, Charlotte, Concord, Goldsboro, Greensboro, Hickory, Raleigh, Wilson, and Winston-Salem
Wastewater Services	Apex, Charlotte, Concord, Goldsboro, Greensboro, Hickory, Raleigh, Wilson, and Winston-Salem
Core Parks and Recreation	Apex, Chapel Hill, Concord, Goldsboro, Greensboro, Greenville, Hickory, Raleigh, Wilson, and Winston-Salem

It also should be noted that not all municipalities submit performance and cost data for each performance measure contained within the respective service area. Therefore, data are missing for selected performance measures regardless of service participation.

Performance and Cost Data

RESIDENTIAL REFUSE COLLECTION

PERFORMANCE MEASURES FOR RESIDENTIAL REFUSE COLLECTION

SERVICE DEFINITION

Residential refuse collection is regularly scheduled collection of household refuse or "garbage" from residential premises and other locations, including small businesses, using containers small enough that residents and/or workers can move or lift them manually. The service excludes collection of waste from dumpsters; regular or special collection of yard waste and leaves; collection of recyclable materials, white goods, or other bulky items; and any special or nonroutine service provided to residences. Transportation of refuse to a landfill or a transfer station is included, but the disposal of refuse and tipping costs is excluded.

NOTES ON PERFORMANCE MEASURES

1. Tons of (Residential) Refuse Collected per 1,000 Population and per 1,000 (Residential) Collection Points

"Tons of refuse collected" is widely used as a measure of workload for this service. A collection, or pickup, point is a single locale (active address) from which residential refuse is collected. It can be a single-family residence, a condominium, an apartment, or a small business that uses containers that residents or sanitation workers can move or lift. Pickup points directly generate collection work, so this measure provides a good assessment of workload. "Tons of refuse collected per 1,000 population" and "per 1,000 collection points" also serve as measures of need for this service. Because of citizen expectations and public health requirements, sanitation crews or contractors must pick up all, or virtually all, household refuse that residents put out for collection.

2. Cost per Ton of Residential Refuse Collected and Cost per Residential Collection Point

These are the project's principal measures of efficiency for this service. Because of differences in the number of people per household and the percentage of the municipal population served by curbside collection, comparisons for these two efficiency measures can vary.

3. Full-Time Equivalent (FTE) Positions

The number of full-time equivalent (FTE) positions for residential refuse collection is the number of employees directly involved in providing the service as approved in the annual operating budget during the fiscal year. This number includes both full-time and part-time workers and both permanent and temporary workers. One FTE equates to 2,080 hours of work per year. Any combination of employees providing 2,080 hours of work annually equals one FTE. Cost data reflect all such workers. The measure "tons collected per collection FTE," however, includes only those workers who actually collect refuse and not supervisory or support personnel.

4. Number of Complaints and Number of Valid Complaints

All of the participating units take calls about residential refuse collection, and nearly all maintain records of one kind or another about such calls. However, the municipalities follow very different procedures in processing and recording these calls and in determining which ones are complaints and which are not. For these reasons, the project is able to present limited comparative data about complaints or valid complaints for residential refuse collection or other solid waste services. Nonetheless, the project recommends that the participating municipalities devise common criteria for identifying complaints and procedures for processing and recording calls.

Residential Refuse Collection

Summary of Key Dimensions of Service

City or Town	Collection Points	Tons Collected	Weekly Routes	Percentage Contracted Service	Crew Size (most commonly used)	City FTE Collection Positions	Main Equipment		Landfill/Transfer	
							Packers	Automated	Trips per Day	Distance
Apex	21,169	16,021	25	100%	Contracted	Contracted	Contracted	Contracted	2	5 miles
Chapel Hill	12,210	7,108	27	0%	1 & 3 person	12.71	7	0	1	18 miles
Charlotte	225,219	224,090	335	5%	1 & 2 person	81	7	60	1.3	23 miles
Concord	35,094	36,427	25	100%	Contracted	Contracted	Contractor - 2	Contractor - 6	1	8 miles
Goldsboro	14,372	12,435	16	0%	1 & 3 person	6	1	3	6	11 miles
Greensboro	88,020	72,216	106	0%	1 & 2 person	31	6	20	1.8	8 miles
Greenville	19,479	19,522	25	0%	1 & 2 person	7	1	5	2	5 miles
Hickory	12,200	11,049	15	0%	1 & 2 person	3.75	1	4	2	5 miles
Raleigh	125,321	100,490	112	0%	1 & 3 person	79	10	22	2	15 miles
Wilson	21,111	23,080	27	0%	1 & 3 person	11	2	5	2	10 miles
Winston-Salem	81,589	69,373	96	0%	1 & 3 person	65	11	13	1	12 miles

NOTES

All of the municipalities currently collect residential refuse once per week.
All of the municipalities have special provisions for collecting from the back or side yards of individuals with disabilities or mobility restrictions.

EXPLANATORY FACTORS

These are factors that the project found affected residential refuse collection performance and cost in one or more of the municipalities:

Backyard or curbside collection
Routing
Climate
Topographic conditions
Population density
Size of crews
Type of equipment used (automated)
Privatization
Participation in recycling program
Economies of scale
Distance to landfill/transfer station
Fee policies (volume-based or other)

Fiscal Year 2020-21

Explanatory Information

Service Level and Delivery

Apex contracts with Waste Industries for refuse collection, disposal, and recycling. Only the refuse collection is reflected on this page.

Residents pay $8.72 per month for collection. Refuse is collected once a week at curbside, although backyard collection is provided for disabled customers at no additional charge. Residents receiving service are provided with one ninety-six-gallon container. The service also includes a small number of businesses in the downtown area that use the standard carts but receive service twice a week.

The contractor collects five days a week from different routes. Trash is trucked to the landfill.

The contractor collected 16,021 tons of residential refuse during the fiscal year, at a cost of $75 per ton. The cost per ton does not include the disposal cost at the landfill.

Conditions Affecting Service, Performance, and Costs

Municipal Profile

Population (OSBM 2020)	59,368
Land Area (Square Miles)	23.61
Persons per Square Mile	2,514

Service Profile

FTE Positions—Collection	Contractor
FTE Positions—Other	Contractor
Type of Equipment	Contractor
Size of Crews (most commonly used)	Contractor
Weekly Routes	25
Average Distance to Disposal Site	5 miles
Average Daily Trips to Disposal Site	2
Percentage of Service Contracted	100%
Collection Frequency	1 x week
General Collection Location	Curbside
Residential Customers (number represents collection points)	21,169
Tons Collected	16,021
Monthly Service Fee	$8.72

Full Cost Profile

Cost Breakdown by Percentage

Personal Services	0.0%
Operating Costs	100.0%
Capital Costs	0.0%
TOTAL	100.0%

Cost Breakdown in Dollars

Personal Services	$0
Operating Costs	$1,206,222
Capital Costs	$0
TOTAL	$1,206,222

Apex

Residential Refuse Collection

Key: Apex ▨   Benchmarking Average —   Fiscal Years 2017 through 2021

Resource Measures

Residential Refuse Collection Costs per Capita

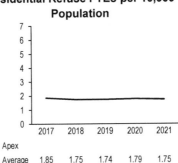

	2017	2018	2019	2020	2021
Apex	$23.64	$21.00	$20.88	$20.19	$20.32
Average	$24.29	$23.74	$24.24	$29.01	$27.66

Residential Refuse FTEs per 10,000 Population

	2017	2018	2019	2020	2021
Apex					
Average	1.85	1.75	1.74	1.79	1.75

Workload Measures

Residential Refuse Tons per 1,000 Population

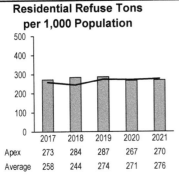

	2017	2018	2019	2020	2021
Apex	273	284	287	267	270
Average	258	244	274	271	276

Residential Refuse Tons per 1,000 Collection Points

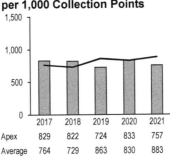

	2017	2018	2019	2020	2021
Apex	829	822	724	833	757
Average	764	729	863	830	883

Efficiency Measures

Residential Refuse Collection Cost per Ton Collected

	2017	2018	2019	2020	2021
Apex	$74	$74	$73	$76	$75
Average	$127	$117	$106	$121	$111

Residential Refuse Collection Cost per Collection Point

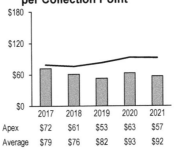

	2017	2018	2019	2020	2021
Apex	$72	$61	$53	$63	$57
Average	$79	$76	$82	$93	$92

Refuse Tons Collected per Municipal Collection FTE

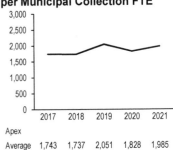

	2017	2018	2019	2020	2021
Apex					
Average	1,743	1,737	2,051	1,828	1,985

Effectiveness Measures

Complaints per 1,000 Collection Points

	2017	2018	2019	2020	2021
Apex	1.3	39.2		54.0	84.3
Average	28.7	34.0	39.1	38.4	44.4

Valid Complaints per 1,000 Collection Points

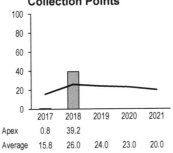

	2017	2018	2019	2020	2021
Apex	0.8	39.2			
Average	15.8	26.0	24.0	23.0	20.0

Fiscal Year 2020-21

Explanatory Information

Service Level and Delivery

Chapel Hill residential refuse collection is performed by the Solid Waste Services Division under the Public Works Department. The Town provides weekly household waste collection Mondays and Tuesdays with no fees charged.

Residential refuse is collected by seven 3-person crews using rear packers two days per week. The packer crews are staffed with three persons: one driver and two collectors. The trucks average one trip to the transfer station with the distance averaging eighteen miles one way. A lift gate truck is also used to collect bulky items and electronics for a fee five days per week. Two pickup trucks are also used to collect medical exemptions, pedestrian trash cans, and streets not accessible to rear packers, with one truck running seven days per week and the other running two days per week.

The town collected 7,108 tons of residential refuse during the fiscal year at a cost of $272 per ton, or $158 per collection point. The cost does not include the disposal cost at the transfer station for the tipping fee. Residents receive one roll-out cart at no charge but can purchase an additional cart for $60 per cart. Residents can also purchase their own trash cans, but these must be 32 gallons or smaller and weigh less than 60 pounds when full.

Conditions Affecting Service, Performance, and Costs

The out-of-town transfer station is the primary disposal location for Chapel Hill. Orange County had the highest waste reduction rate (64 percent) in North Carolina in FY 2014–15. The town provides special exemptions for backyard collections for 519 collection points, which represent 4.3 percent of the total collection points.

Municipal Profile

Population (OSBM 2020)	62,080
Land Area (Square Miles)	21.31
Persons per Square Mile	2,914

Service Profile

FTE Positions—Collection	12.7
FTE Positions—Other	1.1
Type of Equipment	7 packers
	1 Lift-Gate Truck and 2 Pickups
Size of Crews (most commonly used)	1 & 3 person
Weekly Routes	27
Average Distance to Disposal Site	18 miles
Average Daily Route Trips to Disposal Site	1
Percentage of Service Contracted	0%
Collection Frequency	1 x week
General Collection Location	Curbside
Residential Customers (number represents collection points)	12,210
Tons Collected	7,108
Monthly Service Fee	No

Full Cost Profile

Cost Breakdown by Percentage	
Personal Services	43.3%
Operating Costs	43.9%
Capital Costs	12.8%
TOTAL	100.0%

Cost Breakdown in Dollars	
Personal Services	$837,503
Operating Costs	$848,962
Capital Costs	$248,275
TOTAL	$1,934,740

Chapel Hill
Residential Refuse Collection

Key: Chapel Hill ▨   Benchmarking Average —   Fiscal Years 2017 through 2021

Resource Measures

Residential Refuse Collection Costs per Capita

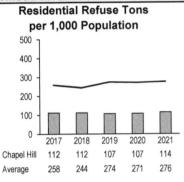

	2017	2018	2019	2020	2021
Chapel Hill	$35.94	$34.06	$33.05	$31.93	$31.17
Average	$24.29	$23.74	$24.24	$29.01	$27.66

Residential Refuse FTEs per 10,000 Population

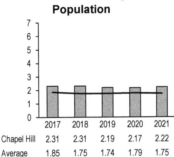

	2017	2018	2019	2020	2021
Chapel Hill	2.31	2.31	2.19	2.17	2.22
Average	1.85	1.75	1.74	1.79	1.75

Workload Measures

Residential Refuse Tons per 1,000 Population

	2017	2018	2019	2020	2021
Chapel Hill	112	112	107	107	114
Average	258	244	274	271	276

Residential Refuse Tons per 1,000 Collection Points

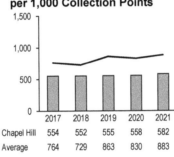

	2017	2018	2019	2020	2021
Chapel Hill	554	552	555	558	582
Average	764	729	863	830	883

Efficiency Measures

Residential Refuse Collection Cost per Ton Collected

	2017	2018	2019	2020	2021
Chapel Hill	$304	$304	$308	$298	$272
Average	$127	$117	$106	$121	$111

Residential Refuse Collection Cost per Collection Point

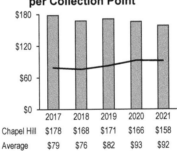

	2017	2018	2019	2020	2021
Chapel Hill	$178	$168	$171	$166	$158
Average	$79	$76	$82	$93	$92

Refuse Tons Collected per Municipal Collection FTE

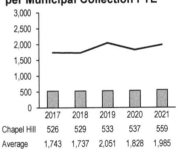

	2017	2018	2019	2020	2021
Chapel Hill	526	529	533	537	559
Average	1,743	1,737	2,051	1,828	1,985

Effectiveness Measures

Complaints per 1,000 Collection Points

	2017	2018	2019	2020	2021
Chapel Hill	17.1	11.7	12.1	11.3	12.8
Average	28.7	34.0	39.1	38.4	44.4

Valid Complaints per 1,000 Collection Points

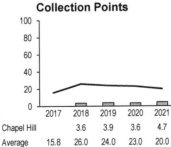

	2017	2018	2019	2020	2021
Chapel Hill		3.6	3.9	3.6	4.7
Average	15.8	26.0	24.0	23.0	20.0

Fiscal Year 2020-21

Explanatory Information

Service Level and Delivery

Charlotte collects residential refuse once a week at curbside. Backyard service is available only to those persons with valid medical reasons and physician certification. The city charges an annual fee of $67.66 for refuse services, which is paid on the property tax bill; the fee applies to both collection and disposal costs and is meant to be just a portion of cost recovery for services.

City crews are composed primarily of one driver, each operating an automated packer. There were sixty of these crews for FY 2020–21. In addition, three crews, each composed of one driver and one laborer, collected refuse using semi-automated packers. These crews are used primarily for backyard service for those citizens with disabilities and some multifamily complexes with less than thirty units. Small business garbage is collected by four crews, each composed of one driver and one laborer, using rear loaders. Costs include reserve crews that were used as needed throughout the year.

The city serviced 335 daily collection routes once each week during the fiscal year, with an average of 1.3 trips to the landfill per day per route at an average one-way distance of twenty-three miles. Each single-family residence is provided one ninety-six-gallon rollout container. An additional receptacle may be purchased for a nominal one-time fee. Charlotte collected 224,090 tons of residential refuse during the fiscal year, at a cost of $98 per ton. The cost per ton does not include the disposal cost representing the landfill tipping fee.

Conditions Affecting Service, Performance, and Costs

Charlotte is highly automated in the area of residential refuse collection. It considers all complaints to be valid complaints.

Municipal Profile

Population (OSBM 2020)	876,694
Land Area (Square Miles)	307.41
Persons per Square Mile	2,852

Service Profile

FTE Positions—Collection	81.0
FTE Positions—Other	7.0
Type of Equipment	60 automated packers
	7 packers
Size of Crews (most commonly used)	1 & 2 person
Weekly Routes	335
Average Distance to Disposal Site	23 miles
Average Daily Trips to Disposal Site	1.3
Percentage of Service Contracted	5%
Collection Frequency	1 x week
General Collection Location	Curbside
Residential Customers (number represents collection points)	225,219
Tons Collected	224,090
Annual Service Fee	$67.66

Full Cost Profile

Cost Breakdown by Percentage	
Personal Services	33.4%
Operating Costs	47.3%
Capital Costs	19.3%
TOTAL	100.0%

Cost Breakdown in Dollars	
Personal Services	$7,328,756
Operating Costs	$10,396,742
Capital Costs	$4,249,330
TOTAL	$21,974,828

Charlotte
Residential Refuse Collection

Key: Charlotte ▨   Benchmarking Average —   Fiscal Years 2017 through 2021

Resource Measures

Residential Refuse Collection Costs per Capita

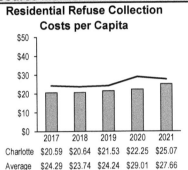

	2017	2018	2019	2020	2021
Charlotte	$20.59	$20.64	$21.53	$22.25	$25.07
Average	$24.29	$23.74	$24.24	$29.01	$27.66

Residential Refuse FTEs per 10,000 Population

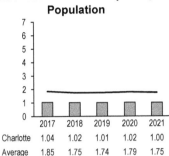

	2017	2018	2019	2020	2021
Charlotte	1.04	1.02	1.01	1.02	1.00
Average	1.85	1.75	1.74	1.79	1.75

Workload Measures

Residential Refuse Tons per 1,000 Population

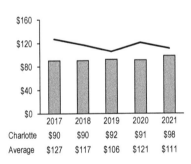

	2017	2018	2019	2020	2021
Charlotte	228	229	234	244	256
Average	258	244	274	271	276

Residential Refuse Tons per 1,000 Collection Points

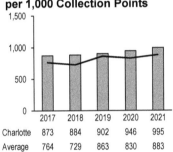

	2017	2018	2019	2020	2021
Charlotte	873	884	902	946	995
Average	764	729	863	830	883

Efficiency Measures

Residential Refuse Collection Cost per Ton Collected

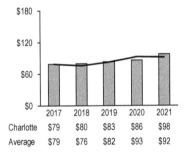

	2017	2018	2019	2020	2021
Charlotte	$90	$90	$92	$91	$98
Average	$127	$117	$106	$121	$111

Residential Refuse Collection Cost per Collection Point

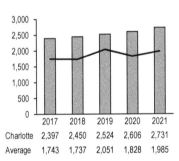

	2017	2018	2019	2020	2021
Charlotte	$79	$80	$83	$86	$98
Average	$79	$76	$82	$93	$92

Refuse Tons Collected per Municipal Collection FTE

	2017	2018	2019	2020	2021
Charlotte	2,397	2,450	2,524	2,606	2,731
Average	1,743	1,737	2,051	1,828	1,985

Effectiveness Measures

Complaints per 1,000 Collection Points

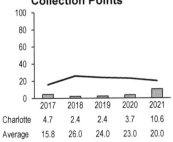

	2017	2018	2019	2020	2021
Charlotte	4.7	2.4	2.4	3.7	10.6
Average	28.7	34.0	39.1	38.4	44.4

Valid Complaints per 1,000 Collection Points

	2017	2018	2019	2020	2021
Charlotte	4.7	2.4	2.4	3.7	10.6
Average	15.8	26.0	24.0	23.0	20.0

Fiscal Year 2020-21

Service Level and Delivery

Residential refuse collection service is provided once a week at curbside to Concord residents. Backyard service is available for the elderly and disabled. The city has provided residential refuse collection service under contract for many years. The cost of the contract for the year was approximately $2.4 million.

The contractor primarily used seven automated packers, each with one person. Residents used one ninety-five-gallon cart, with extra carts available for larger families or unusual circumstances.

The contractor serviced twenty-five collection routes each week, with an average distance per route per day to the landfill of eight miles. The packers made an average of one trip to the landfill per day per route. The contractor collected 36,427 tons of residential refuse during the fiscal year, at a cost of $83 per ton.

Conditions Affecting Service, Performance, and Costs

Concord is one of only two jurisdictions participating in the benchmarking project that contracts 100 percent of its residential refuse collection service. Therefore, "tons collected per collection FTE" is not used for Concord as a performance measure, as this reflects only municipal workers.

Concord's "total tons collected" includes bulk trash, which is collected along with residential refuse and cannot be separated for reporting purposes.

Concord defines valid complaints to mean any missed collection or request for service as determined by the city to result from contractor negligence or omission.

Municipal Profile

Population (OSBM 2020)	105,936
Land Area (Square Miles)	63.65
Persons per Square Mile	1,664

Service Profile

FTE Positions—Collection	0.6 City
FTE Positions—Other	4.65 City
Type of Equipment	7 automated packers
	2 packers
Size of Crews (most commonly used)	Contractor
Weekly Routes	25
Average Distance to Disposal Site	8 miles
Average Daily Trips to Disposal Site	1
Percentage of Service Contracted	100%
Collection Frequency	1 x week
General Collection Location	Curbside
Residential Customers (number represents collection points)	35,094
Tons Collected	36,427
Monthly Service Fee	$2.24

Full Cost Profile

Cost Breakdown by Percentage	
Personal Services	5.9%
Operating Costs	93.4%
Capital Costs	0.7%
TOTAL	100.0%

Cost Breakdown in Dollars	
Personal Services	$178,982
Operating Costs	$2,837,244
Capital Costs	$21,353
TOTAL	$3,037,579

Concord

Residential Refuse Collection

Resource Measures

Residential Refuse Collection Costs per Capita

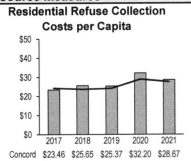

	2017	2018	2019	2020	2021
Concord	$23.46	$25.65	$25.37	$32.20	$28.67
Average	$24.29	$23.74	$24.24	$29.01	$27.66

Residential Refuse FTEs per 10,000 Population

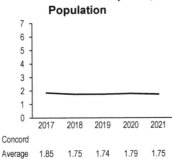

	2017	2018	2019	2020	2021
Concord					
Average	1.85	1.75	1.74	1.79	1.75

Workload Measures

Residential Refuse Tons per 1,000 Population

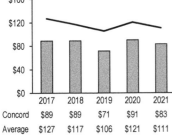

	2017	2018	2019	2020	2021
Concord	275	287	356	356	344
Average	258	244	274	271	276

Residential Refuse Tons per 1,000 Collection Points

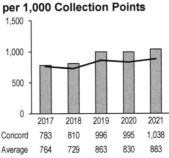

	2017	2018	2019	2020	2021
Concord	783	810	996	995	1,038
Average	764	729	863	830	883

Efficiency Measures

Residential Refuse Collection Cost per Ton Collected

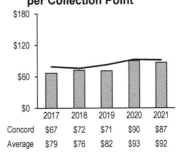

	2017	2018	2019	2020	2021
Concord	$89	$89	$71	$91	$83
Average	$127	$117	$106	$121	$111

Residential Refuse Collection Cost per Collection Point

	2017	2018	2019	2020	2021
Concord	$67	$72	$71	$90	$87
Average	$79	$76	$82	$93	$92

Refuse Tons Collected per Municipal Collection FTE

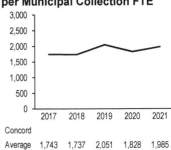

	2017	2018	2019	2020	2021
Concord					
Average	1,743	1,737	2,051	1,828	1,985

Effectiveness Measures

Complaints per 1,000 Collection Points

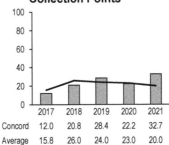

	2017	2018	2019	2020	2021
Concord	40.5	54.9	92.8	64.7	93.1
Average	28.7	34.0	39.1	38.4	44.4

Valid Complaints per 1,000 Collection Points

	2017	2018	2019	2020	2021
Concord	12.0	20.8	28.4	22.2	32.7
Average	15.8	26.0	24.0	23.0	20.0

Explanatory Information

Service Level and Delivery

Goldsboro provides residential refuse collection once a week at curbside for residents. Collection is done by the Solid Waste Division of the Public Works Department. Backyard collection is available for the disabled. Currently the city charges a monthly fee of $22, which includes refuse, recycling, and leaf and limb pickup.

There are three automated trucks with a single driver and one crew with a driver and two collectors using a rear loader. Collection trucks run four days per week. Crews drive eleven miles to a transfer station.

The city collected 12,435 tons of residential refuse during the fiscal year from 14,372 collection points at a cost of $140 per ton. The collection costs do not include a disposal cost at the transfer station.

Conditions Affecting Service, Performance, and Costs

The City of Goldsboro joined the Benchmarking Project in July 2017, with the first year of data showing for FY 2016–17.

Goldsboro contracts refuse collection for one small neighborhood where a hill and tight roads make it infeasible to use city trucks.

Municipal Profile

Population (OSBM 2020)	34,156
Land Area (Square Miles)	29.45
Persons per Square Mile	1,160

Service Profile

FTE Positions—Collection	6.0
FTE Positions—Other	1.2
Type of Equipment	3 automated packers
	1 packer
Size of Crews (most commonly used)	1 & 3 person
Weekly Routes	16
Average Distance to Disposal Site	11 miles
Average Daily Trips to Disposal Site	6
Percentage of Service Contracted	0.1%
Collection Frequency	1 x week
General Collection Location	Curbside
Residential Customers (number represents collection points)	14,372
Tons Collected	12,435
Monthly Service Fee	$22

Full Cost Profile

Cost Breakdown by Percentage

Personal Services	61.2%
Operating Costs	38.8%
Capital Costs	0.0%
TOTAL	100.0%

Cost Breakdown in Dollars

Personal Services	$1,066,292
Operating Costs	$675,079
Capital Costs	$0
TOTAL	$1,741,371

Goldsboro

Residential Refuse Collection

Resource Measures

Residential Refuse Collection Costs per Capita

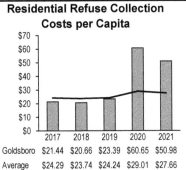

	2017	2018	2019	2020	2021
Goldsboro	$21.44	$20.66	$23.39	$60.65	$50.98
Average	$24.29	$23.74	$24.24	$29.01	$27.66

Residential Refuse FTEs per 10,000 Population

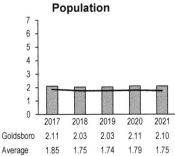

	2017	2018	2019	2020	2021
Goldsboro	2.11	2.03	2.03	2.11	2.10
Average	1.85	1.75	1.74	1.79	1.75

Workload Measures

Residential Refuse Tons per 1,000 Population

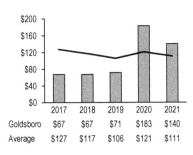

	2017	2018	2019	2020	2021
Goldsboro	323	307	328	332	364
Average	258	244	274	271	276

Residential Refuse Tons per 1,000 Collection Points

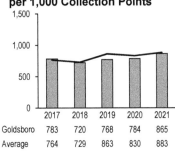

	2017	2018	2019	2020	2021
Goldsboro	783	720	768	784	865
Average	764	729	863	830	883

Efficiency Measures

Residential Refuse Collection Cost per Ton Collected

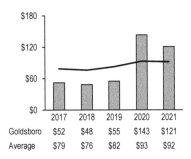

	2017	2018	2019	2020	2021
Goldsboro	$67	$67	$71	$183	$140
Average	$127	$117	$106	$121	$111

Residential Refuse Collection Cost per Collection Point

	2017	2018	2019	2020	2021
Goldsboro	$52	$48	$55	$143	$121
Average	$79	$76	$82	$93	$92

Refuse Tons Collected per Municipal Collection FTE

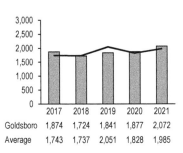

	2017	2018	2019	2020	2021
Goldsboro	1,874	1,724	1,841	1,877	2,072
Average	1,743	1,737	2,051	1,828	1,985

Effectiveness Measures

Complaints per 1,000 Collection Points

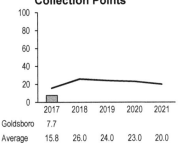

	2017	2018	2019	2020	2021
Goldsboro	81.0				
Average	28.7	34.0	39.1	38.4	44.4

Valid Complaints per 1,000 Collection Points

	2017	2018	2019	2020	2021
Goldsboro	7.7				
Average	15.8	26.0	24.0	23.0	20.0

Explanatory Information

Service Level and Delivery

Greensboro provides once-a-week collection of residential refuse at curbside. Each resident is provided up to two ninety-gallon carts. Currently there is no fee for residential collection of refuse.

There were twenty-three city crews for the fiscal year. Eighteen crews each have one driver operating an automated packer. Five crews use rear loaders.

The city used sixty-eight collection routes during the fiscal year, with each packer making an average of 1.8 trips per day to a municipal solid waste transfer station and the travel distance averaging eight miles.

The city collected 72,216 tons of residential refuse during the fiscal year at a cost of $66 per ton.

Greensboro defines automated packers as one-armed automated-loading packers that are operated by one person. Rear loaders are rear-loading packer trucks.

Conditions Affecting Service, Performance, and Costs

Greensboro is highly automated in the area of residential refuse collection.

Municipal Profile

Population (OSBM 2020)	299,556
Land Area (Square Miles)	129.62
Persons per Square Mile	2,311

Service Profile

FTE Positions—Collection	31.0
FTE Positions—Other	6.0
Type of Equipment	20 automated packers
	6 packers
Size of Crews (most commonly used)	1 & 2 person
Weekly Routes	106
Average Distance to Disposal Site	8.0
Average Daily Trips to Disposal Site	1.8
Percentage of Service Contracted	0.0%
Collection Frequency	1 x week
General Collection Location	Curbside
Residential Customers (number represents collection points)	88020
Tons Collected	72,216
Monthly Service Fee	$2.50

Full Cost Profile

Cost Breakdown by Percentage	
Personal Services	38.7%
Operating Costs	61.3%
Capital Costs	0.0%
TOTAL	100.0%

Cost Breakdown in Dollars	
Personal Services	$1,846,060
Operating Costs	$2,924,933
Capital Costs	$0
TOTAL	$4,770,993

Greensboro   **Residential Refuse Collection**

Resource Measures

Residential Refuse Collection Costs per Capita

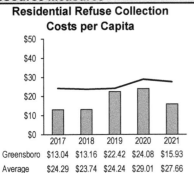

	2017	2018	2019	2020	2021
Greensboro	$13.04	$13.16	$22.42	$24.08	$15.93
Average	$24.29	$23.74	$24.24	$29.01	$27.66

Residential Refuse FTEs per 10,000 Population

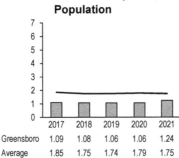

	2017	2018	2019	2020	2021
Greensboro	1.09	1.08	1.06	1.06	1.24
Average	1.85	1.75	1.74	1.79	1.75

Workload Measures

Residential Refuse Tons per 1,000 Population

	2017	2018	2019	2020	2021
Greensboro	203	206	210	230	241
Average	258	244	274	271	276

Residential Refuse Tons per 1,000 Collection Points

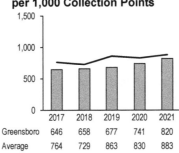

	2017	2018	2019	2020	2021
Greensboro	646	658	677	741	820
Average	764	729	863	830	883

Efficiency Measures

Residential Refuse Collection Cost per Ton Collected

	2017	2018	2019	2020	2021
Greensboro	$64	$64	$107	$105	$66
Average	$127	$117	$106	$121	$111

Residential Refuse Collection Cost per Collection Point

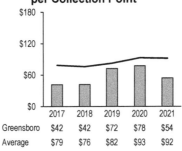

	2017	2018	2019	2020	2021
Greensboro	$42	$42	$72	$78	$54
Average	$79	$76	$82	$93	$92

Refuse Tons Collected per Municipal Collection FTE

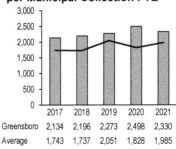

	2017	2018	2019	2020	2021
Greensboro	2,134	2,196	2,273	2,498	2,330
Average	1,743	1,737	2,051	1,828	1,985

Effectiveness Measures

Complaints per 1,000 Collection Points

	2017	2018	2019	2020	2021
Greensboro	26.2	28.2	42.9	44.7	54.9
Average	28.7	34.0	39.1	38.4	44.4

Valid Complaints per 1,000 Collection Points

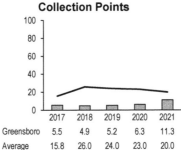

	2017	2018	2019	2020	2021
Greensboro	5.5	4.9	5.2	6.3	11.3
Average	15.8	26.0	24.0	23.0	20.0

Explanatory Information

Service Level and Delivery

Greenville collects refuse from residential premises once a week at curbside. Curbside collection is priced at $16 per month. Curbside recycling of white goods and electronics is included in the residential refuse fee.

The city uses five one-person crews operating automated trucks and one truck with a crew of three persons using rear-loading vehicles. The crews run collection routes four days a week.

Twenty-four collection routes were used during the fiscal year, with an average of two trips to the transfer station per day per route. The average distance to the transfer station per route was five-and-a-half miles.

Greenville collected 19,522 tons of residential refuse during the fiscal year at a cost of $92 per ton. The cost per ton does not include the disposal cost representing the tipping fee at the transfer station.

Conditions Affecting Service, Performance, and Costs

The apparent drop in the data in the graphs that look at tons collected is due to reporting improvements. In earlier years, Greenville could not easily separate out refuse collected from multifamily units. Improvements in what the county landfill is able to track and report back to the city mean that the most recent years include just single-family units. The refuse tonnage, however, for FY 2017–18 was not separated out and represents an estimate. No data were reported for FY 2019-20 for the city of Greenville.

Municipal Profile

Population (OSBM 2020)	87,428
Land Area (Square Miles)	35.66
Persons per Square Mile	2,452

Service Profile

FTE Positions—Collection	7.00
FTE Positions—Other	2.50
Type of Equipment	5 automated packers
	1 packer
Size of Crews (most commonly used)	1 & 2 person
Weekly Routes	25
Average Distance to Disposal Site	5 miles
Average Daily Trips to Disposal Site	2
Percentage of Service Contracted	0%
Collection Frequency	1 x week
General Collection Location	Curbside
Residential Customers (number represents collection points)	19,479
Tons Collected	19,522
Monthly Service Fee	$16.00

Full Cost Profile

Cost Breakdown by Percentage	
Personal Services	35.8%
Operating Costs	45.8%
Capital Costs	18.4%
TOTAL	100.0%

Cost Breakdown in Dollars	
Personal Services	$645,246
Operating Costs	$827,336
Capital Costs	$332,093
TOTAL	$1,804,675

Greenville

Residential Refuse Collection

Key: Greenville ▨   Benchmarking Average —   Fiscal Years 2017 through 2021

Resource Measures

Residential Refuse Collection Costs per Capita

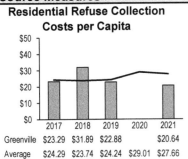

	2017	2018	2019	2020	2021
Greenville	$23.29	$31.89	$22.88		$20.64
Average	$24.29	$23.74	$24.24	$29.01	$27.66

Residential Refuse FTEs per 10,000 Population

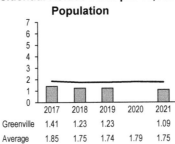

	2017	2018	2019	2020	2021
Greenville	1.41	1.23	1.23		1.09
Average	1.85	1.75	1.74	1.79	1.75

Workload Measures

Residential Refuse Tons per 1,000 Population

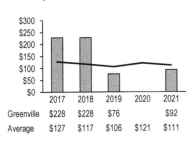

	2017	2018	2019	2020	2021
Greenville	327	140	302		223
Average	258	244	274	271	276

Residential Refuse Tons per 1,000 Collection Points

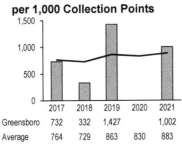

	2017	2018	2019	2020	2021
Greensboro	732	332	1,427		1,002
Average	764	729	863	830	883

Efficiency Measures

Residential Refuse Collection Cost per Ton Collected

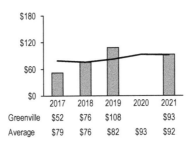

	2017	2018	2019	2020	2021
Greenville	$228	$228	$76		$92
Average	$127	$117	$106	$121	$111

Residential Refuse Collection Cost per Collection Point

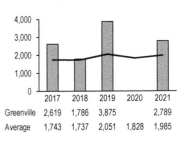

	2017	2018	2019	2020	2021
Greenville	$52	$76	$108		$93
Average	$79	$76	$82	$93	$92

Refuse Tons Collected per Municipal Collection FTE

	2017	2018	2019	2020	2021
Greenville	2,619	1,786	3,875		2,789
Average	1,743	1,737	2,051	1,828	1,985

Effectiveness Measures

Complaints per 1,000 Collection Points

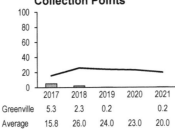

	2017	2018	2019	2020	2021
Greenville	5.3	5.6	6.4		5.6
Average	28.7	34.0	39.1	38.4	44.4

Valid Complaints per 1,000 Collection Points

	2017	2018	2019	2020	2021
Greenville	5.3	2.3	0.2		0.2
Average	15.8	26.0	24.0	23.0	20.0

Explanatory Information

Service Level and Delivery

Hickory collects refuse from residential premises once a week at curbside, although backyard collection is provided for elderly and disabled citizens. A monthly solid waste fee of $24 per cart was charged for residential refuse collection service during FY 2020–21. Each residence uses a cart provided by the city for residential refuse collection. Each cart has a capacity of ninety-six gallons and is provided at no charge. Upon request, a second cart is provided to the customer for an additional solid-waste fee.

The city used four one-person crews operating automated packers, with three of these trucks running full-time and one one-fourth of the time. A regular packer truck with one driver and one crew member works about half-time collecting on one-way streets and dead ends.

Fifteen collection routes were used during the fiscal year, with an average of two trips to the transfer station per day per route. The average distance to the transfer station per route was five miles.

Hickory collected 11,049 tons of residential refuse during the fiscal year, at a cost of $34 per ton. The cost per ton does not include the disposal cost representing the tipping fee at the Catawba County landfill.

Hickory defines automated packers as trucks with mechanical arms.

Conditions Affecting Service, Performance, and Costs

Hickory is highly automated in the area of residential refuse collection.

Municipal Profile

Population (OSBM 2020)	43,578
Land Area (Square Miles)	30.50
Persons per Square Mile	1,429

Service Profile

FTE Positions—Collection	3.75
FTE Positions—Other	0.82
Type of Equipment	4 automated packers
	1 packer
Size of Crews (most commonly used)	1 & 2 person
Weekly Routes	15
Average Distance to Disposal Site	5 miles
Average Daily Trips to Disposal Site	2
Percentage of Service Contracted	0%
Collection Frequency	1 x week
General Collection Location	Curbside
Residential Customers (number represents collection points)	12,200
Tons Collected	11,049
Monthly Service Fee	$24.00

Full Cost Profile

Cost Breakdown by Percentage	
Personal Services	44.4%
Operating Costs	42.9%
Capital Costs	12.6%
TOTAL	100.0%

Cost Breakdown in Dollars	
Personal Services	$166,409
Operating Costs	$160,658
Capital Costs	$47,355
TOTAL	$374,422

Hickory

Residential Refuse Collection

Key: Hickory ▦   Benchmarking Average —   Fiscal Years 2017 through 2021

Resource Measures

Residential Refuse Collection Costs per Capita

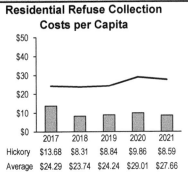

	2017	2018	2019	2020	2021
Hickory	$13.68	$8.31	$8.84	$9.86	$8.59
Average	$24.29	$23.74	$24.24	$29.01	$27.66

Residential Refuse FTEs per 10,000 Population

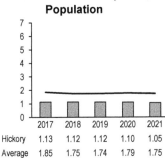

	2017	2018	2019	2020	2021
Hickory	1.13	1.12	1.12	1.10	1.05
Average	1.85	1.75	1.74	1.79	1.75

Workload Measures

Residential Refuse Tons per 1,000 Population

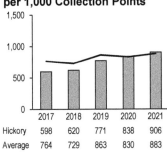

	2017	2018	2019	2020	2021
Hickory	180	182	225	245	254
Average	258	244	274	271	276

Residential Refuse Tons per 1,000 Collection Points

	2017	2018	2019	2020	2021
Hickory	598	620	771	838	906
Average	764	729	863	830	883

Efficiency Measures

Residential Refuse Collection Cost per Ton Collected

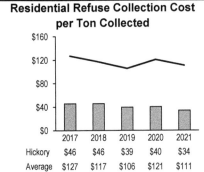

	2017	2018	2019	2020	2021
Hickory	$46	$46	$39	$40	$34
Average	$127	$117	$106	$121	$111

Residential Refuse Collection Cost per Collection Point

	2017	2018	2019	2020	2021
Hickory	$45	$28	$30	$34	$31
Average	$79	$76	$82	$93	$92

Refuse Tons Collected per Municipal Collection FTE

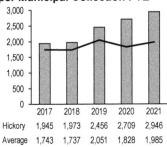

	2017	2018	2019	2020	2021
Hickory	1,945	1,973	2,456	2,709	2,946
Average	1,743	1,737	2,051	1,828	1,985

Effectiveness Measures

Complaints per 1,000 Collection Points

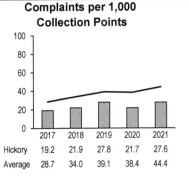

	2017	2018	2019	2020	2021
Hickory	19.2	21.9	27.8	21.7	27.6
Average	28.7	34.0	39.1	38.4	44.4

Valid Complaints per 1,000 Collection Points

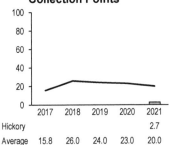

	2017	2018	2019	2020	2021
Hickory					2.7
Average	15.8	26.0	24.0	23.0	20.0

Fiscal Year 2020-21

Explanatory Information

Service Level and Delivery

Raleigh provides residential refuse collection service once per week at curbside. Backyard collection service is provided for customers who have been certified by a physician as being unable to move a cart to the curb and who have no able-bodied resident to provide assistance. The city charges a monthly fee of $15.45 for refuse collection.

The city employed twenty-two automated trucks with a single driver and ten crews of three on semi-automated trucks for primary collection. A total of 112 collection routes were used per week with a average truck making two trips per day to the disposal site, covering a distance of fifteen miles.

Each customer has up to two ninety-five-gallon roll-out carts provided and paid for by the city. The city collected 100,490 tons of residential refuse during the fiscal year, at a cost per ton of $140, or $112 per collection point. Not included in the cost per ton was a landfill tipping fee.

Conditions Affecting Service, Performance, and Costs

Municipal Profile

Population (OSBM 2020)	468,977
Land Area (Square Miles)	146.47
Persons per Square Mile	3,202

Service Profile

FTE Positions—Collection	79.0
FTE Positions—Other	6.0
Type of Equipment	22 automated packers
	10 packers
Size of Crews (most commonly used)	1 & 3 person
Weekly Routes	112
Average Distance to Disposal Site	15 miles
Average Daily Trips to Disposal Site	2
Percentage of Service Contracted	0%
Collection Frequency	1 x week
General Collection Location	Curbside
Residential Customers	125,321
(number represents collection points)	
Tons Collected	100,490
Monthly Service Fee	$15.45

Full Cost Profile

Cost Breakdown by Percentage	
Personal Services	35.2%
Operating Costs	30.8%
Capital Costs	34.0%
TOTAL	100.0%

Cost Breakdown in Dollars	
Personal Services	$4,947,350
Operating Costs	$4,320,428
Capital Costs	$4,775,851
TOTAL	$14,043,629

Raleigh
Residential Refuse Collection

Key: Raleigh ▨   Benchmarking Average —   Fiscal Years 2017 through 2021

Resource Measures

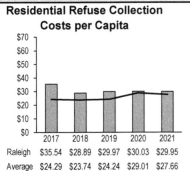

Residential Refuse Collection Costs per Capita

	2017	2018	2019	2020	2021
Raleigh	$35.54	$28.89	$29.97	$30.03	$29.95
Average	$24.29	$23.74	$24.24	$29.01	$27.66

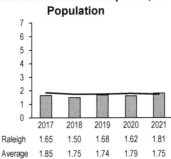

Residential Refuse FTEs per 10,000 Population

	2017	2018	2019	2020	2021
Raleigh	1.65	1.50	1.68	1.62	1.81
Average	1.85	1.75	1.74	1.79	1.75

Workload Measures

Residential Refuse Tons per 1,000 Population

	2017	2018	2019	2020	2021
Raleigh	210	200	199	199	214
Average	258	244	274	271	276

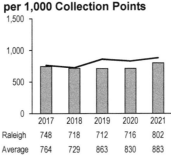

Residential Refuse Tons per 1,000 Collection Points

	2017	2018	2019	2020	2021
Raleigh	748	718	712	716	802
Average	764	729	863	830	883

Efficiency Measures

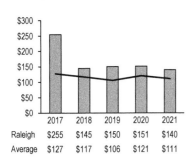

Residential Refuse Collection Cost per Ton Collected

	2017	2018	2019	2020	2021
Raleigh	$255	$145	$150	$151	$140
Average	$127	$117	$106	$121	$111

Residential Refuse Collection Cost per Collection Point

	2017	2018	2019	2020	2021
Raleigh	$126	$104	$107	$108	$112
Average	$79	$76	$82	$93	$92

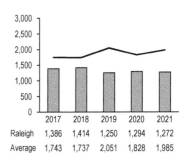

Refuse Tons Collected per Municipal Collection FTE

	2017	2018	2019	2020	2021
Raleigh	1,386	1,414	1,250	1,294	1,272
Average	1,743	1,737	2,051	1,828	1,985

Effectiveness Measures

Complaints per 1,000 Collection Points

	2017	2018	2019	2020	2021
Raleigh	46.3	52.5	48.4	72.1	67.0
Average	28.7	34.0	39.1	38.4	44.4

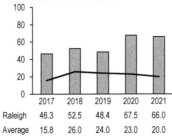

Valid Complaints per 1,000 Collection Points

	2017	2018	2019	2020	2021
Raleigh	46.3	52.5	48.4	67.5	66.0
Average	15.8	26.0	24.0	23.0	20.0

Residential Refuse Collection   31

Fiscal Year 2020-21

Explanatory Information

Service Level and Delivery

Residential refuse collection service is provided once a week at curbside to Wilson residents. Senior citizens and disabled persons may apply for and receive backyard pickup. There is currently a monthly $20.00 fee per household for the residential refuse collection service.

During the fiscal year, the city used five one-person crews working from automated packers. The city also used two three-person crews, each composed of one driver and two collectors working from semi-automated rear loaders. Residents are required to use ninety-six-gallon roll-out containers.

The city serviced twenty-seven collection routes each week during the fiscal year. The packers made an average of two trips to the disposal facility per day per route, with the distance to the transfer station being ten miles.

Wilson collected 23,080 tons of residential refuse during the fiscal year, at a cost of $60 per ton. The cost per ton does not include the disposal cost representing the tipping fee at the transfer station.

Conditions Affecting Service, Performance, and Costs

During FY 2017–18, Wilson made sweeping route changes and added additional entry level positions and two new supervisors.

Wilson began using a new system for tracking all call-ins into "FixIt Wilson" during FY 2017–18. Complaints include missed trash, spilled trash, improper place of container, vehicle or other obstructions blocking pickup, and other issues. Not all of these represent problems with the collection staff. This change in the system increased the reported number of complaints or problems. The City of Wilson considers all complaints to be valid complaints.

Municipal Profile

Population (OSBM 2020)	47,769
Land Area (Square Miles)	31.02
Persons per Square Mile	1,540

Service Profile

FTE Positions—Collection	11.0
FTE Positions—Other	1.0
Type of Equipment	5 automated packers
	2 packers
Size of Crews (most commonly used)	1 & 3 person
Weekly Routes	27
Average Distance to Disposal Site	10 miles
Average Daily Trips to Disposal Site	2
Percentage of Service Contracted	0%
Collection Frequency	1 x week
General Collection Location	Curbside
Residential Customers (number represents collection points)	21,111
Tons Collected	23,080
Monthly Service Fee	$20.00

Full Cost Profile

Cost Breakdown by Percentage	
Personal Services	38.5%
Operating Costs	43.1%
Capital Costs	18.3%
TOTAL	100.0%

Cost Breakdown in Dollars	
Personal Services	$531,616
Operating Costs	$595,062
Capital Costs	$252,494
TOTAL	$1,379,172

Wilson

Residential Refuse Collection

Key: Wilson █   Benchmarking Average —   Fiscal Years 2017 through 2021

Resource Measures

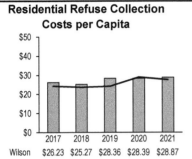

Residential Refuse Collection Costs per Capita

	2017	2018	2019	2020	2021
Wilson	$26.23	$25.27	$28.36	$28.39	$28.87
Average	$24.29	$23.74	$24.24	$29.01	$27.66

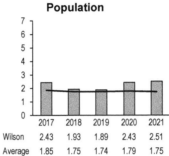

Residential Refuse FTEs per 10,000 Population

	2017	2018	2019	2020	2021
Wilson	2.43	1.93	1.89	2.43	2.51
Average	1.85	1.75	1.74	1.79	1.75

Workload Measures

Residential Refuse Tons per 1,000 Population

	2017	2018	2019	2020	2021
Wilson	467	491	512	467	483
Average	258	244	274	271	276

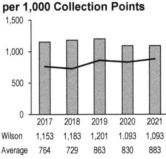

Residential Refuse Tons per 1,000 Collection Points

	2017	2018	2019	2020	2021
Wilson	1,153	1,183	1,201	1,093	1,093
Average	764	729	863	830	883

Efficiency Measures

Residential Refuse Collection Cost per Ton Collected

	2017	2018	2019	2020	2021
Wilson	$51	$51	$55	$61	$60
Average	$127	$117	$106	$121	$111

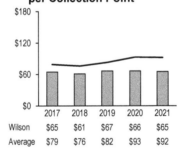

Residential Refuse Collection Cost per Collection Point

	2017	2018	2019	2020	2021
Wilson	$65	$61	$67	$66	$65
Average	$79	$76	$82	$93	$92

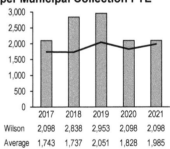

Refuse Tons Collected per Municipal Collection FTE

	2017	2018	2019	2020	2021
Wilson	2,098	2,838	2,953	2,098	2,098
Average	1,743	1,737	2,051	1,828	1,985

Effectiveness Measures

Complaints per 1,000 Collection Points

	2017	2018	2019	2020	2021
Wilson	45.1	92.5	87.8	42.7	42.7
Average	28.7	34.0	39.1	38.4	44.4

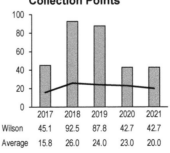

Valid Complaints per 1,000 Collection Points

	2017	2018	2019	2020	2021
Wilson	45.1	92.5	87.8	42.7	42.7
Average	15.8	26.0	24.0	23.0	20.0

Residential Refuse Collection   33

Fiscal Year 2020-21

Explanatory Information

Service Level and Delivery

Winston-Salem collects residential refuse once per week from curbside. The city implemented a voluntary curbside collection program in March 2005. In October 2010, the city began the transition to mandatory curbside collection. The transition to a curbside-only collection system was completed during FY 2011–12.

The city uses thirteen one-person crews to collect residential refuse plus eleven three-person crews, each composed of a driver and two collectors equipped with rear-loading packers.

Residents may use three thirty-two-gallon containers or one ninety-six-gallon roll-out cart. There was no fee for the residential refuse service during the fiscal year.

The city collected 69,373 tons of residential refuse during the fiscal year from 81,589 collection points. The cost per ton was $159, which does not include the tipping fee for disposal at the landfill. The city serviced ninety-six collection routes during the fiscal year, with an average of one trip per route per day to the landfill. The average distance to the landfill was twelve miles.

Conditions Affecting Service, Performance, and Costs

Municipal Profile

Population (OSBM 2020)	249,986
Land Area (Square Miles)	132.59
Persons per Square Mile	1,885

Service Profile

FTE Positions—Collection	65.0
FTE Positions—Other	3.0
Type of Equipment	13 automated packers
	11 packers
Size of Crews (most commonly used)	1 & 3 person
Weekly Routes	96
Average Distance to Disposal Site	12 miles
Average Daily Trips to Disposal Site	1
Percentage of Service Contracted	0%
Collection Frequency	1 x week
General Collection Location	Curbside
Residential Customers	81,589
(number represents collection points)	
Tons Collected	69,373
Monthly Service Fee	No

Full Cost Profile

Cost Breakdown by Percentage	
Personal Services	39.2%
Operating Costs	47.7%
Capital Costs	13.2%
TOTAL	100.0%

Cost Breakdown in Dollars	
Personal Services	$4,319,818
Operating Costs	$5,258,939
Capital Costs	$1,450,415
TOTAL	$11,029,172

Resource Measures

Residential Refuse Collection Costs per Capita

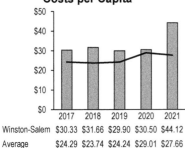

	2017	2018	2019	2020	2021
Winston-Salem	$30.33	$31.66	$29.90	$30.50	$44.12
Average	$24.29	$23.74	$24.24	$29.01	$27.66

Residential Refuse FTEs per 10,000 Population

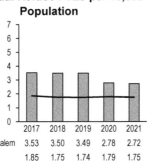

	2017	2018	2019	2020	2021
Winston-Salem	3.53	3.50	3.49	2.78	2.72
Average	1.85	1.75	1.74	1.79	1.75

Workload Measures

Residential Refuse Tons per 1,000 Population

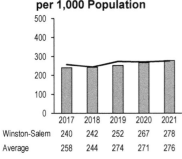

	2017	2018	2019	2020	2021
Winston-Salem	240	242	252	267	278
Average	258	244	274	271	276

Residential Refuse Tons per 1,000 Collection Points

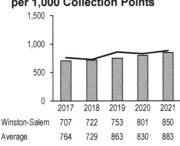

	2017	2018	2019	2020	2021
Winston-Salem	707	722	753	801	850
Average	764	729	863	830	883

Efficiency Measures

Residential Refuse Collection Cost per Ton Collected

	2017	2018	2019	2020	2021
Winston-Salem	$131	$131	$119	$114	$159
Average	$127	$117	$106	$121	$111

Residential Refuse Collection Cost per Collection Point

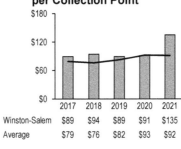

	2017	2018	2019	2020	2021
Winston-Salem	$89	$94	$89	$91	$135
Average	$79	$76	$82	$93	$92

Refuse Tons Collected per Municipal Collection FTE

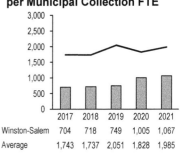

	2017	2018	2019	2020	2021
Winston-Salem	704	718	749	1,005	1,067
Average	1,743	1,737	2,051	1,828	1,985

Effectiveness Measures

Complaints per 1,000 Collection Points

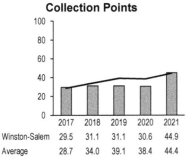

	2017	2018	2019	2020	2021
Winston-Salem	29.5	31.1	31.1	30.6	44.9
Average	28.7	34.0	39.1	38.4	44.4

Valid Complaints per 1,000 Collection Points

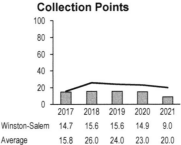

	2017	2018	2019	2020	2021
Winston-Salem	14.7	15.6	15.6	14.9	9.0
Average	15.8	26.0	24.0	23.0	20.0

Performance and Cost Data

HOUSEHOLD RECYCLING

PERFORMANCE MEASURES FOR HOUSEHOLD RECYCLING

SERVICE DEFINITION

Household Recycling includes both curbside collection and processing of household recyclable materials from residences and certain other locations and the drop-off of such materials by citizens at recycling stations or centers. The recyclable materials collected are mainly aluminum and steel cans, plastics, glass bottles, newspapers, magazines, and cardboard. The curbside portion of this service involves regularly scheduled collection that utilizes containers small enough that residents and/or workers can move or lift them. The service definition excludes collection of yard waste, leaves, and commercial recycling.

NOTES ON PERFORMANCE MEASURES

1. Workload and Efficiency Measures

The same sorts of workload and efficiency measures are used for household recycling as for residential refuse collection. The project's workload measures for household recycling are tons of recyclable materials collected per 1,000 population and per 1,000 collection points, and the efficiency measures for this service are cost per ton of recyclable materials collected, cost per collection point, and tons of household recyclable materials collected per full-time equivalent (FTE) position directly involved in household recycling. FTEs for recycling are calculated in the same way as they are for residential refuse collection. Only those FTE positions that actually collect recyclables are used for the measure "tons collected per FTE."

2. Tons of Solid Waste Landfilled per 1,000 Population

"Tons solid waste landfilled per 1,000 population" is used as a workload measure. Although not all residential refuse is recyclable, much more of it is likely to be recycled in the future as recycling technology improves and markets for recyclable materials grow. Thus, tons of solid waste landfilled per 1,000 population serves as a useful indicator of the need for household recycling.

3. Community Set-Out Rate in Household Recycling

The project uses this as a measure of the effectiveness of household recycling. Residents in municipalities with curbside recycling choose whether to participate in the program and decide the extent of their participation. As the portion of households participating in household recycling grows, the more effective recycling is likely to be in reducing the volume of residential refuse. This measure combines the set-out rate for those participating and the participation rate to estimate the percentage of potential households that are actually recycling.

4. Tons of Household Recyclable Materials Collected as a Percentage of the Sum of Tons of Residential Refuse Collected Plus Tons of Household Recyclable Materials Collected

This measure assesses the magnitude of household recycling in relation to residential refuse collected for disposal. A household recycling program is effective to the extent it diverts residential refuse from the disposal stream.

Household Recycling

Summary of Key Dimensions of Service

City or Town	Drop-Off Sites		Collection Frequency	Collection Points	Community Set-Out Rate	Tons Collected	Percentage of Waste Stream Diverted from Landfill	Percentage Service Contracted	Municipal FTE Collection Positions
	City Owned	Other							
Apex	0	0	1 x week	21,504	95%	4,205	21%	100%	NA
Charlotte	0	9	1 x 2 weeks	224,062	85%	46,714	17%	100%	NA
Concord	0	1	1 x 2 weeks	35,094	60%	5,480	13%	100%	1.3
Goldsboro	0	0	1 x 2 weeks	14,372	NA	1,026	8%	0.1%	4.0
Greensboro	2	0	1 x 2 weeks	88,020	51%	13,363	16%	0.0%	16
Greenville	220	0	1 x week	19,132	65%	2,511	11%	0.0%	6
Hickory	2	0	1 x 2 weeks	12,200	73%	2,663	19%	94%	0.5
Raleigh	2	1	1 x 2 weeks	184,460	NA	30,906	24%	0%	33
Wilson	0	0	1 x 2 weeks	21,111	53%	1,705	7%	0%	7
Winston-Salem	7	0	1 x 2 weeks	81,589	64%	15,430	18%	100%	NA

NOTES
Community Set-Out Rate is a combination of the participation rate and the participant's set-out rate.

EXPLANATORY FACTORS
These are factors that the project found affected household recycling collection performance and cost in one or more of the municipalities:

Types of items eligible for recycling
Landfill tipping fees for solid waste
Commitment of city officials to recycling
Number of drop-off centers
Community education
Market prices for recyclable materials
Demographic makeup of community

Fiscal Year 2020-21

Explanatory Information

Service Level and Delivery

Apex contracts with Waste Industries for refuse collection, disposal, and recycling. Only the recycling collection is reflected on this page. The town offers curbside recycling to all residents. Residents pay a $4.89 fee per container per month. Most residents have a sixty-four-gallon cart though some have eighteen-gallon containers.

The following materials are collected:

- plastics
- paperboard
- chipboard
- paper tubes
- corrugated cardboard
- aluminum
- tin and steel cans
- glass
- newspaper
- magazines and catalogs
- phone books

Residents living within Apex are encouraged to participate in the curbside recycling program. The program serves 21,504 residences.

Conditions Affecting Service, Performance, and Costs

Municipal Profile

Population (OSBM 2020)	59,368
Land Area (Square Miles)	23.61
Persons per Square Mile	2,514

Service Profile

FTE Positions—Collection	Contractor
FTE Positions—Other	Contractor
Number of City Drop-Off Centers	0
Other Drop-Off Centers	0
Percentage of Service Contracted	100%
Collection Frequency	1 x week
General Collection Location	Curbside
Recyclables Sorted at Curb	No
Collection Points	21,504
Tons of Recyclables Collected	
Curbside	4,205
City Drop-Off Centers	0
Total Tons Collected	4,205
Monthly Service Fee	$4.89
Revenue from Sale of Recyclables	$0
Sale Revenue as Percentage of Cost	NA

Full Cost Profile

Cost Breakdown by Percentage	
Personal Services	0.0%
Operating Costs	100.0%
Capital Costs	0.0%
TOTAL	100.0%
Cost Breakdown in Dollars	
Personal Services	$0
Operating Costs	$1,218,174
Capital Costs	$0
TOTAL	$1,218,174

Apex   Household Recycling

Key: Apex ▨   Benchmarking Average —   Fiscal Years 2017 through 2021

Resource Measures

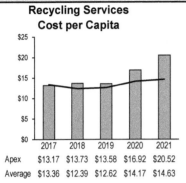

Recycling Services Cost per Capita

	2017	2018	2019	2020	2021
Apex	$13.17	$13.73	$13.58	$16.92	$20.52
Average	$13.36	$12.39	$12.62	$14.17	$14.63

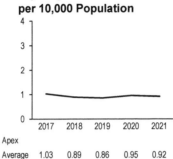

Recycling Services FTEs per 10,000 Population

	2017	2018	2019	2020	2021
Apex					
Average	1.03	0.89	0.86	0.95	0.92

Workload Measures

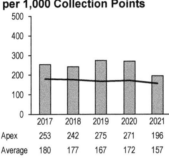

Tons Recyclables Collected per 1,000 Population

	2017	2018	2019	2020	2021
Apex	84.6	82.1	80.1	88.0	70.8
Average	57.4	56.1	52.8	57.0	50.4

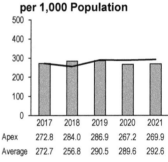

Tons Recyclables Collected per 1,000 Collection Points

	2017	2018	2019	2020	2021
Apex	253	242	275	271	196
Average	180	177	167	172	157

Tons Solid Waste Landfilled per 1,000 Population

	2017	2018	2019	2020	2021
Apex	272.8	284.0	286.9	267.2	269.9
Average	272.7	256.8	290.5	289.6	292.6

Efficiency Measures

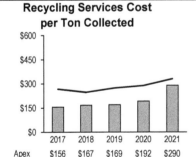

Recycling Services Cost per Ton Collected

	2017	2018	2019	2020	2021
Apex	$156	$167	$169	$192	$290
Average	$267	$247	$273	$288	$330

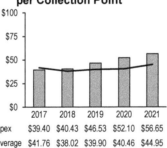

Recycling Services Cost per Collection Point

	2017	2018	2019	2020	2021
Apex	$39.40	$40.43	$46.53	$52.10	$56.65
Average	$41.76	$38.02	$39.90	$40.46	$44.95

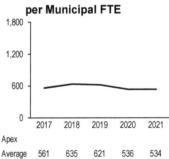

Tons Collected Curbside per Municipal FTE

	2017	2018	2019	2020	2021
Apex					
Average	561	635	621	536	534

Effectiveness Measures

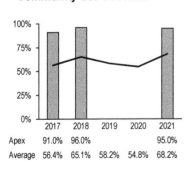

Community Set-Out Rate

	2017	2018	2019	2020	2021
Apex	91.0%	96.0%			95.0%
Average	56.4%	65.1%	58.2%	54.8%	68.2%

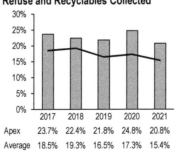

Tons Recycled as Percentage of Tons Refuse and Recyclables Collected

	2017	2018	2019	2020	2021
Apex	23.7%	22.4%	21.8%	24.8%	20.8%
Average	18.5%	19.3%	16.5%	17.3%	15.4%

Fiscal Year 2020-21

Explanatory Information

Service Level and Delivery

Charlotte provides curbside recycling collection to single-family residential customers once every two weeks. Recycling collection is entirely provided by a contractor. Materials collected in the recycling program include the following:

- glass
- plastic
- aluminum
- newspaper
- magazines
- catalogs
- phone books
- cardboard
- milk cartons
- aerosol cans
- juice boxes

The majority of users have ninety-five or ninety-six-gallon roll-out containers.

The county operates several recycling drop-off centers that are available for use by citizens of Charlotte and Mecklenburg County. Tonnage from the drop-off centers is not included in this report.

Conditions Affecting Service, Performance, and Costs

The set-out rate is calculated daily, as the trucks are outfitted with Radio Frequency Identification (RFID) readers and the recycling carts have RFID chips installed.

Municipal Profile

Population (OSBM 2020)	876,694
Land Area (Square Miles)	307.41
Persons per Square Mile	2,852

Service Profile

FTE Positions—Collection	Contractor
FTE Positions—Other	Contractor
Number of City Drop-Off Centers	0
Other Drop-Off Centers	9
Percentage of Service Contracted	100%
Collection Frequency	Every 2 weeks
General Collection Location	Curbside
Recyclables Sorted at Curb	No
Collection Points	224,062
Tons of Recyclables Collected	
Curbside	46,714
City Drop-Off Centers	0
Total Tons Collected	46,714
Monthly Service Fee	0
Revenue from Sale of Recyclables	$0
Sale Revenue as Percentage of Cost	NA

Full Cost Profile

Cost Breakdown by Percentage	
Personal Services	0.0%
Operating Costs	99.3%
Capital Costs	0.7%
TOTAL	100.0%
Cost Breakdown in Dollars	
Personal Services	$0
Operating Costs	$7,535,379
Capital Costs	$52,177
TOTAL	$7,587,556

Charlotte

Household Recycling

Resource Measures

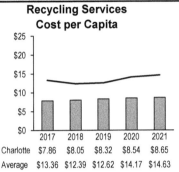

Recycling Services Cost per Capita

	2017	2018	2019	2020	2021
Charlotte	$7.86	$8.05	$8.32	$8.54	$8.65
Average	$13.36	$12.39	$12.62	$14.17	$14.63

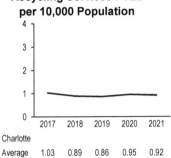

Recycling Services FTEs per 10,000 Population

	2017	2018	2019	2020	2021
Charlotte					
Average	1.03	0.89	0.86	0.95	0.92

Workload Measures

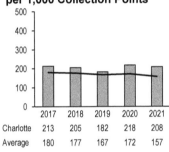

Tons Recyclables Collected per 1,000 Population

	2017	2018	2019	2020	2021
Charlotte	55.2	52.7	47.0	55.9	53.3
Average	57.4	56.1	52.8	57.0	50.4

Tons Recyclables Collected per 1,000 Collection Points

	2017	2018	2019	2020	2021
Charlotte	213	205	182	218	208
Average	180	177	167	172	157

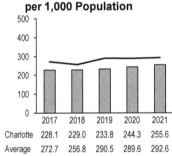

Tons Solid Waste Landfilled per 1,000 Population

	2017	2018	2019	2020	2021
Charlotte	228.1	229.0	233.8	244.3	255.6
Average	272.7	256.8	290.5	289.6	292.6

Efficiency Measures

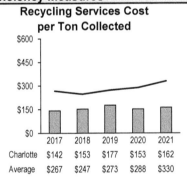

Recycling Services Cost per Ton Collected

	2017	2018	2019	2020	2021
Charlotte	$142	$153	$177	$153	$162
Average	$267	$247	$273	$288	$330

Recycling Services Cost per Collection Point

	2017	2018	2019	2020	2021
Charlotte	$30.28	$31.24	$32.28	$33.24	$33.86
Average	$41.76	$38.02	$39.90	$40.46	$44.95

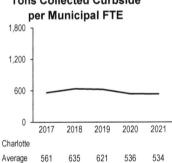

Tons Collected Curbside per Municipal FTE

	2017	2018	2019	2020	2021
Charlotte					
Average	561	635	621	536	534

Effectiveness Measures

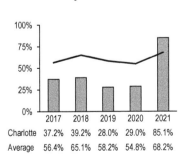

Community Set-Out Rate

	2017	2018	2019	2020	2021
Charlotte	37.2%	39.2%	28.0%	29.0%	85.1%
Average	56.4%	65.1%	58.2%	54.8%	68.2%

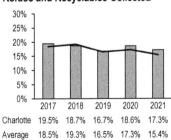

Tons Recycled as Percentage of Tons Refuse and Recyclables Collected

	2017	2018	2019	2020	2021
Charlotte	19.5%	18.7%	16.7%	18.6%	17.3%
Average	18.5%	19.3%	16.5%	17.3%	15.4%

Explanatory Information

Service Level and Delivery

Concord provides biweekly curbside collection of recyclable materials from households. The city uses a contractor to provide recycling collection. Residents place materials into a ninety-five-gallon cart. The recyclable materials collected include:

- glass
- newspaper
- magazines
- mixed paper and mail
- No. 1 and No. 2 plastics
- metal and aluminum food and beverage containers

Concord uses a contract collector for regular residential curbside recycling. The materials are collected on a commingled basis biweekly from each participating resident and delivered to a materials recovery facility (MRF) in Charlotte for separation and marketing.

The city received $60,137 from the sale of recyclables during the year, offsetting some of the costs.

Conditions Affecting Service, Performance, and Costs

Municipal Profile

Population (OSBM 2020)	105,936
Land Area (Square Miles)	63.65
Persons per Square Mile	1,664

Service Profile

FTE Positions—Collection	1.3
FTE Positions—Other	4.78
Number of City Drop-Off Centers	0
Other Drop-Off Centers	1
Percentage of Service Contracted	100%
Collection Frequency	Every 2 weeks
General Collection Location	Curbside
Recyclables Sorted at Curb	No
Collection Points	35,094
Tons of Recyclables Collected	
Curbside	5,480
City Drop-Off Centers	0
Total Tons Collected	5,480
Monthly Service Fee	2.24
Revenue from Sale of Recyclables	$60,137
Sale Revenue as Percentage of Cost	2.9%

Full Cost Profile

Cost Breakdown by Percentage	
Personal Services	9.8%
Operating Costs	89.3%
Capital Costs	0.9%
TOTAL	100.0%

Cost Breakdown in Dollars	
Personal Services	$202,271
Operating Costs	$1,849,130
Capital Costs	$18,578
TOTAL	$2,069,979

Concord

Household Recycling

Key: Concord ▨   Benchmarking Average —   Fiscal Years 2017 through 2021

Resource Measures

Recycling Services Cost per Capita

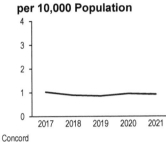

	2017	2018	2019	2020	2021
Concord	$12.78	$13.62	$15.83	$20.68	$19.54
Average	$13.36	$12.39	$12.62	$14.17	$14.63

Recycling Services FTEs per 10,000 Population

	2017	2018	2019	2020	2021
Concord					
Average	1.03	0.89	0.86	0.95	0.92

Workload Measures

Tons Recyclables Collected per 1,000 Population

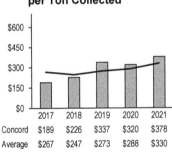

	2017	2018	2019	2020	2021
Concord	67.6	60.2	47.0	64.7	51.7
Average	57.4	56.1	52.8	57.0	50.4

Tons Recyclables Collected per 1,000 Collection Points

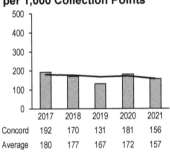

	2017	2018	2019	2020	2021
Concord	192	170	131	181	156
Average	180	177	167	172	157

Tons Solid Waste Landfilled per 1,000 Population

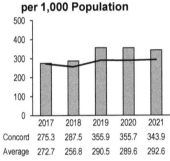

	2017	2018	2019	2020	2021
Concord	275.3	287.5	355.9	355.7	343.9
Average	272.7	256.8	290.5	289.6	292.6

Efficiency Measures

Recycling Services Cost per Ton Collected

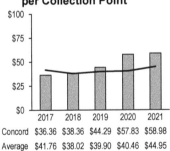

	2017	2018	2019	2020	2021
Concord	$189	$226	$337	$320	$378
Average	$267	$247	$273	$288	$330

Recycling Services Cost per Collection Point

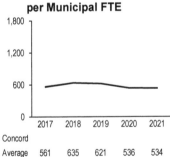

	2017	2018	2019	2020	2021
Concord	$36.36	$38.36	$44.29	$57.83	$58.98
Average	$41.76	$38.02	$39.90	$40.46	$44.95

Tons Collected Curbside per Municipal FTE

	2017	2018	2019	2020	2021
Concord					
Average	561	635	621	536	534

Effectiveness Measures

Community Set-Out Rate

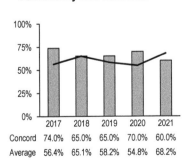

	2017	2018	2019	2020	2021
Concord	74.0%	65.0%	65.0%	70.0%	60.0%
Average	56.4%	65.1%	58.2%	54.8%	68.2%

Tons Recycled as Percentage of Tons Refuse and Recyclables Collected

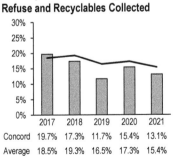

	2017	2018	2019	2020	2021
Concord	19.7%	17.3%	11.7%	15.4%	13.1%
Average	18.5%	19.3%	16.5%	17.3%	15.4%

Fiscal Year 2020-21

Explanatory Information

Service Level and Delivery

Goldsboro operates a recycling system with curbside collection for residents. Recycling is picked up by the Solid Waste Division of the Public Works Department. Collection is done every two weeks. Residents pay a fee that covers all solid waste services, including recycling. Residents use a ninety-five-gallon container provided by the city.

Goldsboro's recycling is not sorted curbside. Materials collected by the household recycling program include:

- No. 1 and No. 2 plastics
- newspaper
- magazines
- telephone books
- cardboard
- aluminum and steel cans
- glass jars and bottles
- plastic soda bottles and milk jugs
- office paper

Conditions Affecting Service, Performance, and Costs

The City of Goldsboro joined the Benchmarking Project in July 2017, with the first year of data showing for FY 2016–17.

Goldsboro contracts recycling collection for one small neighborhood where a hill and tight roads make it infeasible to use city trucks.

.

Municipal Profile

Population (OSBM 2020)	34,156
Land Area (Square Miles)	29.45
Persons per Square Mile	1,160

Service Profile

FTE Positions—Collection	4.0
FTE Positions—Other	1.2
Number of City Drop-Off Centers	0
Other Drop-Off Centers	0
Percentage of Service Contracted	0.1%
Collection Frequency	Every 2 weeks
General Collection Location	Curbside
Recyclables Sorted at Curb	No
Collection Points	14,372
Tons of Recyclables Collected	
Curbside	1,026
City Drop-Off Centers	0
Total Tons Collected	1,026
Monthly Service Fee	0
Revenue from Sale of Recyclables	$0
Sale Revenue as Percentage of Cost	NA

Full Cost Profile

Cost Breakdown by Percentage	
Personal Services	61.2%
Operating Costs	38.8%
Capital Costs	0.0%
TOTAL	100.0%
Cost Breakdown in Dollars	
Personal Services	$441,224
Operating Costs	$279,340
Capital Costs	$0
TOTAL	$720,564

Goldsboro

Household Recycling

Resource Measures

Recycling Services Cost per Capita

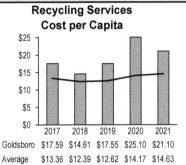

	2017	2018	2019	2020	2021
Goldsboro	$17.59	$14.61	$17.55	$25.10	$21.10
Average	$13.36	$12.39	$12.62	$14.17	$14.63

Recycling Services FTEs per 10,000 Population

	2017	2018	2019	2020	2021
Goldsboro	1.53	1.43	1.44	1.53	1.53
Average	1.03	0.89	0.86	0.95	0.92

Workload Measures

Tons Recyclables Collected per 1,000 Population

	2017	2018	2019	2020	2021
Goldsboro	31.2	32.6	30.3	31.4	30.0
Average	57.4	56.1	52.8	57.0	50.4

Tons Recyclables Collected per 1,000 Collection Points

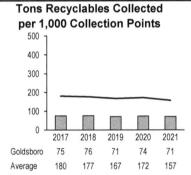

	2017	2018	2019	2020	2021
Goldsboro	75	76	71	74	71
Average	180	177	167	172	157

Tons Solid Waste Landfilled per 1,000 Population

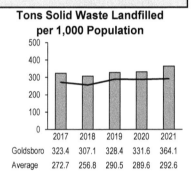

	2017	2018	2019	2020	2021
Goldsboro	323.4	307.1	328.4	331.6	364.1
Average	272.7	256.8	290.5	289.6	292.6

Efficiency Measures

Recycling Services Cost per Ton Collected

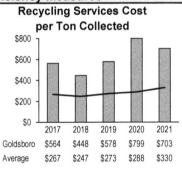

	2017	2018	2019	2020	2021
Goldsboro	$564	$448	$578	$799	$703
Average	$267	$247	$273	$288	$330

Recycling Services Cost per Collection Point

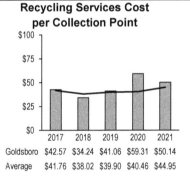

	2017	2018	2019	2020	2021
Goldsboro	$42.57	$34.24	$41.06	$59.31	$50.14
Average	$41.76	$38.02	$39.90	$40.46	$44.95

Tons Collected Curbside per Municipal FTE

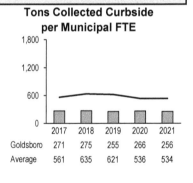

	2017	2018	2019	2020	2021
Goldsboro	271	275	255	266	256
Average	561	635	621	536	534

Effectiveness Measures

Community Set-Out Rate

	2017	2018	2019	2020	2021
Goldsboro					
Average	56.4%	65.1%	58.2%	54.8%	68.2%

Tons Recycled as Percentage of Tons Refuse and Recyclables Collected

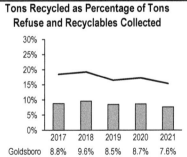

	2017	2018	2019	2020	2021
Goldsboro	8.8%	9.6%	8.5%	8.7%	7.6%
Average	18.5%	19.3%	16.5%	17.3%	15.4%

Fiscal Year 2020-21

Explanatory Information

Service Level and Delivery

Greensboro operates a voluntary commingled collection process for its recycling customers. Recycling services are provided to the community by means of single ninety-six or sixty-four-gallon automated containers and by green translucent bags. Partnerships also are maintained with fire departments, the county school system, the extension office, and the parks department for providing drop-off sites. There are two city-owned drop-off sites, but these collected tons are not reported in Greensboro's data.

Recycling pickup is done every other week. Recycling materials are not sorted curbside. Instead, they are set out in one container, picked up by an automated-collection crew, and taken to an off-site contractor that sorts and recycles the materials. Greensboro provides the collection pickup and delivery to the contractor's location, while the contractor provides for recovery of materials and disposal of the residuals it is unable to recycle.

Materials collected by Greensboro's household recycling program include:

- No. 1 and No. 2 plastics
- newspaper
- magazines
- telephone books
- cardboard
- aluminum and steel cans
- chipboard (cereal boxes)
- glass jars and bottles
- plastic soda bottles and milk jugs
- office paper
- empty aerosol cans

Greensboro contracts with a private firm for separation, packaging, and sale of recyclable materials. City payments to the contractor for the fiscal year are included in total cost. Greensboro gets additional revenues from the sale of recyclables from nonresidential sources, but these are not counted here.

Conditions Affecting Service, Performance, and Costs

Greensboro is highly automated in gathering materials from its recycling program.

The set-out rate was based on a manual count done on a biweekly basis.

Municipal Profile

Population (OSBM 2020)	299,556
Land Area (Square Miles)	129.62
Persons per Square Mile	2,311

Service Profile

FTE Positions—Collection	16.0
FTE Positions—Other	3.0
Number of City Drop-Off Centers	2
Other Drop-Off Centers	0
Percentage of Service Contracted	0%
Collection Frequency	Every 2 weeks
General Collection Location	Curbside
Recyclables Sorted at Curb	No
Collection Points	88,020
Tons of Recyclables Collected	
Curbside	13,363
City Drop-Off Centers	0
Total Tons Collected	13,363
Monthly Service Fee	2.5
Revenue from Sale of Recyclables	$0
Sale Revenue as Percentage of Cost	NA

Full Cost Profile

Cost Breakdown by Percentage	
Personal Services	26.0%
Operating Costs	74.0%
Capital Costs	0.0%
TOTAL	100.0%
Cost Breakdown in Dollars	
Personal Services	$930,057
Operating Costs	$2,648,847
Capital Costs	$0
TOTAL	$3,578,904

Greensboro

Household Recycling

Resource Measures

Recycling Services Cost per Capita

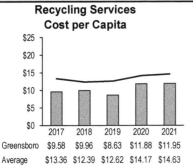

	2017	2018	2019	2020	2021
Greensboro	$9.58	$9.96	$8.63	$11.88	$11.95
Average	$13.36	$12.39	$12.62	$14.17	$14.63

Recycling Services FTEs per 10,000 Population

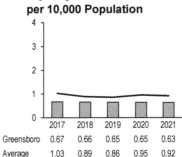

	2017	2018	2019	2020	2021
Greensboro	0.67	0.66	0.65	0.65	0.63
Average	1.03	0.89	0.86	0.95	0.92

Workload Measures

Tons Recyclables Collected per 1,000 Population

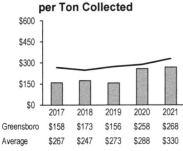

	2017	2018	2019	2020	2021
Greensboro	60.5	57.5	55.4	46.1	44.6
Average	57.4	56.1	52.8	57.0	50.4

Tons Recyclables Collected per 1,000 Collection Points

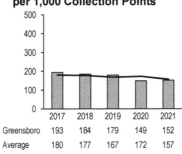

	2017	2018	2019	2020	2021
Greensboro	193	184	179	149	152
Average	180	177	167	172	157

Tons Solid Waste Landfilled per 1,000 Population

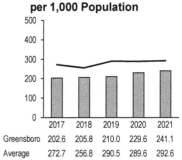

	2017	2018	2019	2020	2021
Greensboro	202.6	205.8	210.0	229.6	241.1
Average	272.7	256.8	290.5	289.6	292.6

Efficiency Measures

Recycling Services Cost per Ton Collected

	2017	2018	2019	2020	2021
Greensboro	$158	$173	$156	$258	$268
Average	$267	$247	$273	$288	$330

Recycling Services Cost per Collection Point

	2017	2018	2019	2020	2021
Greensboro	$30.52	$31.86	$27.84	$38.31	$40.66
Average	$41.76	$38.02	$39.90	$40.46	$44.95

Tons Collected Curbside per Municipal FTE

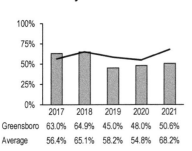

	2017	2018	2019	2020	2021
Greensboro	1,148	1,104	1,079	903	835
Average	561	635	621	536	534

Effectiveness Measures

Community Set-Out Rate

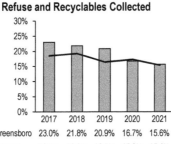

	2017	2018	2019	2020	2021
Greensboro	63.0%	64.9%	45.0%	48.0%	50.6%
Average	56.4%	65.1%	58.2%	54.8%	68.2%

Tons Recycled as Percentage of Tons Refuse and Recyclables Collected

	2017	2018	2019	2020	2021
Greensboro	23.0%	21.8%	20.9%	16.7%	15.6%
Average	18.5%	19.3%	16.5%	17.3%	15.4%

Explanatory Information

Service Level and Delivery

Greenville offers once-a-week curbside or backyard collection of recyclable materials to its residents through a city-run program. Residents can choose to have backyard collection for a fee. The recycling fee is included in the solid-waste fee for residential refuse collection. The recycling materials include:

- newspaper and magazines
- cardboard
- aluminum and steel cans
- No. 1 and No. 2 plastics
- glass of all colors
- white goods

Greenville's household recycling program also uses three city-owned drop-off recycling centers and over 200 other sites connected to multifamily complexes. Tonnage and cost for these other drop-off sites are not included in the performance and cost data.

Conditions Affecting Service, Performance, and Costs

No data were reported for FY 2019-20 for the city of Greenville.

Municipal Profile

Population (OSBM 2020)	87,428
Land Area (Square Miles)	35.66
Persons per Square Mile	2,452

Service Profile

FTE Positions—Collection	6.0
FTE Positions—Other	1.5
Number of City Drop-Off Centers	220
Other Drop-Off Centers	0
Percentage of Service Contracted	0%
Collection Frequency	Every 2 weeks
General Collection Location	Curbside
Recyclables Sorted at Curb	No
Collection Points	19,132
Tons of Recyclables Collected	
Curbside	2,511
City Drop-Off Centers	0
Total Tons Collected	2,511
Monthly Service Fee	na
Revenue from Sale of Recyclables	$0
Sale Revenue as Percentage of Cost	NA

Full Cost Profile

Cost Breakdown by Percentage	
Personal Services	35.4%
Operating Costs	46.3%
Capital Costs	18.2%
TOTAL	100.0%

Cost Breakdown in Dollars	
Personal Services	$509,405
Operating Costs	$665,991
Capital Costs	$262,164
TOTAL	$1,437,560

Key: Greenville ▨   Benchmarking Average —   Fiscal Years 2017 through 2021

Resource Measures

Recycling Services Cost per Capita

	2017	2018	2019	2020	2021
Greenville	$22.94	$14.39	$21.40		$16.44
Average	$13.36	$12.39	$12.62	$14.17	$14.63

Recycling Services FTEs per 10,000 Population

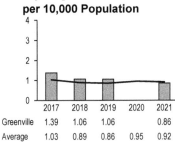

	2017	2018	2019	2020	2021
Greenville	1.39	1.06	1.06		0.86
Average	1.03	0.89	0.86	0.95	0.92

Workload Measures

Tons Recyclables Collected per 1,000 Population

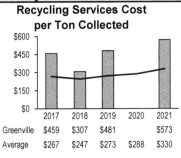

	2017	2018	2019	2020	2021
Greenville	49.9	46.8	44.5		28.7
Average	57.4	56.1	52.8	57.0	50.4

Tons Recyclables Collected per 1,000 Collection Points

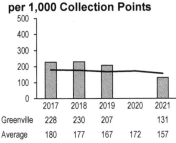

	2017	2018	2019	2020	2021
Greenville	228	230	207		131
Average	180	177	167	172	157

Tons Solid Waste Landfilled per 1,000 Population

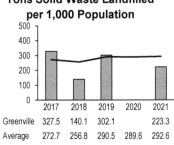

	2017	2018	2019	2020	2021
Greenville	327.5	140.1	302.1		223.3
Average	272.7	256.8	290.5	289.6	292.6

Efficiency Measures

Recycling Services Cost per Ton Collected

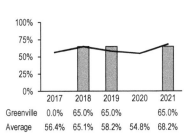

	2017	2018	2019	2020	2021
Greenville	$459	$307	$481		$573
Average	$267	$247	$273	$288	$330

Recycling Services Cost per Collection Point

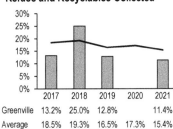

	2017	2018	2019	2020	2021
Greenville	$104.61	$70.59	$99.80		$75.14
Average	$41.76	$38.02	$39.90	$40.46	$44.95

Tons Collected Curbside per Municipal FTE

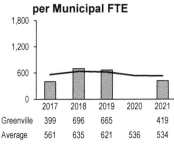

	2017	2018	2019	2020	2021
Greenville	399	696	665		419
Average	561	635	621	536	534

Effectiveness Measures

Community Set-Out Rate

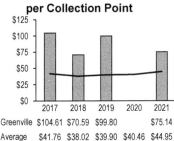

	2017	2018	2019	2020	2021
Greenville	0.0%	65.0%	65.0%		65.0%
Average	56.4%	65.1%	58.2%	54.8%	68.2%

Tons Recycled as Percentage of Tons Refuse and Recyclables Collected

	2017	2018	2019	2020	2021
Greenville	13.2%	25.0%	12.8%		11.4%
Average	18.5%	19.3%	16.5%	17.3%	15.4%

Fiscal Year 2020-21

Service Level and Delivery

Hickory offers curbside collection of recyclable materials every other week to its residents through a contractual agreement. The recycling materials collected include:

- newspaper and magazines
- aluminum and steel cans
- No. 1 and No. 2 plastics
- glass—all colors
- phone books and junk mail

Hickory's household recycling program also uses two drop-off recycling centers. One is staffed, and the other is not. These centers collect antifreeze and oil in addition to the same household materials that are collected at the curb. Tonnage and costs for this service are included in the performance and cost data.

A separate commercial recycling program that services businesses and multifamily units is operated by the city. The program utilizes city workers and equipment to collect cardboard and paper in addition to the curbside materials. The performance and cost data do not include the commercial program.

The city charges residents a monthly fee for recycling, which is included in the monthly solid-waste fee. In the fiscal year, the city collected $49,697 in revenue from the sale of recyclables, partially offsetting program costs.

Conditions Affecting Service, Performance, and Costs

The set-out rate is calculated on a monthly basis by the contractor. While not tracked, missed recycling pickups are minimal and average less than one per month.

Municipal Profile

Population (OSBM 2020)	43,578
Land Area (Square Miles)	30.50
Persons per Square Mile	1,429

Service Profile

FTE Positions—Collection	0.5 City
FTE Positions—Other	0.27 City
Number of City Drop-Off Centers	2
Other Drop-Off Centers	0
Percentage of Service Contracted	94%
Collection Frequency	Every 2 weeks
General Collection Location	Curbside
Recyclables Sorted at Curb	No
Collection Points	12,200
Tons of Recyclables Collected	
Curbside	2,497
City Drop-Off Centers	166
Total Tons Collected	2,663
Monthly Service Fee	0
Revenue from Sale of Recyclables	$49,697
Sale Revenue as Percentage of Cost	9.8%

Full Cost Profile

Cost Breakdown by Percentage	
Personal Services	8.9%
Operating Costs	88.7%
Capital Costs	2.4%
TOTAL	100.0%
Cost Breakdown in Dollars	
Personal Services	$45,098
Operating Costs	$448,298
Capital Costs	$11,997
TOTAL	$505,393

Hickory

Household Recycling

Key: Hickory ▨   Benchmarking Average —   Fiscal Years 2017 through 2021

Resource Measures

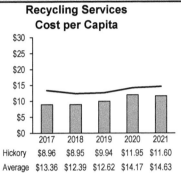

Recycling Services Cost per Capita

	2017	2018	2019	2020	2021
Hickory	$8.96	$8.95	$9.94	$11.95	$11.60
Average	$13.36	$12.39	$12.62	$14.17	$14.63

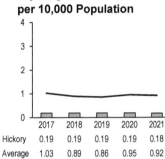

Recycling Services FTEs per 10,000 Population

	2017	2018	2019	2020	2021
Hickory	0.19	0.19	0.19	0.19	0.18
Average	1.03	0.89	0.86	0.95	0.92

Workload Measures

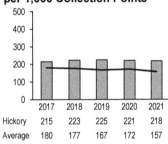

Tons Recyclables Collected per 1,000 Population

	2017	2018	2019	2020	2021
Hickory	64.8	65.6	65.5	64.7	61.1
Average	57.4	56.1	52.8	57.0	50.4

Tons Recyclables Collected per 1,000 Collection Points

	2017	2018	2019	2020	2021
Hickory	215	223	225	221	218
Average	180	177	167	172	157

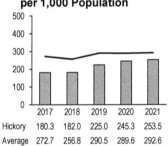

Tons Solid Waste Landfilled per 1,000 Population

	2017	2018	2019	2020	2021
Hickory	180.3	182.0	225.0	245.3	253.5
Average	272.7	256.8	290.5	289.6	292.6

Efficiency Measures

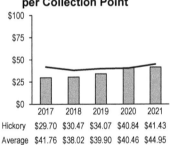

Recycling Services Cost per Ton Collected

	2017	2018	2019	2020	2021
Hickory	$138	$136	$152	$185	$190
Average	$267	$247	$273	$288	$330

Recycling Services Cost per Collection Point

	2017	2018	2019	2020	2021
Hickory	$29.70	$30.47	$34.07	$40.84	$41.43
Average	$41.76	$38.02	$39.90	$40.46	$44.95

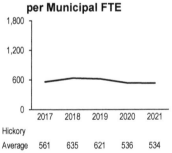

Tons Collected Curbside per Municipal FTE

	2017	2018	2019	2020	2021
Hickory					
Average	561	635	621	536	534

Effectiveness Measures

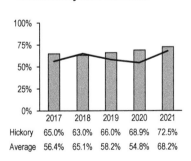

Community Set-Out Rate

	2017	2018	2019	2020	2021
Hickory	65.0%	63.0%	66.0%	68.9%	72.5%
Average	56.4%	65.1%	58.2%	54.8%	68.2%

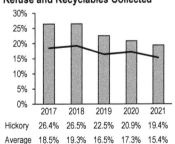

Tons Recycled as Percentage of Tons Refuse and Recyclables Collected

	2017	2018	2019	2020	2021
Hickory	26.4%	26.5%	22.5%	20.9%	19.4%
Average	18.5%	19.3%	16.5%	17.3%	15.4%

Fiscal Year 2020-21

Explanatory Information

Service Level and Delivery

Raleigh provides curbside collection of recyclables every other week. Three drop-off centers for use by all residents and small businesses are also available. Customers are allowed two ninety-five-gallon carts. A few townhome locations use smaller eighteen-gallon bins due to the difficulty of moving carts to a pickup location.

Recyclables collected include:

- plastic
- glass
- metal and aluminum cans
- magazines
- newspaper
- phone books
- cardboard
- mixed paper

Conditions Affecting Service, Performance, and Costs

Municipal Profile

Population (OSBM 2020)	468,977
Land Area (Square Miles)	146.47
Persons per Square Mile	3,202

Service Profile

FTE Positions—Collection	33.0
FTE Positions—Other	3.0
Number of City Drop-Off Centers	2
Other Drop-Off Centers	1
Percentage of Service Contracted	0%
Collection Frequency	Every 2 weeks
General Collection Location	Curbside
Recyclables Sorted at Curb	No
Collection Points	184,460
Tons of Recyclables Collected	
Curbside	30,205
City Drop-Off Centers	701
Total Tons Collected	30,906
Monthly Service Fee	$4.60
Revenue from Sale of Recyclables	$0
Sale Revenue as Percentage of Cost	NA

Full Cost Profile

Cost Breakdown by Percentage	
Personal Services	30.7%
Operating Costs	49.2%
Capital Costs	20.2%
TOTAL	100.0%
Cost Breakdown in Dollars	
Personal Services	$2,302,705
Operating Costs	$3,691,321
Capital Costs	$1,516,237
TOTAL	$7,510,263

Raleigh

Household Recycling

Key: Raleigh ▣   Benchmarking Average —   Fiscal Years 2017 through 2021

Resource Measures

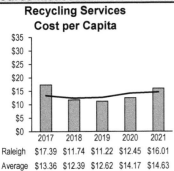

Recycling Services Cost per Capita

	2017	2018	2019	2020	2021
Raleigh	$17.39	$11.74	$11.22	$12.45	$16.01
Average	$13.36	$12.39	$12.62	$14.17	$14.63

Recycling Services FTEs per 10,000 Population

	2017	2018	2019	2020	2021
Raleigh	0.87	0.87	0.90	0.88	0.77
Average	1.03	0.89	0.86	0.95	0.92

Workload Measures

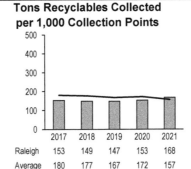

Tons Recyclables Collected per 1,000 Population

	2017	2018	2019	2020	2021
Raleigh	63.3	60.6	60.2	61.2	65.9
Average	57.4	56.1	52.8	57.0	50.4

Tons Recyclables Collected per 1,000 Collection Points

	2017	2018	2019	2020	2021
Raleigh	153	149	147	153	168
Average	180	177	167	172	157

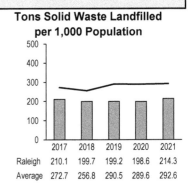

Tons Solid Waste Landfilled per 1,000 Population

	2017	2018	2019	2020	2021
Raleigh	210.1	199.7	199.2	198.6	214.3
Average	272.7	256.8	290.5	289.6	292.6

Efficiency Measures

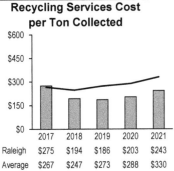

Recycling Services Cost per Ton Collected

	2017	2018	2019	2020	2021
Raleigh	$275	$194	$186	$203	$243
Average	$267	$247	$273	$288	$330

Recycling Services Cost per Collection Point

	2017	2018	2019	2020	2021
Raleigh	$42.02	$28.79	$27.48	$31.06	$40.71
Average	$41.76	$38.02	$39.90	$40.46	$44.95

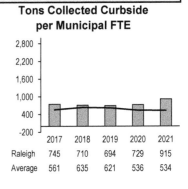

Tons Collected Curbside per Municipal FTE

	2017	2018	2019	2020	2021
Raleigh	745	710	694	729	915
Average	561	635	621	536	534

Effectiveness Measures

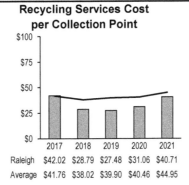

Community Set-Out Rate

	2017	2018	2019	2020	2021
Raleigh	68.0%	72.0%	72.0%		
Average	56.4%	65.1%	58.2%	54.8%	68.2%

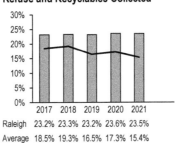

Tons Recycled as Percentage of Tons Refuse and Recyclables Collected

	2017	2018	2019	2020	2021
Raleigh	23.2%	23.3%	23.2%	23.6%	23.5%
Average	18.5%	19.3%	16.5%	17.3%	15.4%

Explanatory Information

Service Level and Delivery

Wilson's household recycling program provides curbside pickup of materials once each week to residents on the same day as residential refuse collection but by different crews. Wilson began a pilot program in July 2015 that shifted to collection being done once every two weeks. This pilot phase initially covered about 2,800 homes, and each received a ninety-six-gallon roll-out cart. About two-thirds of households are serviced every other week and one-third are serviced weekly with households having the smaller bins. The city is beginning to replace all the remaining smaller bins and move all residents to a bi-weekly collection cycle. The recycling program is part of the Division of Environmental Services.

The following materials are collected:

- aluminum and steel cans
- No. 1 and No. 2 plastic containers
- newsprint
- clear, green, and brown glass
- waste oil, fluorescent bulbs, electronics, and small appliances, which are collected curbside on a call-in basis

Conditions Affecting Service, Performance, and Costs

The set-out rate was calculated on a monthly basis by drivers on the recycling trucks using counters.

The initial pilot phase for recycling began in July 2015 and helped lower overall costs notably.

Municipal Profile

Population (OSBM 2020)	47,769
Land Area (Square Miles)	31.02
Persons per Square Mile	1,540

Service Profile

FTE Positions—Collection	7.0
FTE Positions—Other	0.5
Number of City Drop-Off Centers	0
Other Drop-Off Centers	0
Percentage of Service Contracted	0%
Collection Frequency	
for 96-gallon carts	Every 2 weeks
for 18-gallon cart	Every week
General Collection Location	Curbside
Recyclables Sorted at Curb	No
Collection Points	21,111
Tons of Recyclables Collected	
Curbside	1,705
City Drop-Off Centers	0
Total Tons Collected	1,705
Monthly Service Fee	$20.00
Revenue from Sale of Recyclables	$0

Full Cost Profile

Cost Breakdown by Percentage	
Personal Services	41.5%
Operating Costs	45.2%
Capital Costs	13.3%
TOTAL	100.0%

Cost Breakdown in Dollars	
Personal Services	$267,178
Operating Costs	$291,147
Capital Costs	$85,633
TOTAL	$643,958

Wilson

Household Recycling

Key: Wilson ▪   Benchmarking Average —   Fiscal Years 2017 through 2021

Resource Measures

Recycling Services Cost per Capita

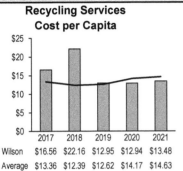

	2017	2018	2019	2020	2021
Wilson	$16.56	$22.16	$12.95	$12.94	$13.48
Average	$13.36	$12.39	$12.62	$14.17	$14.63

Recycling Services FTEs per 10,000 Population

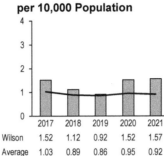

	2017	2018	2019	2020	2021
Wilson	1.52	1.12	0.92	1.52	1.57
Average	1.03	0.89	0.86	0.95	0.92

Workload Measures

Tons Recyclables Collected per 1,000 Population

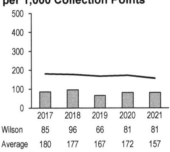

	2017	2018	2019	2020	2021
Wilson	34.5	39.7	33.5	34.5	35.7
Average	57.4	56.1	52.8	57.0	50.4

Tons Recyclables Collected per 1,000 Collection Points

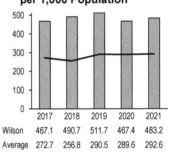

	2017	2018	2019	2020	2021
Wilson	85	96	66	81	81
Average	180	177	167	172	157

Tons Solid Waste Landfilled per 1,000 Population

	2017	2018	2019	2020	2021
Wilson	467.1	490.7	511.7	467.4	483.2
Average	272.7	256.8	290.5	289.6	292.6

Efficiency Measures

Recycling Services Cost per Ton Collected

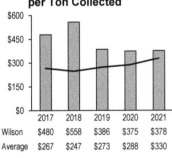

	2017	2018	2019	2020	2021
Wilson	$480	$558	$386	$375	$378
Average	$267	$247	$273	$288	$330

Recycling Services Cost per Collection Point

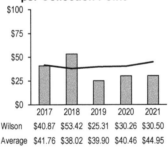

	2017	2018	2019	2020	2021
Wilson	$40.87	$53.42	$25.31	$30.26	$30.50
Average	$41.76	$38.02	$39.90	$40.46	$44.95

Tons Collected Curbside per Municipal FTE

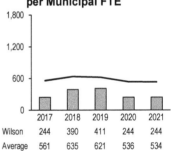

	2017	2018	2019	2020	2021
Wilson	244	390	411	244	244
Average	561	635	621	536	534

Effectiveness Measures

Community Set-Out Rate

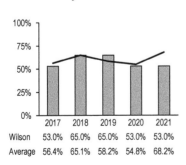

	2017	2018	2019	2020	2021
Wilson	53.0%	65.0%	65.0%	53.0%	53.0%
Average	56.4%	65.1%	58.2%	54.8%	68.2%

Tons Recycled as Percentage of Tons Refuse and Recyclables Collected

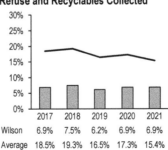

	2017	2018	2019	2020	2021
Wilson	6.9%	7.5%	6.2%	6.9%	6.9%
Average	18.5%	19.3%	16.5%	17.3%	15.4%

Fiscal Year 2020-21

Explanatory Information

Service Level and Delivery

Winston-Salem provides biweekly curbside household recycling service to its single-family residences using ninety-six-gallon carts. The city provides nine drop-off sites for cardboard at its fire stations plus two full-service drop-off sites. Items collected in the city's curbside household recycling program include:

- aluminum and steel cans
- all plastic bottles
- green, amber, and clear glass
- newspaper
- magazines, telephone books, and junk mail
- chipboard
- corrugated cardboard (no bundling requirement)
- office paper
- aerosol cans

The city contracts for 100 percent of its curbside household recycling program. The city does not charge a recycling fee. Revenue to the city for the sale of recyclables was $307,572 during the year, partially offsetting program costs.

Conditions Affecting Service, Performance, and Costs

Complaints include calls reported to the city. The contractor has a separate customer service hotline.

Municipal Profile

Population (OSBM 2020)	249,986
Land Area (Square Miles)	132.59
Persons per Square Mile	1,885

Service Profile

FTE Positions—Collection	Contractor
FTE Positions—Other	1.0
Number of City Drop-Off Centers	7
Other Drop-Off Centers	0
Percentage of Service Contracted	100%
Collection Frequency	Every 2 weeks
General Collection Location	Curbside
Recyclables Sorted at Curb	No
Collection Points	81,589
Tons of Recyclables Collected	
Curbside	15,288
City Drop-Off Centers	142
Total Tons Collected	15,430
Monthly Service Fee	0
Revenue from Sale of Recyclables	$307,572
Sale Revenue as Percentage of Cost	17.6%

Full Cost Profile

Cost Breakdown by Percentage	
Personal Services	5.1%
Operating Costs	94.9%
Capital Costs	0.0%
TOTAL	100.0%
Cost Breakdown in Dollars	
Personal Services	$88,376
Operating Costs	$1,660,005
Capital Costs	$0
TOTAL	$1,748,381

Winston-Salem

Household Recycling

Resource Measures

Recycling Services Cost per Capita

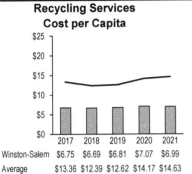

	2017	2018	2019	2020	2021
Winston-Salem	$6.75	$6.69	$6.81	$7.07	$6.99
Average	$13.36	$12.39	$12.62	$14.17	$14.63

Recycling Services FTEs per 10,000 Population

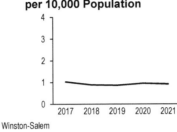

	2017	2018	2019	2020	2021
Winston-Salem					
Average	1.03	0.89	0.86	0.95	0.92

Workload Measures

Tons Recyclables Collected per 1,000 Population

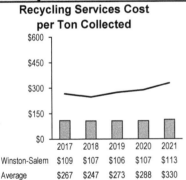

	2017	2018	2019	2020	2021
Winston-Salem	62.0	62.7	64.2	66.4	61.7
Average	57.4	56.1	52.8	57.0	50.4

Tons Recyclables Collected per 1,000 Collection Points

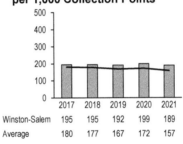

	2017	2018	2019	2020	2021
Winston-Salem	195	195	192	199	189
Average	180	177	167	172	157

Tons Solid Waste Landfilled per 1,000 Population

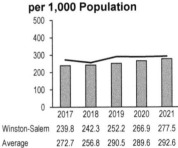

	2017	2018	2019	2020	2021
Winston-Salem	239.8	242.3	252.2	266.9	277.5
Average	272.7	256.8	290.5	289.6	292.6

Efficiency Measures

Recycling Services Cost per Ton Collected

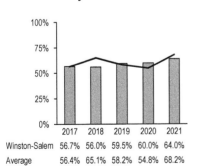

	2017	2018	2019	2020	2021
Winston-Salem	$109	$107	$106	$107	$113
Average	$267	$247	$273	$288	$330

Recycling Services Cost per Collection Point

	2017	2018	2019	2020	2021
Winston-Salem	$21.24	$20.82	$20.31	$21.22	$21.43
Average	$41.76	$38.02	$39.90	$40.46	$44.95

Tons Collected Curbside per Municipal FTE

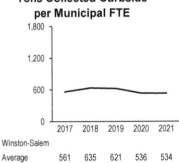

	2017	2018	2019	2020	2021
Winston-Salem					
Average	561	635	621	536	534

Effectiveness Measures

Community Set-Out Rate

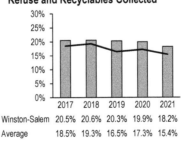

	2017	2018	2019	2020	2021
Winston-Salem	56.7%	56.0%	59.5%	60.0%	64.0%
Average	56.4%	65.1%	58.2%	54.8%	68.2%

Tons Recycled as Percentage of Tons Refuse and Recyclables Collected

	2017	2018	2019	2020	2021
Winston-Salem	20.5%	20.6%	20.3%	19.9%	18.2%
Average	18.5%	19.3%	16.5%	17.3%	15.4%

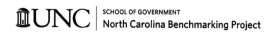

Performance and Cost Data

YARD WASTE / LEAF COLLECTION

PERFORMANCE MEASURES FOR
YARD WASTE/LEAF COLLECTION

SERVICE DEFINITION

Yard Waste/Leaf Collection includes regularly scheduled or special collection of these items. Such collection may occur from the curb, backyard, or another locale. Yard waste and leaves may be bagged, placed in containers, or loose. The service definition excludes the collection of white goods and other bulky items. Although some municipalities collect yard waste and leaves with household refuse or other trash, they separate the items at some point in the collection process because yard waste and leaves cannot be placed in landfills.

NOTES ON PERFORMANCE MEASURES

1. Tons Collected per 1,000 Population and per 1,000 Collection Points

These are the same performance measures that are used for residential refuse collection, except that tonnage here is for yard waste, leaves, and miscellaneous trash rather than residential refuse. "Collection points" refer to the number of residential premises served by regularly scheduled collection of yard waste, leaves, and miscellaneous trash.

2. Cost per Ton Collected

Cost is measured using the project's full cost accounting model, calculating direct, indirect, and capital costs. Tons are as defined above.

3. Tons Collected per Collection FTE

The number of full-time equivalent (FTE) positions refers to the number of employees or laborers who were directly involved in the collection of yard waste, leaves, and miscellaneous trash during the fiscal year. This number includes temporary, permanent, full-time, and part-time workers. Such workers can be sanitation, street, or other municipal employees. One FTE equals 2,080 hours of work per year. Any combination of employees providing 2,080 hours of work per year is one FTE.

4. Complaints (and Valid Complaints) per 10,000 Collection Points

Complaints are those tracked by each jurisdiction, using its own criteria and procedures. Collection points are as defined above. The municipalities follow very different procedures in processing and recording these calls and in determining which ones are complaints and which are not. For these reasons, the project is able to present only limited comparative data about complaints or valid complaints. Nonetheless, the project recommends that the participating municipalities devise common criteria for identifying complaints and procedures for processing and recording calls.

Yard Waste/Leaf Collection

Summary of Key Dimensions of Service

City or Town	Yard Waste Collection		Seasonal Loose Leaf Collection	Collection Points	Tons Collected		Collection FTE Positions
	Location	Frequency			Yard Waste	Seasonal Leaves	
Apex	Curbside	1 x week	NA	21,073	7,299	NA	16.0
Chapel Hill	Curbside	1 x week	2-6 sweeps	12,210	2,348	3,932	13.5
Charlotte	Curbside	1 x week	NA	224,062	51,042	NA	70.0
Concord	Curbside	1 x week	3 sweeps	35,094	8,530	1,817	22.4
Goldsboro	Curbside	1 x 2 weeks	1 x 2 weeks	14,372	4,408	4,136	14.0
Greensboro	Curbside	1 x week	2 sweeps	88,020	12,895	11,861	42.2
Greenville	Curbside	1 x week	1 x 2 weeks	20,000	52,047	956	20.3
Hickory	Curbside	1 x week	2 sweeps	12,200	10,246	3,023	4.3
Raleigh	Curbside	1 x week	2 sweeps	123,500	13,730	11,352	96.0
Wilson	Curbside	1 x week	1 x 3 weeks	21,500	9,211	1,204	15.0
Winston-Salem	Curbside	Yard Waste Cart 1 x week Brush every 10 days	1 x 3 weeks	81,589 for Leaves and brush, 15,022 for Yard Waste	7,191	11,814	70.8

NOTES
Municipalities with no reported seasonal leaf collection collect leaves as part of their yard waste collection programs.

EXPLANATORY FACTORS
These are factors that the project found affected yard waste and leaf collection performance and cost in one or more of the municipalities:

Whether or not a fee is charged for collection
Residential/commercial/industrial nature of the community
Policies regarding sizes and types of items collected
Extent of seasonal leaf collection service
Landfill policies and tipping fees

Explanatory Information

Service Level and Delivery

The Town of Apex collects yard waste curbside once per week for all city residents. The town collects vegetative matter from residential landscaping. The town does not operate a seasonal leaf collection, but leaves are collected year-round as part of the weekly service. Land clearing debris is not collected. The town charges $7.83 per month for the collection of yard waste.

There are three grass/vacuum trucks, two two-person limb-chipping crews, and one grapple-truck operator for larger items. These crews cover the town every week using a five-day-a-week schedule.

Conditions Affecting Service, Performance, and Costs

Municipal Profile

Population (OSBM 2020)	59,368
Land Area (Square Miles)	23.61
Persons per Square Mile	2,514

Service Profile

FTE Positions—Collection	17.0
FTE Positions—Other	2.8
Collection Frequency	
Yard Waste	1 x week
Collection Points	21,073
Tons Collected	
Yard Waste	7,299
Seasonal Leaves	with yard waste
Total Tons Collected	7,299
Monthly Service Fee	$7.83

Full Cost Profile

Cost Breakdown by Percentage	
Personal Services	47.4%
Operating Costs	35.7%
Capital Costs	16.9%
TOTAL	100.0%

Cost Breakdown in Dollars	
Personal Services	$1,232,892
Operating Costs	$927,101
Capital Costs	$439,567
TOTAL	$2,599,560

Apex

Yard Waste/Leaf Collection

Resource Measures

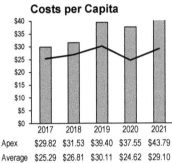

Yard Waste and Leaf Collection Costs per Capita

	2017	2018	2019	2020	2021
Apex	$29.82	$31.53	$39.40	$37.55	$43.79
Average	$25.29	$26.81	$30.11	$24.62	$29.10

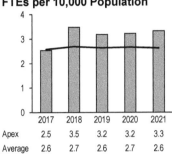

Yard Waste and Leaf Collection FTEs per 10,000 Population

	2017	2018	2019	2020	2021
Apex	2.5	3.5	3.2	3.2	3.3
Average	2.6	2.7	2.6	2.7	2.6

Workload Measures

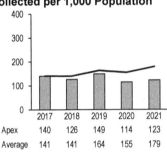

Yard Waste and Leaf Tons Collected per 1,000 Population

	2017	2018	2019	2020	2021
Apex	140	126	149	114	123
Average	141	141	164	155	179

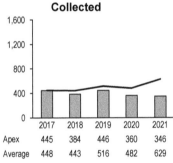

Yard Waste and Leaf Tons Collected

	2017	2018	2019	2020	2021
Apex	445	384	446	360	346
Average	448	443	516	482	629

Efficiency Measures

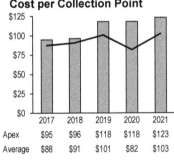

Yard Waste and Leaf Collection Cost per Collection Point

	2017	2018	2019	2020	2021
Apex	$95	$96	$118	$118	$123
Average	$88	$91	$101	$82	$103

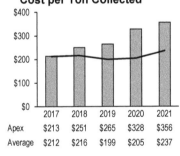

Yard Waste and Leaf Collection Cost per Ton Collected

	2017	2018	2019	2020	2021
Apex	$213	$251	$265	$328	$356
Average	$212	$216	$199	$205	$237

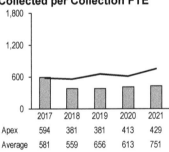

Yard Waste and Leaf Tons Collected per Collection FTE

	2017	2018	2019	2020	2021
Apex	594	381	381	413	429
Average	581	559	656	613	751

Effectiveness Measures

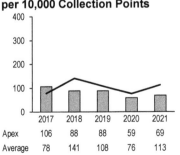

Collection Complaints per 10,000 Collection Points

	2017	2018	2019	2020	2021
Apex	106	88	88	59	69
Average	78	141	108	76	113

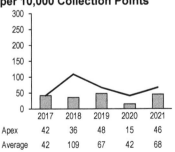

Valid Complaints per 10,000 Collection Points

	2017	2018	2019	2020	2021
Apex	42	36	48	15	46
Average	42	109	67	42	68

Fiscal Year 2020-21

Explanatory Information

Service Level and Delivery

Yard waste collection is managed by the Solid Waste Services Division of the Public Works Department. Yard waste includes organic materials, such as leaves, stems, grass, limbs, and other residential organic matter. The town does not collect large logs or stumps, or debris from lot clearing.

Yard waste is collected once per week curbside with no monthly fee. Yard waste is collected by seven three-person crews using rear packers two days per week. The town collects small-yard-waste materials placed in roll carts, other rigid containers, or paper yard waste bags. The town collects large yard waste materials in loose piles. Yard waste piles larger than three cubic yards are collected for a fee. The town does not collect yard waste in plastic bags.

Residents can rent a 10-cubic-yard roll-off container or schedule a paid knuckle boom collection for large projects. These larger loads are collected by a one-person crew using a knuckle boom truck and a hook-lift truck five days per week. Residents pay a fee of $35 per day or $60 per week to rent a roll-off container for collection. The fee for a knuckle boom collection is $125.

Seasonal leaf collection is managed by the Streets and Construction Services Division of the Public Works Department. Seasonal leaf collection is run with five or six cycles in a season from mid-October to early March. Only loose leaves and pine straw free of limbs or other debris are collected curbside. Leaf crews consist of a driver, a raker, and a machine operator. Crews may make use of seasonal labor, and three to six crews are used depending on the volume of leaves at the curb for collection. During peak leaf fall, crews also pull the curb line in conjunction with street sweepers from the Stormwater Program of the Public Works Department.

Conditions Affecting Service, Performance, and Costs

Municipal Profile

Population (OSBM 2020)	62,080
Land Area (Square Miles)	21.31
Persons per Square Mile	2,914

Service Profile

FTE Positions—Collection	14.5
FTE Positions—Other	0.3
Collection Frequency	
Yard Waste	1 x week
Seasonal Leaf Collection	5-6 sweeps
Collection Points	12,230
Tons Collected	
Yard Waste	2,348
Seasonal Leaves	3,932
Total Tons Collected	6,280
Monthly Service Fee	Resdients may purchase cart for $50 but not required

Full Cost Profile

Cost Breakdown by Percentage	
Personal Services	39.0%
Operating Costs	44.3%
Capital Costs	16.7%
TOTAL	100.0%

Cost Breakdown in Dollars	
Personal Services	$993,453
Operating Costs	$1,129,288
Capital Costs	$426,700
TOTAL	$2,549,441

Chapel Hill

Yard Waste/Leaf Collection

Key: Chapel Hill ▒   Benchmarking Average —   Fiscal Years 2017 through 2021

Resource Measures

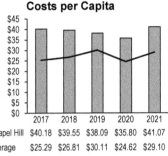

Yard Waste and Leaf Collection Costs per Capita

	2017	2018	2019	2020	2021
Chapel Hill	$40.18	$39.55	$38.09	$35.80	$41.07
Average	$25.29	$26.81	$30.11	$24.62	$29.10

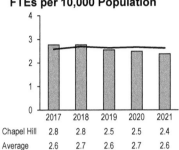

Yard Waste and Leaf Collection FTEs per 10,000 Population

	2017	2018	2019	2020	2021
Chapel Hill	2.8	2.8	2.5	2.5	2.4
Average	2.6	2.7	2.6	2.7	2.6

Workload Measures

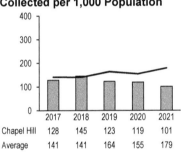

Yard Waste and Leaf Tons Collected per 1,000 Population

	2017	2018	2019	2020	2021
Chapel Hill	128	145	123	119	101
Average	141	141	164	155	179

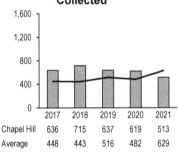

Yard Waste and Leaf Tons Collected

	2017	2018	2019	2020	2021
Chapel Hill	636	715	637	619	513
Average	448	443	516	482	629

Efficiency Measures

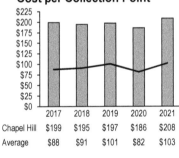

Yard Waste and Leaf Collection Cost per Collection Point

	2017	2018	2019	2020	2021
Chapel Hill	$199	$195	$197	$186	$208
Average	$88	$91	$101	$82	$103

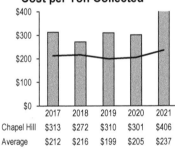

Yard Waste and Leaf Collection Cost per Ton Collected

	2017	2018	2019	2020	2021
Chapel Hill	$313	$272	$310	$301	$406
Average	$212	$216	$199	$205	$237

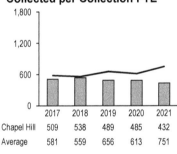

Yard Waste and Leaf Tons Collected per Collection FTE

	2017	2018	2019	2020	2021
Chapel Hill	509	538	489	485	432
Average	581	559	656	613	751

Effectiveness Measures

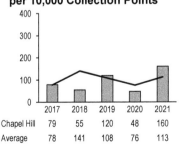

Collection Complaints per 10,000 Collection Points

	2017	2018	2019	2020	2021
Chapel Hill	79	55	120	48	160
Average	78	141	108	76	113

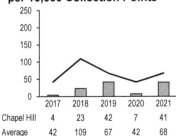

Valid Complaints per 10,000 Collection Points

	2017	2018	2019	2020	2021
Chapel Hill	4	23	42	7	41
Average	42	109	67	42	68

Fiscal Year 2020-21

Explanatory Information

Service Level and Delivery

Charlotte collects yard waste once per week curbside. The city performs all yard waste collection.

Yard waste includes leaves, stems, grass, limbs, and other residential organic matter. Limbs should be separated into piles small enough for one individual to handle. Leaves and grass clippings must be placed in untied plastic bags or in uncovered trash cans. Yard waste placed at the curb by a commercial landscaping service will not be collected by the city. The city of Charlotte used thirty-five two-person crews working from rear loaders to service the entire city. Additional trucks and staff are allocated as a yard waste reserve.

Leaves are collected in bags and are debagged at the curb as part of the regular yard waste service. A special seasonal leaf collection is not done by the City of Charlotte.

Conditions Affecting Service, Performance, and Costs

Municipal Profile

Population (OSBM 2020)	876,694
Land Area (Square Miles)	307.41
Persons per Square Mile	2,852

Service Profile

FTE Positions—Collection	73.00
FTE Positions—Other	0.00
Collection Frequency	
Yard Waste	1 x week
Collection Points	224,062
Tons Collected	
Yard Waste	51,042
Seasonal Leaves	with yard waste
Total Tons Collected	51,042
Monthly Service Fee	No

Full Cost Profile

Cost Breakdown by Percentage	
Personal Services	33.9%
Operating Costs	53.4%
Capital Costs	12.6%
TOTAL	100.0%

Cost Breakdown in Dollars	
Personal Services	$5,210,731
Operating Costs	$8,207,659
Capital Costs	$1,939,105
TOTAL	$15,357,495

Charlotte

Yard Waste/Leaf Collection

Key: Charlotte ▨   Benchmarking Average —   Fiscal Years 2017 through 2021

Resource Measures

Yard Waste and Leaf Collection Costs per Capita

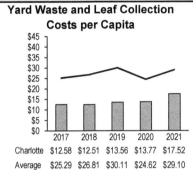

	2017	2018	2019	2020	2021
Charlotte	$12.58	$12.51	$13.56	$13.77	$17.52
Average	$25.29	$26.81	$30.11	$24.62	$29.10

Yard Waste and Leaf Collection FTEs per 10,000 Population

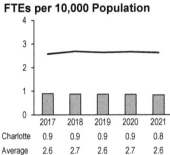

	2017	2018	2019	2020	2021
Charlotte	0.9	0.9	0.9	0.9	0.8
Average	2.6	2.7	2.6	2.7	2.6

Workload Measures

Yard Waste and Leaf Tons Collected per 1,000 Population

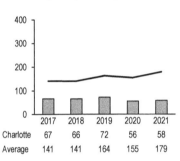

	2017	2018	2019	2020	2021
Charlotte	67	66	72	56	58
Average	141	141	164	155	179

Yard Waste and Leaf Tons Collected per 1,000 Collection Points

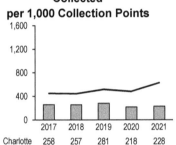

	2017	2018	2019	2020	2021
Charlotte	258	257	281	218	228
Average	448	443	516	482	629

Efficiency Measures

Yard Waste and Leaf Collection Cost per Collection Point

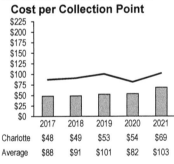

	2017	2018	2019	2020	2021
Charlotte	$48	$49	$53	$54	$69
Average	$88	$91	$101	$82	$103

Yard Waste and Leaf Collection Cost per Ton Collected

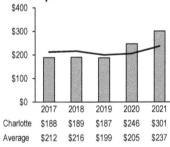

	2017	2018	2019	2020	2021
Charlotte	$188	$189	$187	$246	$301
Average	$212	$216	$199	$205	$237

Yard Waste and Leaf Tons Collected per Collection FTE

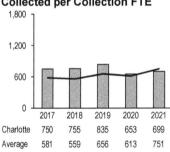

	2017	2018	2019	2020	2021
Charlotte	750	755	835	653	699
Average	581	559	656	613	751

Effectiveness Measures

Collection Complaints per 10,000 Collection Points

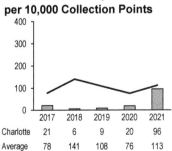

	2017	2018	2019	2020	2021
Charlotte	21	6	9	20	96
Average	78	141	108	76	113

Valid Complaints per 10,000 Collection Points

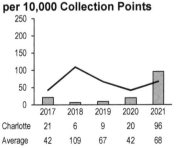

	2017	2018	2019	2020	2021
Charlotte	21	6	9	20	96
Average	42	109	67	42	68

Fiscal Year 2020-21

Explanatory Information

Service Level and Delivery
Concord collects all yard waste once per week. Yard waste includes limbs, logs, grass clippings, shrubbery clippings, and leaves.

Concord uses three two-person crews with rearloaders and five two-person crews with knuckleboom trucks to collect limbs and brush on a weekly basis.

Concord's seasonal loose-leaf collection runs from November through mid-February. Each street is serviced following a publicized schedule a minimum of three times for loose-leaf collection during this period. Residents who bag their leaves receive weekly collection along with the normal yard waste collection program.

Conditions Affecting Service, Performance, and Costs
Concord provides a high level of service in this area, which make the costs per collection point and per ton appear high.

Municipal Profile

Population (OSBM 2020)	105,936
Land Area (Square Miles)	63.65
Persons per Square Mile	1,664

Service Profile

FTE Positions—Collection	23.70
FTE Positions—Other	2.07
Collection Frequency	
Yard Waste	1 x week
Seasonal Leaf Collection	3 sweeps
Collection Points	35,094
Tons Collected	
Yard Waste	8,530
Seasonal Leaves	1,817
Total Tons Collected	10,347
Monthly Service Fee	No

Full Cost Profile

Cost Breakdown by Percentage	
Personal Services	55.0%
Operating Costs	28.6%
Capital Costs	16.4%
TOTAL	100.0%
Cost Breakdown in Dollars	
Personal Services	$1,714,641
Operating Costs	$889,856
Capital Costs	$511,068
TOTAL	$3,115,565

Concord   Yard Waste/Leaf Collection

Resource Measures

Yard Waste and Leaf Collection Costs per Capita

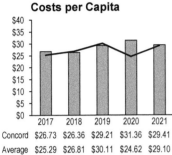

	2017	2018	2019	2020	2021
Concord	$26.73	$26.36	$29.21	$31.36	$29.41
Average	$25.29	$26.81	$30.11	$24.62	$29.10

Yard Waste and Leaf Collection FTEs per 10,000 Population

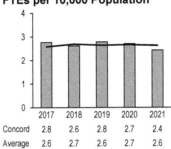

	2017	2018	2019	2020	2021
Concord	2.8	2.6	2.8	2.7	2.4
Average	2.6	2.7	2.6	2.7	2.6

Workload Measures

Yard Waste and Leaf Tons Collected per 1,000 Population

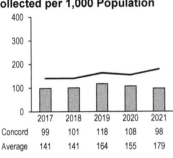

	2017	2018	2019	2020	2021
Concord	99	101	118	108	98
Average	141	141	164	155	179

Yard Waste and Leaf Tons Collected

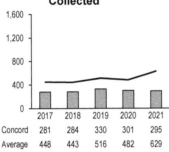

	2017	2018	2019	2020	2021
Concord	281	284	330	301	295
Average	448	443	516	482	629

Efficiency Measures

Yard Waste and Leaf Collection Cost per Collection Point

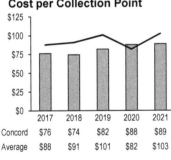

	2017	2018	2019	2020	2021
Concord	$76	$74	$82	$88	$89
Average	$88	$91	$101	$82	$103

Yard Waste and Leaf Collection Cost per Ton Collected

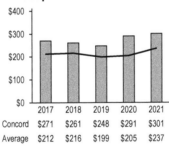

	2017	2018	2019	2020	2021
Concord	$271	$261	$248	$291	$301
Average	$212	$216	$199	$205	$237

Yard Waste and Leaf Tons Collected per Collection FTE

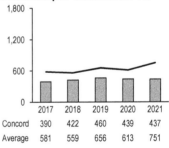

	2017	2018	2019	2020	2021
Concord	390	422	460	439	437
Average	581	559	656	613	751

Effectiveness Measures

Collection Complaints per 10,000 Collection Points

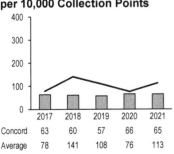

	2017	2018	2019	2020	2021
Concord	63	60	57	66	65
Average	78	141	108	76	113

Valid Complaints per 10,000 Collection Points

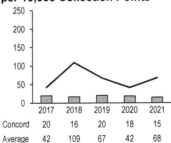

	2017	2018	2019	2020	2021
Concord	20	16	20	18	15
Average	42	109	67	42	68

Goldsboro

Yard Waste/Leaf Collection

Fiscal Year 2020-21

Explanatory Information

Service Level and Delivery

Goldsboro provides yard waste and seasonal leaf collection through the Solid Waste Division of the Public Works Department. Yard waste includes grass clippings, vines, garden and hedge trimmings, shrubbery, and other vegetative debris. Yard waste must be placed at the curbside in loose piles.

Yard waste is collected by four two-person crews consisting of one driver and one collector. Yard waste is collected every two weeks, rotating through different sections of the city.

Seasonal leaf collection is done during the months of October through February. Collection is done every two weeks. Five crews are used for seasonal leaf collection consisting of one driver and two collectors per crew. One of the seasonal collectors is a temporary employee, while the driver and the other collector are permanent employees. Leaves must be placed loose or in a leaf cage at the curb.

Conditions Affecting Service, Performance, and Costs

The City of Goldsboro joined the Benchmarking Project in July 2017, with the first year of data showing for FY 2016–17.

Municipal Profile

Population (OSBM 2020)	34,156
Land Area (Square Miles)	29.45
Persons per Square Mile	1,160

Service Profile

FTE Positions—Collection	15.00
FTE Positions—Other	0.33
Collection Frequency	
Yard Waste	1 x 2 weeks
Seasonal Leaf Collection	1 x 2 weeks
Collection Points	14,372
Tons Collected	
Yard Waste	4,408
Seasonal Leaves	4,136
Total Tons Collected	8,544
Monthly Service Fee	No

Full Cost Profile

Cost Breakdown by Percentage	
Personal Services	61.2%
Operating Costs	38.8%
Capital Costs	0.0%
TOTAL	100.0%
Cost Breakdown in Dollars	
Personal Services	$330,919
Operating Costs	$209,502
Capital Costs	$0
TOTAL	$540,421

Goldsboro

Yard Waste/Leaf Collection

Resource Measures

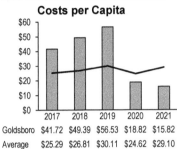

Yard Waste and Leaf Collection Costs per Capita

	2017	2018	2019	2020	2021
Goldsboro	$41.72	$49.39	$56.53	$18.82	$15.82
Average	$25.29	$26.81	$30.11	$24.62	$29.10

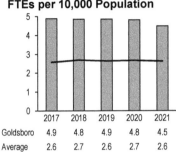

Yard Waste and Leaf Collection FTEs per 10,000 Population

	2017	2018	2019	2020	2021
Goldsboro	4.9	4.8	4.9	4.8	4.5
Average	2.6	2.7	2.6	2.7	2.6

Workload Measures

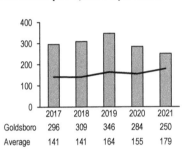

Yard Waste and Leaf Tons Collected per 1,000 Population

	2017	2018	2019	2020	2021
Goldsboro	296	309	346	284	250
Average	141	141	164	155	179

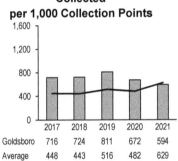

Yard Waste and Leaf Tons Collected per 1,000 Collection Points

	2017	2018	2019	2020	2021
Goldsboro	716	724	811	672	594
Average	448	443	516	482	629

Efficiency Measures

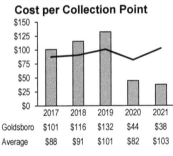

Yard Waste and Leaf Collection Cost per Collection Point

	2017	2018	2019	2020	2021
Goldsboro	$101	$116	$132	$44	$38
Average	$88	$91	$101	$82	$103

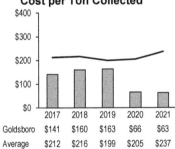

Yard Waste and Leaf Collection Cost per Ton Collected

	2017	2018	2019	2020	2021
Goldsboro	$141	$160	$163	$66	$63
Average	$212	$216	$199	$205	$237

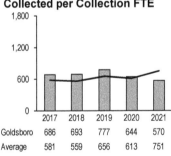

Yard Waste and Leaf Tons Collected per Collection FTE

	2017	2018	2019	2020	2021
Goldsboro	686	693	777	644	570
Average	581	559	656	613	751

Effectiveness Measures

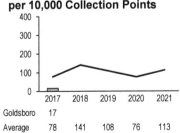

Collection Complaints per 10,000 Collection Points

	2017	2018	2019	2020	2021
Goldsboro	17				
Average	78	141	108	76	113

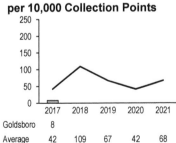

Valid Complaints per 10,000 Collection Points

	2017	2018	2019	2020	2021
Goldsboro	8				
Average	42	109	67	42	68

Fiscal Year 2020-21

Explanatory Information

Service Level and Delivery

Greensboro collects yard waste once per week curbside, either in clear plastic bags, thirty-five-gallon containers, or tied in bundles not to exceed 50 pounds or 5 feet in length. Yard waste includes grass, weeds, leaves, tree trimmings, plants, shrubbery trimmings, and other materials generated in yard maintenance. Yard waste does include some bagged leaves during the fall, and this waste is not broken out separately into leaf collection.

The city provides yard waste service to all single-family residences inside the city limits. Yard waste crews include ten two-person crews that rotate between driver and collector. The crews work four days per week, ten hours per day.

Seasonal leaf collection (October through January) is provided by Greensboro's Field Operations Division. Leaves are picked up a minimum of two times from November until mid-January by vacuuming the leaves from the curb.

Conditions Affecting Service, Performance, and Costs

Municipal Profile

Population (OSBM 2020)	299,556
Land Area (Square Miles)	129.62
Persons per Square Mile	2,311

Service Profile

FTE Positions—Collection	44.79
FTE Positions—Other	1.15
Collection Frequency	
Yard Waste	1 x week
Seasonal Leaf Collection	2 sweeps
Collection Points	88,020
Tons Collected	
Yard Waste	12,895
Seasonal Leaves	11,861
Total Tons Collected	24,756
Monthly Service Fee	No

Full Cost Profile

Cost Breakdown by Percentage	
Personal Services	36.2%
Operating Costs	63.8%
Capital Costs	0.0%
TOTAL	100.0%

Cost Breakdown in Dollars	
Personal Services	$1,243,997
Operating Costs	$2,189,079
Capital Costs	$0
TOTAL	$3,433,076

Greensboro

Yard Waste/Leaf Collection

Resource Measures

Yard Waste and Leaf Collection Costs per Capita

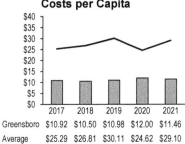

	2017	2018	2019	2020	2021
Greensboro	$10.92	$10.50	$10.98	$12.00	$11.46
Average	$25.29	$26.81	$30.11	$24.62	$29.10

Yard Waste and Leaf Collection FTEs per 10,000 Population

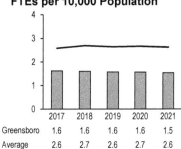

	2017	2018	2019	2020	2021
Greensboro	1.6	1.6	1.6	1.6	1.5
Average	2.6	2.7	2.6	2.7	2.6

Workload Measures

Yard Waste and Leaf Tons Collected per 1,000 Population

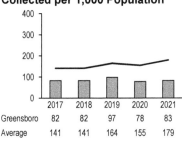

	2017	2018	2019	2020	2021
Greensboro	82	82	97	78	83
Average	141	141	164	155	179

Yard Waste and Leaf Tons Collected

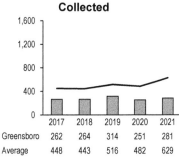

	2017	2018	2019	2020	2021
Greensboro	262	264	314	251	281
Average	448	443	516	482	629

Efficiency Measures

Yard Waste and Leaf Collection Cost per Collection Point

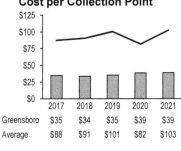

	2017	2018	2019	2020	2021
Greensboro	$35	$34	$35	$39	$39
Average	$88	$91	$101	$82	$103

Yard Waste and Leaf Collection Cost per Ton Collected

	2017	2018	2019	2020	2021
Greensboro	$133	$127	$113	$154	$139
Average	$212	$216	$199	$205	$237

Yard Waste and Leaf Tons Collected per Collection FTE

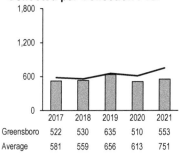

	2017	2018	2019	2020	2021
Greensboro	522	530	635	510	553
Average	581	559	656	613	751

Effectiveness Measures

Collection Complaints per 10,000 Collection Points

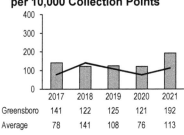

	2017	2018	2019	2020	2021
Greensboro	141	122	125	121	192
Average	78	141	108	76	113

Valid Complaints per 10,000 Collection Points

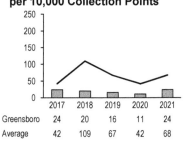

	2017	2018	2019	2020	2021
Greensboro	24	20	16	11	24
Average	42	109	67	42	68

Fiscal Year 2020-21

Explanatory Information

Service Level and Delivery
Greenville collects yard waste once per week curbside. Yard waste includes tree limbs up to 6 feet in length or 4 inches in diameter, bushes, grass clippings, and other vegetative matter. The city does not charge a separate fee for yard waste, leaves, or bulky items. It is part of the solid-waste fee.

Greenville uses two-person crews to collect yard waste. Crews are made up of a driver and a collection worker. Each crew has an assigned route for each day.

The city's seasonal leaf collection service runs from November to February. Leaves are collected weekly from the backs of curbs. The city uses five crews, each having a driver and two collection workers. The leaf collection crews are all seasonal employees.

Conditions Affecting Service, Performance, and Costs
No data were reported for FY 2019-20 for the city of Greenville.

Municipal Profile

Population (OSBM 2020)	87,428
Land Area (Square Miles)	35.66
Persons per Square Mile	2,452

Service Profile

FTE Positions—Collection	20.30
FTE Positions—Other	6.0
Collection Frequency	
Yard Waste	1 x week
Seasonal Leaf Collection	Every two weeks
Collection Points	20,000
Tons Collected	
Yard Waste	52,047
Seasonal Leaves	956
Total Tons Collected	53,003
Monthly Service Fee	No

Full Cost Profile

Cost Breakdown by Percentage	
Personal Services	36.2%
Operating Costs	45.2%
Capital Costs	18.6%
TOTAL	100.0%

Cost Breakdown in Dollars	
Personal Services	$1,786,311
Operating Costs	$2,227,629
Capital Costs	$919,387
TOTAL	$4,933,327

Greenville

Yard Waste/Leaf Collection

Resource Measures

Yard Waste and Leaf Collection Costs per Capita

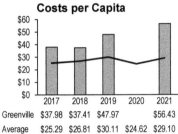

	2017	2018	2019	2020	2021
Greenville	$37.98	$37.41	$47.97		$56.43
Average	$25.29	$26.81	$30.11	$24.62	$29.10

Yard Waste and Leaf Collection FTEs per 10,000 Population

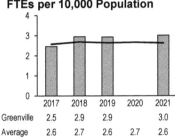

	2017	2018	2019	2020	2021
Greenville	2.5	2.9	2.9		3.0
Average	2.6	2.7	2.6	2.7	2.6

Workload Measures

Yard Waste and Leaf Tons Collected per 1,000 Population

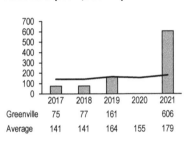

	2017	2018	2019	2020	2021
Greenville	75	77	161		606
Average	141	141	164	155	179

Yard Waste and Leaf Tons Collected per 1,000 Collection Points

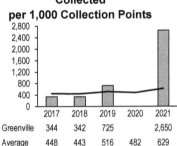

	2017	2018	2019	2020	2021
Greenville	344	342	725		2,650
Average	448	443	516	482	629

Efficiency Measures

Yard Waste and Leaf Collection Cost per Collection Point

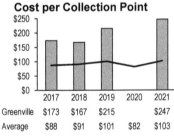

	2017	2018	2019	2020	2021
Greenville	$173	$167	$215		$247
Average	$88	$91	$101	$82	$103

Yard Waste and Leaf Collection Cost per Ton Collected

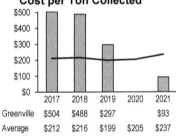

	2017	2018	2019	2020	2021
Greenville	$504	$488	$297		$93
Average	$212	$216	$199	$205	$237

Yard Waste and Leaf Tons Collected per Collection FTE

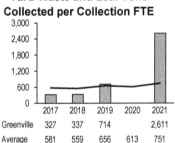

	2017	2018	2019	2020	2021
Greenville	327	337	714		2,611
Average	581	559	656	613	751

Effectiveness Measures

Collection Complaints per 10,000 Collection Points

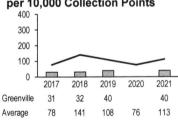

	2017	2018	2019	2020	2021
Greenville	31	32	40		40
Average	78	141	108	76	113

Valid Complaints per 10,000 Collection Points

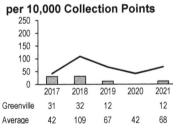

	2017	2018	2019	2020	2021
Greenville	31	32	12		12
Average	42	109	67	42	68

Fiscal Year 2020-21

Explanatory Information

Service Level and Delivery

Hickory collects yard waste once per week curbside. Yard waste includes tree limbs less than 6 feet in length and 6 inches in diameter, shrubs, grass clippings, leaves, and other vegetative matter. The city does not charge a separate fee for yard waste, leaves, or bulky items. It is part of the solid-waste fee. Residents use either clear plastic bags or open containers.

Hickory is divided into five sections for the yard-waste program. Three routes are serviced each day within each section, using three rear loaders with crews comprised of one driver and one laborer each. Large piles are collected with a knuckle boom loader with one driver on a scheduled basis working about half-time.

All yard waste is collected and stockpiled at the city yard-waste facility. Debris is ground into mulch or compost and sold back to citizens or used for city projects.

The city's seasonal-leaf-collection service runs from November to January. There are two sweeps down each city street during this time. City crews use leaf vacuums to collect leaves in box trucks. Hickory uses temporary contract workers to help with leaf collection. These seasonal employees are counted in the total employee count, but only for the one-fourth of the year they work.

Conditions Affecting Service, Performance, and Costs

Hickory's yard waste collection is set up to provide regular service but also takes requests for service when collection is needed. These calls for service cannot be separated out from actual complaints, so complaint data cannot be reported for this service area.

Municipal Profile

Population (OSBM 2020)	43,578
Land Area (Square Miles)	30.50
Persons per Square Mile	1,429

Service Profile

FTE Positions—Collection	9.75
FTE Positions—Other	0.7
Collection Frequency	
Yard Waste	1 x week
Seasonal Leaf Collection	2 sweeps
Collection Points	12,200
Tons Collected	
Yard Waste	10,246
Seasonal Leaves	3,023
Total Tons Collected	13,270
Monthly Service Fee	No

Full Cost Profile

Cost Breakdown by Percentage	
Personal Services	46.0%
Operating Costs	40.9%
Capital Costs	13.1%
TOTAL	100.0%
Cost Breakdown in Dollars	
Personal Services	$462,397
Operating Costs	$410,728
Capital Costs	$131,585
TOTAL	$1,004,710

Hickory

Yard Waste/Leaf Collection

Key: Hickory   Benchmarking Average —   Fiscal Years 2017 through 2021

Resource Measures

Yard Waste and Leaf Collection Costs per Capita

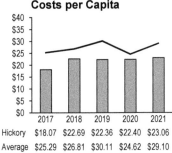

	2017	2018	2019	2020	2021
Hickory	$18.07	$22.69	$22.36	$22.40	$23.06
Average	$25.29	$26.81	$30.11	$24.62	$29.10

Yard Waste and Leaf Collection FTEs per 10,000 Population

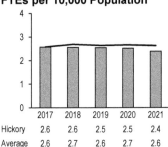

	2017	2018	2019	2020	2021
Hickory	2.6	2.6	2.5	2.5	2.4
Average	2.6	2.7	2.6	2.7	2.6

Workload Measures

Yard Waste and Leaf Tons Collected per 1,000 Population

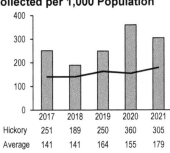

	2017	2018	2019	2020	2021
Hickory	251	189	250	360	305
Average	141	141	164	155	179

Yard Waste and Leaf Tons Collected

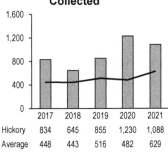

	2017	2018	2019	2020	2021
Hickory	834	645	855	1,230	1,088
Average	448	443	516	482	629

Efficiency Measures

Yard Waste and Leaf Collection Cost per Collection Point

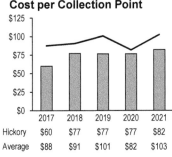

	2017	2018	2019	2020	2021
Hickory	$60	$77	$77	$77	$82
Average	$88	$91	$101	$82	$103

Yard Waste and Leaf Collection Cost per Ton Collected

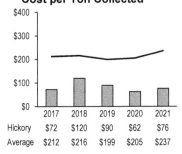

	2017	2018	2019	2020	2021
Hickory	$72	$120	$90	$62	$76
Average	$212	$216	$199	$205	$237

Yard Waste and Leaf Tons Collected per Collection FTE

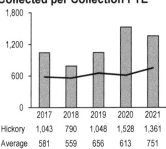

	2017	2018	2019	2020	2021
Hickory	1,043	790	1,048	1,528	1,361
Average	581	559	656	613	751

Effectiveness Measures

Collection Complaints per 10,000 Collection Points

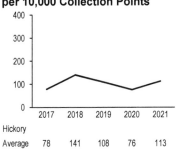

	2017	2018	2019	2020	2021
Hickory					
Average	78	141	108	76	113

Valid Complaints per 10,000 Collection Points

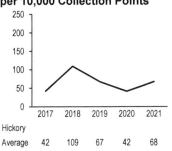

	2017	2018	2019	2020	2021
Hickory					
Average	42	109	67	42	68

Raleigh

Yard Waste/Leaf Collection

Fiscal Year 2020-21

Explanatory Information

Service Level and Delivery
Yard waste is picked up weekly at the curb in Raleigh by the Solid Waste Services Department. Yard waste must be bagged or containerized with a limit of fifteen bags. Bags must be clear or biodegradable.

The city uses twelve three-person crews to collect yard waste on the same day as trash collection. Temporary crews are added during leaf season as yard waste volume picks up.

Loose leaf collection is done by the Transportation Field Services Division. Loose leaves are collected curbside during leaf season, which runs from November to February. Two sweeps of the city are completed during leaf season. The first sweep is usually completed by mid-January, and the second sweep is usually completed by the end of February. Loose leaves must be placed at the street and must be free of debris to be collected.

Conditions Affecting Service, Performance, and Costs

Municipal Profile

Population (OSBM 2020)	468,977
Land Area (Square Miles)	146.47
Persons per Square Mile	3,202

Service Profile

FTE Positions—Collection	103.0
FTE Positions—Other	4.5
Collection Frequency	
Yard Waste	1 x week
Seasonal Leaf Collection	2 sweeps
Collection Points	123,500
Tons Collected	
Yard Waste	13,730
Seasonal Leaves	11,352
Total Tons Collected	25,082
Monthly Service Fee	
Yard Waste	Yes
Seasonal Leaf Collection	No

Full Cost Profile

Cost Breakdown by Percentage	
Personal Services	51.4%
Operating Costs	36.0%
Capital Costs	12.6%
TOTAL	100.0%

Cost Breakdown in Dollars	
Personal Services	$4,039,819
Operating Costs	$2,829,257
Capital Costs	$994,050
TOTAL	$7,863,126

Raleigh

Yard Waste/Leaf Collection

Resource Measures

Yard Waste and Leaf Collection Costs per Capita

	2017	2018	2019	2020	2021
Raleigh	$14.59	$15.66	$17.35	$16.14	$16.77
Average	$25.29	$26.81	$30.11	$24.62	$29.10

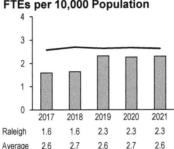

Yard Waste and Leaf Collection FTEs per 10,000 Population

	2017	2018	2019	2020	2021
Raleigh	1.6	1.6	2.3	2.3	2.3
Average	2.6	2.7	2.6	2.7	2.6

Workload Measures

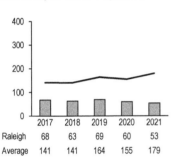

Yard Waste and Leaf Tons Collected per 1,000 Population

	2017	2018	2019	2020	2021
Raleigh	68	63	69	60	53
Average	141	141	164	155	179

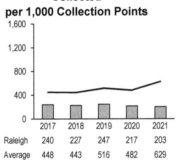

Yard Waste and Leaf Tons Collected per 1,000 Collection Points

	2017	2018	2019	2020	2021
Raleigh	240	227	247	217	203
Average	448	443	516	482	629

Efficiency Measures

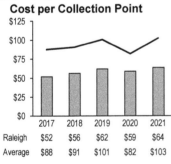

Yard Waste and Leaf Collection Cost per Collection Point

	2017	2018	2019	2020	2021
Raleigh	$52	$56	$62	$59	$64
Average	$88	$91	$101	$82	$103

Yard Waste and Leaf Collection Cost per Ton Collected

	2017	2018	2019	2020	2021
Raleigh	$216	$248	$251	$271	$313
Average	$212	$216	$199	$205	$237

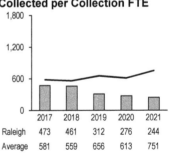

Yard Waste and Leaf Tons Collected per Collection FTE

	2017	2018	2019	2020	2021
Raleigh	473	461	312	276	244
Average	581	559	656	613	751

Effectiveness Measures

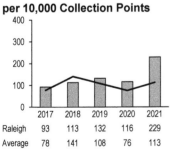

Collection Complaints per 10,000 Collection Points

	2017	2018	2019	2020	2021
Raleigh	93	113	132	116	229
Average	78	141	108	76	113

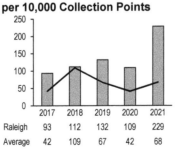

Valid Complaints per 10,000 Collection Points

	2017	2018	2019	2020	2021
Raleigh	93	112	132	109	229
Average	42	109	67	42	68

Fiscal Year 2020-21

Explanatory Information

Service Level and Delivery

Yard waste is containerized in bags, sheets, roll-out containers, or other container types for collection by rear-loader packers. Yard waste is collected once per week by compost crews on the same day as residential refuse collection.

The city uses two three-person crews on Tuesdays and Fridays and three or four three-person crews on Mondays and Thursdays to collect yard waste. Each crew is composed of one driver and two workers. These crews rotate collection between residential refuse and yard waste. A one-person crew uses a knuckle boom truck to collect large limbs daily.

The city's leaf season is from mid-October to mid-January. Leaves are collected loose at the curb on a one-to-three-week cycle. The city uses leaf vacuum machines and compacting leaf trucks to collect loose leaves.

Six to eight three-person crews are used to collect loose leaves. The drivers are permanent employees. Collectors are seasonal employees.

Conditions Affecting Service, Performance, and Costs

Wilson began using a new automated system for tracking all call-ins into "Fix-It Wilson" during FY 2017–2018. The contacts for yard waste include all items related to limbs, leaves, and compost. Previously all complaints were received by telephone and documented by hand in a notebook. The jump in complaints is connected to the implementation of this new system rather than changes in service.

Municipal Profile

Population (OSBM 2020)	47,769
Land Area (Square Miles)	31.02
Persons per Square Mile	1,540

Service Profile

FTE Positions—Collection	15.5
FTE Positions—Other	0.0
Collection Frequency	
Yard Waste	1 x week
Seasonal Leaf Collection	1 x 3 weeks
Collection Points	21,500
Tons Collected	
Yard Waste	9,211
Seasonal Leaves	1,204
Total Tons Collected	10,415
Monthly Service Fee	Included in solid waste fee

Full Cost Profile

Cost Breakdown by Percentage	
Personal Services	45.9%
Operating Costs	41.2%
Capital Costs	12.9%
TOTAL	100.0%

Cost Breakdown in Dollars	
Personal Services	$762,348
Operating Costs	$684,825
Capital Costs	$213,522
TOTAL	$1,660,695

Wilson

Yard Waste/Leaf Collection

Resource Measures

Yard Waste and Leaf Collection Costs per Capita

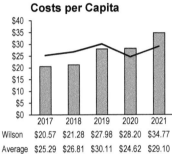

	2017	2018	2019	2020	2021
Wilson	$20.57	$21.28	$27.98	$28.20	$34.77
Average	$25.29	$26.81	$30.11	$24.62	$29.10

Yard Waste and Leaf Collection FTEs per 10,000 Population

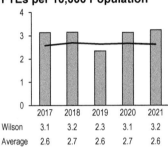

	2017	2018	2019	2020	2021
Wilson	3.1	3.2	2.3	3.1	3.2
Average	2.6	2.7	2.6	2.7	2.6

Workload Measures

Yard Waste and Leaf Tons Collected per 1,000 Population

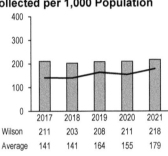

	2017	2018	2019	2020	2021
Wilson	211	203	208	211	218
Average	141	141	164	155	179

Yard Waste and Leaf Tons Collected

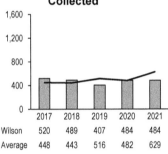

	2017	2018	2019	2020	2021
Wilson	520	489	407	484	484
Average	448	443	516	482	629

Efficiency Measures

Yard Waste and Leaf Collection Cost per Collection Point

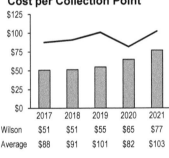

	2017	2018	2019	2020	2021
Wilson	$51	$51	$55	$65	$77
Average	$88	$91	$101	$82	$103

Yard Waste and Leaf Collection Cost per Ton Collected

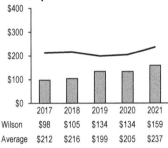

	2017	2018	2019	2020	2021
Wilson	$98	$105	$134	$134	$159
Average	$212	$216	$199	$205	$237

Yard Waste and Leaf Tons Collected per Collection FTE

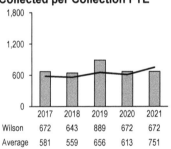

	2017	2018	2019	2020	2021
Wilson	672	643	889	672	672
Average	581	559	656	613	751

Effectiveness Measures

Collection Complaints per 10,000 Collection Points

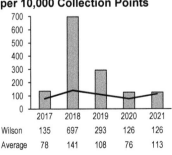

	2017	2018	2019	2020	2021
Wilson	135	697	293	126	126
Average	78	141	108	76	113

Valid Complaints per 10,000 Collection Points

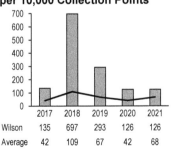

	2017	2018	2019	2020	2021
Wilson	135	697	293	126	126
Average	42	109	67	42	68

Winston-Salem

Yard Waste/Leaf Collection

Fiscal Year 2020-21

Explanatory Information

Service Level and Delivery

The city operates a curbside collection program for brush, leaves, and bulky items. Brush is collected throughout the year, while leaves and bulky items are collected on a seasonal basis. Brush is defined as small tree limbs, branches, and shrubbery clippings. Tree and shrubbery limbs cannot be larger than 6 inches in diameter or 6 feet in length. A city ordinance requires that brush be collected once every ten working days except during leaf season. There are no separate fees for the curbside collection program. The brush collection program gathered 21,942 tons across the city.

The yard-waste-cart program provides weekly collection of containerized yard waste placed in ninety-six-gallon carts. The city uses six one-person crews using automated packers and one two-person crew using a rear-loading packer to service these carts. Collection is provided Monday through Thursday. Carts are delivered on Friday. Residents who participate in the yard-waste-cart program pay an annual $60 fee. Residents also pay for the ninety-six-gallon carts at a cost of $60 if the cart is picked up or $65 if the cart is delivered. A household can have up to three carts. The yard cart program serviced 15,022 customers in the fiscal year..

The city's seasonal-leaf-collection program picks up leaves that are deposited at the curb between November 1 and January 15. Loose leaves are vacuumed two to three times during this time period. Containerized leaves are collected throughout the year as part of the yard waste program. The city uses thirty-two crews for seasonal leaf collection, with a combination of equipment operators, maintenance workers, and both permanent and seasonal workers.

Conditions Affecting Service, Performance, and Costs

The performance measure "cost per collection point" is based on a total of 81,589 collection points.

Municipal Profile

Population (OSBM 2020)	249,986
Land Area (Square Miles)	132.59
Persons per Square Mile	1,885

Service Profile

FTE Positions—Collection	74.5
FTE Positions—Other	1.4
Collection Frequency	
Yard Waste	1 x week
Seasonal Leaf Collection	1 x 3 weeks
Brush	1 x 10 days
Collection Points	81,589
Tons Collected	
Yard Waste	7,191
Seasonal Leaves	11,814
Total Tons Collected	19,006
Monthly Service Fee	$60 per year for cart

Full Cost Profile

Cost Breakdown by Percentage	
Personal Services	52.0%
Operating Costs	28.9%
Capital Costs	19.1%
TOTAL	100.0%
Cost Breakdown in Dollars	
Personal Services	$3,903,800
Operating Costs	$2,169,600
Capital Costs	$1,435,908
TOTAL	$7,509,308

Resource Measures

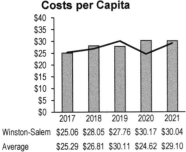

Yard Waste and Leaf Collection Costs per Capita

	2017	2018	2019	2020	2021
Winston-Salem	$25.06	$28.05	$27.76	$30.17	$30.04
Average	$25.29	$26.81	$30.11	$24.62	$29.10

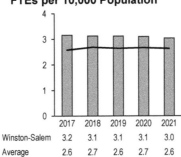

Yard Waste and Leaf Collection FTEs per 10,000 Population

	2017	2018	2019	2020	2021
Winston-Salem	3.2	3.1	3.1	3.1	3.0
Average	2.6	2.7	2.6	2.7	2.6

Workload Measures

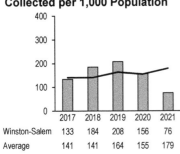

Yard Waste and Leaf Tons Collected per 1,000 Population

	2017	2018	2019	2020	2021
Winston-Salem	133	184	208	156	76
Average	141	141	164	155	179

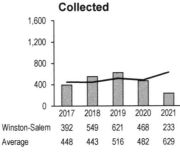

Yard Waste and Leaf Tons Collected

	2017	2018	2019	2020	2021
Winston-Salem	392	549	621	468	233
Average	448	443	516	482	629

Efficiency Measures

Yard Waste and Leaf Collection Cost per Collection Point

	2017	2018	2019	2020	2021
Winston-Salem	$74	$84	$83	$91	$92
Average	$88	$91	$101	$82	$103

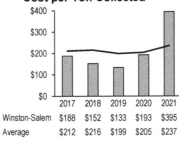

Yard Waste and Leaf Collection Cost per Ton Collected

	2017	2018	2019	2020	2021
Winston-Salem	$188	$152	$133	$193	$395
Average	$212	$216	$199	$205	$237

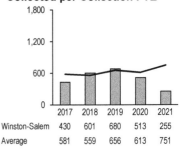

Yard Waste and Leaf Tons Collected per Collection FTE

	2017	2018	2019	2020	2021
Winston-Salem	430	601	680	513	255
Average	581	559	656	613	751

Effectiveness Measures

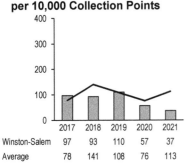

Collection Complaints per 10,000 Collection Points

	2017	2018	2019	2020	2021
Winston-Salem	97	93	110	57	37
Average	78	141	108	76	113

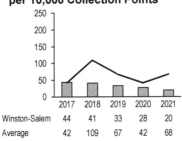

Valid Complaints per 10,000 Collection Points

	2017	2018	2019	2020	2021
Winston-Salem	44	41	33	28	20
Average	42	109	67	42	68

Performance and Cost Data

POLICE SERVICES

PERFORMANCE MEASURES FOR POLICE SERVICES

SERVICE DEFINITION
Police Services consist of all police activities performed by sworn and non-sworn personnel. This includes, but is not limited to, activities performed by patrol, traffic, investigations, special units, support staff, supervisors, and police administration. This definition captures all functions of the police department except for emergency communications.

NOTES ON PERFORMANCE MEASURES

1. Dispatched Calls
These are calls resulting in the dispatch of an officer. Most dispatches result from calls coming into the emergency communications center or the police department, but some are self-initiated by officers on duty. Multiple calls resulting in the dispatch of several officers are counted as one dispatched call.

2. Uniform Crime Reporting (UCR) Part I Crimes
Uniform Crime Reporting (UCR) Part I crimes include crimes against persons (criminal homicide, forcible rape, robbery, and aggravated assault) and crimes against property (burglary, larceny, motor vehicle theft, and arson).

3. Incident-Based Reporting (IBR) Part I Crimes
Incident-Based Reporting (IBR) Part I crimes include crimes against persons (criminal homicide, forcible rape, robbery, and aggravated assault) and crimes against property (burglary, larceny, motor vehicle theft, and arson). The difference between the UCR method and the IBR method for reporting crimes is that IBR counts crime and arrest activities at the incident level, as opposed to counting only the most serious crime with multiple offenses.

4. Full-Time Equivalent (FTE) Positions: Sworn Officers
The number of full-time equivalent (FTE) positions is the number of budgeted positions for sworn officers during the fiscal year.

5. Response Time to High-Priority Calls
Each police department defines high-priority calls somewhat differently. The definitions generally refer to crimes in progress or situations where there are risks of injury or threats to life or property. Response time commences with the dispatch of an officer and ends with the arrival of the officer at the scene of the incident. The officer may be dispatched while on patrol or from the police station.

Police Services

Summary of Key Dimensions of Service

City or Town	Police Department Accredited?	Number of Sworn Officers	Average Length of Service for Sworn Officers (Years)	Number of Patrol Vehicles	Reporting Format	Part I Crimes			Part II Crimes	Dispatched Calls	Number of Traffic Accidents
						Against Persons	Against Property	Total			
Apex	Yes	96.0	13.2	116	IBR	44	702	746	1,485	67,205	964
Chapel Hill	No	117	13.4	73	IBR	99	1,114	1,213	2,144	24,084	1,233
Concord	No	195	9.1	207	IBR	94	1,313	1,407	2,293	128,560	3,388
Goldsboro	Yes	108	10.6	107	IBR	273	1,634	1,907	2,435	45,240	2,165
Greensboro	Yes	690	11.6	223	IBR	2,545	10,933	13,478	16,154	241,032	10,150
Greenville	Yes	204	10.0	222	IBR	433	2,617	3,050	8,597	117,882	4,030
Hickory	No	122	8.5	143	IBR	185	1,845	2,030	4,585	107,438	2,402
Raleigh	Yes	800	14.6	785	NIBRS	1,700	9,851	11,551	NA	292,110	19,531
Wilson	Yes	125	12.3	148	IBR	225	1,412	1,637	2,966	109,241	2,505
Winston-Salem	Yes	538	11.7	437	NIBRS	3,133	11,237	14,370	35,002	192,924	9,289

EXPLANATORY FACTORS

These are factors that the project found affected police services performance and cost in one or more of the municipalities:

Demographic makeup of the community
Community policing policies
Population density and land area
Downtown area characteristics
Use of incident-based reporting
Presence of unique problems in particular areas, such as drugs or gangs
Emphasis on quick response to all calls
Vehicle take-home policy
Beat structure
Use of special units

Explanatory Information

Service Level and Delivery

The Town of Apex Police Department provides an array of police services, including patrol, investigations, a special-response unit, and school resource officers at the high school and middle schools located in the town.

The city had ninety-six sworn officer positions authorized for the year, with an average length of service of 13.2 years. Police services occupies a headquarters located in downtown Apex, newly built in 2010, which houses all divisions in the department. There are also two unmanned substations attached to town fire stations.

Officers in Apex in the patrol division work twelve-hour modified DuPont schedules. Each patrol squad is also assigned a flex officer. The traffic unit works a modified DuPont schedule based on crash statistics. The investigations division works Monday through Friday from 8 a.m. to 5 p.m., with one investigator working from 2 p.m. to 11 p.m. The investigator working the late shift is also the on-call investigator, and this position rotates every week.

Patrol and investigation units are assigned individual vehicles. Command staff also have individually assigned vehicles, which are the only take-home vehicles in the fleet.

The police department was successful in clearing a total of 228 Part I cases during the fiscal year.

The definition of a high-priority call in Apex is any call by which the immediate arrival and presence of the police may prevent death or injury or alleviate the threat of death or injury.

Conditions Affecting Service, Performance, and Costs

Municipal Profile

Population (OSBM 2020)	59,368
Land Area (Square Miles)	23.61
Persons per Square Mile	2,514

Service Profile

FTE Positions—Sworn	96.0
FTE Positions—Other	9.0
Marked and Unmarked Patrol Vehicles	116
Part I Crimes Reported	
Homicide	1
Rape	9
Robbery	6
Assault	28
Burglary	60
Larceny	617
Auto Theft	23
Arson	2
TOTAL	746
Part II Crimes Reported	1,485
Part I Crimes Cleared	
Persons	28
Property	200
TOTAL	228
Reporting Format	IBR
Number of Calls Dispatched	67,205
Number of Traffic Accidents	964
Property Damage for Accidents	$4,735,004

Full Cost Profile

Cost Breakdown by Percentage	
Personal Services	66.8%
Operating Costs	20.5%
Capital Costs	12.8%
TOTAL	100.0%

Cost Breakdown in Dollars	
Personal Services	$9,557,562
Operating Costs	$2,927,991
Capital Costs	$1,830,104
TOTAL	$14,315,657

Key: Apex ▨   Benchmarking Average —   Fiscal Years 2017 through 2021

Resource Measures

Police Services Costs per Capita

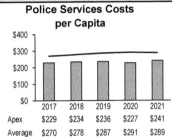

	2017	2018	2019	2020	2021
Apex	$229	$234	$236	$227	$241
Average	$270	$278	$287	$291	$289

Total Police Services Personnel per 10,000 Population

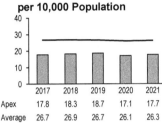

	2017	2018	2019	2020	2021
Apex	17.8	18.3	18.7	17.1	17.7
Average	26.7	26.9	26.7	26.1	26.3

Sworn Police Officers per 10,000 Population

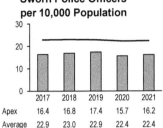

	2017	2018	2019	2020	2021
Apex	16.4	16.8	17.4	15.7	16.2
Average	22.9	23.0	22.9	22.4	22.4

Workload Measures

Calls Dispatched per 1,000 Population

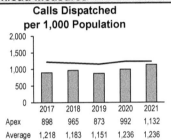

	2017	2018	2019	2020	2021
Apex	898	965	873	992	1,132
Average	1,218	1,183	1,151	1,236	1,236

Part I Crimes per 1,000 Population

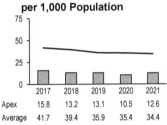

	2017	2018	2019	2020	2021
Apex	15.8	13.2	13.1	10.5	12.6
Average	41.7	39.4	35.9	35.4	34.4

Efficiency Measures

Police Services Cost per Call Dispatched

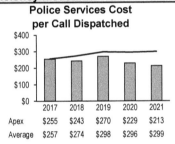

	2017	2018	2019	2020	2021
Apex	$255	$243	$270	$229	$213
Average	$257	$274	$298	$296	$299

Calls Dispatched per Sworn Officer

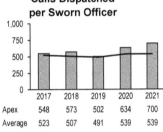

	2017	2018	2019	2020	2021
Apex	548	573	502	634	700
Average	523	507	491	539	539

Police Services Cost per Part I Case Cleared

	2017	2018	2019	2020	2021
Apex	$43,413	$58,864	$46,407	$64,228	$62,788
Average	$25,031	$29,606	$33,208	$33,378	$39,435

Part I Cases Cleared per Sworn Officer

	2017	2018	2019	2020	2021
Apex	3.2	2.4	2.9	2.3	2.4
Average	5.3	5.0	4.5	4.5	3.9

Effectiveness Measures

Percentage of Part I Cases Cleared of Those Reported

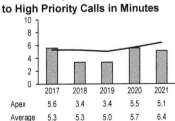

	2017	2018	2019	2020	2021
Apex	33.4%	30.1%	30.1%	33.6%	30.6%
Average	30.2%	30.1%	30.0%	31.8%	27.2%

Response Time to High Priority Calls in Minutes

	2017	2018	2019	2020	2021
Apex	5.6	3.4	3.4	5.5	5.1
Average	5.3	5.3	5.0	5.7	6.4

Fiscal Year 2020-21

Explanatory Information

Service Level and Delivery
The Town of Chapel Hill Police Department provides an array of police services, including patrol, investigations, a special-response unit, bicycle patrol, drug enforcement, limited laboratory work, and a canine unit.

The town had 117 sworn officer positions authorized for the fiscal year, with an average length of service of 13.4 years. Police headquarters is located in a separate building. The department also operates one substation at the local mall, which is not regularly staffed.

In order to provide continuous service to the citizens of Chapel Hill, officers work twelve hour shifts and are assigned to either day (6 a.m. to 6 p.m.) or night (6 p.m. to 6 a.m.) shifts. Each shift selects a number of officers to report one to two hours early to cover calls that occur leading up to shift change.

Vehicles are allocated to divisions in the department and are assigned by unit-level supervisors. Individual assignments are made for certain positions, but the only officers allowed to take home vehicles are K9 units, administrative officers, and on-call investigators.

The town defines a high-priority call as one that requires immediate police attention to protect persons or render emergency aid.

The police department was successful in clearing a total of 211 Part I cases during the fiscal year.

Conditions Affecting Service, Performance, and Costs
The average response time to high-priority calls reflects the response time of the first arriving unit. Self-initiated calls with a response time of zero are included in the average response time to high-priority calls.

Municipal Profile

Population (OSBM 2020)	62,080
Land Area (Square Miles)	21.31
Persons per Square Mile	2,914

Service Profile

FTE Positions—Sworn	117.0
FTE Positions—Other	16.0
Marked and Unmarked Patrol Vehicles	73
Part I Crimes Reported	
Homicide	1
Rape	10
Robbery	24
Assault	64
Burglary	179
Larceny	867
Auto Theft	67
Arson	1
TOTAL	1,213
Part II Crimes Reported	2,144
Part I Crimes Cleared	
Persons	42
Property	169
TOTAL	211
Reporting Format	IBR
Number of Calls Dispatched	24,084
Number of Traffic Accidents	1,233
Property Damage for Accidents	$3,838,626

Full Cost Profile

Cost Breakdown by Percentage	
Personal Services	65.9%
Operating Costs	27.6%
Capital Costs	6.5%
TOTAL	100.0%

Cost Breakdown in Dollars	
Personal Services	$10,514,332
Operating Costs	$4,399,310
Capital Costs	$1,045,186
TOTAL	$15,958,828

Chapel Hill

Police Services

Key: Chapel Hill Benchmarking Average — Fiscal Years 2017 through 2021

Resource Measures

Police Services Costs per Capita

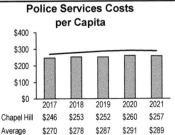

	2017	2018	2019	2020	2021
Chapel Hill	$246	$253	$252	$260	$257
Average	$270	$278	$287	$291	$289

Total Police Services Personnel per 10,000 Population

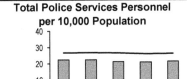

	2017	2018	2019	2020	2021
Chapel Hill	22.4	22.4	21.2	20.9	21.4
Average	26.7	26.9	26.7	26.1	26.3

Sworn Police Officers per 10,000 Population

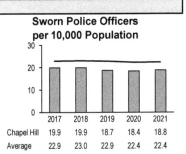

	2017	2018	2019	2020	2021
Chapel Hill	19.9	19.9	18.7	18.4	18.8
Average	22.9	23.0	22.9	22.4	22.4

Workload Measures

Calls Dispatched per 1,000 Population

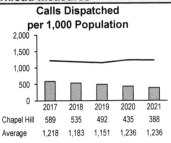

	2017	2018	2019	2020	2021
Chapel Hill	589	535	492	435	388
Average	1,218	1,183	1,151	1,236	1,236

Part I Crimes per 1,000 Population

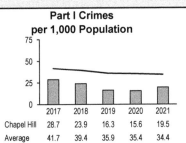

	2017	2018	2019	2020	2021
Chapel Hill	28.7	23.9	16.3	15.6	19.5
Average	41.7	39.4	35.9	35.4	34.4

Efficiency Measures

Police Services Cost per Call Dispatched

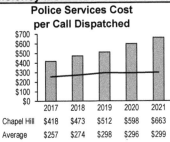

	2017	2018	2019	2020	2021
Chapel Hill	$418	$473	$512	$598	$663
Average	$257	$274	$298	$296	$299

Calls Dispatched per Sworn Officer

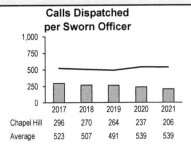

	2017	2018	2019	2020	2021
Chapel Hill	296	270	264	237	206
Average	523	507	491	539	539

Police Services Cost per Part I Case Cleared

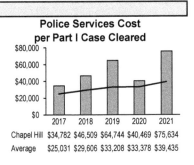

	2017	2018	2019	2020	2021
Chapel Hill	$34,782	$46,509	$64,744	$40,469	$75,634
Average	$25,031	$29,606	$33,208	$33,378	$39,435

Part I Cases Cleared per Sworn Officer

	2017	2018	2019	2020	2021
Chapel Hill	3.6	2.7	2.1	3.5	1.8
Average	5.3	5.0	4.5	4.5	3.9

Effectiveness Measures

Percentage of Part I Cases Cleared of Those Reported

	2017	2018	2019	2020	2021
Chapel Hill	24.7%	22.8%	23.9%	41.3%	17.4%
Average	30.2%	30.1%	30.0%	31.8%	27.2%

Response Time to High Priority Calls in Minutes

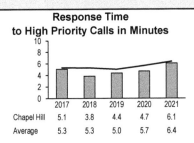

	2017	2018	2019	2020	2021
Chapel Hill	5.1	3.8	4.4	4.7	6.1
Average	5.3	5.3	5.0	5.7	6.4

Fiscal Year 2020-21

Explanatory Information

Service Level and Delivery

Concord's police department provides an array of police services, including patrol, investigations, a traffic unit, a telephone response unit, a canine unit, a special-response unit, a bicycle patrol unit, a drug enforcement unit, a limited forensic laboratory, and other programs, such as school resource officers.

The city had 195 sworn officer positions authorized for the fiscal year, with an average length of service of 9.1 years. The police headquarters is in a separate building located downtown. Five substations are used: three in fire stations, one in a shopping mall, and one in the Transit Center.

Uniformed patrol officers work twelve-hour rotating shifts. Investigators work five eight-hour days on first and second shifts. District Commanders have the authority to change individual schedules to meet peak demands.

The city defines high-priority emergency calls as those involving an assault in progress, personal injury, breaking and entering, or robbery in progress.

Concord uses a one-on-one car plan. Officers may take their vehicles home if they live thirty miles from the Police Department headquarters using straight line distance.

The police department was successful in clearing a total of 482 Part I cases during the fiscal year.

Conditions Affecting Service, Performance, and Costs

The average response time to high-priority calls reflects the response time of the first arriving unit. Self-initiated calls are not included.

Concord's high clearance rate has been driven by a focus on clearing larceny cases by arrest or by exhausting leads as quickly as possible. Because larcenies are the largest category of Part I crimes, this effort has substantially improved the overall clearance rate. The lower clearance rates in the last few years are driven mostly by more accurate data reporting rather than a drop in results.

Municipal Profile

Population (OSBM 2020)	105,936
Land Area (Square Miles)	63.65
Persons per Square Mile	1,664

Service Profile

FTE Positions—Sworn	195.00
FTE Positions—Other	21.0
Marked and Unmarked Patrol Vehicles	207

Part I Crimes Reported

Homicide	6
Rape	6
Robbery	33
Assault	49
Burglary	120
Larceny	1,067
Auto Theft	123
Arson	3
TOTAL	1,407

Part II Crimes Reported	2,293

Part I Crimes Cleared

Persons	53
Property	429
TOTAL	482

Reporting Format	IBR
Number of Calls Dispatched	128,560
Number of Traffic Accidents	3,388
Property Damage for Accidents	$14,647,515

Full Cost Profile

Cost Breakdown by Percentage

Personal Services	67.4%
Operating Costs	23.6%
Capital Costs	9.0%
TOTAL	100.0%

Cost Breakdown in Dollars

Personal Services	$18,197,970
Operating Costs	$6,387,267
Capital Costs	$2,427,860
TOTAL	$27,013,097

Concord

Police Services

Resource Measures

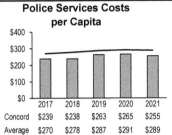

Police Services Costs per Capita

	2017	2018	2019	2020	2021
Concord	$239	$238	$263	$265	$255
Average	$270	$278	$287	$291	$289

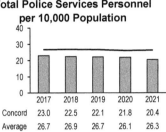

Total Police Services Personnel per 10,000 Population

	2017	2018	2019	2020	2021
Concord	23.0	22.5	22.1	21.8	20.4
Average	26.7	26.9	26.7	26.1	26.3

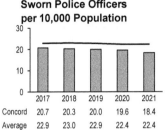

Sworn Police Officers per 10,000 Population

	2017	2018	2019	2020	2021
Concord	20.7	20.3	20.0	19.6	18.4
Average	22.9	23.0	22.9	22.4	22.4

Workload Measures

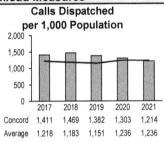

Calls Dispatched per 1,000 Population

	2017	2018	2019	2020	2021
Concord	1,411	1,469	1,382	1,303	1,214
Average	1,218	1,183	1,151	1,236	1,236

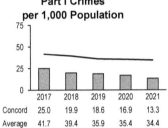

Part I Crimes per 1,000 Population

	2017	2018	2019	2020	2021
Concord	25.0	19.9	18.6	16.9	13.3
Average	41.7	39.4	35.9	35.4	34.4

Efficiency Measures

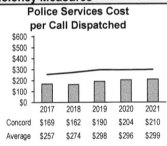

Police Services Cost per Call Dispatched

	2017	2018	2019	2020	2021
Concord	$169	$162	$190	$204	$210
Average	$257	$274	$298	$296	$299

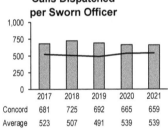

Calls Dispatched per Sworn Officer

	2017	2018	2019	2020	2021
Concord	681	725	692	665	659
Average	523	507	491	539	539

Police Services Cost per Part I Case Cleared

	2017	2018	2019	2020	2021
Concord	$30,846	$35,154	$32,628	$42,269	$56,044
Average	$25,031	$29,606	$33,208	$33,378	$39,435

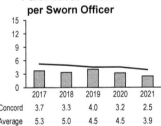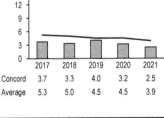

Part I Cases Cleared per Sworn Officer

	2017	2018	2019	2020	2021
Concord	3.7	3.3	4.0	3.2	2.5
Average	5.3	5.0	4.5	4.5	3.9

Effectiveness Measures

Percentage of Part I Cases Cleared of Those Reported

	2017	2018	2019	2020	2021
Concord	32.0%	34.1%	43.2%	37.2%	34.3%
Average	30.2%	30.1%	30.0%	31.8%	27.2%

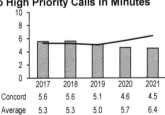

Response Time to High Priority Calls in Minutes

	2017	2018	2019	2020	2021
Concord	5.6	5.6	5.1	4.6	4.5
Average	5.3	5.3	5.0	5.7	6.4

Fiscal Year 2020-21

Explanatory Information

Service Level and Delivery

Goldsboro provides comprehensive police services, including patrol, investigations, a canine unit, a bicycle patrol unit, a drug enforcement unit, animal control, and a limited-service forensics unit. The bicycle unit is made up of officers assigned to the housing unit and selective enforcement unit and is not a stand-alone unit.

The city had 108 sworn officers authorized for the fiscal year, with an average length of service of 10.6 years. The police department is housed in a complex that is shared with the fire department, with each department having its own entrance but sharing a gym and locker rooms.

Uniformed officers work a total of 2,052 hours per year while investigators work a total of 2,080 hours. Schedules can be adjusted at any time according to call demand, special events, or special incidents. Officers are assigned a vehicle once they are out of field training. They can drive a vehicle home if they live within Wayne County.

Conditions Affecting Service, Performance, and Costs

The City of Goldsboro joined the Benchmarking Project in July 2017, with the first year of data showing for FY 2016–17.

Municipal Profile

Population (OSBM 2020)	34,156
Land Area (Square Miles)	29.45
Persons per Square Mile	1,160

Service Profile

FTE Positions—Sworn	108.0
FTE Positions—Other	13.0
Marked and Unmarked Patrol Vehicles	107
Part I Crimes Reported	
Homicide	6
Rape	17
Robbery	46
Assault	204
Burglary	345
Larceny	1,196
Auto Theft	91
Arson	2
TOTAL	1,907
Part II Crimes Reported	2,435
Part I Crimes Cleared	
Persons	75
Property	335
TOTAL	410
Reporting Format	IBR
Number of Calls Dispatched	45,240
Number of Traffic Accidents	2,165
Property Damage for Accidents	$553,795

Full Cost Profile

Cost Breakdown by Percentage

Personal Services	85.4%
Operating Costs	14.6%
Capital Costs	0.0%
TOTAL	100.0%

Cost Breakdown in Dollars

Personal Services	$7,413,897
Operating Costs	$1,268,977
Capital Costs	$0
TOTAL	$8,682,874

Goldsboro

Police Services

Key: Goldsboro ▨   Benchmarking Average —   Fiscal Years 2017 through 2021

Resource Measures

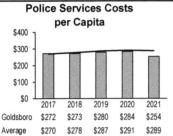

Police Services Costs per Capita

	2017	2018	2019	2020	2021
Goldsboro	$272	$273	$280	$284	$254
Average	$270	$278	$287	$291	$289

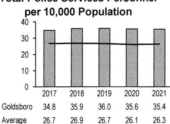

Total Police Services Personnel per 10,000 Population

	2017	2018	2019	2020	2021
Goldsboro	34.8	35.9	36.0	35.6	35.4
Average	26.7	26.9	26.7	26.1	26.3

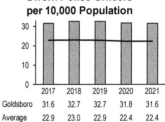

Sworn Police Officers per 10,000 Population

	2017	2018	2019	2020	2021
Goldsboro	31.6	32.7	32.7	31.8	31.6
Average	22.9	23.0	22.9	22.4	22.4

Workload Measures

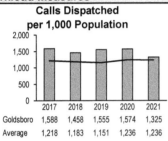

Calls Dispatched per 1,000 Population

	2017	2018	2019	2020	2021
Goldsboro	1,588	1,458	1,555	1,574	1,325
Average	1,218	1,183	1,151	1,236	1,236

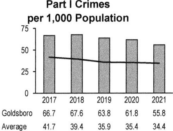

Part I Crimes per 1,000 Population

	2017	2018	2019	2020	2021
Goldsboro	66.7	67.6	63.8	61.8	55.8
Average	41.7	39.4	35.9	35.4	34.4

Efficiency Measures

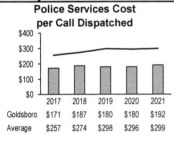

Police Services Cost per Call Dispatched

	2017	2018	2019	2020	2021
Goldsboro	$171	$187	$180	$180	$192
Average	$257	$274	$298	$296	$299

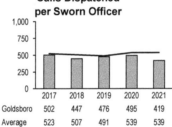

Calls Dispatched per Sworn Officer

	2017	2018	2019	2020	2021
Goldsboro	502	447	476	495	419
Average	523	507	491	539	539

Police Services Cost per Part I Case Cleared

	2017	2018	2019	2020	2021
Goldsboro	$15,735	$15,039	$17,835	$19,529	$21,178
Average	$25,031	$29,606	$33,208	$33,378	$39,435

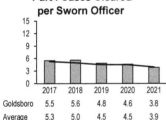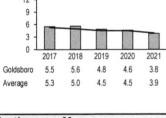

Part I Cases Cleared per Sworn Officer

	2017	2018	2019	2020	2021
Goldsboro	5.5	5.6	4.8	4.6	3.8
Average	5.3	5.0	4.5	4.5	3.9

Effectiveness Measures

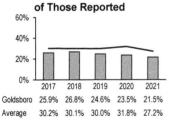

Percentage of Part I Cases Cleared of Those Reported

	2017	2018	2019	2020	2021
Goldsboro	25.9%	26.8%	24.6%	23.5%	21.5%
Average	30.2%	30.1%	30.0%	31.8%	27.2%

Response Time to High Priority Calls in Minutes

	2017	2018	2019	2020	2021
Goldsboro		4.6	4.6	6.2	5.5
Average	5.3	5.3	5.0	5.7	6.4

Greensboro   **Police Services**

Fiscal Year 2020-21

Service Level and Delivery

Greensboro provides comprehensive police services, including patrol, investigations, a traffic unit, a telephone response unit, a forensics laboratory, a canine unit, a motorcycle unit, a special-response unit, a bicycle patrol unit, a drug enforcement unit, and a student outreach and recruiting program.

The city had 690 sworn officer positions authorized for the fiscal year, with an average length of service of 11.6 years. The police department is housed in a stand-alone headquarters facility. The city also has four substations that serve as remote line-up facilities.

Patrol officers work a four-days-on and four-days-off fixed schedule. There are four shifts each day, with each patrol officer shift lasting eleven hours. Investigators and administrative personnel work Monday through Friday from 8 a.m. to 5 p.m. Schedules can be adjusted at any time according to call demand, special events, or special incidents.

Line patrol officers do take vehicles home during their tour of duty. Patrol supervisors, division commanders, and some investigators take vehicles home, depending on their assignments.

Greensboro defines a high-priority emergency call as one in which there is a potential for imminent serious injury or death. The police department was successful in clearing a total of 3,105 Part I cases during the fiscal year.

Conditions Affecting Service, Performance, and Costs

The average response time to high-priority calls reflects the response time of the first arriving unit. Self-initiated calls with a response time of zero are included in the average response time to high-priority calls, with the exception of traffic stops and report-only calls.

Municipal Profile

Population (OSBM 2020)	299,556
Land Area (Square Miles)	129.62
Persons per Square Mile	2,311

Service Profile

FTE Positions—Sworn	690.0
FTE Positions—Other	114.0
Marked and Unmarked Patrol Vehicles	223
Part I Crimes Reported	
Homicide	59
Rape	81
Robbery	528
Assault	1,877
Burglary	2,036
Larceny	7,646
Auto Theft	1,149
Arson	102
TOTAL	13,478
Part II Crimes Reported	16,154
Part I Crimes Cleared	
Persons	682
Property	2,423
TOTAL	3,105
Reporting Format	IBR
Number of Calls Dispatched	241,032
Number of Traffic Accidents	10,150
Property Damage for Accidents	$37,706,790

Full Cost Profile

Cost Breakdown by Percentage	
Personal Services	77.3%
Operating Costs	22.7%
Capital Costs	0.0%
TOTAL	100.0%
Cost Breakdown in Dollars	
Personal Services	$65,504,440
Operating Costs	$19,255,155
Capital Costs	$0
TOTAL	$84,759,595

Greensboro

Police Services

Resource Measures

Police Services Costs per Capita

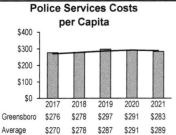

	2017	2018	2019	2020	2021
Greensboro	$276	$278	$297	$291	$283
Average	$270	$278	$287	$291	$289

Total Police Services Personnel per 10,000 Population

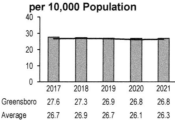

	2017	2018	2019	2020	2021
Greensboro	27.6	27.3	26.9	26.8	26.8
Average	26.7	26.9	26.7	26.1	26.3

Sworn Police Officers per 10,000 Population

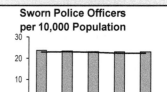

	2017	2018	2019	2020	2021
Greensboro	23.7	23.4	23.1	23.0	23.0
Average	22.9	23.0	22.9	22.4	22.4

Workload Measures

Calls Dispatched per 1,000 Population

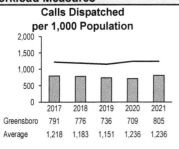

	2017	2018	2019	2020	2021
Greensboro	791	776	736	709	805
Average	1,218	1,183	1,151	1,236	1,236

Part I Crimes per 1,000 Population

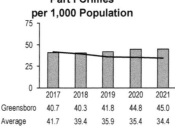

	2017	2018	2019	2020	2021
Greensboro	40.7	40.3	41.8	44.8	45.0
Average	41.7	39.4	35.9	35.4	34.4

Efficiency Measures

Police Services Cost per Call Dispatched

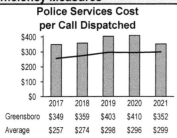

	2017	2018	2019	2020	2021
Greensboro	$349	$359	$403	$410	$352
Average	$257	$274	$298	$296	$299

Calls Dispatched per Sworn Officer

	2017	2018	2019	2020	2021
Greensboro	334	332	319	309	349
Average	523	507	491	539	539

Police Services Cost per Part I Case Cleared

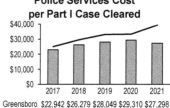

	2017	2018	2019	2020	2021
Greensboro	$22,942	$26,279	$28,049	$29,310	$27,298
Average	$25,031	$29,606	$33,208	$33,378	$39,435

Part I Cases Cleared per Sworn Officer

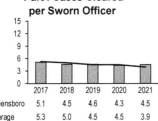
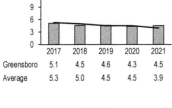

	2017	2018	2019	2020	2021
Greensboro	5.1	4.5	4.6	4.3	4.5
Average	5.3	5.0	4.5	4.5	3.9

Effectiveness Measures

Percentage of Part I Cases Cleared of Those Reported

	2017	2018	2019	2020	2021
Greensboro	29.6%	26.3%	25.3%	22.2%	23.0%
Average	30.2%	30.1%	30.0%	31.8%	27.2%

Response Time to High Priority Calls in Minutes

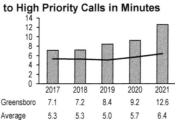

	2017	2018	2019	2020	2021
Greensboro	7.1	7.2	8.4	9.2	12.6
Average	5.3	5.3	5.0	5.7	6.4

Explanatory Information

Service Level and Delivery
Greenville provides a full array of police services, including patrol, investigations, a canine unit, a special-response unit, bicycle patrol, and drug enforcement.

The city had 204 sworn officer positions authorized for the fiscal year, with an average length of service of ten years. The police department occupies space in the city government building.

Patrol officers work a rotating schedule of two on/two off/three on/two off/two on/three off. There are four shifts each day for patrol officers, with the shifts lasting eleven hours. Investigators and administrative personnel work Monday through Friday, in eight-hour shifts. Schedules are subject to change based on call demand, special events, or unusual events.

Some patrol officers have take-home vehicles. There are seven or eight take-home cars per shift. They are assigned by seniority and whether or not the officer lives in the city limits. Officers on a shift who do not have a take-home car are assigned a pool car to drive each day. All investigators and administrative personnel (with one exception) have take-home cars.

Greenville defines high-priority emergency calls as those situations that present a potential for imminent serious injury or death. These calls are dispatched to the first available patrol unit, which may require a citywide dispatch.

The police department was successful in clearing a total of 865 Part I cases during the fiscal year.

Conditions Affecting Service, Performance, and Costs
The average response time to high-priority calls reflects the response time of the first arriving unit. Self-initiated calls are not included in the response times. No data were reported for FY 2019-20 for the city of Greenville.

Municipal Profile

Population (OSBM 2020)	87,428
Land Area (Square Miles)	35.66
Persons per Square Mile	2,452

Service Profile

FTE Positions—Sworn	204.0
FTE Positions—Other	51.0
Marked and Unmarked Patrol Vehicles	222
Part I Crimes Reported	
Homicide	8
Rape	23
Robbery	80
Assault	322
Burglary	378
Larceny	2,088
Auto Theft	135
Arson	16
TOTAL	3,050
Part II Crimes Reported	8,597
Part I Crimes Cleared	
Persons	201
Property	664
TOTAL	865
Reporting Format	IBR
Number of Calls Dispatched	117,882
Number of Traffic Accidents	4,030
Property Damage for Accidents	$13,000,000

Full Cost Profile

Cost Breakdown by Percentage	
Personal Services	66.7%
Operating Costs	21.1%
Capital Costs	12.2%
TOTAL	100.0%

Cost Breakdown in Dollars	
Personal Services	$17,890,915
Operating Costs	$5,673,019
Capital Costs	$3,277,451
TOTAL	$26,841,385

Greenville

Police Services

Key: Greenville ▓ Benchmarking Average — Fiscal Years 2017 through 2021

Resource Measures

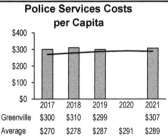

Police Services Costs per Capita

	2017	2018	2019	2020	2021
Greenville	$300	$310	$299		$307
Average	$270	$278	$287	$291	$289

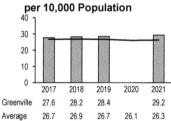

Total Police Services Personnel per 10,000 Population

	2017	2018	2019	2020	2021
Greenville	27.6	28.2	28.4		29.2
Average	26.7	26.9	26.7	26.1	26.3

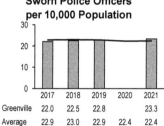

Sworn Police Officers per 10,000 Population

	2017	2018	2019	2020	2021
Greenville	22.0	22.5	22.8		23.3
Average	22.9	23.0	22.9	22.4	22.4

Workload Measures

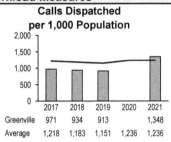

Calls Dispatched per 1,000 Population

	2017	2018	2019	2020	2021
Greenville	971	934	913		1,348
Average	1,218	1,183	1,151	1,236	1,236

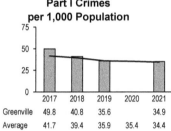

Part I Crimes per 1,000 Population

	2017	2018	2019	2020	2021
Greenville	49.8	40.8	35.6		34.9
Average	41.7	39.4	35.9	35.4	34.4

Efficiency Measures

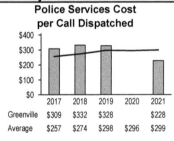

Police Services Cost per Call Dispatched

	2017	2018	2019	2020	2021
Greenville	$309	$332	$328		$228
Average	$257	$274	$298	$296	$299

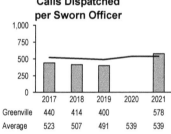

Calls Dispatched per Sworn Officer

	2017	2018	2019	2020	2021
Greenville	440	414	400		578
Average	523	507	491	539	539

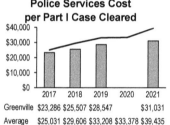

Police Services Cost per Part I Case Cleared

	2017	2018	2019	2020	2021
Greenville	$23,286	$25,507	$28,547		$31,031
Average	$25,031	$29,606	$33,208	$33,378	$39,435

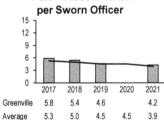

Part I Cases Cleared per Sworn Officer

	2017	2018	2019	2020	2021
Greenville	5.8	5.4	4.6		4.2
Average	5.3	5.0	4.5	4.5	3.9

Effectiveness Measures

Percentage of Part I Cases Cleared of Those Reported

	2017	2018	2019	2020	2021
Greenville	25.8%	29.8%	29.4%		28.4%
Average	30.2%	30.1%	30.0%	31.8%	27.2%

Response Time to High Priority Calls in Minutes

	2017	2018	2019	2020	2021
Greenville	1.5	4.8	4.2		8.3
Average	5.3	5.3	5.0	5.7	6.4

Fiscal Year 2020-21

Explanatory Information

Service Level and Delivery
Hickory provides a full array of police services, including patrol, investigations, a traffic unit, a small laboratory facility, a canine unit, a special-response unit, bicycle patrol, a jail/holding facility, animal control, drug enforcement, and a DARE program.

The city had 122 sworn officer positions authorized for the fiscal year, with an average length of service of 8.5 years. The police department occupies its own three-story facility, completed in January 1996. Each of the five community police areas has an office located in its respective community. These offices are not staffed. They are used for interviews, to obtain information, to store supplies, and to make phone calls.

Patrol officers work a fourteen-day, 80.5-hour cycle. During this period, officers work seven 11.5-hour days. Each of the five districts is commanded by a lieutenant who establishes schedules based on need.

Investigators work Monday through Friday, either from 8:30 a.m. to 5:00 p.m. or 3:30 p.m. to 12:00 a.m. for the second-shift on-call investigators.

Hickory uses the one-officer, one-car plan. Officers take vehicles home if they live in or within one mile of the city. Officers who are members of specialized units needed for emergency response, such as special operations, K-9, or criminial investigations, may also take their vehicles home.

Hickory defines high-priority emergency calls as those situations that present an in-progress threat to life or serious property loss. Officers are authorized to utilize blue lights and sirens during responses and may exceed posted speed limits by up to 20 miles per hour.

The police department was successful in clearing a total of 566 Part I cases during the fiscal year.

Conditions Affecting Service, Performance, and Costs
The average response time to high-priority calls reflects the response time of the first arriving unit. Self-initiated calls with a response time of zero are included in the average response time to high-priority calls.

Municipal Profile

Population (OSBM 2020)	43,578
Land Area (Square Miles)	30.50
Persons per Square Mile	1,429

Service Profile

FTE Positions—Sworn	122.0
FTE Positions—Other	35.0
Marked and Unmarked Patrol Vehicles	143
Part I Crimes Reported	
Homicide	6
Rape	17
Robbery	38
Assault	124
Burglary	306
Larceny	1,359
Auto Theft	167
Arson	13
TOTAL	2,030
Part II Crimes Reported	4,585
Part I Crimes Cleared	
Persons	88
Property	478
TOTAL	566
Reporting Format	IBR
Number of Calls Dispatched	107,438
Number of Traffic Accidents	2,402
Property Damage for Accidents	$9,618,110

Full Cost Profile

Cost Breakdown by Percentage

Personal Services	67.7%
Operating Costs	24.1%
Capital Costs	8.2%
TOTAL	100.0%

Cost Breakdown in Dollars

Personal Services	$9,196,105
Operating Costs	$3,268,784
Capital Costs	$1,109,216
TOTAL	$13,574,105

Hickory

Police Services

Resource Measures

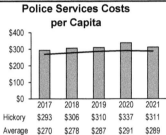

Police Services Costs per Capita

	2017	2018	2019	2020	2021
Hickory	$293	$306	$310	$337	$311
Average	$270	$278	$287	$291	$289

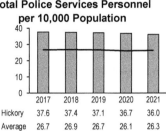

Total Police Services Personnel per 10,000 Population

	2017	2018	2019	2020	2021
Hickory	37.6	37.4	37.1	36.7	36.0
Average	26.7	26.9	26.7	26.1	26.3

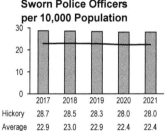

Sworn Police Officers per 10,000 Population

	2017	2018	2019	2020	2021
Hickory	28.7	28.5	28.3	28.0	28.0
Average	22.9	23.0	22.9	22.4	22.4

Workload Measures

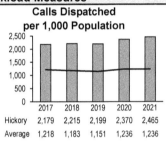

Calls Dispatched per 1,000 Population

	2017	2018	2019	2020	2021
Hickory	2,179	2,215	2,199	2,370	2,465
Average	1,218	1,183	1,151	1,236	1,236

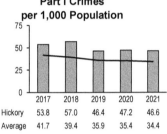

Part I Crimes per 1,000 Population

	2017	2018	2019	2020	2021
Hickory	53.8	57.0	46.4	47.2	46.6
Average	41.7	39.4	35.9	35.4	34.4

Efficiency Measures

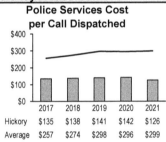

Police Services Cost per Call Dispatched

	2017	2018	2019	2020	2021
Hickory	$135	$138	$141	$142	$126
Average	$257	$274	$298	$296	$299

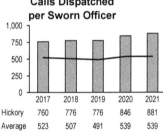

Calls Dispatched per Sworn Officer

	2017	2018	2019	2020	2021
Hickory	760	776	776	846	881
Average	523	507	491	539	539

Police Services Cost per Part I Case Cleared

	2017	2018	2019	2020	2021
Hickory	$15,338	$12,330		$19,646	$23,983
Average	$25,031	$29,606	$33,208	$33,378	$39,435

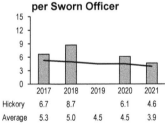

Part I Cases Cleared per Sworn Officer

	2017	2018	2019	2020	2021
Hickory	6.7	8.7		6.1	4.6
Average	5.3	5.0	4.5	4.5	3.9

Effectiveness Measures

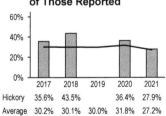

Percentage of Part I Cases Cleared of Those Reported

	2017	2018	2019	2020	2021
Hickory	35.6%	43.5%		36.4%	27.9%
Average	30.2%	30.1%	30.0%	31.8%	27.2%

Response Time to High Priority Calls in Minutes

	2017	2018	2019	2020	2021
Hickory	6.6	7.8	4.4	4.3	4.2
Average	5.3	5.3	5.0	5.7	6.4

Fiscal Year 2020-21

Explanatory Information

Service Level and Delivery
Raleigh's police department provides an array of police services, including patrol, investigations, canine unit, special-response unit, mounted equine unit, motorcycle unit, drug enforcement units, and other programs.

The city had 800 sworn officer positions authorized for the fiscal year, with an average length of service of 14.6 years. The police department has twelve substations around the city.

Patrol officers work a twelve-hour schedule, rotating between days and nights every twenty-eight days. Detectives work an 8.4-hour schedule each weekday, rotating between a day shift and an evening shift. Most detectives are in a pool that shares responsibilities to cover weekend duty and midnight shifts.

The Field Operations Division has a take-home vehicle program for officers with two years of service and living inside the city limits with a safe driving record. Detectives and Special Operation Divisions have take-home vehicles for units on call or call-back status.

The police department was successful in clearing a total of 2,698 Part I cases during the fiscal year.

The city defines high-priority emergency calls as those involving crimes that are in progress or calls that are life-threatening or potentially life-threatening.

Conditions Affecting Service, Performance, and Costs
The average response time to high-priority calls reflects the response time of each arriving unit. Self-initiated calls are not included in the average response time to high-priority calls.

Municipal Profile

Population (OSBM 2020)	468,977
Land Area (Square Miles)	146.47
Persons per Square Mile	3,202

Service Profile

FTE Positions—Sworn	800.0
FTE Positions—Other	108.0
Marked and Unmarked Patrol Vehicles	785
Part I Crimes Reported	
Homicide	29
Rape	173
Robbery	507
Assault	991
Burglary	1,180
Larceny	7,576
Auto Theft	1,064
Arson	31
TOTAL	11,551
Part II Crimes Reported	NA
Part I Crimes Cleared	
Persons	710
Property	1,988
TOTAL	2,698
Reporting Format	NIBRS
Number of Calls Dispatched	292,110
Number of Traffic Accidents	19,531
Property Damage for Accidents	$4,297,191

Full Cost Profile

Cost Breakdown by Percentage	
Personal Services	76.1%
Operating Costs	15.1%
Capital Costs	8.7%
TOTAL	100.0%

Cost Breakdown in Dollars	
Personal Services	$94,410,290
Operating Costs	$18,786,407
Capital Costs	$10,851,832
TOTAL	$124,048,529

Raleigh

Police Services

Key: Raleigh   Benchmarking Average —   Fiscal Years 2017 through 2021

Resource Measures

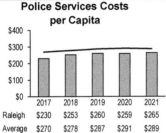

Police Services Costs per Capita

	2017	2018	2019	2020	2021
Raleigh	$230	$253	$260	$259	$265
Average	$270	$278	$287	$291	$289

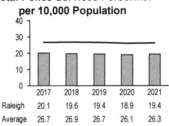

Total Police Services Personnel per 10,000 Population

	2017	2018	2019	2020	2021
Raleigh	20.1	19.6	19.4	18.9	19.4
Average	26.7	26.9	26.7	26.1	26.3

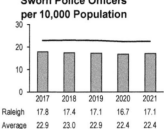

Sworn Police Officers per 10,000 Population

	2017	2018	2019	2020	2021
Raleigh	17.8	17.4	17.1	16.7	17.1
Average	22.9	23.0	22.9	22.4	22.4

Workload Measures

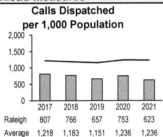

Calls Dispatched per 1,000 Population

	2017	2018	2019	2020	2021
Raleigh	807	766	657	753	623
Average	1,218	1,183	1,151	1,236	1,236

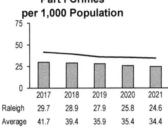

Part I Crimes per 1,000 Population

	2017	2018	2019	2020	2021
Raleigh	29.7	28.9	27.9	25.8	24.6
Average	41.7	39.4	35.9	35.4	34.4

Efficiency Measures

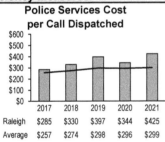

Police Services Cost per Call Dispatched

	2017	2018	2019	2020	2021
Raleigh	$285	$330	$397	$344	$425
Average	$257	$274	$298	$296	$299

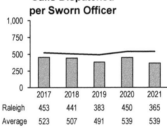

Calls Dispatched per Sworn Officer

	2017	2018	2019	2020	2021
Raleigh	453	441	383	450	365
Average	523	507	491	539	539

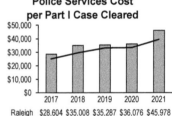

Police Services Cost per Part I Case Cleared

	2017	2018	2019	2020	2021
Raleigh	$28,604	$35,008	$35,287	$36,076	$45,978
Average	$25,031	$29,606	$33,208	$33,378	$39,435

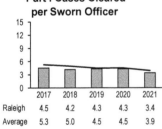

Part I Cases Cleared per Sworn Officer

	2017	2018	2019	2020	2021
Raleigh	4.5	4.2	4.3	4.3	3.4
Average	5.3	5.0	4.5	4.5	3.9

Effectiveness Measures

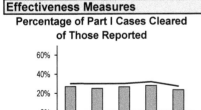

Percentage of Part I Cases Cleared of Those Reported

	2017	2018	2019	2020	2021
Raleigh	27.1%	25.0%	26.5%	27.9%	23.4%
Average	30.2%	30.1%	30.0%	31.8%	27.2%

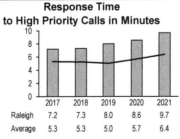

Response Time to High Priority Calls in Minutes

	2017	2018	2019	2020	2021
Raleigh	7.2	7.3	8.0	8.6	9.7
Average	5.3	5.3	5.0	5.7	6.4

Police Services   105

Wilson

Police Services

Fiscal Year 2020-21

Explanatory Information

Service Level and Delivery

Wilson's police department provides an array of police services, including patrol, investigations, a telephone response unit, a forensics laboratory, a canine unit, a part-time mounted equine unit, a special-response unit, street crimes, drug enforcement, and other services.

The city had 125 sworn officer positions authorized for the fiscal year, with an average length of service of 12.3 years. The main police department headquarters is located in downtown Wilson, housing administration, records, property, major-case investigations, police information services, victim services, evidence, and recruitment and training. There are five substations.

Patrol officers work twelve-hour shifts, working fourteen days of a twenty-eight day cycle (168 hours). Shifts are either 7 a.m. to 7 p.m. or 7 p.m. to 7 a.m. and are rotated every two weeks. Department needs may cause shifts to vary. Investigators generally work eight-hour shifts five days per week. Shifts are 8 a.m. to 5 p.m.

Each patrol officer is assigned a vehicle and may take the vehicle home if he or she resides in the city. Officers living outside the city limits park their vehicles at businesses.

The police department was successful in clearing a total of 689 Part I cases during the fiscal year.

Wilson defines high-priority emergency calls as calls related to crimes in progress that require immediate response: murder, rape, robbery, burglary, arson/fire, and assaults.

Conditions Affecting Service, Performance, and Costs

The average response time to high-priority calls reflects the response time of the first unit to arrive. Self-initiated calls with a response time of zero are not included in the average response time to high-priority calls.

Municipal Profile

Population (OSBM 2020)	47,769
Land Area (Square Miles)	31.02
Persons per Square Mile	1,540

Service Profile

FTE Positions—Sworn	125.0
FTE Positions—Other	17.0
Marked and Unmarked Patrol Vehicles	148
Part I Crimes Reported	
Homicide	5
Rape	10
Robbery	38
Assault	172
Burglary	207
Larceny	1,081
Auto Theft	115
Arson	9
TOTAL	1,637
Part II Crimes Reported	2,966
Part I Crimes Cleared	
Persons	160
Property	529
TOTAL	689
Reporting Format	IBR
Number of Calls Dispatched	109,241
Number of Traffic Accidents	2,505
Property Damage for Accidents	NA

Full Cost Profile

Cost Breakdown by Percentage

Personal Services	70.5%
Operating Costs	24.0%
Capital Costs	5.5%
TOTAL	100.0%

Cost Breakdown in Dollars

Personal Services	$13,155,062
Operating Costs	$4,486,468
Capital Costs	$1,023,886
TOTAL	$18,665,416

Wilson

Police Services

Resource Measures

Police Services Costs per Capita

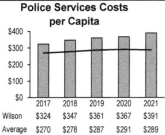

	2017	2018	2019	2020	2021
Wilson	$324	$347	$361	$367	$391
Average	$270	$278	$287	$291	$289

Total Police Services Personnel per 10,000 Population

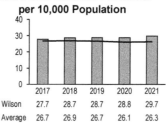

	2017	2018	2019	2020	2021
Wilson	27.7	28.7	28.7	28.8	29.7
Average	26.7	26.9	26.7	26.1	26.3

Sworn Police Officers per 10,000 Population

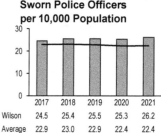

	2017	2018	2019	2020	2021
Wilson	24.5	25.4	25.5	25.3	26.2
Average	22.9	23.0	22.9	22.4	22.4

Workload Measures

Calls Dispatched per 1,000 Population

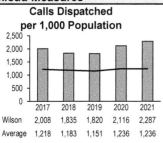

	2017	2018	2019	2020	2021
Wilson	2,008	1,835	1,820	2,116	2,287
Average	1,218	1,183	1,151	1,236	1,236

Part I Crimes per 1,000 Population

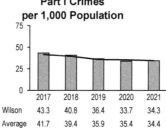

	2017	2018	2019	2020	2021
Wilson	43.3	40.8	36.4	33.7	34.3
Average	41.7	39.4	35.9	35.4	34.4

Efficiency Measures

Police Services Cost per Call Dispatched

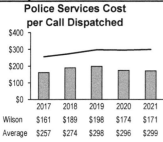

	2017	2018	2019	2020	2021
Wilson	$161	$189	$198	$174	$171
Average	$257	$274	$298	$296	$299

Calls Dispatched per Sworn Officer

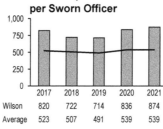

	2017	2018	2019	2020	2021
Wilson	820	722	714	836	874
Average	523	507	491	539	539

Police Services Cost per Part I Case Cleared

	2017	2018	2019	2020	2021
Wilson	$20,033	$24,656	$28,401	$28,802	$27,091
Average	$25,031	$29,606	$33,208	$33,378	$39,435

Part I Cases Cleared per Sworn Officer

	2017	2018	2019	2020	2021
Wilson	6.6	5.5	5.0	5.0	5.5
Average	5.3	5.0	4.5	4.5	3.9

Effectiveness Measures

Percentage of Part I Cases Cleared of Those Reported

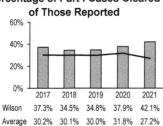

	2017	2018	2019	2020	2021
Wilson	37.3%	34.5%	34.8%	37.9%	42.1%
Average	30.2%	30.1%	30.0%	31.8%	27.2%

Response Time to High Priority Calls in Minutes

	2017	2018	2019	2020	2021
Wilson	5.3	4.5	4.2	4.2	3.9
Average	5.3	5.3	5.0	5.7	6.4

Fiscal Year 2020-21

Explanatory Information

Service Level and Delivery

Winston-Salem provides an array of police services to its citizens, including patrol, investigations, a traffic enforcement unit, a DWI Task Force, a telephone response unit, a canine unit, a special-response unit, bicycle patrol, drug enforcement, a gang unit, and other crime prevention programs.

The city had 538 sworn officer positions authorized for the fiscal year, with an average length of service of 11.7 years. The police department occupies the public safety center. It houses the police department, emergency communications, and the fire department administration. The special investigations division occupies offices in leased space in another facility. A downtown bike patrol office is maintained in the central downtown area.

The department employs a forward-rotating schedule of five shifts. Officers work five days on and four days off. Shifts are ten hours in length. The majority of investigators work Monday through Friday from 8 a.m. to 5 p.m.

Patrol vehicles are assigned to individual officers. Officers residing within Forsyth County take their vehicles home. If officers reside outside of the county, they park their vehicles in a residential or business area within the city limits.

The police department was successful in clearing a total of 3,440 Part I crimes during the fiscal year.

Winston-Salem defines highest-priority emergency calls as those dealing with a significant threat of imminent injury to persons or with crimes against persons that are in progress or have just occurred and where the suspect is still there.

Conditions Affecting Service, Performance, and Costs

The average response time to high-priority calls reflects the response time of the first arriving unit. Self-initiated calls with a response time of zero are included in the average response time to high-priority calls.

The Winston-Salem Police Department does not investigate arsons, so arsons are not included in the crimes reported here. Arson investigations are handled by the Winston-Salem Fire Department.

Municipal Profile

Population (OSBM 2020)	249,986
Land Area (Square Miles)	132.59
Persons per Square Mile	1,885

Service Profile

FTE Positions—Sworn	538.0
FTE Positions—Other	125.0
Marked and Unmarked Patrol Vehicles	437
Part I Crimes Reported	
Homicide	33
Rape	112
Robbery	296
Assault	2,692
Burglary	1,859
Larceny	8,425
Auto Theft	953
Arson	NA
TOTAL	14,370
Part II Crimes Reported	35,002
Part I Crimes Cleared	
Persons	1,017
Property	2,423
TOTAL	3,440
Reporting Format	NIBRS
Number of Calls Dispatched	192,924
Number of Traffic Accidents	9,289
Property Damage for Accidents	$34,752,997

Full Cost Profile

Cost Breakdown by Percentage

Personal Services	76.7%
Operating Costs	15.2%
Capital Costs	8.1%
TOTAL	100.0%

Cost Breakdown in Dollars

Personal Services	$61,556,692
Operating Costs	$12,177,549
Capital Costs	$6,504,847
TOTAL	$80,239,088

Winston-Salem

Police Services

Key: Winston-Salem ▨   Benchmarking Average —   Fiscal Years 2017 through 2021

Resource Measures

Police Services Costs per Capita

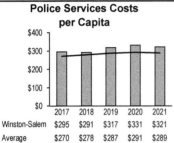

	2017	2018	2019	2020	2021
Winston-Salem	$295	$291	$317	$331	$321
Average	$270	$278	$287	$291	$289

Total Police Services Personnel per 10,000 Population

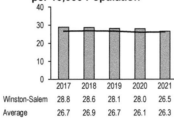

	2017	2018	2019	2020	2021
Winston-Salem	28.8	28.6	28.1	28.0	26.5
Average	26.7	26.9	26.7	26.1	26.3

Sworn Police Officers per 10,000 Population

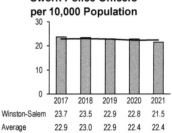

	2017	2018	2019	2020	2021
Winston-Salem	23.7	23.5	22.9	22.8	21.5
Average	22.9	23.0	22.9	22.4	22.4

Workload Measures

Calls Dispatched per 1,000 Population

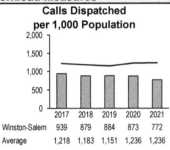

	2017	2018	2019	2020	2021
Winston-Salem	939	879	884	873	772
Average	1,218	1,183	1,151	1,236	1,236

Part I Crimes per 1,000 Population

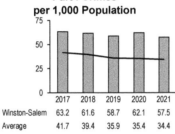

	2017	2018	2019	2020	2021
Winston-Salem	63.2	61.6	58.7	62.1	57.5
Average	41.7	39.4	35.9	35.4	34.4

Efficiency Measures

Police Services Cost per Call Dispatched

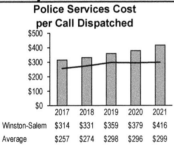

	2017	2018	2019	2020	2021
Winston-Salem	$314	$331	$359	$379	$416
Average	$257	$274	$298	$296	$299

Calls Dispatched per Sworn Officer

	2017	2018	2019	2020	2021
Winston-Salem	396	375	386	383	359
Average	523	507	491	539	539

Police Services Cost per Part I Case Cleared

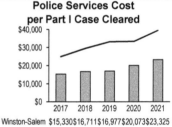

	2017	2018	2019	2020	2021
Winston-Salem	$15,330	$16,711	$16,977	$20,073	$23,325
Average	$25,031	$29,606	$33,208	$33,378	$39,435

Part I Cases Cleared per Sworn Officer

	2017	2018	2019	2020	2021
Winston-Salem	8.1	7.4	8.1	7.2	6.4
Average	5.3	5.0	4.5	4.5	3.9

Effectiveness Measures

Percentage of Part I Cases Cleared of Those Reported

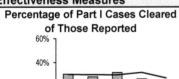

	2017	2018	2019	2020	2021
Winston-Salem	30.4%	28.3%	31.8%	26.5%	23.9%
Average	30.2%	30.1%	30.0%	31.8%	27.2%

Response Time to High Priority Calls in Minutes

	2017	2018	2019	2020	2021
Winston-Salem	4.0	3.9	3.9	3.8	4.1
Average	5.3	5.3	5.0	5.7	6.4

Performance and Cost Data

EMERGENCY COMMUNICATIONS

PERFORMANCE MEASURES FOR EMERGENCY COMMUNICATIONS

SERVICE DEFINITION

Emergency Communication refer to the receipt and handling of 911 and other calls by an emergency communications center. Such a center must answer all calls, including those that come in over 911 lines and others that come in over regular phone lines. Some calls result in the dispatch of a police or other emergency response unit. Others do not.

NOTES ON PERFORMANCE MEASURES

1. Number of Calls Answered and Number of Calls Dispatched per 1,000 Population

These are used as measures of workload. All calls coming into a police emergency communications center must be answered; therefore, these measures assess service workload. Calls coming into a center also reflect the actual or existing, if not full potential, need for emergency communications services. Many calls coming into a center are dispatched. Others come in over regular telephone lines, and still others may be referred to the center by an external call-taker, such as a county emergency communications center.

2. Telecommunicators

Telecommunicators are the personnel who handle the calls in the communication centers. They may take calls, dispatch calls, or do both. Telecommunicators receive specialized training. They work on a shift schedule that generally allows 24/7 coverage.

3. Average Number of Seconds from Initial Ring to Answer and Percentage of Calls Answered within Twenty Seconds

These are effectiveness measures that assess how quickly telecommunicators answer calls.

4. Average Processing Time (Seconds)

This is an effectiveness measure representing the average time in seconds between when the telecommunicator answers the telephone and when computer-aided dispatch (CAD) entry begins. This measure is often referred to as "talk time."

5. For Calls Dispatched, Average Number of Seconds from CAD Entry to Dispatch—Highest-Priority Calls

Some calls result in the dispatch of a police or other emergency response unit to a life-threatening or other similar emergency situation. Other calls result in a dispatch to a serious—but not emergency—situation. Other calls do not result in a dispatch. This measure assesses dispatch time for high-priority, emergency situations.

Emergency Communications

Summary of Key Dimensions of Service

City or Town	Population Served	Number of FTEs	Average Length of Service for Call Takers (in Years)	Total Incoming Calls Handled	Total E-911 Calls Handled	Total Dispatches	Outgoing Calls Other than Dispatches
Apex	59,368	13.0	13.9	37,017	3,704	67,325	10,700
Concord	105,936	25.5	10.6	97,091	29,860	140,645	30,945
Greensboro	542,255	98.0	11.2	524,938	331,068	424,889	180,726
Greenville	87,428	21.0	na	92,531	26,123	na	20,161
Hickory	43,578	15.0	3.9	na	na	107,438	na
Raleigh	1,134,824	129.0	5.1	772,003	515,516	440,294	284,016
Winston-Salem	249,986	47.0	9.0	444,704	206,928	209,737	68,955

NOTES

The population served by the municipal emergency communications center may go beyond municipal boundaries up to the entire county in cases where the service is a consolidated center.

EXPLANATORY FACTORS

These are factors that the project found affected emergency communication performance and cost in one or more of the municipalities:

Types of emergency response units dispatched, such as police, fire, and EMS
Number and proportion of nonemergency calls received by center
Types of assistance or advice, such as medical, that telecommunicators provide over the phone
Technology available to telecommunication centers
City's definition of what constitutes an "emergency" and "highest priority" call
Service to city only or to city and outlying areas
Training of telecommunicators
Demographic makeup of community
Organizational configuration and staffing for service

Fiscal Year 2020-21

Explanatory Information

Service Level and Delivery

The Apex Emergency Communications Center is a division within the Apex Police Department. This center is a secondary public safety answering point within Wake County, using Raleigh computer-aided dispatch (CAD) as a remote position. The communications center dispatches calls for police, fire, public works, and utilities.

The town owns a 150-foot radio tower that is tied into the Wake County radio system. The system is an 800 MHz system tied into the state VIPER system for radio operations.

Apex's emergency communications center handled a total of 37,017 incoming calls in the fiscal year and dispatched 67,325 calls. The city defines highest-priority emergency calls as those with immediate life or property risk or in-progress calls.

Conditions Affecting Service, Performance, and Costs

CAD entry for Apex does not begin immediately but is activated by operators.

Municipal Profile

Population (OSBM 2020)	59,368
Land Area (Square Miles)	23.61
Persons per Square Mile	2,514
County	Wake

Service Profile

Primary or Secondary Answering Point	Secondary
Calls Dispatched	
Police	Yes
Fire	No
Other	Yes
FTE Positions	
Telecommunicators/Call-Takers	10.20
Other	2.80
Total Positions	13.00
Average Length of Service for Call-Takers	13.9 years
Total Incoming Calls	37,017
Total 911 Calls	3,704
Total Calls Dispatched	67,325
Outgoing Calls Other than Dispatch	10,700
Revenue from E-911 Fees	None

Full Cost Profile

Cost Breakdown by Percentage	
Personal Services	64.4%
Operating Costs	27.9%
Capital Costs	7.7%
TOTAL	100.0%
Cost Breakdown in Dollars	
Personal Services	$935,925
Operating Costs	$405,158
Capital Costs	$111,788
TOTAL	$1,452,871

Apex

Emergency Communications

Resource Measures

Emergency Communications Services Costs per Capita

	2017	2018	2019	2020	2021
Apex	$20.19	$22.13	$22.25	$22.77	$24.47
Average	$18.18	$18.67	$20.39	$19.83	$20.91

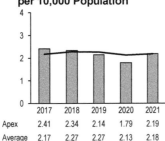

Emergency Communications FTEs per 10,000 Population

	2017	2018	2019	2020	2021
Apex	2.41	2.34	2.14	1.79	2.19
Average	2.17	2.27	2.27	2.13	2.18

Workload Measures

Total Calls Answered per 1,000 Population

	2017	2018	2019	2020	2021
Apex	1,033	847	782	636	624
Average	1,255	1,204	1,120	1,042	1,004

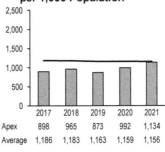

Calls Dispatched per 1,000 Population

	2017	2018	2019	2020	2021
Apex	898	965	873	992	1,134
Average	1,186	1,183	1,163	1,159	1,156

E-911 Calls as a Percentage of All Incoming Calls

	2017	2018	2019	2020	2021
Apex	7.8%	9.1%	9.3%	10.0%	10.0%
Average	38.8%	37.8%	38.8%	43.1%	40.9%

Efficiency Measures

Calls Answered per Telecommunicator

	2017	2018	2019	2020	2021
Apex	4,638	4,369	4,399	4,241	3,629
Average	7,000	6,638	6,363	6,425	5,936

Calls Dispatched per Telecommunicator

	2017	2018	2019	2020	2021
Apex	4,030	4,977	4,912	6,612	6,600
Average	5,614	5,365	5,348	5,650	5,564

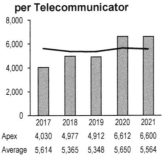

Emergency Communications Cost per Call Dispatched

	2017	2018	2019	2020	2021
Apex	$22.49	$22.93	$25.50	$22.95	$21.58
Average	$18.02	$18.40	$20.48	$19.57	$21.43

Effectiveness Measures

Number of Seconds from Initial Ring to Answer

	2017	2018	2019	2020	2021
Apex	4	1	7	6	6
Average	5	4	6	5	5

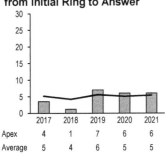

Percent of E-911 Calls Answered within Twenty Seconds

	2017	2018	2019	2020	2021
Apex	99.4%	99.2%	99.9%	99.5%	99.9%
Average	98.8%	98.8%	98.5%	98.8%	98.7%

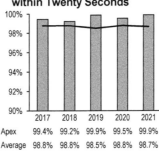

Average Time in Seconds from CAD Entry to Dispatch for Priority One Calls

	2017	2018	2019	2020	2021
Apex	42	43	70	40	43
Average	71	86	84	61	67

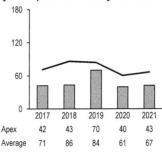

Concord
Emergency Communications

Fiscal Year 2020-21

Explanatory Information

Service Level and Delivery

Concord's emergency communications center handles E-911 and non-emergency calls for the city. The emergency communications function of the city is separate from the police and fire functions and does not answer or transfer administrative calls for those departments. The emergency communications center does answer calls for utility and other city departments after hours, which is reflected in the number of incoming calls.

The city uses an 800 MHz system, which is a twelve-channel, five-site system shared with Cabarrus County and the City of Kannapolis.

Concord's center handled a total of 97,091 calls in the fiscal year, dispatching 140,645 calls.

Conditions Affecting Service, Performance, and Costs

Municipal Profile

Population (OSBM 2020)	105,936
Land Area (Square Miles)	63.65
Persons per Square Mile	1,664
County	Cabarrus

Service Profile

Primary or Secondary Answering Point	Primary
Calls Dispatched	
Police	Yes
Fire	Yes
Other	Yes
FTE Positions	
Telecommunicators/Call-Takers	23.5
Other	2.0
Total Positions	25.5
Average Length of Service for Call-Takers	10.6 years
Total Incoming Calls	97,091
Total 911 Calls	29,860
Total Calls Dispatched	140,645
Outgoing Calls Other than Dispatch	30,945
Revenue from E-911 Fees	None

Full Cost Profile

Cost Breakdown by Percentage	
Personal Services	81.3%
Operating Costs	16.9%
Capital Costs	1.8%
TOTAL	100.0%
Cost Breakdown in Dollars	
Personal Services	$1,657,531
Operating Costs	$344,340
Capital Costs	$36,007
TOTAL	$2,037,878

Concord

Emergency Communications

Resource Measures

Emergency Communications Services Costs per Capita

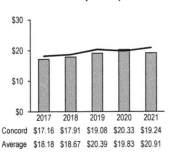

	2017	2018	2019	2020	2021
Concord	$17.16	$17.91	$19.08	$20.33	$19.24
Average	$18.18	$18.67	$20.39	$19.83	$20.91

Emergency Communications FTEs per 10,000 Population

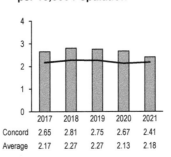

	2017	2018	2019	2020	2021
Concord	2.65	2.81	2.75	2.67	2.41
Average	2.17	2.27	2.27	2.13	2.18

Workload Measures

Total Calls Answered per 1,000 Population

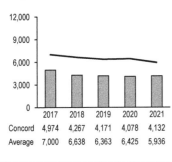

	2017	2018	2019	2020	2021
Concord	1,204	1,104	1,059	1,004	917
Average	1,255	1,204	1,120	1,042	1,004

Calls Dispatched per 1,000 Population

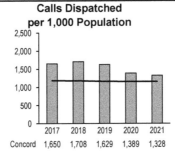

	2017	2018	2019	2020	2021
Concord	1,650	1,708	1,629	1,389	1,328
Average	1,186	1,183	1,163	1,159	1,156

E-911 Calls as a Percentage of All Incoming Calls

	2017	2018	2019	2020	2021
Concord	27.1%	28.3%	29.7%	30.3%	30.8%
Average	38.8%	37.8%	38.8%	43.1%	40.9%

Efficiency Measures

Calls Answered per Telecommunicator

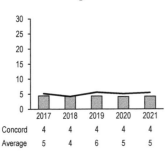

	2017	2018	2019	2020	2021
Concord	4,974	4,267	4,171	4,078	4,132
Average	7,000	6,638	6,363	6,425	5,936

Calls Dispatched per Telecommunicator

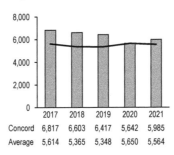

	2017	2018	2019	2020	2021
Concord	6,817	6,603	6,417	5,642	5,985
Average	5,614	5,365	5,348	5,650	5,564

Emergency Communications Cost per Call Dispatched

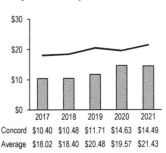

	2017	2018	2019	2020	2021
Concord	$10.40	$10.48	$11.71	$14.63	$14.49
Average	$18.02	$18.40	$20.48	$19.57	$21.43

Effectiveness Measures

Number of Seconds from Initial Ring to Answer

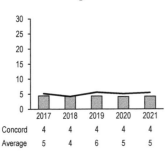

	2017	2018	2019	2020	2021
Concord	4	4	4	4	4
Average	5	4	6	5	5

Percent of E-911 Calls Answered within Twenty Seconds

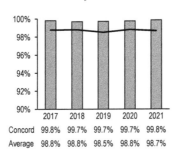

	2017	2018	2019	2020	2021
Concord	99.8%	99.7%	99.7%	99.7%	99.8%
Average	98.8%	98.8%	98.5%	98.8%	98.7%

Average Time in Seconds from CAD Entry to Dispatch for Priority One Calls

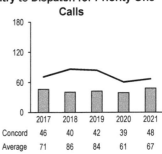

	2017	2018	2019	2020	2021
Concord	46	40	42	39	48
Average	71	86	84	61	67

Explanatory Information

Service Level and Delivery

Guilford Metro 911 operates under an interlocal agreement between the City of Greensboro and Guilford County. The public safety answering point serves as a separate department providing emergency communications for the City of Greensboro, Guilford County, and Gibsonville (except for the City of High Point police and fire departments). The services include dispatch and call intake for all law agencies, fire agencies, and EMS. The consolidation process enabled the first update of all 911 equipment in ten years and the creation of a backup E-911 center to improve disaster preparedness. These changes contributed to slightly higher operational costs.

Guilford Metro 911 uses a Motorola Trunked P25 Regional radio system. The system has nine tower sites and is jointly owned with Guilford County.

Greensboro's communications center handled a total of 524,938 incoming calls in the fiscal year, dispatching 424,889 calls. The city defines highest-priority emergency calls as call types that require the fastest response, such as shootings, robberies, and domestic violence.

Greensboro received $2,204,248 in E-911 revenues to support system operations.

Conditions Affecting Service, Performance, and Costs

Municipal Profile

Population (OSBM 2020)–Guilford County	542,255
Land Area (Square Miles)	649.42
Persons per Square Mile	835
County	Guilford

Service Profile

Primary or Secondary Answering Point	Primary
Calls Dispatched	
Police	Yes
Fire	Yes
Other	Yes
FTE Positions	
Telecommunicators/Call-Takers	92.0
Other	6.0
Total Positions	98.0
Average Length of Service for Call-Takers	11.2 years
Total Incoming Calls	524,938
Total 911 Calls	331,068
Total Calls Dispatched	424,889
Outgoing Calls Other than Dispatch	180,726
Revenue from E-911 Fees	$2,204,248

Full Cost Profile

Cost Breakdown by Percentage	
Personal Services	84.3%
Operating Costs	15.7%
Capital Costs	0.0%
TOTAL	100.0%
Cost Breakdown in Dollars	
Personal Services	$7,133,030
Operating Costs	$1,323,517
Capital Costs	$0
TOTAL	$8,456,547

Greensboro   Emergency Communications

Resource Measures

Emergency Communications Services Costs per Capita

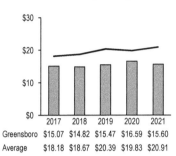

	2017	2018	2019	2020	2021
Greensboro	$15.07	$14.82	$15.47	$16.59	$15.60
Average	$18.18	$18.67	$20.39	$19.83	$20.91

Emergency Communications FTEs per 10,000 Population

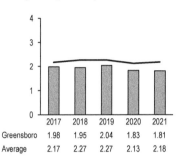

	2017	2018	2019	2020	2021
Greensboro	1.98	1.95	2.04	1.83	1.81
Average	2.17	2.27	2.27	2.13	2.18

Workload Measures

Total Calls Answered per 1,000 Population

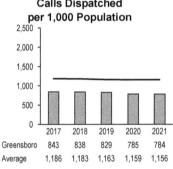

	2017	2018	2019	2020	2021
Greensboro	1,196	1,115	1,105	979	968
Average	1,255	1,204	1,120	1,042	1,004

Calls Dispatched per 1,000 Population

	2017	2018	2019	2020	2021
Greensboro	843	838	829	785	784
Average	1,186	1,183	1,163	1,159	1,156

E-911 Calls as a Percentage of All Incoming Calls

	2017	2018	2019	2020	2021
Greensboro	57.0%	56.4%	56.1%	61.7%	63.1%
Average	38.8%	37.8%	38.8%	43.1%	40.9%

Efficiency Measures

Calls Answered per Telecommunicator

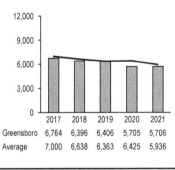

	2017	2018	2019	2020	2021
Greensboro	6,764	6,396	6,406	5,705	5,706
Average	7,000	6,638	6,363	6,425	5,936

Calls Dispatched per Telecommunicator

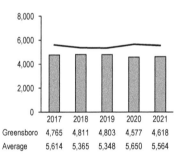

	2017	2018	2019	2020	2021
Greensboro	4,765	4,811	4,803	4,577	4,618
Average	5,614	5,365	5,348	5,650	5,564

Emergency Communications Cost per Call Dispatched

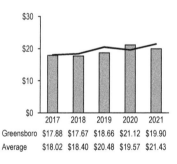

	2017	2018	2019	2020	2021
Greensboro	$17.88	$17.67	$18.66	$21.12	$19.90
Average	$18.02	$18.40	$20.48	$19.57	$21.43

Effectiveness Measures

Number of Seconds from Initial Ring to Answer

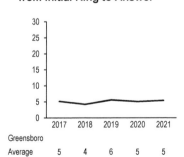

	2017	2018	2019	2020	2021
Greensboro					
Average	5	4	6	5	5

Percent of E-911 Calls Answered within Twenty Seconds

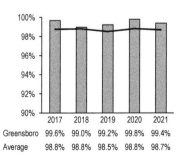

	2017	2018	2019	2020	2021
Greensboro	99.6%	99.0%	99.2%	99.8%	99.4%
Average	98.8%	98.8%	98.5%	98.8%	98.7%

Average Time in Seconds from CAD Entry to Dispatch for Priority One Calls

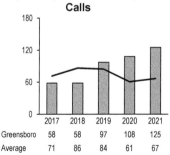

	2017	2018	2019	2020	2021
Greensboro	58	58	97	108	125
Average	71	86	84	61	67

Explanatory Information

Service Level and Delivery

Greenville's emergency communications center is a secondary public safety answering point, with Pitt County being the primary answering point. Pitt County initially receives all 911 calls and dispatches fire and EMS calls inside the city limits. All 911 calls for police services are transferred to the Greenville Police Department emergency communications center for dispatch. Calls can also be made directly to the police department over a dedicated emergency line.

The city does not own its own communications system and infrastructure. Greenville operates on the VIPER system maintained by the North Carolina State Highway Patrol. This system is fully maintained and operated by the state. The system has one tower located within the city limits and fully supports communication interoperability among all law enforcement agencies in Pitt County and with Greenville Fire/Rescue and East Care medical transport.

Greenville's center took in 92,531 incoming calls in the fiscal year. The number of dispatched calls was not available.

Conditions Affecting Service, Performance, and Costs

Telecommunicators in Greenville are also tasked with overseeing public safety cameras through several large monitors. When needed, they are instructed to log events requiring a response as service calls. This video monitoring results in higher staffing needs in the emergency communications center.

No data were reported for FY 2019-20 for the city of Greenville.

Municipal Profile

Population (OSBM 2020)	87,428
Land Area (Square Miles)	35.66
Persons per Square Mile	2,452
County	Pitt

Service Profile

Primary or Secondary Answering Point	Secondary
Calls Dispatched	
Police	Yes
Fire	No
Other	No
FTE Positions	
Telecommunicators/Call-Takers	20.0
Other	1.0
Total Positions	21.0
Average Length of Service for Call-Takers	NA
Total Incoming Calls	92,531
Total 911 Calls	26,123
Total Calls Dispatched	NA
Outgoing Calls Other than Dispatch	20,161
Revenue from E-911 Fees	None

Full Cost Profile

Cost Breakdown by Percentage	
Personal Services	74.1%
Operating Costs	25.9%
Capital Costs	0.0%
TOTAL	100.0%

Cost Breakdown in Dollars	
Personal Services	$1,469,900
Operating Costs	$514,002
Capital Costs	$0
TOTAL	$1,983,902

Greenville   Emergency Communications

Key: Greenville   ▨   Benchmarking Average   —   Fiscal Years 2017 through 2021

Resource Measures

Emergency Communications Services Costs per Capita

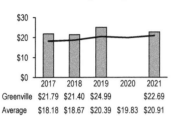

	2017	2018	2019	2020	2021
Greenville	$21.79	$21.40	$24.99		$22.69
Average	$18.18	$18.67	$20.39	$19.83	$20.91

Emergency Communications FTEs per 10,000 Population

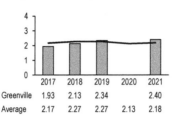

	2017	2018	2019	2020	2021
Greenville	1.93	2.13	2.34		2.40
Average	2.17	2.27	2.27	2.13	2.18

Workload Measures

Total Calls Answered per 1,000 Population

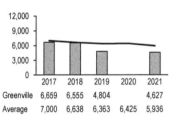

	2017	2018	2019	2020	2021
Greenville	1,211	1,396	1,070		1,058
Average	1,255	1,204	1,120	1,042	1,004

Calls Dispatched per 1,000 Population

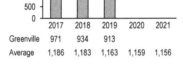

	2017	2018	2019	2020	2021
Greenville	971	934	913		
Average	1,186	1,183	1,163	1,159	1,156

E-911 Calls as a Percentage of All Incoming Calls

	2017	2018	2019	2020	2021
Greenville	27.6%	22.8%	25.7%		28.2%
Average	38.8%	37.8%	38.8%	43.1%	40.9%

Efficiency Measures

Calls Answered per Telecommunicator

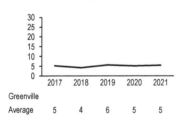

	2017	2018	2019	2020	2021
Greenville	6,659	6,555	4,804		4,627
Average	7,000	6,638	6,363	6,425	5,936

Calls Dispatched per Telecommunicator

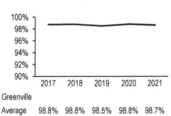

	2017	2018	2019	2020	2021
Greenville	5,339	4,384	4,097		
Average	5,614	5,365	5,348	5,650	5,564

Emergency Communications Cost per Call Dispatched

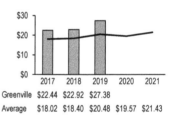

	2017	2018	2019	2020	2021
Greenville	$22.44	$22.92	$27.38		
Average	$18.02	$18.40	$20.48	$19.57	$21.43

Effectiveness Measures

Number of Seconds from Initial Ring to Answer

	2017	2018	2019	2020	2021
Greenville					
Average	5	4	6	5	5

Percent of E-911 Calls Answered within Twenty Seconds

	2017	2018	2019	2020	2021
Greenville					
Average	98.8%	98.8%	98.5%	98.8%	98.7%

Average Time in Seconds from CAD Entry to Dispatch for Priority One Calls

	2017	2018	2019	2020	2021
Greenville					
Average	71	86	84	61	67

Explanatory Information

Service Level and Delivery

Hickory's emergency communications center is a secondary public safety answering point, with Catawba County being the primary answering point. Catawaba County initially receives all 911 calls and dispatches fire and EMS calls inside the city limits. All 911 calls for police services are transferred to the emergency communications center for dispatch. Any emergency calls for other city services are transferred to the emergency communications center between 3:30 p.m. and 7:00 a.m.

The city owns its communications system and infrastructure. It uses an Ericsson 800 MHz radio system. There is one 1,350-foot tower and antennas at two other sites. The system serves approximately 200 users in five city departments.

Hickory's communications dispatched 107,438 calls during the year. The number of incoming class was not available.

Hickory received $90,725 in E-911 revenues to support system operations.

Conditions Affecting Service, Performance, and Costs

Incoming calls in Hickory are down over time because of changes in how calls are routed. Several special units now have their own administrative phones, so calls no longer come through the emergency communications center. Additionally, the animal control unit's operations were moved out of the police department, so their calls are now being fed through code enforcement.

Municipal Profile

Population (OSBM 2020)	43,578
Land Area (Square Miles)	30.50
Persons per Square Mile	1,429
County	Catawba

Service Profile

Primary or Secondary Answering Point	Secondary
Calls Dispatched	
Police	Yes
Fire	No
Other	No
FTE Positions	
Telecommunicators/Call-Takers	15.0
Other	0.0
Total Positions	15.0
Average Length of Service for Call-Takers	3.9 years
Total Incoming Calls	NA
Total 911 Calls	NA
Total Calls Dispatched	107,438
Outgoing Calls Other than Dispatch	NA
Revenue from E-911 Fees	$90,725

Full Cost Profile

Cost Breakdown by Percentage	
Personal Services	66.1%
Operating Costs	25.3%
Capital Costs	8.6%
TOTAL	100.0%

Cost Breakdown in Dollars	
Personal Services	$816,559
Operating Costs	$313,201
Capital Costs	$105,976
TOTAL	$1,235,736

Hickory
Emergency Communications

Key: Hickory ▨   Benchmarking Average —   Fiscal Years 2017 through 2021

Resource Measures

Emergency Communications Services Costs per Capita

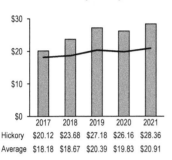

	2017	2018	2019	2020	2021
Hickory	$20.12	$23.68	$27.18	$26.16	$28.36
Average	$18.18	$18.67	$20.39	$19.83	$20.91

Emergency Communications FTEs per 10,000 Population

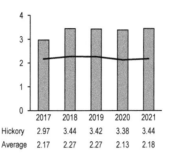

	2017	2018	2019	2020	2021
Hickory	2.97	3.44	3.42	3.38	3.44
Average	2.17	2.27	2.27	2.13	2.18

Workload Measures

Total Calls Answered per 1,000 Population

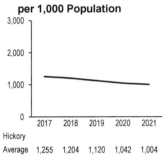

	2017	2018	2019	2020	2021
Hickory					
Average	1,255	1,204	1,120	1,042	1,004

Calls Dispatched per 1,000 Population

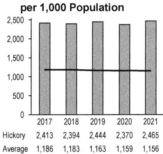

	2017	2018	2019	2020	2021
Hickory	2,413	2,394	2,444	2,370	2,465
Average	1,186	1,183	1,163	1,159	1,156

E-911 Calls as a Percentage of All Incoming Calls

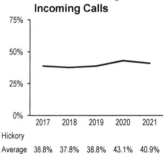

	2017	2018	2019	2020	2021
Hickory					
Average	38.8%	37.8%	38.8%	43.1%	40.9%

Efficiency Measures

Calls Answered per Telecommunicator

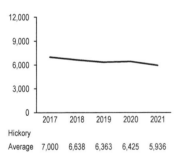

	2017	2018	2019	2020	2021
Hickory					
Average	7,000	6,638	6,363	6,425	5,936

Calls Dispatched per Telecommunicator

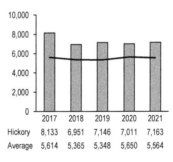

	2017	2018	2019	2020	2021
Hickory	8,133	6,951	7,146	7,011	7,163
Average	5,614	5,365	5,348	5,650	5,564

Emergency Communications Cost per Call Dispatched

	2017	2018	2019	2020	2021
Hickory	$8.34	$9.89	$11.12	$11.04	$11.50
Average	$18.02	$18.40	$20.48	$19.57	$21.43

Effectiveness Measures

Number of Seconds from Initial Ring to Answer

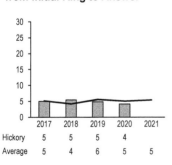

	2017	2018	2019	2020	2021
Hickory	5	5	5	4	
Average	5	4	6	5	5

Percent of E-911 Calls Answered within Twenty Seconds

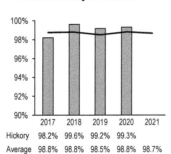

	2017	2018	2019	2020	2021
Hickory	98.2%	99.6%	99.2%	99.3%	
Average	98.8%	98.8%	98.5%	98.8%	98.7%

Average Time in Seconds from CAD Entry to Dispatch for Priority One Calls

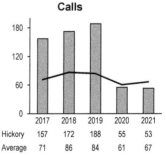

	2017	2018	2019	2020	2021
Hickory	157	172	188	55	53
Average	71	86	84	61	67

Raleigh   Emergency Communications

Fiscal Year 2020-21

Explanatory Information

Service Level and Delivery

The Emergency Communications Center (ECC) is the answering and dispatch agency for all of Wake County. It provides dispatch services for forty-four law enforcement, fire, EMS, rescue, and public-service agencies. The ECC takes 911 calls for the Wake County Sheriff's Department, but these calls are transferred to the sheriff's telecommunicators.

The Town of Cary provides its own services for fire and police, but the ECC provides EMS call service for Cary.

The ECC uses a combination of city-owned and leased tower and transmitter sites. The system uses an 800 MHz system. Over 7,000 mobile and portable radios have been issued to public safety and non-public safety users within Wake County for use of the system.

The ECC handled a total of 772,003 incoming calls in the fiscal year, dispatching 440,294 calls. The ECC defines highest-priority emergency calls as all fire and EMS calls and also police calls with a priority of "0" or "1" as defined by the police agency being dispatched.

Raleigh received $2,630,143 in E-911 revenues to support system operations.

Conditions Affecting Service, Performance, and Costs

Municipal Profile

Population (OSBM 2017)-Wake County	1,134,824
Land Area (Square Miles)	831.92
Persons per Square Mile	1,364
County	Wake

Service Profile

Primary or Secondary Answering Point	Primary
Calls Dispatched	
Police	Yes
Fire	Yes
Other	Yes
FTE Positions	
Telecommunicators/Call-Takers	101.0
Other	28.0
Total Positions	129.0
Average Length of Service for Call-Takers	5.1 years
Total Incoming Calls	772,003
Total 911 Calls	515,516
Total Calls Dispatched	440,294
Outgoing Calls Other than Dispatch	284,016
Revenue from E-911 Fees	$2,630,143

Full Cost Profile

Cost Breakdown by Percentage	
Personal Services	60.6%
Operating Costs	37.9%
Capital Costs	1.4%
TOTAL	100.0%
Cost Breakdown in Dollars	
Personal Services	$9,050,273
Operating Costs	$5,664,397
Capital Costs	$212,190
TOTAL	$14,926,860

Emergency Communications

Key: Raleigh ▨   Benchmarking Average —   Fiscal Years 2017 through 2021

Resource Measures

Emergency Communications Services Costs per Capita

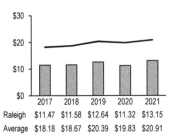

	2017	2018	2019	2020	2021
Raleigh	$11.47	$11.58	$12.64	$11.32	$13.15
Average	$18.18	$18.67	$20.39	$19.83	$20.91

Emergency Communications FTEs per 10,000 Population

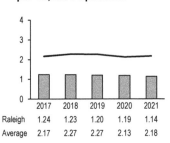

	2017	2018	2019	2020	2021
Raleigh	1.24	1.23	1.20	1.19	1.14
Average	2.17	2.27	2.27	2.13	2.18

Workload Measures

Total Calls Answered per 1,000 Population

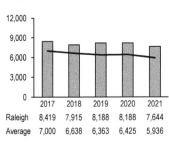

	2017	2018	2019	2020	2021
Raleigh	828	767	778	770	680
Average	1,255	1,204	1,120	1,042	1,004

Calls Dispatched per 1,000 Population

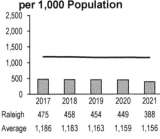

	2017	2018	2019	2020	2021
Raleigh	475	458	454	449	388
Average	1,186	1,183	1,163	1,159	1,156

E-911 Calls as a Percentage of All Incoming Calls

	2017	2018	2019	2020	2021
Raleigh	68.0%	65.7%	66.3%	66.3%	66.8%
Average	38.8%	37.8%	38.8%	43.1%	40.9%

Efficiency Measures

Calls Answered per Telecommunicator

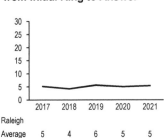

	2017	2018	2019	2020	2021
Raleigh	8,419	7,915	8,188	8,188	7,644
Average	7,000	6,638	6,363	6,425	5,936

Calls Dispatched per Telecommunicator

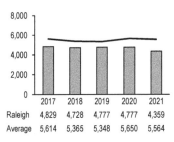

	2017	2018	2019	2020	2021
Raleigh	4,829	4,728	4,777	4,777	4,359
Average	5,614	5,365	5,348	5,650	5,564

Emergency Communications Cost per Call Dispatched

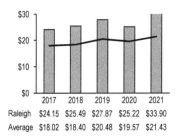

	2017	2018	2019	2020	2021
Raleigh	$24.15	$25.49	$27.87	$25.22	$33.90
Average	$18.02	$18.40	$20.48	$19.57	$21.43

Effectiveness Measures

Number of Seconds from Initial Ring to Answer

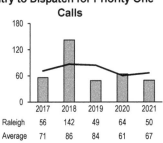

	2017	2018	2019	2020	2021
Raleigh					
Average	5	4	6	5	5

Percent of E-911 Calls Answered within Twenty Seconds

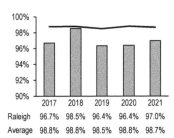

	2017	2018	2019	2020	2021
Raleigh	96.7%	98.5%	96.4%	96.4%	97.0%
Average	98.8%	98.8%	98.5%	98.8%	98.7%

Average Time in Seconds from CAD Entry to Dispatch for Priority One Calls

	2017	2018	2019	2020	2021
Raleigh	56	142	49	64	50
Average	71	86	84	61	67

Fiscal Year 2020-21

Service Level and Delivery

Winston-Salem's Emergency Communications Division is part of the city's police department and handles 911 and non-emergency calls for police and fire. Calls received for EMS, the sheriff's office, county fire, and the highway patrol are transferred to the appropriate agency. All telecommunicators are hired and trained as call-takers and dispatchers.

The city owns the infrastructure but contracts with local vendors to provide telecommunications services. The City of Winston-Salem and Forsyth County implemented a voice radio system in October 2004. The Motorola ASTRO 800 MHz Trunked Simulcast system is made up of eight tower sites utilizing fifteen channels. The Winston-Salem Police Department uses a non-trunked 800 MHz system for the mobile data system, with one transmitter site using three channels.

Winston-Salem's center handled a total of 444,704 calls in the fiscal year, dispatching 209,737 calls. The city defines highest-priority emergency calls as calls with a significant threat of imminent injury to persons or calls for crimes against persons that are in progress or have just occurred and the suspect is still there.

Winston-Salem received $446,454 in E-911 revenues to support system operations.

Conditions Affecting Service, Performance, and Costs

The Emergency Communications Division has been short operators from its authorized total during some of the years.

The system has not been able to provide data on calls answered in the 20-second interval in the past, but improvements now show this data.

Municipal Profile

Population (OSBM 2020)	249,986
Land Area (Square Miles)	132.59
Persons per Square Mile	1,885
County	Forsyth

Service Profile

Primary or Secondary Answering Point	Primary
Calls Dispatched	
Police	Yes
Fire	Yes
Other	No
FTE Positions	
Telecommunicators/Call-Takers	45.0
Other	2.0
Total Positions	47.0
Average Length of Service for Call-Takers	9.0 years
Total Incoming Calls	444,704
Total 911 Calls	206,928
Total Calls Dispatched	209,737
Outgoing Calls Other than Dispatch	68,955
Revenue from E-911 Fees	$446,454

Full Cost Profile

Cost Breakdown by Percentage	
Personal Services	68.3%
Operating Costs	27.4%
Capital Costs	4.3%
TOTAL	100.0%

Cost Breakdown in Dollars	
Personal Services	$3,898,157
Operating Costs	$1,565,763
Capital Costs	$245,558
TOTAL	$5,709,478

Winston-Salem   Emergency Communications

Key: Winston-Salem ▓   Benchmarking Average —   Fiscal Years 2017 through 2021

Resource Measures

Emergency Communications Services Costs per Capita

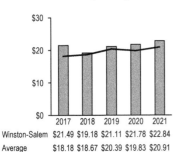

	2017	2018	2019	2020	2021
Winston-Salem	$21.49	$19.18	$21.11	$21.78	$22.84
Average	$18.18	$18.67	$20.39	$19.83	$20.91

Emergency Communications FTEs per 10,000 Population

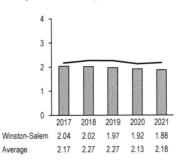

	2017	2018	2019	2020	2021
Winston-Salem	2.04	2.02	1.97	1.92	1.88
Average	2.17	2.27	2.27	2.13	2.18

Workload Measures

Total Calls Answered per 1,000 Population

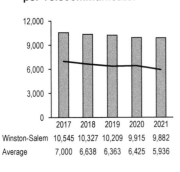

	2017	2018	2019	2020	2021
Winston-Salem	2,060	1,997	1,929	1,823	1,779
Average	1,255	1,204	1,120	1,042	1,004

Calls Dispatched per 1,000 Population

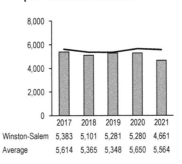

	2017	2018	2019	2020	2021
Winston-Salem	1,052	986	998	971	839
Average	1,186	1,183	1,163	1,159	1,156

E-911 Calls as a Percentage of All Incoming Calls

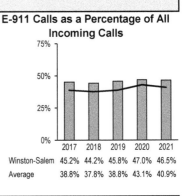

	2017	2018	2019	2020	2021
Winston-Salem	45.2%	44.2%	45.8%	47.0%	46.5%
Average	38.8%	37.8%	38.8%	43.1%	40.9%

Efficiency Measures

Calls Answered per Telecommunicator

	2017	2018	2019	2020	2021
Winston-Salem	10,545	10,327	10,209	9,915	9,882
Average	7,000	6,638	6,363	6,425	5,936

Calls Dispatched per Telecommunicator

	2017	2018	2019	2020	2021
Winston-Salem	5,383	5,101	5,281	5,280	4,661
Average	5,614	5,365	5,348	5,650	5,564

Emergency Communications Cost per Call Dispatched

	2017	2018	2019	2020	2021
Winston-Salem	$20.43	$19.44	$21.15	$22.44	$27.22
Average	$18.02	$18.40	$20.48	$19.57	$21.43

Effectiveness Measures

Number of Seconds from Initial Ring to Answer

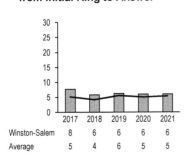

	2017	2018	2019	2020	2021
Winston-Salem	8	6	6	6	6
Average	5	4	6	5	5

Percent of E-911 Calls Answered within Twenty Seconds

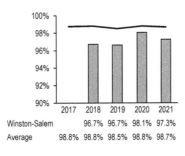

	2017	2018	2019	2020	2021
Winston-Salem		96.7%	96.7%	98.1%	97.3%
Average		98.8%	98.8%	98.5%	98.8%	98.7%

Average Time in Seconds from CAD Entry to Dispatch for Priority One Calls

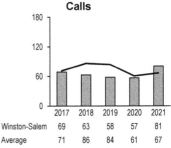

	2017	2018	2019	2020	2021
Winston-Salem	69	63	58	57	81
Average	71	86	84	61	67

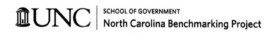

SCHOOL OF GOVERNMENT
North Carolina Benchmarking Project

Performance and Cost Data

ASPHALT MAINTENANCE AND REPAIR

SERVICE DEFINITION

Asphalt Maintenance and Repair includes the activities of pothole repair, repaving, surface treatment, structure adjustments, milling, and utility cuts. It does not include work on reconstruction, handicap ramps, storm drainage, sidewalks, curb and gutter, right-of-way maintenance, street cleaning and sweeping, pavement marking, lane widening, unpaved street maintenance, or snow and ice removal.

NOTES ON PERFORMANCE MEASURES

1. Lane Miles Maintained

This measure refers to the total number lane miles that a municipality maintains, including state streets and municipal streets. The standard lane mile is 12 feet in width and 5,280 feet in length. Some jurisdictions do not track lane miles. Therefore, a methodology must be employed to calculate lane miles for participation.

2. Potholes and Utility Cuts per Lane Mile

Breaks in pavement due to potholes or to intentional utility cuts affect asphalt maintenance workload in the short term and long term because of breaks in the pavement integrity.

3. Cost of Road Treatment per Lane Mile

This is the cost of different types of asphalt treatment that a municipality may use to maintain or repair roads. Treatments include preservation work, such as crack or slurry sealing; resurfacing, which is typically one to two inches of new asphalt; and rehabilitation, which combines resurfacing with milling work to repair more damaged roads.

4. Cost of Asphalt Maintenance and Repair

Total cost of asphalt maintenance and repair represents the total direct, indirect, and capital costs taken from the accounting form. "Cost of maintenance" represents total cost from the accounting form minus cost of any treatment efforts by contract and municipal crews.

5. Percentage of Street Segments Rated 85 or Better and Below 45

Many municipalities use standard rating systems for assessing street pavement condition. These systems apply professionally determined criteria and embody scales that provide relatively objective ratings. These measures indicate the proportion of street segments that are rated 85 or better, which is good condition, and those rated below 45, which is poor condition, on the most-recent street pavement assessment.

6. Percentage of Potholes Repaired within Twenty-Four Hours

Repair of potholes in a timely manner is important for maintaining pavement integrity and for minimizing further damage to the street and vehicles.

Asphalt Maintenance and Repair

Summary of Key Dimensions of Service

City or Town	Lane Miles Maintained	Total Lane Miles Treated by Type			Percent Treated			FTE Positions for City Staff
		Preservation	Resurfacing	Rehabilitation	Preservation	Resurfacing	Rehabilitation	
Apex	449.53	8.7	3.9	0.0	1.9%	0.9%	0.0%	14.0
Chapel Hill	334.50	0.0	0.0	9.2	0.0%	0.0%	2.8%	14.0
Charlotte	5,479.91	1.5	6.9	137.4	0.0%	0.1%	2.5%	120.0
Concord	743.42	8.2	0.0	35.9	1.1%	0.0%	4.8%	12.3
Goldsboro	324.00	0.0	0.0	0.0	0.0%	0.0%	0.0%	6.8
Greensboro	2,443.00	21.2	64.2	0.0	0.9%	2.6%	0.0%	51.0
Greenville	718.11	5.8	0.0	10.6	0.8%	0.0%	1.5%	6.0
Hickory	719.52	0.0	6.2	1.8	0.0%	0.9%	0.3%	7.0
Raleigh	2,368.00	78.0	33.0	1.0	3.3%	1.4%	0.0%	41.0
Wilson	698.13	2.7	0.0	0.0	0.4%	0.0%	0.0%	5.5
Winston-Salem	2,890.10	26.4	0.0	87.0	0.9%	0.0%	3.0%	44.4

EXPLANATORY FACTORS

These are factors that the project found affected asphalt maintenance and repair performance and cost in one or more of the municipalities:

- Costs of materials in different cities
- Weather conditions and terrain
- Vehicle burden placed on streets
- Age of street infrastructure
- Depth of materials applied in repaving
- Extent of contracting

Explanatory Information

Service Level and Delivery

The Town of Apex's Streets Department was responsible for maintaining approximately 449.5 lane miles during the fiscal year. The Streets Department is part of the Public Works and Utilities Division for the town.

The town resurfaced 3.9 lane miles during the year. The town also did preservation work on 8.7 lane miles. This represented treatment of about 2.8 percent of total lane miles maintained.

The city reported that 42 percent of its lane miles were rated 85 or better on the pavement condition rating. The rating was performed by US Infrastructure of Carolina, Inc., using surveying done in 2020.

The number of potholes reported for the fiscal year was sixty-eight. The town only repairs within one day those potholes that are considered large and dangerous. Smaller potholes are repaired when the streets crews can get to them.

The Streets Department also repaired twenty-five utility cuts and thirty-eight maintenance patches.

Conditions Affecting Service, Performance, and Costs

Hurricane Matthew in September 2016 had impacts on Apex, which raised the event to a Federal Emergency Management Agency (FEMA) event and response.

Municipal Profile

Population (OSBM 2020)	59,368
Land Area (Square Miles)	23.61
Persons per Square Mile	2,514
Topography	Flat; gently rolling
Climate	Temperate; little ice and snow

Service Profile

FTE Positions—Crews	12.00
FTE Positions—Other	2.00
Lane Miles Maintained	449.5
Lane Miles Treated	
Preservation	8.7
Resurfacing	3.9
Rehabilitation	0.0
TOTAL	12.6
Total Costs for All Treatment Types	$993,140
Potholes Repaired	68
Number of Utility Cuts	25
Number of Maintenance Patches (exclusive of potholes and utility cuts)	38
Average Cost per Ton of Hot Asphalt during Year	$75.76

Full Cost Profile

Cost Breakdown by Percentage	
Personal Services	21.0%
Operating Costs	74.4%
Capital Costs	4.5%
TOTAL	100.0%
Cost Breakdown in Dollars	
Personal Services	$355,601
Operating Costs	$1,257,507
Capital Costs	$76,535
TOTAL	$1,689,643

Apex

Asphalt Maintenance and Repair

Key: Apex ▨   Benchmarking Average —   Fiscal Years 2017 through 2021

Resource Measures

Asphalt Maintenance and Repair Services Costs per Capita

	2017	2018	2019	2020	2021
Apex	$36.24	$37.60	$27.68	$30.99	$28.46
Average	$43.59	$44.18	$51.29	$39.86	$32.35

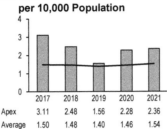

Asphalt Maintenance and Repair FTEs per 10,000 Population

	2017	2018	2019	2020	2021
Apex	3.11	2.48	1.56	2.28	2.36
Average	1.50	1.48	1.40	1.46	1.54

Service Costs per Lane Mile of Road Maintained

	2017	2018	2019	2020	2021
Apex	$4,949	$4,714	$3,530	$4,404	$3,759
Average	$5,810	$6,013	$6,162	$4,759	$3,968

Workload Measures

Number of Lane Miles Maintained per 1,000 Population

	2017	2018	2019	2020	2021
Apex	7.3	8.0	7.8	7.0	7.6
Average	8.6	8.7	9.2	9.2	9.1

Reported Potholes per Lane Mile Maintained

	2017	2018	2019	2020	2021
Apex	0.47	0.57	0.20	0.15	0.15
Average	1.42	1.27	1.34	0.92	1.22

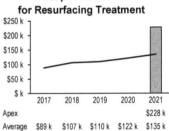

Repaired Utility Cuts per Lane Mile Maintained

	2017	2018	2019	2020	2021
Apex	0.09	0.08	0.11	0.13	0.06
Average	0.51	0.43	0.34	0.38	0.33

Efficiency Measures

Cost of Maintenance per Lane Mile Maintained

	2017	2018	2019	2020	2021
Apex	$3,545	$2,050	$1,852	$2,948	$1,549
Average	$2,574	$2,391	$2,442	$2,446	$2,158

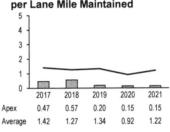

Cost per Lane Mile for Preservation Treatment

	2017	2018	2019	2020	2021
Apex			$9,508	$6,165	$11,762
Average	$6,231	$9,697	$5,320	$8,025	$8,764

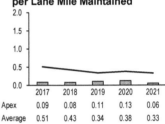

Cost per Lane Mile for Resurfacing Treatment

	2017	2018	2019	2020	2021
Apex					$228 k
Average	$89 k	$107 k	$110 k	$122 k	$135 k

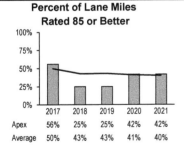

Cost per Lane Mile for Rehabilitation Treatment

	2017	2018	2019	2020	2021
Apex	$308 k	$308 k	$110 k	$78 k	
Average	$115 k	$115 k	$268 k	$92 k	$116 k

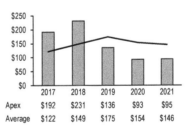

Cost per Ton for Contract Resurfacing

	2017	2018	2019	2020	2021
Apex	$192	$231	$136	$93	$95
Average	$122	$149	$175	$154	$146

Effectiveness Measures

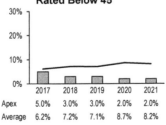

Percent of Lane Miles Rated 85 or Better

	2017	2018	2019	2020	2021
Apex	56%	25%	25%	42%	42%
Average	50%	43%	43%	41%	40%

Percent of Lane Miles Rated Below 45

	2017	2018	2019	2020	2021
Apex	5.0%	3.0%	3.0%	2.0%	2.0%
Average	6.2%	7.2%	7.1%	8.7%	8.2%

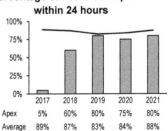

Percentage of Potholes Repaired within 24 hours

	2017	2018	2019	2020	2021
Apex	5%	60%	80%	75%	80%
Average	89%	87%	83%	84%	88%

Fiscal Year 2020-21

Service Level and Delivery

Asphalt maintenance is performed by the Town of Chapel Hill Streets and Construction Services Division of the Public Works Department. The town provides services in asphalt maintenance, sidewalk maintenance, storm debris cleanup, gravel road maintenance, snow and ice removal, and cleanup following special events.

During the fiscal year the town was responsible for maintaining approximately 334.5 lane miles. During the year 9.2 lane miles were treated by contract crews doing rehabilitation work, or about 2.8 percent of total lane miles.

The town reported that 38 percent of its lane miles rated 85 or above on its most-recent pavement condition rating conducted in 2020. The roads were rated by US Infrastructure of Carolina using the system relying on the Institute for Transportation Research and Education (ITRE) degradation curves.

The number of potholes reported for the year was seventy-two. Permit holders repaired fifty-eight utility cuts during the year in the town. A permit is required for any non-town entity cutting inside the right-of-way. The permit holder is responsible for all repairs. Because one permit can involve multiple cuts, the actual number of cuts is higher than the number listed. The streets inspector monitors the work and bills the responsible party. The Public Works Engineering Division inspects larger projects involving a water or sewer line replacement.

Conditions Affecting Service, Performance, and Costs

Though the FY 2015–16 Chapel Hill budget included $585,222 for annual resurfacing work, this funding was encumbered and carried forward into FY 2016–17 and was not reflected in the costs for this service area for that report year. A total of 5.5 lane miles were resurfaced using FY 2015–16 funds but at the beginning of FY 2016–17. These costs were reported in that year.

The town experienced two significant snow storms in the FY 2017–18 fiscal year, which impacted operations and funding.

Municipal Profile

Population (OSBM 2020)	62,080
Land Area (Square Miles)	21.31
Persons per Square Mile	2,914
Topography	Flat; gently rolling
Climate	Temperate; little ice and snow

Service Profile

FTE Positions—Crews	11.00
FTE Positions—Other	3.00
Lane Miles Maintained	334.5
Lane Miles Treated	
Preservation	0.0
Resurfacing	0.0
Rehabilitation	9.2
TOTAL	9.2
Total Costs for All Treatment Types	$707,885
Potholes Repaired	72
Number of Utility Cuts	58
Number of Maintenance Patches (exclusive of potholes and utility cuts)	NA
Average Cost per Ton of Hot Asphalt during Year	$59.00

Full Cost Profile

Cost Breakdown by Percentage

Personal Services	33.5%
Operating Costs	43.7%
Capital Costs	22.8%
TOTAL	100.0%

Cost Breakdown in Dollars

Personal Services	$435,943
Operating Costs	$569,866
Capital Costs	$296,765
TOTAL	$1,302,574

Asphalt Maintenance and Repair

Key: Chapel Hill ▪   Benchmarking Average —   Fiscal Years 2017 through 2021

Resource Measures

Asphalt Maintenance and Repair Services Costs per Capita

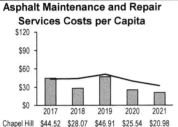

	2017	2018	2019	2020	2021
Chapel Hill	$44.52	$28.07	$46.91	$25.54	$20.98
Average	$43.59	$44.18	$51.29	$39.86	$32.35

Asphalt Maintenance and Repair FTEs per 10,000 Population

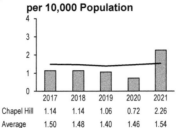

	2017	2018	2019	2020	2021
Chapel Hill	1.14	1.14	1.06	0.72	2.26
Average	1.50	1.48	1.40	1.46	1.54

Service Costs per Lane Mile of Road Maintained

	2017	2018	2019	2020	2021
Chapel Hill	$7,992	$5,044	$8,890	$4,875	$3,894
Average	$5,810	$6,013	$6,162	$4,759	$3,968

Workload Measures

Number of Lane Miles Maintained per 1,000 Population

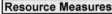

	2017	2018	2019	2020	2021
Chapel Hill	5.6	5.6	5.3	5.2	5.4
Average	8.6	8.7	9.2	9.2	9.1

Reported Potholes per Lane Mile Maintained

	2017	2018	2019	2020	2021
Chapel Hill		0.23	0.29	0.18	0.22
Average	1.42	1.27	1.34	0.92	1.22

Repaired Utility Cuts per Lane Mile Maintained

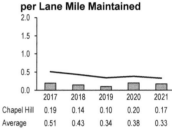

	2017	2018	2019	2020	2021
Chapel Hill	0.19	0.14	0.10	0.20	0.17
Average	0.51	0.43	0.34	0.38	0.33

Efficiency Measures

Cost of Maintenance per Lane Mile Maintained

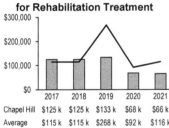

	2017	2018	2019	2020	2021
Chapel Hill	$3,479	$3,282	$4,452	$3,260	$1,778
Average	$2,574	$2,391	$2,442	$2,446	$2,158

Cost per Lane Mile for Preservation Treatment

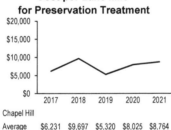

	2017	2018	2019	2020	2021
Chapel Hill					
Average	$6,231	$9,697	$5,320	$8,025	$8,764

Cost per Lane Mile for Resurfacing Treatment

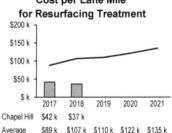

	2017	2018	2019	2020	2021
Chapel Hill	$42 k	$37 k			
Average	$89 k	$107 k	$110 k	$122 k	$135 k

Cost per Lane Mile for Rehabilitation Treatment

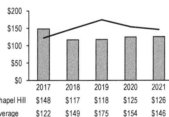

	2017	2018	2019	2020	2021
Chapel Hill	$125 k	$125 k	$133 k	$68 k	$66 k
Average	$115 k	$115 k	$268 k	$92 k	$116 k

Cost per Ton for Contract Resurfacing

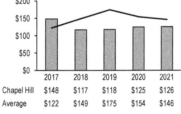

	2017	2018	2019	2020	2021
Chapel Hill	$148	$117	$118	$125	$126
Average	$122	$149	$175	$154	$146

Effectiveness Measures

Percent of Lane Miles Rated 85 or Better

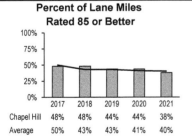

	2017	2018	2019	2020	2021
Chapel Hill	48%	48%	44%	44%	38%
Average	50%	43%	43%	41%	40%

Percent of Lane Miles Rated Below 45

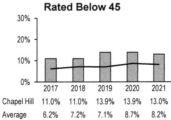

	2017	2018	2019	2020	2021
Chapel Hill	11.0%	11.0%	13.9%	13.9%	13.0%
Average	6.2%	7.2%	7.1%	8.7%	8.2%

Percentage of Potholes Repaired within 24 hours

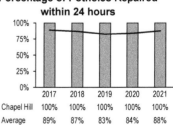

	2017	2018	2019	2020	2021
Chapel Hill	100%	100%	100%	100%	100%
Average	89%	87%	83%	84%	88%

Explanatory Information

Service Level and Delivery

The City of Charlotte Street Maintenance Division provides service in the areas of maintenance and repair of street drainage structures; sidewalks; storm debris cleanup; and specialty repair items, such as brick walls, decorative pavers, fences, and guardrails. During the fiscal year, the city was responsible for maintaining approximately 5,479 lane miles and treated 146 lane miles, equating to approximately 2.7 percent of total lane miles.

Of the treatment work done during the year, 1.53 lane miles received preservation work completed by city crews, such as crack sealing or thin overlays. Resurfacing work covered 6.9 lane miles and was done by contractors and city crews. Additionally, 127.4 lane miles were rehabilitated by contractors with milling followed by resurfacing. City crews completed a further 10 lane miles of rehabilitation work as well.

The city reported that 40.81 percent of its lane miles rated 85 or above on its most-recent pavement condition rating conducted in 2019.

The number of potholes reported for the fiscal year was 1,919. A total of 1,213 utility cuts was also repaired during the year by contractors and the Street Maintenance Division.

Conditions Affecting Service, Performance, and Costs

Municipal Profile

Population (OSBM 2020)	876,694
Land Area (Square Miles)	307.41
Persons per Square Mile	2,852
Topography	Flat; gently rolling
Climate	Temperate; little ice and snow

Service Profile

FTE Positions—Crews	101.00
FTE Positions—Other	19.00
Lane Miles Maintained	5,479.9
Lane Miles Treated	
Preservation	1.5
Resurfacing	6.9
Rehabilitation	137.4
TOTAL	145.8
Total Costs for All Treatment Types	$13,933,694
Potholes Repaired	1,919
Number of Utility Cuts	1,213
Number of Maintenance Patches (exclusive of potholes and utility cuts)	na
Average Cost per Ton of Hot Asphalt during Year	$47.26

Full Cost Profile

Cost Breakdown by Percentage	
Personal Services	28.5%
Operating Costs	60.0%
Capital Costs	11.5%
TOTAL	100.0%
Cost Breakdown in Dollars	
Personal Services	$8,363,013
Operating Costs	$17,624,580
Capital Costs	$3,366,686
TOTAL	$29,354,279

Asphalt Maintenance and Repair

Key: Charlotte ▨   Benchmarking Average —   Fiscal Years 2017 through 2021

Resource Measures

Asphalt Maintenance and Repair Services Costs per Capita
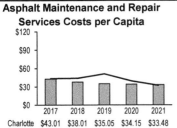

	2017	2018	2019	2020	2021
Charlotte	$43.01	$38.01	$35.05	$34.15	$33.48
Average	$43.59	$44.18	$51.29	$39.86	$32.35

Asphalt Maintenance and Repair FTEs per 10,000 Population
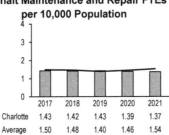

	2017	2018	2019	2020	2021
Charlotte	1.43	1.42	1.43	1.39	1.37
Average	1.50	1.48	1.40	1.46	1.54

Service Costs per Lane Mile of Road Maintained

	2017	2018	2019	2020	2021
Charlotte	$6,709	$5,982	$5,522	$5,418	$5,357
Average	$5,810	$6,013	$6,162	$4,759	$3,968

Workload Measures

Number of Lane Miles Maintained per 1,000 Population
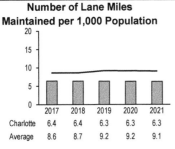

	2017	2018	2019	2020	2021
Charlotte	6.4	6.4	6.3	6.3	6.3
Average	8.6	8.7	9.2	9.2	9.1

Reported Potholes per Lane Mile Maintained

	2017	2018	2019	2020	2021
Charlotte	0.22	0.28	0.53	0.41	0.35
Average	1.42	1.27	1.34	0.92	1.22

Repaired Utility Cuts per Lane Mile Maintained
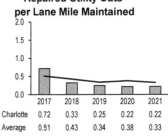

	2017	2018	2019	2020	2021
Charlotte	0.72	0.33	0.25	0.22	0.22
Average	0.51	0.43	0.34	0.38	0.33

Efficiency Measures

Cost of Maintenance per Lane Mile Maintained
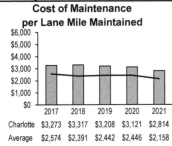

	2017	2018	2019	2020	2021
Charlotte	$3,273	$3,317	$3,208	$3,121	$2,814
Average	$2,574	$2,391	$2,442	$2,446	$2,158

Cost per Lane Mile for Preservation Treatment
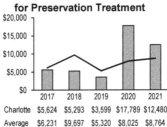

	2017	2018	2019	2020	2021
Charlotte	$5,624	$5,293	$3,599	$17,789	$12,480
Average	$6,231	$9,697	$5,320	$8,025	$8,764

Cost per Lane Mile for Resurfacing Treatment

	2017	2018	2019	2020	2021
Charlotte	$49 k	$52 k	$46 k	$69 k	$87 k
Average	$89 k	$107 k	$110 k	$122 k	$135 k

Cost per Lane Mile for Rehabilitation Treatment

	2017	2018	2019	2020	2021
Charlotte	$67 k	$67 k	$79 k	$89 k	$97 k
Average	$115 k	$115 k	$268 k	$92 k	$116 k

Cost per Ton for Contract Resurfacing
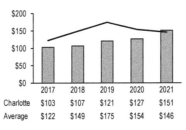

	2017	2018	2019	2020	2021
Charlotte	$103	$107	$121	$127	$151
Average	$122	$149	$175	$154	$146

Effectiveness Measures

Percent of Lane Miles Rated 85 or Better
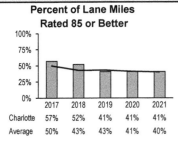

	2017	2018	2019	2020	2021
Charlotte	57%	52%	41%	41%	41%
Average	50%	43%	43%	41%	40%

Percent of Lane Miles Rated Below 45

	2017	2018	2019	2020	2021
Charlotte	0.5%	0.8%	0.2%	0.2%	0.2%
Average	6.2%	7.2%	7.1%	8.7%	8.2%

Percentage of Potholes Repaired within 24 hours
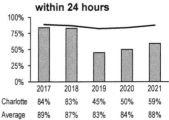

	2017	2018	2019	2020	2021
Charlotte	84%	83%	45%	50%	59%
Average	89%	87%	83%	84%	88%

Fiscal Year 2020-21

Explanatory Information

Service Level and Delivery

The City of Concord was responsible for maintaining approximately 743 lane miles during the fiscal year.

The city reported that 31 percent of its lane miles rated 85 or above on its most-recent pavement condition rating conducted by a consultant using radar-equiped vehicles using the ITRE rating system.

The number of potholes reported for the year was 179, including those reported by citizens and the city. Concord also reported 528 utility cuts that were repaired and 88 maintenance patches for work other than potholes or utility cuts.

Conditions Affecting Service, Performance, and Costs

The costs associated with asphalt maintenance and resurfacing are influenced by competition among providers due to the location of three asphalt plants within the city limits.

Municipal Profile

Population (OSBM 2020)	105,936
Land Area (Square Miles)	63.65
Persons per Square Mile	1,664
Topography	Flat; gently rolling
Climate	Temperate; little ice and snow

Service Profile

FTE Positions—Crews	10.75
FTE Positions—Other	1.55
Lane Miles Maintained	743.4
Lane Miles Treated	
Preservation	8.2
Resurfacing	0.0
Rehabilitation	35.9
TOTAL	44.1
Total Costs for All Treatment Types	$2,220,170
Potholes Repaired	179
Number of Utility Cuts	528
Number of Maintenance Patches (exclusive of potholes and utility cuts)	88
Average Cost per Ton of Hot Asphalt during Year	$65.00

Full Cost Profile

Cost Breakdown by Percentage	
Personal Services	24.2%
Operating Costs	70.7%
Capital Costs	5.1%
TOTAL	100.0%

Cost Breakdown in Dollars	
Personal Services	$929,397
Operating Costs	$2,719,654
Capital Costs	$197,386
TOTAL	$3,846,437

Concord

Asphalt Maintenance and Repair

Key: Concord ▨   Benchmarking Average —   Fiscal Years 2017 through 2021

Resource Measures

Asphalt Maintenance and Repair Services Costs per Capita

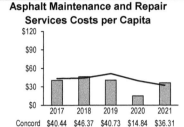

	2017	2018	2019	2020	2021
Concord	$40.44	$46.37	$40.73	$14.84	$36.31
Average	$43.59	$44.18	$51.29	$39.86	$32.35

Asphalt Maintenance and Repair FTEs per 10,000 Population

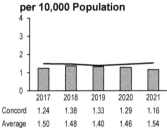

	2017	2018	2019	2020	2021
Concord	1.24	1.38	1.33	1.29	1.16
Average	1.50	1.48	1.40	1.46	1.54

Service Costs per Lane Mile of Road Maintained

	2017	2018	2019	2020	2021
Concord	$5,046	$5,973	$5,299	$1,988	$5,174
Average	$5,810	$6,013	$6,162	$4,759	$3,968

Workload Measures

Number of Lane Miles Maintained per 1,000 Population

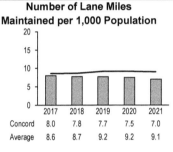

	2017	2018	2019	2020	2021
Concord	8.0	7.8	7.7	7.5	7.0
Average	8.6	8.7	9.2	9.2	9.1

Reported Potholes per Lane Mile Maintained

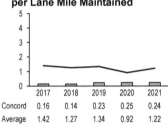

	2017	2018	2019	2020	2021
Concord	0.16	0.14	0.23	0.25	0.24
Average	1.42	1.27	1.34	0.92	1.22

Repaired Utility Cuts per Lane Mile Maintained

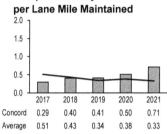

	2017	2018	2019	2020	2021
Concord	0.29	0.40	0.41	0.50	0.71
Average	0.51	0.43	0.34	0.38	0.33

Efficiency Measures

Cost of Maintenance per Lane Mile Maintained

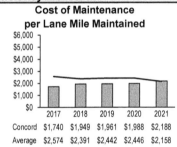

	2017	2018	2019	2020	2021
Concord	$1,740	$1,949	$1,961	$1,988	$2,188
Average	$2,574	$2,391	$2,442	$2,446	$2,158

Cost per Lane Mile for Preservation Treatment

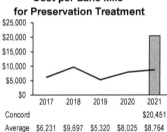

	2017	2018	2019	2020	2021
Concord					$20,451
Average	$6,231	$9,697	$5,320	$8,025	$8,764

Cost per Lane Mile for Resurfacing Treatment

	2017	2018	2019	2020	2021
Concord	$66 k	$113 k	$95 k		
Average	$89 k	$107 k	$110 k	$122 k	$135 k

Cost per Lane Mile for Rehabilitation Treatment

	2017	2018	2019	2020	2021
Concord	$10 k	$10 k			$57 k
Average	$115 k	$115 k	$268 k	$92 k	$116 k

Cost per Ton for Contract Resurfacing

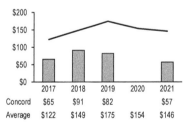

	2017	2018	2019	2020	2021
Concord	$65	$91	$82		$57
Average	$122	$149	$175	$154	$146

Effectiveness Measures

Percent of Lane Miles Rated 85 or Better

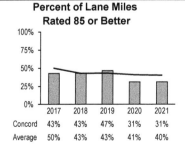

	2017	2018	2019	2020	2021
Concord	43%	43%	47%	31%	31%
Average	50%	43%	43%	41%	40%

Percent of Lane Miles Rated Below 45

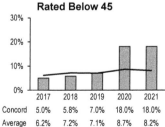

	2017	2018	2019	2020	2021
Concord	5.0%	5.8%	7.0%	18.0%	18.0%
Average	6.2%	7.2%	7.1%	8.7%	8.2%

Percentage of Potholes Repaired within 24 hours

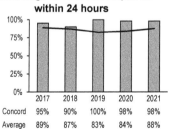

	2017	2018	2019	2020	2021
Concord	95%	90%	100%	98%	98%
Average	89%	87%	83%	84%	88%

Fiscal Year 2020-21

Explanatory Information

Service Level and Delivery
The City of Goldsboro was responsible for maintaining 324 lane miles during the fiscal year. Goldsboro did not undertake any road treatment projects during the fiscal year.

The number of potholes reported for the year was 693. The city has one person driving around the city every day looking for potholes that need to be repaired and fixing them on the spot. A total of 144 utility cuts were also repaired, with city crews repairing water and sewer cuts reported by the city's Distribution and Collections Division.

Conditions Affecting Service, Performance, and Costs
The City of Goldsboro joined the Benchmarking Project in July 2017, with the first year of data showing for FY 2016–17.

Hurricane Matthew in October 2016 impacted asphalt work significantly. Crews were diverted to recovery efforts such as tree removal. Additionally, fifty-one sinkholes developed over the year in roads due to storm-water-infrastructure failures under the asphalt surfaces.

The amount of street work done in FY 2017–18 was up significantly due the use of street bonds to fund the work.

Municipal Profile

Population (OSBM 2020)	34,156
Land Area (Square Miles)	29.45
Persons per Square Mile	1,160
Topography	Flat
Climate	Temperate; little ice and snow

Service Profile

FTE Positions—Crews	5.00
FTE Positions—Other	1.83
Lane Miles Maintained	324.0
Lane Miles Treated	
Preservation	0.0
Resurfacing	0.0
Rehabilitation	0.0
TOTAL	0.0
Total Costs for All Treatment Types	$0
Potholes Repaired	693
Number of Utility Cuts	144
Number of Maintenance Patches (exclusive of potholes and utility cuts)	47
Average Cost per Ton of Hot Asphalt during Year	$72.00

Full Cost Profile

Cost Breakdown by Percentage	
Personal Services	81.8%
Operating Costs	13.0%
Capital Costs	5.2%
TOTAL	100.0%
Cost Breakdown in Dollars	
Personal Services	$749,699
Operating Costs	$118,956
Capital Costs	$47,608
TOTAL	$916,263

Goldsboro

Asphalt Maintenance and Repair

Key: Goldsboro ▪ Benchmarking Average — Fiscal Years 2017 through 2021

Resource Measures

Asphalt Maintenance and Repair Services Costs per Capita

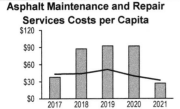

	2017	2018	2019	2020	2021
Goldsboro	$37.86	$87.22	$92.43	$92.17	$26.83
Average	$43.59	$44.18	$51.29	$39.86	$32.35

Asphalt Maintenance and Repair FTEs per 10,000 Population

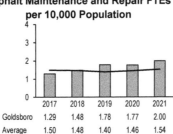

	2017	2018	2019	2020	2021
Goldsboro	1.29	1.48	1.78	1.77	2.00
Average	1.50	1.48	1.40	1.46	1.54

Service Costs per Lane Mile of Road Maintained

	2017	2018	2019	2020	2021
Goldsboro	$8,094	$18,072	$9,576	$9,643	$2,828
Average	$5,810	$6,013	$6,162	$4,759	$3,968

Workload Measures

Number of Lane Miles Maintained per 1,000 Population

	2017	2018	2019	2020	2021
Goldsboro	4.7	4.8	9.7	9.6	9.5
Average	8.6	8.7	9.2	9.2	9.1

Reported Potholes per Lane Mile Maintained

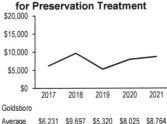

	2017	2018	2019	2020	2021
Goldsboro	4.02	3.70	0.97	0.97	2.14
Average	1.42	1.27	1.34	0.92	1.22

Repaired Utility Cuts per Lane Mile Maintained

	2017	2018	2019	2020	2021
Goldsboro	0.82	1.10	0.42	0.42	0.44
Average	0.51	0.43	0.34	0.38	0.33

Efficiency Measures

Cost of Maintenance per Lane Mile Maintained

	2017	2018	2019	2020	2021
Goldsboro	$6,237	$2,143	$1,484	$1,551	$2,828
Average	$2,574	$2,391	$2,442	$2,446	$2,158

Cost per Lane Mile for Preservation Treatment

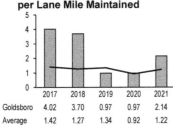

	2017	2018	2019	2020	2021
Goldsboro					
Average	$6,231	$9,697	$5,320	$8,025	$8,764

Cost per Lane Mile for Resurfacing Treatment

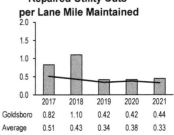

	2017	2018	2019	2020	2021
Goldsboro	$39 k	$103 k			
Average	$89 k	$107 k	$110 k	$122 k	$135 k

Cost per Lane Mile for Rehabilitation Treatment

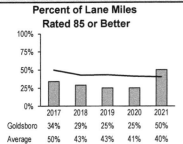

	2017	2018	2019	2020	2021
Goldsboro	$47 k	$47 k	$123 k	$123 k	
Average	$115 k	$115 k	$268 k	$92 k	$116 k

Cost per Ton for Contract Resurfacing

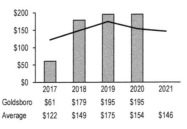

	2017	2018	2019	2020	2021
Goldsboro	$61	$179	$195	$195	
Average	$122	$149	$175	$154	$146

Effectiveness Measures

Percent of Lane Miles Rated 85 or Better

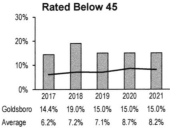

	2017	2018	2019	2020	2021
Goldsboro	34%	29%	25%	25%	50%
Average	50%	43%	43%	41%	40%

Percent of Lane Miles Rated Below 45

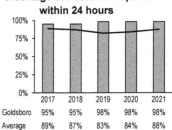

	2017	2018	2019	2020	2021
Goldsboro	14.4%	19.0%	15.0%	15.0%	15.0%
Average	6.2%	7.2%	7.1%	8.7%	8.2%

Percentage of Potholes Repaired within 24 hours

	2017	2018	2019	2020	2021
Goldsboro	95%	95%	98%	98%	98%
Average	89%	87%	83%	84%	88%

Explanatory Information

Service Level and Delivery

The City of Greensboro was responsible for maintaining 2,443 lane miles during the fiscal year. Greensboro treated a total of 85.4 lane miles during the year, equating to about 3.5 percent of total lane miles.

Of the treatment work done on Greensboro's streets, 21.2 of the lane miles had preservation work performed, such as crack sealing or thin overlays. All of this preservation work was done by city crews. Resurfacing work was done on 64.2 lane miles by contract crews.

The number of potholes reported for the year was 3,615. A total of 289 utility cuts were also repaired, with city crews repairing water and sewer cuts but private contractors repairing others after getting permits from the city. A further 76 maintenance patches were completed beyond the number of potholes and utility cuts.

Conditions Affecting Service, Performance, and Costs

Changes in tracking software have improved the accuracy of potholes reported and asphalt used over time.

Municipal Profile

Population (OSBM 2020)	299,556
Land Area (Square Miles)	129.62
Persons per Square Mile	2,311
Topography	Flat; gently rolling
Climate	Temperate; little ice and snow

Service Profile

FTE Positions—Crews	45.00
FTE Positions—Other	6.00
Lane Miles Maintained	2,443.0
Lane Miles Treated	
Preservation	21.2
Resurfacing	64.2
Rehabilitation	0.0
TOTAL	85.4
Total Costs for All Treatment Types	$6,401,374
Potholes Repaired	3,615
Number of Utility Cuts	289
Number of Maintenance Patches (exclusive of potholes and utility cuts)	76
Average Cost per Ton of Hot Asphalt during Year	$68.48

Full Cost Profile

Cost Breakdown by Percentage	
Personal Services	23.3%
Operating Costs	76.7%
Capital Costs	0.0%
TOTAL	100.0%

Cost Breakdown in Dollars	
Personal Services	$2,697,725
Operating Costs	$8,903,208
Capital Costs	$0
TOTAL	$11,600,933

Asphalt Maintenance and Repair

Resource Measures

Asphalt Maintenance and Repair Services Costs per Capita

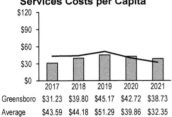

	2017	2018	2019	2020	2021
Greensboro	$31.23	$39.80	$45.17	$42.72	$38.73
Average	$43.59	$44.18	$51.29	$39.86	$32.35

Asphalt Maintenance and Repair FTEs per 10,000 Population

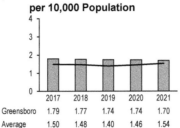

	2017	2018	2019	2020	2021
Greensboro	1.79	1.77	1.74	1.74	1.70
Average	1.50	1.48	1.40	1.46	1.54

Service Costs per Lane Mile of Road Maintained

	2017	2018	2019	2020	2021
Greensboro	$3,652	$4,716	$5,432	$5,162	$4,749
Average	$5,810	$6,013	$6,162	$4,759	$3,968

Workload Measures

Number of Lane Miles Maintained per 1,000 Population

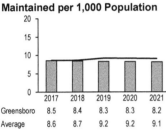

	2017	2018	2019	2020	2021
Greensboro	8.5	8.4	8.3	8.3	8.2
Average	8.6	8.7	9.2	9.2	9.1

Reported Potholes per Lane Mile Maintained

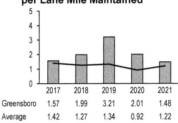

	2017	2018	2019	2020	2021
Greensboro	1.57	1.99	3.21	2.01	1.48
Average	1.42	1.27	1.34	0.92	1.22

Repaired Utility Cuts per Lane Mile Maintained

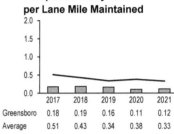

	2017	2018	2019	2020	2021
Greensboro	0.18	0.19	0.16	0.11	0.12
Average	0.51	0.43	0.34	0.38	0.33

Efficiency Measures

Cost of Maintenance per Lane Mile Maintained

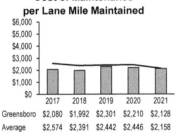

	2017	2018	2019	2020	2021
Greensboro	$2,080	$1,992	$2,301	$2,210	$2,128
Average	$2,574	$2,391	$2,442	$2,446	$2,158

Cost per Lane Mile for Preservation Treatment

	2017	2018	2019	2020	2021
Greensboro	$2,148	$3,128	$4,044	$4,507	$5,043
Average	$6,231	$9,697	$5,320	$8,025	$8,764

Cost per Lane Mile for Resurfacing Treatment

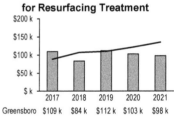

	2017	2018	2019	2020	2021
Greensboro	$109 k	$84 k	$112 k	$103 k	$98 k
Average	$89 k	$107 k	$110 k	$122 k	$135 k

Cost per Lane Mile for Rehabilitation Treatment

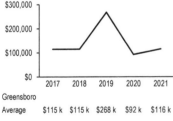

	2017	2018	2019	2020	2021
Greensboro					
Average	$115 k	$115 k	$268 k	$92 k	$116 k

Cost per Ton for Contract Resurfacing

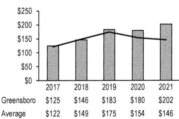

	2017	2018	2019	2020	2021
Greensboro	$125	$146	$183	$180	$202
Average	$122	$149	$175	$154	$146

Effectiveness Measures

Percent of Lane Miles Rated 85 or Better

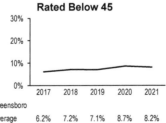

	2017	2018	2019	2020	2021
Greensboro					
Average	50%	43%	43%	41%	40%

Percent of Lane Miles Rated Below 45

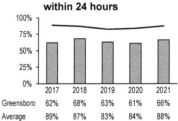

	2017	2018	2019	2020	2021
Greensboro					
Average	6.2%	7.2%	7.1%	8.7%	8.2%

Percentage of Potholes Repaired within 24 hours

	2017	2018	2019	2020	2021
Greensboro	62%	68%	63%	61%	66%
Average	89%	87%	83%	84%	88%

Greenville

Asphalt Maintenance and Repair

Fiscal Year 2020-21

Explanatory Information

Service Level and Delivery

The City of Greenville was responsible for maintaining approximately 718 lane miles during the fiscal year. During the year, Greenville reported that 16.4 lane miles were given some form of treatment, or 2.3 percent of total lane miles.

Preservation work, such as crack sealing or thin overlays, totaled 5.8 lane miles done by city staff. A total of 10.6 lane miles received rehabilitation treatment, which involves milling and resurfacing.

The city reported a total of 1,400 potholes repaired, 173 utility cuts, and 72 maintenance patches.

Greenville reported that 27 percent of lane miles were rated 85 or better on its most-recent pavement condition rating, conducted in 2019 by a consultant.

Conditions Affecting Service, Performance, and Costs

Above-average rainfall and extreme temperatures during the winter months has resulted in higher-than-normal numbers of pothole repairs and pavement failures.

No data were reported for FY 2019-20 for the city of Greenville.

Municipal Profile

Population (OSBM 2020)	87,428
Land Area (Square Miles)	35.66
Persons per Square Mile	2,452
Topography	Flat
Climate	Temperate; little ice and snow

Service Profile

FTE Positions—Crews	4.00
FTE Positions—Other	2.00
Lane Miles Maintained	718.1
Lane Miles Treated	
Preservation	5.8
Resurfacing	0.0
Rehabilitation	10.6
TOTAL	16.4
Total Costs for All Treatment Types	$1,355,135
Potholes Repaired	1,400
Number of Utility Cuts	173
Number of Maintenance Patches (exclusive of potholes and utility cuts)	72
Average Cost per Ton of Hot Asphalt during Year	$100.00

Full Cost Profile

Cost Breakdown by Percentage	
Personal Services	23.5%
Operating Costs	57.1%
Capital Costs	19.3%
TOTAL	100.0%

Cost Breakdown in Dollars	
Personal Services	$773,927
Operating Costs	$1,878,869
Capital Costs	$634,876
TOTAL	$3,287,672

Greenville

Asphalt Maintenance and Repair

Key: Greenville █   Benchmarking Average —   Fiscal Years 2017 through 2021

Resource Measures

Asphalt Maintenance and Repair Services Costs per Capita

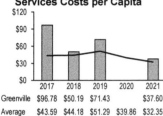

	2017	2018	2019	2020	2021
Greenville	$96.78	$50.19	$71.43		$37.60
Average	$43.59	$44.18	$51.29	$39.86	$32.35

Asphalt Maintenance and Repair FTEs per 10,000 Population

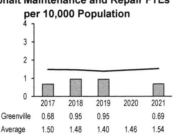

	2017	2018	2019	2020	2021
Greenville	0.68	0.95	0.95		0.69
Average	1.50	1.48	1.40	1.46	1.54

Service Costs per Lane Mile of Road Maintained

	2017	2018	2019	2020	2021
Greenville	$12,585	$6,538	$9,395		$4,578
Average	$5,810	$6,013	$6,162	$4,759	$3,968

Workload Measures

Number of Lane Miles Maintained per 1,000 Population

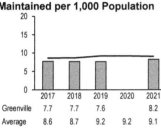

	2017	2018	2019	2020	2021
Greenville	7.7	7.7	7.6		8.2
Average	8.6	8.7	9.2	9.2	9.1

Reported Potholes per Lane Mile Maintained

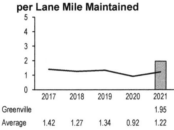

	2017	2018	2019	2020	2021
Greenville					1.95
Average	1.42	1.27	1.34	0.92	1.22

Repaired Utility Cuts per Lane Mile Maintained

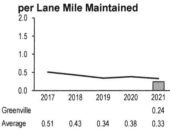

	2017	2018	2019	2020	2021
Greenville					0.24
Average	0.51	0.43	0.34	0.38	0.33

Efficiency Measures

Cost of Maintenance per Lane Mile Maintained

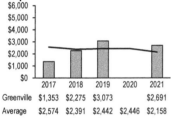

	2017	2018	2019	2020	2021
Greenville	$1,353	$2,275	$3,073		$2,691
Average	$2,574	$2,391	$2,442	$2,446	$2,158

Cost per Lane Mile for Preservation Treatment

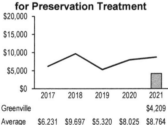

	2017	2018	2019	2020	2021
Greenville					$4,209
Average	$6,231	$9,697	$5,320	$8,025	$8,764

Cost per Lane Mile for Resurfacing Treatment

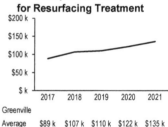

	2017	2018	2019	2020	2021
Greenville					
Average	$89 k	$107 k	$110 k	$122 k	$135 k

Cost per Lane Mile for Rehabilitation Treatment

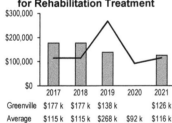

	2017	2018	2019	2020	2021
Greenville	$177 k	$177 k	$138 k		$126 k
Average	$115 k	$115 k	$268 k	$92 k	$116 k

Cost per Ton for Contract Resurfacing

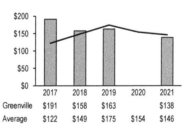

	2017	2018	2019	2020	2021
Greenville	$191	$158	$163		$138
Average	$122	$149	$175	$154	$146

Effectiveness Measures

Percent of Lane Miles Rated 85 or Better

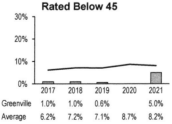

	2017	2018	2019	2020	2021
Greenville	46%	46%	63%		27%
Average	50%	43%	43%	41%	40%

Percent of Lane Miles Rated Below 45

	2017	2018	2019	2020	2021
Greenville	1.0%	1.0%	0.6%		5.0%
Average	6.2%	7.2%	7.1%	8.7%	8.2%

Percentage of Potholes Repaired within 24 hours

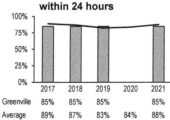

	2017	2018	2019	2020	2021
Greenville	85%	85%	85%		85%
Average	89%	87%	83%	84%	88%

Hickory

Asphalt Maintenance and Repair

Fiscal Year 2020-21

Explanatory Information

Service Level and Delivery

The City of Hickory was responsible for maintaining approximately 720 lane miles during the fiscal year, including 238.8 lane miles of state roads. The city treated a total of eight lane miles, equating to 1.1 percent of total lane miles.

City crews resurfaced 6.2 lane miles and did rehabilitation work on an additional 1.8 lane miles. The city reported that 37 percent of its lane miles rated 85 or above on its most-recent pavement condition rating, conducted in 2017. The city used the Institute for Transportation Research and Education (ITRE) to conduct its rating system.

The number of potholes reported in the city for the year was 348, including self-reported and citizen-reported potholes.

Conditions Affecting Service, Performance, and Costs

Winter weather has caused maintenance problems in a number of the fiscal years reported here.

Municipal Profile

Population (OSBM 2020)	43,578
Land Area (Square Miles)	30.50
Persons per Square Mile	1,429
Topography	Gently rolling
Climate	Temperate; some ice and snow

Service Profile

FTE Positions—Crews	6.00
FTE Positions—Other	1.00
Lane Miles Maintained	719.5
Lane Miles Treated	
Preservation	0.0
Resurfacing	6.2
Rehabilitation	1.8
TOTAL	8.0
Total Costs for All Treatment Types	$866,265
Potholes Repaired	348
Number of Utility Cuts	NA
Number of Maintenance Patches (exclusive of potholes and utility cuts)	NA
Average Cost per Ton of Hot Asphalt during Year	$131.07

Full Cost Profile

Cost Breakdown by Percentage	
Personal Services	15.4%
Operating Costs	78.9%
Capital Costs	5.7%
TOTAL	100.0%

Cost Breakdown in Dollars	
Personal Services	$237,302
Operating Costs	$1,213,335
Capital Costs	$87,622
TOTAL	$1,538,259

Resource Measures

Asphalt Maintenance and Repair Services Costs per Capita

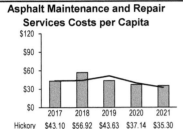

	2017	2018	2019	2020	2021
Hickory	$43.10	$56.92	$43.63	$37.14	$35.30
Average	$43.59	$44.18	$51.29	$39.86	$32.35

Asphalt Maintenance and Repair FTEs per 10,000 Population

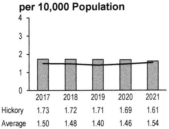

	2017	2018	2019	2020	2021
Hickory	1.73	1.72	1.71	1.69	1.61
Average	1.50	1.48	1.40	1.46	1.54

Service Costs per Lane Mile of Road Maintained

	2017	2018	2019	2020	2021
Hickory	$2,423	$3,208	$2,476	$2,137	$2,138
Average	$5,810	$6,013	$6,162	$4,759	$3,968

Workload Measures

Number of Lane Miles Maintained per 1,000 Population

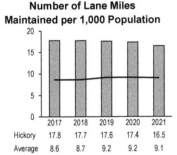

	2017	2018	2019	2020	2021
Hickory	17.8	17.7	17.6	17.4	16.5
Average	8.6	8.7	9.2	9.2	9.1

Reported Potholes per Lane Mile Maintained

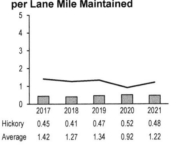

	2017	2018	2019	2020	2021
Hickory	0.45	0.41	0.47	0.52	0.48
Average	1.42	1.27	1.34	0.92	1.22

Repaired Utility Cuts per Lane Mile Maintained

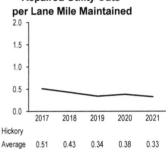

	2017	2018	2019	2020	2021
Hickory					
Average	0.51	0.43	0.34	0.38	0.33

Efficiency Measures

Cost of Maintenance per Lane Mile Maintained

	2017	2018	2019	2020	2021
Hickory	$1,366	$1,928	$1,160	$885	$934
Average	$2,574	$2,391	$2,442	$2,446	$2,158

Cost per Lane Mile for Preservation Treatment

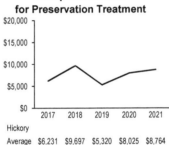

	2017	2018	2019	2020	2021
Hickory					
Average	$6,231	$9,697	$5,320	$8,025	$8,764

Cost per Lane Mile for Resurfacing Treatment

	2017	2018	2019	2020	2021
Hickory	$44 k	$52 k	$105 k	$104 k	$108 k
Average	$89 k	$107 k	$110 k	$122 k	$135 k

Cost per Lane Mile for Rehabilitation Treatment

	2017	2018	2019	2020	2021
Hickory				$104 k	$109 k
Average	$115 k	$115 k	$268 k	$92 k	$116 k

Cost per Ton for Contract Resurfacing

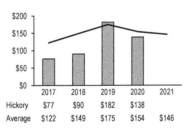

	2017	2018	2019	2020	2021
Hickory	$77	$90	$182	$138	
Average	$122	$149	$175	$154	$146

Effectiveness Measures

Percent of Lane Miles Rated 85 or Better

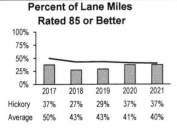

	2017	2018	2019	2020	2021
Hickory	37%	27%	29%	37%	37%
Average	50%	43%	43%	41%	40%

Percent of Lane Miles Rated Below 45

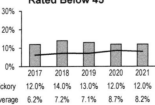

	2017	2018	2019	2020	2021
Hickory	12.0%	14.0%	13.0%	12.0%	12.0%
Average	6.2%	7.2%	7.1%	8.7%	8.2%

Percentage of Potholes Repaired within 24 hours

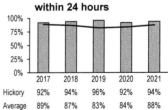

	2017	2018	2019	2020	2021
Hickory	92%	94%	96%	92%	94%
Average	89%	87%	83%	84%	88%

Raleigh

Asphalt Maintenance and Repair

Fiscal Year 2020-21

Explanatory Information

Service Level and Delivery

The City of Raleigh's Department of Transportation is responsible for for street maintenance. During the year, the city was responsible for maintaining approximately 2,368 lane miles.

The city used contractors to do preservation work on 78 lane miles. An additional 33 lane miles were resurfaced by contractors during the year. Finally, one lane received rehabilitation work, which includes milling and resurfacing. All of this road treatment work represented about 4.7 percent of total lane miles.

The city reported that 45 percent of its lane miles rated 85 or above on its most-recent pavement condition rating, conducted in 2019. The city used city staff conducting a windshield survey following the Institute for Transportation Research and Education (ITRE) rating system.

The number of potholes reported for the year was 2,938. A total of 1,294 utility cuts were also made, with the city repairing all of these. Additionally, 160 maintenance patches were completed, which were exclusive of potholes and utility cut repairs.

Conditions Affecting Service, Performance, and Costs

Municipal Profile

Population (OSBM 2020)	468,977
Land Area (Square Miles)	146.47
Persons per Square Mile	3,202
Topography	Flat; gently rolling
Climate	Temperate; little ice and snow

Service Profile

FTE Positions—Crews	33.00
FTE Positions—Other	8.00
Lane Miles Maintained	2,368.0
Lane Miles Treated	
Preservation	78.0
Resurfacing	33.0
Rehabilitation	1.0
TOTAL	112.0
Total Costs for All Treatment Types	$5,952,064
Potholes Repaired	2,938
Number of Utility Cuts	1,294
Number of Maintenance Patches (exclusive of potholes and utility cuts)	160
Average Cost per Ton of Hot Asphalt during Year	$47.62

Full Cost Profile

Cost Breakdown by Percentage	
Personal Services	23.4%
Operating Costs	60.3%
Capital Costs	16.3%
TOTAL	100.0%
Cost Breakdown in Dollars	
Personal Services	$3,235,939
Operating Costs	$8,341,673
Capital Costs	$2,247,505
TOTAL	$13,825,117

Resource Measures

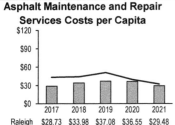

Asphalt Maintenance and Repair Services Costs per Capita

	2017	2018	2019	2020	2021
Raleigh	$28.73	$33.98	$37.08	$36.55	$29.48
Average	$43.59	$44.18	$51.29	$39.86	$32.35

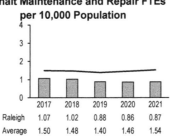

Asphalt Maintenance and Repair FTEs per 10,000 Population

	2017	2018	2019	2020	2021
Raleigh	1.07	1.02	0.88	0.86	0.87
Average	1.50	1.48	1.40	1.46	1.54

Service Costs per Lane Mile of Road Maintained

	2017	2018	2019	2020	2021
Raleigh	$5,621	$6,656	$7,432	$7,378	$5,838
Average	$5,810	$6,013	$6,162	$4,759	$3,968

Workload Measures

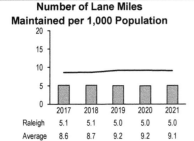

Number of Lane Miles Maintained per 1,000 Population

	2017	2018	2019	2020	2021
Raleigh	5.1	5.1	5.0	5.0	5.0
Average	8.6	8.7	9.2	9.2	9.1

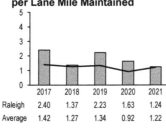

Reported Potholes per Lane Mile Maintained

	2017	2018	2019	2020	2021
Raleigh	2.40	1.37	2.23	1.63	1.24
Average	1.42	1.27	1.34	0.92	1.22

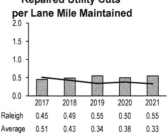

Repaired Utility Cuts per Lane Mile Maintained

	2017	2018	2019	2020	2021
Raleigh	0.45	0.49	0.55	0.50	0.55
Average	0.51	0.43	0.34	0.38	0.33

Efficiency Measures

Cost of Maintenance per Lane Mile Maintained

	2017	2018	2019	2020	2021
Raleigh	$2,662	$3,603	$4,511	$5,581	$3,325
Average	$2,574	$2,391	$2,442	$2,446	$2,158

Cost per Lane Mile for Preservation Treatment

	2017	2018	2019	2020	2021
Raleigh				$4,451	$7,005
Average	$6,231	$9,697	$5,320	$8,025	$8,764

Cost per Lane Mile for Resurfacing Treatment

	2017	2018	2019	2020	2021
Raleigh	$261 k	$295 k	$212 k	$154 k	$155 k
Average	$89 k	$107 k	$110 k	$122 k	$135 k

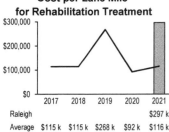

Cost per Lane Mile for Rehabilitation Treatment

	2017	2018	2019	2020	2021
Raleigh					$297 k
Average	$115 k	$115 k	$268 k	$92 k	$116 k

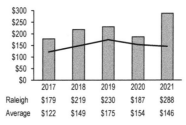

Cost per Ton for Contract Resurfacing

	2017	2018	2019	2020	2021
Raleigh	$179	$219	$230	$187	$288
Average	$122	$149	$175	$154	$146

Effectiveness Measures

Percent of Lane Miles Rated 85 or Better

	2017	2018	2019	2020	2021
Raleigh	70%	64%	64%	54%	45%
Average	50%	43%	43%	41%	40%

Percent of Lane Miles Rated Below 45

	2017	2018	2019	2020	2021
Raleigh	2.0%	1.3%	1.3%	1.0%	1.4%
Average	6.2%	7.2%	7.1%	8.7%	8.2%

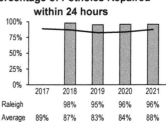

Percentage of Potholes Repaired within 24 hours

	2017	2018	2019	2020	2021
Raleigh		98%	95%	96%	96%
Average	89%	87%	83%	84%	88%

Wilson

Asphalt Maintenance and Repair

Fiscal Year 2020-21

Explanatory Information

Service Level and Delivery

The City of Wilson was responsible for maintaining approximately 698 lane miles of city streets during the year. The city treated a total of 2.7 lane miles during the year, or 0.4 percent of the total lane miles maintained. City crews performed preservation work on 2.7 lane miles. Preservation techniques include methods such as crack sealing or thin overlays.

The city reported that 47 percent of its lane miles rated 85 or above on its most-recent pavement condition rating, conducted in 2018. The city relied on a consultant for the rating, who used a customized rating based on the Institute for Transportation Research and Education (ITRE) system.

The number of potholes reported for the year was 1,484. The percentage of potholes repaired within twenty-four hours was 90 percent. Repairs to 894 utility cuts were also made during the year.

Conditions Affecting Service, Performance, and Costs

The cost of asphalt and maintenance materials is directly related to fluctuations in the price of petroleum.

Municipal Profile

Population (OSBM 2020)	47,769
Land Area (Square Miles)	31.02
Persons per Square Mile	1,540
Topography	Flat
Climate	Temperate; little ice and snow

Service Profile

FTE Positions—Crews	5.00
FTE Positions—Other	0.50
Lane Miles Maintained	698.1
Lane Miles Treated	
Preservation	2.7
Resurfacing	0.0
Rehabilitation	0.0
TOTAL	2.7
Total Costs for All Treatment Types	$19,503
Potholes Repaired	3,115
Number of Utility Cuts	552
Number of Maintenance Patches (exclusive of potholes and utility cuts)	437
Average Cost per Ton of Hot Asphalt during Year	$74.55

Full Cost Profile

Cost Breakdown by Percentage	
Personal Services	27.9%
Operating Costs	67.6%
Capital Costs	4.5%
TOTAL	100.0%

Cost Breakdown in Dollars	
Personal Services	$451,497
Operating Costs	$1,095,559
Capital Costs	$73,229
TOTAL	$1,620,285

Wilson

Asphalt Maintenance and Repair

Key: Wilson ▦   Benchmarking Average —   Fiscal Years 2017 through 2021

Resource Measures

Asphalt Maintenance and Repair Services Costs per Capita

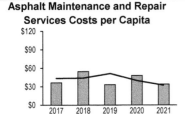

	2017	2018	2019	2020	2021
Wilson	$36.32	$54.57	$33.28	$48.05	$33.92
Average	$43.59	$44.18	$51.29	$39.86	$32.35

Asphalt Maintenance and Repair FTEs per 10,000 Population

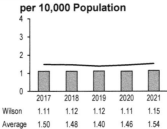

	2017	2018	2019	2020	2021
Wilson	1.11	1.12	1.12	1.11	1.15
Average	1.50	1.48	1.40	1.46	1.54

Service Costs per Lane Mile of Road Maintained

	2017	2018	2019	2020	2021
Wilson	$2,580	$3,859	$2,347	$3,404	$2,321
Average	$5,810	$6,013	$6,162	$4,759	$3,968

Workload Measures

Number of Lane Miles Maintained per 1,000 Population

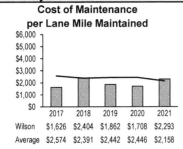

	2017	2018	2019	2020	2021
Wilson	14.1	14.1	14.2	14.1	14.6
Average	8.6	8.7	9.2	9.2	9.1

Reported Potholes per Lane Mile Maintained

	2017	2018	2019	2020	2021
Wilson	2.38	2.83	3.99	2.13	4.46
Average	1.42	1.27	1.34	0.92	1.22

Repaired Utility Cuts per Lane Mile Maintained

	2017	2018	2019	2020	2021
Wilson	1.64	0.99	0.99	1.28	0.79
Average	0.51	0.43	0.34	0.38	0.33

Efficiency Measures

Cost of Maintenance per Lane Mile Maintained

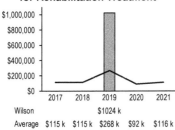

	2017	2018	2019	2020	2021
Wilson	$1,626	$2,404	$1,862	$1,708	$2,293
Average	$2,574	$2,391	$2,442	$2,446	$2,158

Cost per Lane Mile for Preservation Treatment

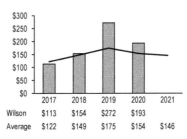

	2017	2018	2019	2020	2021
Wilson	$14,360	$20,671	$3,536	$8,498	$7,332
Average	$6,231	$9,697	$5,320	$8,025	$8,764

Cost per Lane Mile for Resurfacing Treatment

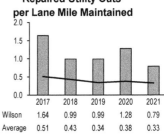

	2017	2018	2019	2020	2021
Wilson	$81 k			$56 k	
Average	$89 k	$107 k	$110 k	$122 k	$135 k

Cost per Lane Mile for Rehabilitation Treatment

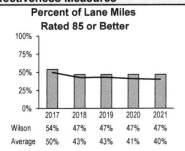

	2017	2018	2019	2020	2021
Wilson			$1024 k		
Average	$115 k	$115 k	$268 k	$92 k	$116 k

Cost per Ton for Contract Resurfacing

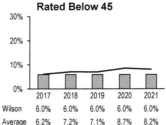

	2017	2018	2019	2020	2021
Wilson	$113	$154	$272	$193	
Average	$122	$149	$175	$154	$146

Effectiveness Measures

Percent of Lane Miles Rated 85 or Better

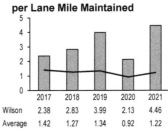

	2017	2018	2019	2020	2021
Wilson	54%	47%	47%	47%	47%
Average	50%	43%	43%	41%	40%

Percent of Lane Miles Rated Below 45

	2017	2018	2019	2020	2021
Wilson	6.0%	6.0%	6.0%	6.0%	6.0%
Average	6.2%	7.2%	7.1%	8.7%	8.2%

Percentage of Potholes Repaired within 24 hours

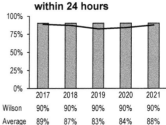

	2017	2018	2019	2020	2021
Wilson	90%	90%	90%	90%	90%
Average	89%	87%	83%	84%	88%

Fiscal Year 2020-21

Explanatory Information

Service Level and Delivery

The City of Winston-Salem was responsible for maintaining approximately 2,890.1 lane miles of city streets during the fiscal year. The city treated 113.4 lane miles, or approximately 3.9% of total lane miles for the city.

Contractors did 26.4 lane miles of preservation work and 87.0 lane miles of rehabilitation, which involves milling and resurfacing.

The city reported that 46 percent of its lane miles rated 85 or above on its most-recent pavement condition rating, conducted in 2020. The city used the Pavement Tracking System (PTS).

The city reported 2,142 potholes for the year. City policy is to repair potholes within twenty-four hours, but the lower response level is a result of calls on weekends and the sick or vacation time of repair crews.

Conditions Affecting Service, Performance, and Costs

Winston-Salem's Department of Transportation has had several major snow storm events and higher-than-normal rainfall in past years, which has affected road repair work and maintenance activities and expenses.

Municipal Profile

Population (OSBM 2020)	249,986
Land Area (Square Miles)	132.59
Persons per Square Mile	1,885
Topography	Gently rolling
Climate	Temperate; some ice and snow

Service Profile

FTE Positions—Crews	40.00
FTE Positions—Other	4.40
Lane Miles Maintained	2,890.1
Lane Miles Treated	
Preservation	26.4
Resurfacing	0.0
Rehabilitation	87.0
TOTAL	113.4
Total Costs for All Treatment Types	$5,182,515
Potholes Repaired	2,142
Number of Utility Cuts	NA
Number of Maintenance Patches (exclusive of potholes and utility cuts)	NA
Average Cost per Ton of Hot Asphalt during Year	$63.84

Full Cost Profile

Cost Breakdown by Percentage	
Personal Services	15.1%
Operating Costs	77.6%
Capital Costs	7.3%
TOTAL	100.0%
Cost Breakdown in Dollars	
Personal Services	$1,311,282
Operating Costs	$6,744,871
Capital Costs	$637,685
TOTAL	$8,693,838

Winston-Salem

Asphalt Maintenance and Repair

Resource Measures

Asphalt Maintenance and Repair Services Costs per Capita

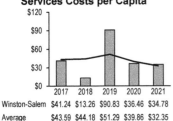

	2017	2018	2019	2020	2021
Winston-Salem	$41.24	$13.26	$90.83	$36.46	$34.78
Average	$43.59	$44.18	$51.29	$39.86	$32.35

Asphalt Maintenance and Repair FTEs per 10,000 Population

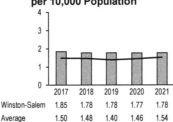

	2017	2018	2019	2020	2021
Winston-Salem	1.85	1.78	1.78	1.77	1.78
Average	1.50	1.48	1.40	1.46	1.54

Service Costs per Lane Mile of Road Maintained

	2017	2018	2019	2020	2021
Winston-Salem	$4,259	$1,382	$7,882	$3,181	$3,008
Average	$5,810	$6,013	$6,162	$4,759	$3,968

Workload Measures

Number of Lane Miles Maintained per 1,000 Population

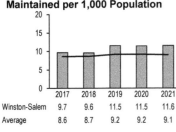

	2017	2018	2019	2020	2021
Winston-Salem	9.7	9.6	11.5	11.5	11.6
Average	8.6	8.7	9.2	9.2	9.1

Reported Potholes per Lane Mile Maintained

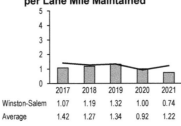

	2017	2018	2019	2020	2021
Winston-Salem	1.07	1.19	1.32	1.00	0.74
Average	1.42	1.27	1.34	0.92	1.22

Repaired Utility Cuts per Lane Mile Maintained

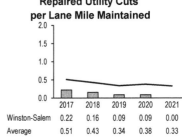

	2017	2018	2019	2020	2021
Winston-Salem	0.22	0.16	0.09	0.09	0.00
Average	0.51	0.43	0.34	0.38	0.33

Efficiency Measures

Cost of Maintenance per Lane Mile Maintained

	2017	2018	2019	2020	2021
Winston-Salem	$955	$1,363	$1,004	$1,210	$1,215
Average	$2,574	$2,391	$2,442	$2,446	$2,158

Cost per Lane Mile for Preservation Treatment

	2017	2018	2019	2020	2021
Winston-Salem	$2,791		$5,914	$6,737	$1,827
Average	$6,231	$9,697	$5,320	$8,025	$8,764

Cost per Lane Mile for Resurfacing Treatment

	2017	2018	2019	2020	2021
Winston-Salem	$105 k	$123 k	$92 k	$246 k	
Average	$89 k	$107 k	$110 k	$122 k	$135 k

Cost per Lane Mile for Rehabilitation Treatment

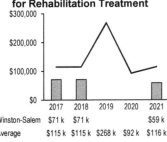

	2017	2018	2019	2020	2021
Winston-Salem	$71 k	$71 k			$59 k
Average	$115 k	$115 k	$268 k	$92 k	$116 k

Cost per Ton for Contract Resurfacing

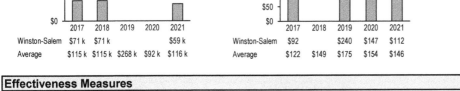

	2017	2018	2019	2020	2021
Winston-Salem	$92		$240	$147	$112
Average	$122	$149	$175	$154	$146

Effectiveness Measures

Percent of Lane Miles Rated 85 or Better

	2017	2018	2019	2020	2021
Winston-Salem	55%	49%	48%	50%	46%
Average	50%	43%	43%	41%	40%

Percent of Lane Miles Rated Below 45

	2017	2018	2019	2020	2021
Winston-Salem	5.0%	10.0%	11.0%	10.0%	9.0%
Average	6.2%	7.2%	7.1%	8.7%	8.2%

Percentage of Potholes Repaired within 24 hours

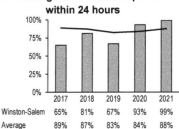

	2017	2018	2019	2020	2021
Winston-Salem	65%	81%	67%	93%	99%
Average	89%	87%	83%	84%	88%

Performance and Cost Data

FIRE SERVICES

PERFORMANCE MEASURES FOR FIRE SERVICES

SERVICE DEFINITION
Fire Services refer to activities and programs relating to the prevention and suppression of fires, responses to calls for service, rescue service (if provided), fire inspections (if provided), responses to hazardous materials calls (if provided), and fire education services. The services provided by fire departments vary from city to city, but the common goal remains the same: to protect the lives and property of the community served.

NOTES ON PERFORMANCE MEASURES

1. Number of Actual Fires per 1,000 Population
The total number of actual fires includes all types of fires, including structural fires.

2. Fire Inspections Completed per 1,000 Population
Fire inspections include Level I, II, and III inspections.

3. Number of Fire Department Responses per 1,000 Population
Responses include those to fires, medical emergencies, false alarms, and other types of situations that result in mobilization of fire equipment and personnel.

4. Cost per Fire Department Response
The cost represents the total cost of fire services and is calculated using a full cost accounting model that captures direct, indirect, and capital costs. Response is as defined above.

5. Number of Inspections Completed per Fire Inspector FTE
One full-time equivalent (FTE) position equals 2,080 hours of work per year. Any combination of employees providing 2,080 hours of work per year is counted as one FTE.

6. Average Turnout and Travel Time for First Unit Dispatched under "Priority One" Situations
Fast response is a critical determinant in how successful fire responders will be. Response time is calculated by adding both the turnout time (the time the dispatch is received until the first unit is out the door) and the travel time (the time the first unit is out the door until the unit arrives on the scene).

7. Percentage of Full Responses within Eight Minutes
The speed of fire department responses can be judged both by the time for the first unit arriving and also by how long it takes a full complement of trucks and personnel to respond to an emergency. The percentage within eight minutes takes into account travel time.

8. Percentage of Fires Confined to Object or Room of Origin

Containment of fires to as small an area as possible limits total damages. The degree of containment depends on how quickly the fire department is called and is also an effectiveness measure that is reported to the state.

9. Percentage of Fires for Which Cause Is Determined

Investigation of the causes of fires can be an important part of prevention and suppression efforts. While the cause of all fires cannot always be determined, being able to identify causes is important if lessons are to be learned from the investigations.

10. Percentage of Fire Code Violations "Cleared" by Correction or Imposition of Penalty within Ninety Days

Fire code violations are violations of state and local laws and regulations as found through fire inspections. The violators are given time to correct the violation before a penalty is imposed. This is an effectiveness measure that provides an indication of timeliness of follow-up.

11. Percentage of Cases with Lost Pulse Where Pulse Is Recovered at Time of Transfer for Transport

Fire departments frequently are the first responders to medical calls, including cases where an individual has no pulse either at the time of arrival or during the response. This effectiveness measure reports the percentage of these cases in which the patient has recovered a pulse by the time responsibility for care has been transferred to emergency responders who will transport the patient to a hospital. Many patients cannot be saved, and recovery of pulse does not guarantee survival at the hospital.

Fire Services

Summary of Key Dimensions of Service

City or Town	Population Served	Land Area Served (in Square Miles)	Value of Property in Service Area (in Billions)	Total Number of Fire Department Responses	Fire Code Violations Found	Number of Community Fire Stations	Number of Fire Services FTEs	ISO* Rating
Apex	66,309	66.3	$11.6	3,510	1,108	5	98	1—town 2—outlying
Chapel Hill	62,676	22.9	$8.5	3,737	224	5	96	2
Charlotte	887,333	312.4	$148.9	124,104	39,653	42 + 1 airport	1,233	1
Concord	109,959	70.1	$14.7	13,609	3,799	10 + 1 airport	244	1
Goldsboro	34,793	29.3	$2.6	2,630	2,965	5	84	2
Greensboro	308,657	140.5	$29.8	34,457	18,199	26	584	1
Greenville	87,819	37.2	$7.5	18,598	4,147	6	164	3
Hickory	48,776	43.4	$5.8	4,577	3,077	6 + 1 airport	139	1
Raleigh	468,977	146.5	$77.4	43,979	21,032	28	626	1
Wilson	47,769	31.0	$4.3	3,812	4,042	5	100	1
Winston-Salem	249,986	132.6	$23.3	16,801	5,899	19	368	2

NOTES
*ISO—Insurance Service Office

EXPLANATORY FACTORS
These are factors that the project found affected fire services performance and cost in one or more of the municipalities:

Population and area served
Value of property area protected in service area
Number of engine companies
Number of fire department responses
Fire code violations
ISO rating
Age of housing stock

Apex

Fire Services

Fiscal Year 2020-21

Explanatory Information

Service Level and Delivery

The mission of the Apex Fire Department is to protect life, property, and the environment from fire, medical emergencies, natural disasters, and other emergencies for those who live, work, and travel in and through the town and surrounding area. In addition to the town, the fire department serves an additional forty-nine square miles in surrounding fire districts.

The fire department uses a shift schedule with one twenty-four-hour shift on schedule and one off every three days, followed by a four-day break. On average, shift personnel work ten to eleven days per twenty-eight-day cycle.

The area within the Town of Apex has an ISO rating of 1, the highest rating possible. The outlying surrounding fire districts that are served by the town have an ISO rating of 2. Both of these ratings were done during 2021 and were an upgrade from the prior ratings for Apex and the surrounding fire districts.

The Apex Fire Department conducted 2,995 fire maintenance, construction, and reinspections during the fiscal year. The fire department handles all inspections within town limits and coordinates with the Wake County Fire Marshal for joint inspections in the extra-territorial jurisdiction for new construction, fire alarms, and sprinkler reviews and inspections. Apex has a fire marshal and one inspector.

All fire investigations in Apex are handled by the Wake County Fire Marshal. Apex assists in investigations but does not provide the investigative reports.

Conditions Affecting Service, Performance, and Costs

Municipal Profile	
Service Population	66,309
Land Area (Square Miles)	66.29
Persons per Square Mile	1,000

Service Profile	
FTE Positions—Firefighters	88.0
FTE Positions—Other	10.0
Fire Stations	5
First-Line Fire Apparatus	
Pumpers	4
Aerial Trucks	2
Quints	0
Squads	0
Rescue	1
Other	6
Fire Department Responses	3,510
Responses for Fires	133
Structural Fires Reported	36
Inspections Completed for Maintenance, Construction, and Reinspections	2,995
Fire Code Violations Reported	1,108
Estimated Fire Loss (millions)	$1.62
Amount of Property Protected in Service Area (billions)	$11.6
Number of Fire Education Programs or Events	28

Full Cost Profile	
Cost Breakdown by Percentage	
Personal Services	69.6%
Operating Costs	20.1%
Capital Costs	10.3%
TOTAL	100.0%
Cost Breakdown in Dollars	
Personal Services	$9,258,184
Operating Costs	$2,670,004
Capital Costs	$1,365,896
TOTAL	$13,294,084

Resource Measures

Fire Services Costs per Capita

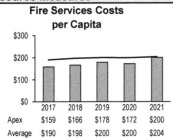

	2017	2018	2019	2020	2021
Apex	$159	$166	$178	$172	$200
Average	$190	$198	$200	$200	$204

Fire Services Total FTEs per 10,000 Population

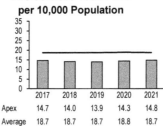

	2017	2018	2019	2020	2021
Apex	14.7	14.0	13.9	14.3	14.8
Average	18.7	18.7	18.7	18.8	18.7

Fire Services Cost per Thousand Dollars of Property Protected

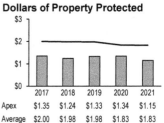

	2017	2018	2019	2020	2021
Apex	$1.35	$1.24	$1.33	$1.34	$1.15
Average	$2.00	$1.98	$1.98	$1.83	$1.83

Workload Measures

Actual Fires per 1,000 Population

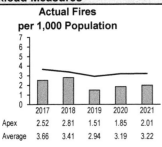

	2017	2018	2019	2020	2021
Apex	2.52	2.81	1.51	1.85	2.01
Average	3.66	3.41	2.94	3.19	3.22

Fire Department Responses per 1,000 Population

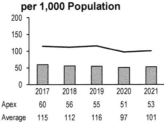

	2017	2018	2019	2020	2021
Apex	60	56	55	51	53
Average	115	112	116	97	101

Fire Inspections Completed per 1,000 Population

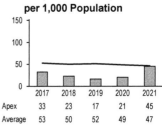

	2017	2018	2019	2020	2021
Apex	33	23	17	21	45
Average	53	50	52	49	47

Efficiency Measures

Fire Services Cost per Fire Department Response

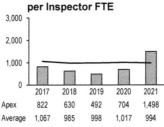

	2017	2018	2019	2020	2021
Apex	$2,659	$2,972	$3,257	$3,369	$3,787
Average	$1,807	$1,951	$1,928	$2,219	$2,311

Inspections Completed per Inspector FTE

	2017	2018	2019	2020	2021
Apex	822	630	492	704	1,498
Average	1,067	985	998	1,017	994

Effectiveness Measures

Average Response Time to Priority One Calls in Minutes

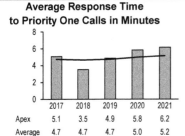

	2017	2018	2019	2020	2021
Apex	5.1	3.5	4.9	5.8	6.2
Average	4.7	4.7	4.7	5.0	5.2

Percentage of Fire Code Violations Cleared within 90 Days

	2017	2018	2019	2020	2021
Apex	73%	82%	89%	97%	98%
Average	63%	78%	63%	61%	67%

Percentage of Fires Confined to Rooms or Objects Involved on Arrival

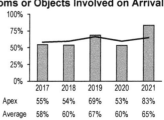

	2017	2018	2019	2020	2021
Apex	55%	54%	69%	53%	83%
Average	58%	60%	67%	60%	65%

Percentage of Fires for Which Cause Was Determined

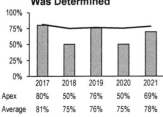

	2017	2018	2019	2020	2021
Apex	80%	50%	76%	50%	69%
Average	81%	75%	76%	75%	78%

Percentage of Full Response within 8 Minutes Travel Time

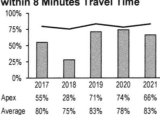

	2017	2018	2019	2020	2021
Apex	55%	28%	71%	74%	66%
Average	80%	75%	83%	78%	83%

Percentage of Lost Pulse Cases Recovered Pulse at Transfer of Care

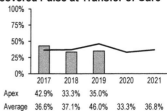

	2017	2018	2019	2020	2021
Apex	42.9%	33.3%	35.0%		
Average	36.6%	37.1%	46.0%	33.3%	36.8%

Fiscal Year 2020-21

Explanatory Information

Service Level and Delivery

The Town of Chapel Hill Fire Department's mission is to minimize the risk of fire and other hazards to the life and property of the citizens of Chapel Hill. To accomplish this mission, the department provides response to and mitigation of fires, medical emergencies, hazardous materials incidents, and other emergencies as they arise.

The fire department is organized into three divisions: operations, administration, and life safety. Operations and life safety are administered by a deputy chief with support staff. Administration consists of the fire chief and support staff.

The fire department works a 3/4 system, where personnel are on duty for 24 hours starting at 7 a.m. The town has five community stations with seven primary vehicles for response.

The town has an ISO rating of 2 received in 2016, which was an upgrade from the year before.

Fire inspections are performed by fire inspectors and are designed to be completed in accordance with the State of North Carolina's inspection schedule. Initial inspections may generate findings for reinspection. The department counts malls as one inspection per occupancy and one per building structure. High rises have one inspection per building plus one per commercial occupancy. Multi-structure apartment complexes have just one inspection per complex.

Conditions Affecting Service, Performance, and Costs

Complete data on fire code violations and fire safety complaints were not available for the last few years.

Municipal Profile

Service Population	62,676
Land Area (Square Miles)	22.91
Persons per Square Mile	2,736

Service Profile

FTE Positions—Firefighters	76.0
FTE Positions—Other	20.0
Fire Stations	5
First-Line Fire Apparatus	
Pumpers	4
Aerial Trucks	2
Quints	0
Squads	0
Rescue	1
Other	0
Fire Department Responses	3,737
Responses for Fires	97
Structural Fires Reported	31
Inspections Completed for Maintenance, Construction, and Reinspections	1,213
Fire Code Violations Reported	224
Estimated Fire Loss (millions)	na
Amount of Property Protected in Service Area (billions)	$8.5
Number of Fire Education Programs or Events	15

Full Cost Profile

Cost Breakdown by Percentage

Personal Services	61.8%
Operating Costs	27.9%
Capital Costs	10.3%
TOTAL	100.0%

Cost Breakdown in Dollars

Personal Services	$7,735,004
Operating Costs	$3,498,188
Capital Costs	$1,291,815
TOTAL	$12,525,007

Chapel Hill

Fire Services

Key: Chapel Hill   Benchmarking Average —   Fiscal Years 2017 through 2021

Resource Measures

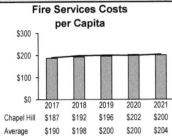

Fire Services Costs per Capita

	2017	2018	2019	2020	2021
Chapel Hill	$187	$192	$196	$202	$200
Average	$190	$198	$200	$200	$204

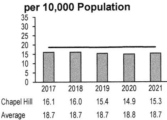

Fire Services Total FTEs per 10,000 Population

	2017	2018	2019	2020	2021
Chapel Hill	16.1	16.0	15.4	14.9	15.3
Average	18.7	18.7	18.7	18.8	18.7

Fire Services Cost per Thousand Dollars of Property Protected

	2017	2018	2019	2020	2021
Chapel Hill	$1.49	$1.44	$1.50	$1.55	$1.47
Average	$2.00	$1.98	$1.98	$1.83	$1.83

Workload Measures

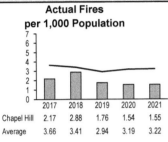

Actual Fires per 1,000 Population

	2017	2018	2019	2020	2021
Chapel Hill	2.17	2.88	1.76	1.54	1.55
Average	3.66	3.41	2.94	3.19	3.22

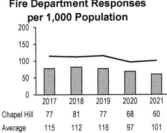

Fire Department Responses per 1,000 Population

	2017	2018	2019	2020	2021
Chapel Hill	77	81	77	68	60
Average	115	112	116	97	101

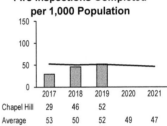

Fire Inspections Completed per 1,000 Population

	2017	2018	2019	2020	2021
Chapel Hill	29	46	52		
Average	53	50	52	49	47

Efficiency Measures

Fire Services Cost per Fire Department Response

	2017	2018	2019	2020	2021
Chapel Hill	$2,432	$2,360	$2,553	$2,958	$3,352
Average	$1,807	$1,951	$1,928	$2,219	$2,311

Inspections Completed per Inspector FTE

	2017	2018	2019	2020	2021
Chapel Hill	310	479	575		
Average	1,067	985	998	1,017	994

Effectiveness Measures

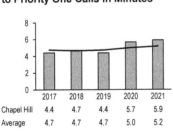

Average Response Time to Priority One Calls in Minutes

	2017	2018	2019	2020	2021
Chapel Hill	4.4	4.7	4.4	5.7	5.9
Average	4.7	4.7	4.7	5.0	5.2

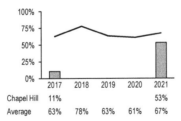

Percentage of Fire Code Violations Cleared within 90 Days

	2017	2018	2019	2020	2021
Chapel Hill	11%				53%
Average	63%	78%	63%	61%	67%

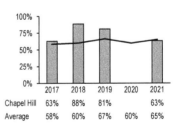

Percentage of Fires Confined to Rooms or Objects Involved on Arrival

	2017	2018	2019	2020	2021
Chapel Hill	63%	88%	81%		63%
Average	58%	60%	67%	60%	65%

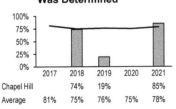

Percentage of Fires for Which Cause Was Determined

	2017	2018	2019	2020	2021
Chapel Hill		74%	19%		85%
Average	81%	75%	76%	75%	78%

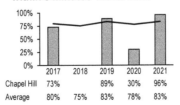

Percentage of Full Response within 8 Minutes Travel Time

	2017	2018	2019	2020	2021
Chapel Hill	73%		89%	30%	96%
Average	80%	75%	83%	78%	83%

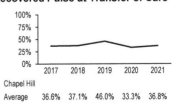

Percentage of Lost Pulse Cases Recovered Pulse at Transfer of Care

	2017	2018	2019	2020	2021
Chapel Hill					
Average	36.6%	37.1%	46.0%	33.3%	36.8%

Charlotte

Fire Services

Fiscal Year 2020-21

Explanatory Information

Service Level and Delivery
The mission of the Charlotte Fire Department is to minimize the risk of fire and other hazards to the life and property of the citizens of Charlotte. To accomplish this mission, the department provides response to and mitigation of fires, medical emergencies, hazardous materials incidents, aircraft emergencies, technical rescues, and other emergencies as they arise. These services are provided immediately to any person who has a need anywhere within the corporate limits of Charlotte.

The divisions of the Charlotte Fire Department are operations (A, B, C), training, administration, communications, logistics, fire prevention, and fire investigation.

The city uses a modified twenty-four-hour/forty-eight-hour shift schedule, using four twenty-four-hour shifts in a twelve-day cycle. The cycle is on one day, off one day, on one day, off two days, on one day, off one day, on one day, and off four days. In addition, firefighters receive a Kelley day (ten hours) off and a Kelley night (fourteen hours) off every seven weeks to maintain the number of hours worked per week at fifty-two.

The city has an ISO rating of 1, which is the highest level possible. The Charlotte Fire Department has been accredited since 2000.

The fire department conducted 39,653 fire maintenance, construction, and reinspections during the fiscal year. All inspections are performed by certified fire inspectors, who are employees of the Fire Prevention Bureau. The inspectors handle certificate-of-occupancy inspections, permit inspections and issuances, regular-code-enforcement inspections, and reinspections. The bureau currently uses separate inspections on each building of an apartment complex.

Conditions Affecting Service, Performance, and Costs
Charlotte staffs a fire station at the airport in addition to forty-two community fire stations.

Municipal Profile	
Service Population	887,333
Land Area (Square Miles)	312.39
Persons per Square Mile	2,840

Service Profile	
FTE Positions—Firefighters	1,104.0
FTE Positions—Other	129.0
Fire Stations	43
First-Line Fire Apparatus	
Pumpers	43
Aerial Trucks	0
Quints	16
Squads	0
Rescue	2
Other	37
Fire Department Responses	124,104
Responses for Fires	2,459
Structural Fires Reported	490
Inspections Completed for Maintenance, Construction, and Reinspections	29,746
Fire Code Violations Reported	39,653
Estimated Fire Loss (millions)	$14.60
Amount of Property Protected in Service Area (billions)	$148.9
Number of Fire Education Programs or Events	200

Full Cost Profile	
Cost Breakdown by Percentage	
Personal Services	66.5%
Operating Costs	21.7%
Capital Costs	11.8%
TOTAL	100.0%
Cost Breakdown in Dollars	
Personal Services	$126,123,346
Operating Costs	$19,308,152
Capital Costs	$7,685,995
TOTAL	$153,117,493

Charlotte

Fire Services

Resource Measures

Fire Services Costs per Capita

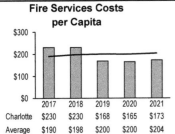

	2017	2018	2019	2020	2021
Charlotte	$230	$230	$168	$165	$173
Average	$190	$198	$200	$200	$204

Fire Services Total FTEs per 10,000 Population

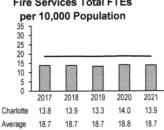

	2017	2018	2019	2020	2021
Charlotte	13.8	13.9	13.3	14.0	13.9
Average	18.7	18.7	18.7	18.8	18.7

Fire Services Cost per Thousand Dollars of Property Protected

	2017	2018	2019	2020	2021
Charlotte	$2.09	$2.03	$1.46	$0.99	$1.03
Average	$2.00	$1.98	$1.98	$1.83	$1.83

Workload Measures

Actual Fires per 1,000 Population

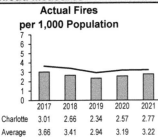

	2017	2018	2019	2020	2021
Charlotte	3.01	2.66	2.34	2.57	2.77
Average	3.66	3.41	2.94	3.19	3.22

Fire Department Responses per 1,000 Population

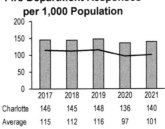

	2017	2018	2019	2020	2021
Charlotte	146	145	148	136	140
Average	115	112	116	97	101

Fire Inspections Completed per 1,000 Population

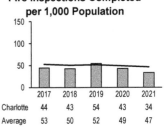

	2017	2018	2019	2020	2021
Charlotte	44	43	54	43	34
Average	53	50	52	49	47

Efficiency Measures

Fire Services Cost per Fire Department Response

	2017	2018	2019	2020	2021
Charlotte	$1,582	$1,594	$1,141	$1,216	$1,234
Average	$1,807	$1,951	$1,928	$2,219	$2,311

Inspections Completed per Inspector FTE

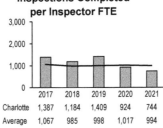

	2017	2018	2019	2020	2021
Charlotte	1,387	1,184	1,409	924	744
Average	1,067	985	998	1,017	994

Effectiveness Measures

Average Response Time to Priority One Calls in Minutes

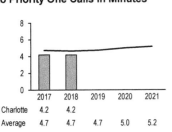

	2017	2018	2019	2020	2021
Charlotte	4.2	4.2			
Average	4.7	4.7	4.7	5.0	5.2

Percentage of Fire Code Violations Cleared within 90 Days

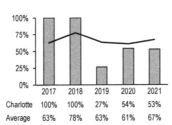

	2017	2018	2019	2020	2021
Charlotte	100%	100%	27%	54%	53%
Average	63%	78%	63%	61%	67%

Percentage of Fires Confined to Rooms or Objects Involved on Arrival

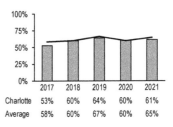

	2017	2018	2019	2020	2021
Charlotte	53%	60%	64%	60%	61%
Average	58%	60%	67%	60%	65%

Percentage of Fires for Which Cause Was Determined

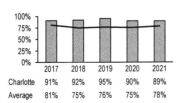

	2017	2018	2019	2020	2021
Charlotte	91%	92%	95%	90%	89%
Average	81%	75%	76%	75%	78%

Percentage of Full Response within 8 Minutes Travel Time

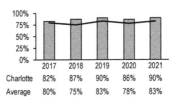

	2017	2018	2019	2020	2021
Charlotte	82%	87%	90%	86%	90%
Average	80%	75%	83%	78%	83%

Percentage of Lost Pulse Cases Recovered Pulse at Transfer of Care

	2017	2018	2019	2020	2021
Charlotte	44.7%	43.4%	63.7%	62.5%	54.2%
Average	36.6%	37.1%	46.0%	33.3%	36.8%

Fiscal Year 2020-21

Explanatory Information

Service Level and Delivery

The City of Concord Fire Department is committed to providing a positive work environment to enable the department and its personnel to strive for and achieve excellence in fire protection services.

The department is committed to the following: providing leadership through a management/employee team organizational concept that is dedicated to modern-day management principles and practices; providing the citizens with the best possible modern-day fire protection and life safety services in a courteous, professional, and cost-effective manner; providing equal opportunity for all employees to excel in their job performance and career development; striving to continually increase the public's awareness through fire prevention activities, public education, and community-based services; maintaining and striving to improve on an open, informative flow of correct information so that all employees and employee teams reach their goals and objectives; subscribing to departmental values of honesty, professionalism, teamwork, loyalty, dedication, and commitment to serving the public; and planning for change to develop and prepare the department to always strive for excellence.

The fire department in Concord contains the following divisions: administration, operations, training, and fire prevention.

The fire department utilizes a shift schedule that includes twenty-four hours on and forty-eight hours off.

The city has an ISO rating of 1, as rated in 2018. This is the highest level rating possible and was an upgrade from the last rating.

The fire department conducted 3,799 fire maintenance, construction, and reinspections during the fiscal year. Inspections are conducted by the Fire Prevention Division. Each inspector has an assigned area of the city and a specific number of inspections to complete. Each occupancy is counted separately in the inspections number. An apartment complex would be considered as one occupancy. Reinspections are conducted within forty-five days to confirm corrections.

Conditions Affecting Service, Performance, and Costs

Concord staffs a fire station at the airport, in addition to ten community fire stations.

Municipal Profile

Service Population	109,959
Land Area (Square Miles)	70.10
Persons per Square Mile	1,569

Service Profile

FTE Positions—Firefighters	224.0
FTE Positions—Other	19.5
Fire Stations	11
First-Line Fire Apparatus	
Pumpers	10
Aerial Trucks	3
Quints	0
Squads	0
Rescue	1
Other	12
Fire Department Responses	13,609
Responses for Fires	229
Structural Fires Reported	41
Inspections Completed for Maintenance, Construction, and Reinspections	2,256
Fire Code Violations Reported	3,799
Estimated Fire Loss (millions)	$2.11
Amount of Property Protected in Service Area (billions)	$14.7
Number of Fire Education Programs or Events	15

Full Cost Profile

Cost Breakdown by Percentage	
Personal Services	67.5%
Operating Costs	21.5%
Capital Costs	11.0%
TOTAL	100.0%

Cost Breakdown in Dollars	
Personal Services	$18,820,201
Operating Costs	$6,002,351
Capital Costs	$3,066,674
TOTAL	$27,889,226

Concord

Fire Services

Resource Measures

Fire Services Costs per Capita

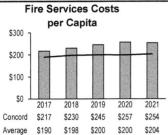

	2017	2018	2019	2020	2021
Concord	$217	$230	$245	$257	$254
Average	$190	$198	$200	$200	$204

Fire Services Total FTEs per 10,000 Population

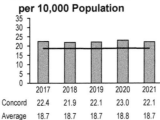

	2017	2018	2019	2020	2021
Concord	22.4	21.9	22.1	23.0	22.1
Average	18.7	18.7	18.7	18.8	18.7

Fire Services Cost per Thousand Dollars of Property Protected

	2017	2018	2019	2020	2021
Concord	$1.98	$1.92	$2.01	$2.10	$1.90
Average	$2.00	$1.98	$1.98	$1.83	$1.83

Workload Measures

Actual Fires per 1,000 Population

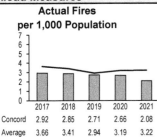

	2017	2018	2019	2020	2021
Concord	2.92	2.85	2.71	2.66	2.08
Average	3.66	3.41	2.94	3.19	3.22

Fire Department Responses per 1,000 Population

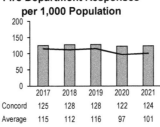

	2017	2018	2019	2020	2021
Concord	125	128	128	122	124
Average	115	112	116	97	101

Fire Inspections Completed per 1,000 Population

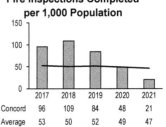

	2017	2018	2019	2020	2021
Concord	96	109	84	48	21
Average	53	50	52	49	47

Efficiency Measures

Fire Services Cost per Fire Department Response

	2017	2018	2019	2020	2021
Concord	$1,733	$1,799	$1,916	$2,095	$2,049
Average	$1,807	$1,951	$1,928	$2,219	$2,311

Inspections Completed per Inspector FTE

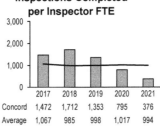

	2017	2018	2019	2020	2021
Concord	1,472	1,712	1,353	795	376
Average	1,067	985	998	1,017	994

Effectiveness Measures

Average Response Time to Priority One Calls in Minutes

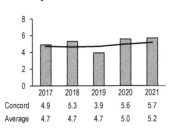

	2017	2018	2019	2020	2021
Concord	4.9	5.3	3.9	5.6	5.7
Average	4.7	4.7	4.7	5.0	5.2

Percentage of Fire Code Violations Cleared within 90 Days

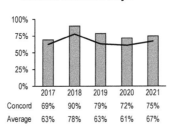

	2017	2018	2019	2020	2021
Concord	69%	90%	79%	72%	75%
Average	63%	78%	63%	61%	67%

Percentage of Fires Confined to Rooms or Objects Involved on Arrival

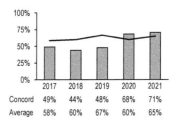

	2017	2018	2019	2020	2021
Concord	49%	44%	48%	68%	71%
Average	58%	60%	67%	60%	65%

Percentage of Fires for Which Cause Was Determined

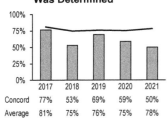

	2017	2018	2019	2020	2021
Concord	77%	53%	69%	59%	50%
Average	81%	75%	76%	75%	78%

Percentage of Full Response within 8 Minutes Travel Time

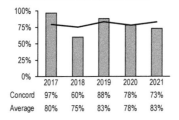

	2017	2018	2019	2020	2021
Concord	97%	60%	88%	78%	73%
Average	80%	75%	83%	78%	83%

Percentage of Lost Pulse Cases Recovered Pulse at Transfer of Care

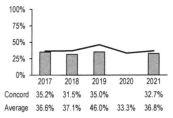

	2017	2018	2019	2020	2021
Concord	35.2%	31.5%	35.0%		32.7%
Average	36.6%	37.1%	46.0%	33.3%	36.8%

Fiscal Year 2020-21

Explanatory Information

Service Level and Delivery

The mission of the Goldsboro Fire Department is to protect lives, the environment, and property by providing prompt, skillful, and cost-effective fire protection, EMS, and life safety services. The department maintains a receptive and ethical work environment that is conducive to the development of innovative and creative solutions by employees to meet the ever-changing needs of the community.

The fire department utilizes a shift schedule that alternates twenty-four hours on and twenty-four hours off for five days, followed by four days off. This works out to fifty-six hour work weeks with shifts starting and ending at 8 a.m.

The city has an ISO rating of 2, as rated in 2020.

The fire department in Goldsboro conducted 1,941 fire maintenance, construction, and reinspections during the fiscal year. General inspections are performed according to the mandated inspection schedule, which is based on occupancy type established in the International Fire Code. Maintenance fire inspections are assigned by the fire marshal to the fire inspectors, fire company inspectors, and the fire marshal's office as well. The fire inspector or fire marshal perform all site plan reviews, fumigation, tent inspections, and construction inspections for fire suppression and sprinklers, tanks, and fire alarm systems.

Conditions Affecting Service, Performance, and Costs

The City of Goldsboro joined the Benchmarking Project in July 2017, with the first year of data showing for FY 2016–17.

Municipal Profile

Service Population	34,793
Land Area (Square Miles)	29.35
Persons per Square Mile	1,186

Service Profile

FTE Positions—Firefighters	75.0
FTE Positions—Other	9.0
Fire Stations	5
First-Line Fire Apparatus	
Pumpers	4
Aerial Trucks	1
Quints	1
Squads	0
Rescue	0
Other	0
Fire Department Responses	2,630
Responses for Fires	178
Structural Fires Reported	42
Inspections Completed for Maintenance, Construction, and Reinspections	1,941
Fire Code Violations Reported	2,965
Estimated Fire Loss (millions)	$0.81
Amount of Property Protected in Service Area (billions)	$2.6
Number of Fire Education Programs or Events	47

Full Cost Profile

Cost Breakdown by Percentage

Personal Services	88.9%
Operating Costs	9.6%
Capital Costs	1.5%
TOTAL	100.0%

Cost Breakdown in Dollars

Personal Services	$5,564,287
Operating Costs	$598,673
Capital Costs	$94,692
TOTAL	$6,257,652

Goldsboro

Fire Services

Resource Measures

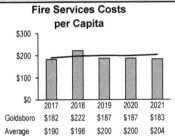

Fire Services Costs per Capita

	2017	2018	2019	2020	2021
Goldsboro	$182	$222	$187	$187	$183
Average	$190	$198	$200	$200	$204

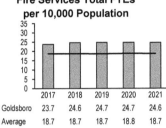

Fire Services Total FTEs per 10,000 Population

	2017	2018	2019	2020	2021
Goldsboro	23.7	24.6	24.7	24.7	24.6
Average	18.7	18.7	18.7	18.8	18.7

Fire Services Cost per Thousand Dollars of Property Protected

	2017	2018	2019	2020	2021
Goldsboro	$2.65	$3.11	$2.60	$2.49	$2.44
Average	$2.00	$1.98	$1.98	$1.83	$1.83

Workload Measures

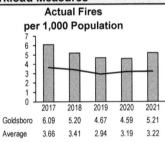

Actual Fires per 1,000 Population

	2017	2018	2019	2020	2021
Goldsboro	6.09	5.20	4.67	4.59	5.21
Average	3.66	3.41	2.94	3.19	3.22

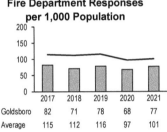

Fire Department Responses per 1,000 Population

	2017	2018	2019	2020	2021
Goldsboro	82	71	78	68	77
Average	115	112	116	97	101

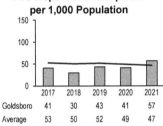

Fire Inspections Completed per 1,000 Population

	2017	2018	2019	2020	2021
Goldsboro	41	30	43	41	57
Average	53	50	52	49	47

Efficiency Measures

Fire Services Cost per Fire Department Response

	2017	2018	2019	2020	2021
Goldsboro	$2,236	$3,125	$2,397	$2,764	$2,379
Average	$1,807	$1,951	$1,928	$2,219	$2,311

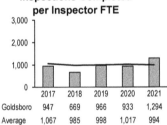

Inspections Completed per Inspector FTE

	2017	2018	2019	2020	2021
Goldsboro	947	669	966	933	1,294
Average	1,067	985	998	1,017	994

Effectiveness Measures

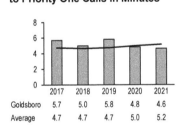

Average Response Time to Priority One Calls in Minutes

	2017	2018	2019	2020	2021
Goldsboro	5.7	5.0	5.8	4.8	4.6
Average	4.7	4.7	4.7	5.0	5.2

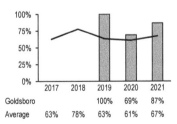

Percentage of Fire Code Violations Cleared within 90 Days

	2017	2018	2019	2020	2021
Goldsboro			100%	69%	87%
Average	63%	78%	63%	61%	67%

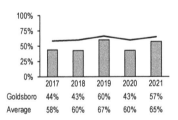

Percentage of Fires Confined to Rooms or Objects Involved on Arrival

	2017	2018	2019	2020	2021
Goldsboro	44%	43%	60%	43%	57%
Average	58%	60%	67%	60%	65%

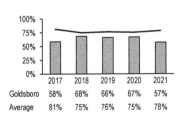

Percentage of Fires for Which Cause Was Determined

	2017	2018	2019	2020	2021
Goldsboro	58%	68%	66%	67%	57%
Average	81%	75%	76%	75%	78%

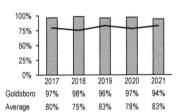

Percentage of Full Response within 8 Minutes Travel Time

	2017	2018	2019	2020	2021
Goldsboro	97%	98%	96%	97%	94%
Average	80%	75%	83%	78%	83%

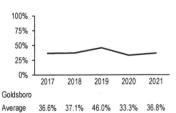

Percentage of Lost Pulse Cases Recovered Pulse at Transfer of Care

	2017	2018	2019	2020	2021
Goldsboro					
Average	36.6%	37.1%	46.0%	33.3%	36.8%

Fiscal Year 2020-21

Explanatory Information

Service Level and Delivery

The mission of the Greensboro Fire Department is to provide the public the best possible service in a courteous, professional, and cost-effective manner; to provide leadership through a well-defined management team committed to the departmental management philosophy; to provide equal opportunity for all employees in job performance and career development; to enhance public awareness through education, activities, and services; to maintain an open, informative flow of information so that all municipal departments may reach their goals and objectives; and to subscribe to honesty, integrity, and fairness.

The fire department contains two branches: emergency services and support services.

The fire department utilizes a shift schedule that includes twenty-four hours on and forty-eight hours off. For the purposes of the Fair Labor Standards Act (FLSA), the department utilizes a twenty-seven-day cycle.

The city has an ISO rating of 1, the highest rating possible, as rated in 2019. The Greensboro Fire Department has been accredited since 1997.

The fire department in Greensboro conducted 10,230 fire maintenance, construction, and reinspections during the fiscal year. General inspections are performed according to the mandated inspection schedule, which is based on the occupancy type established in the International Fire Code. Complaints are addressed within twenty-four hours and are handled twenty-four hours a day as shift personnel are available. Inspectors generally work in districts and work in specialized areas, including educational, institutional, high rise, privilege licenses, and certificates of compliance. Apartment complexes are assigned one file number for the entire complex.

Conditions Affecting Service, Performance, and Costs

For clearance of fire code violations, Greensboro requires the violation to be cleared by witness of an inspector in person. With a backlog of inspections, this has meant some violations have not been cleared per the definition but may have been addressed.

Municipal Profile

Service Population	308,657
Land Area (Square Miles)	140.52
Persons per Square Mile	2,197

Service Profile

FTE Positions—Firefighters	527.0
FTE Positions—Other	57.0
Fire Stations	26
First-Line Fire Apparatus	
Pumpers	24
Aerial Trucks	0
Quints	11
Squads	0
Rescue	1
Other	0
Fire Department Responses	34,457
Responses for Fires	1,066
Structural Fires Reported	265
Inspections Completed for Maintenance, Construction, and Reinspections	10,230
Fire Code Violations Reported	18,199
Estimated Fire Loss (millions)	$7.76
Amount of Property Protected in Service Area (billions)	$29.8
Number of Fire Education Programs or Events	959

Full Cost Profile

Cost Breakdown by Percentage	
Personal Services	81.5%
Operating Costs	18.5%
Capital Costs	0.0%
TOTAL	100.0%

Cost Breakdown in Dollars	
Personal Services	$50,593,409
Operating Costs	$11,455,975
Capital Costs	$0
TOTAL	$62,049,384

Greensboro

Fire Services

Resource Measures

Fire Services Costs per Capita

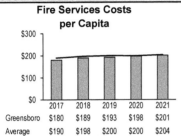

	2017	2018	2019	2020	2021
Greensboro	$180	$189	$193	$198	$201
Average	$190	$198	$200	$200	$204

Fire Services Total FTEs per 10,000 Population

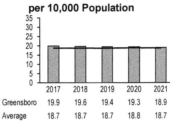

	2017	2018	2019	2020	2021
Greensboro	19.9	19.6	19.4	19.3	18.9
Average	18.7	18.7	18.7	18.8	18.7

Fire Services Cost per Thousand Dollars of Property Protected

	2017	2018	2019	2020	2021
Greensboro	$2.00	$2.00	$2.02	$2.05	$2.08
Average	$2.00	$1.98	$1.98	$1.83	$1.83

Workload Measures

Actual Fires per 1,000 Population

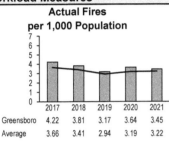

	2017	2018	2019	2020	2021
Greensboro	4.22	3.81	3.17	3.64	3.45
Average	3.66	3.41	2.94	3.19	3.22

Fire Department Responses per 1,000 Population

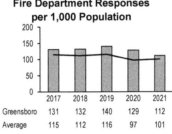

	2017	2018	2019	2020	2021
Greensboro	131	132	140	129	112
Average	115	112	116	97	101

Fire Inspections Completed per 1,000 Population

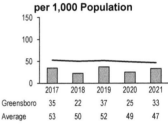

	2017	2018	2019	2020	2021
Greensboro	35	22	37	25	33
Average	53	50	52	49	47

Efficiency Measures

Fire Services Cost per Fire Department Response

	2017	2018	2019	2020	2021
Greensboro	$1,376	$1,438	$1,375	$1,535	$1,801
Average	$1,807	$1,951	$1,928	$2,219	$2,311

Inspections Completed per Inspector FTE

	2017	2018	2019	2020	2021
Greensboro	599	393	701	478	639
Average	1,067	985	998	1,017	994

Effectiveness Measures

Average Response Time to Priority One Calls in Minutes

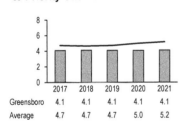

	2017	2018	2019	2020	2021
Greensboro	4.1	4.1	4.1	4.1	4.1
Average	4.7	4.7	4.7	5.0	5.2

Percentage of Fire Code Violations Cleared within 90 Days

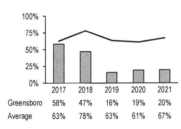

	2017	2018	2019	2020	2021
Greensboro	58%	47%	16%	19%	20%
Average	63%	78%	63%	61%	67%

Percentage of Fires Confined to Rooms or Objects Involved on Arrival

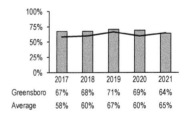

	2017	2018	2019	2020	2021
Greensboro	67%	68%	71%	69%	64%
Average	58%	60%	67%	60%	65%

Percentage of Fires for Which Cause Was Determined

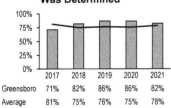

	2017	2018	2019	2020	2021
Greensboro	71%	82%	86%	86%	82%
Average	81%	75%	76%	75%	78%

Percentage of Full Response within 8 Minutes Travel Time

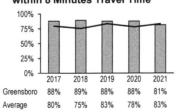

	2017	2018	2019	2020	2021
Greensboro	88%	89%	88%	88%	81%
Average	80%	75%	83%	78%	83%

Percentage of Lost Pulse Cases Recovered Pulse at Transfer of Care

	2017	2018	2019	2020	2021
Greensboro	34.8%	30.4%		23.7%	25.4%
Average	36.6%	37.1%	46.0%	33.3%	36.8%

Fiscal Year 2020-21

Service Level and Delivery

The primary goals of the Greenville Fire and Rescue Department are to prevent fires and save lives and property by providing emergency response services for fires or medical emergencies. The city provides fire services in areas beyond the city boundaries, covering thirty-two square miles.

Emergency personnel work a 24.25-hour shift, followed by 47.75 hours off.

The city has an ISO rating of 3, as rated in 2015. Greenville became an accredited department in 2019.

The fire department in Greenville conducted 3,287 fire maintenance, construction, and reinspections during the fiscal year. The Life Safety Services Division handles all inspection-related matters following the International Fire Code.

Conditions Affecting Service, Performance, and Costs

Greenville is the only city in the Benchmarking Project that has emergency medical services transports (EMS) provided through the city fire department. In the other jurisdictions, EMS transports are provided by county departments.

Complications with data tracking prevented Greenville from being able to submit numbers on fire incidents and several other measures for previous fiscal years.

No data were reported for FY 2019-20 for the city of Greenville.

Municipal Profile

Service Population	87,819
Land Area (Square Miles)	37.16
Persons per Square Mile	2,363

Service Profile

FTE Positions—Firefighters	144.0
FTE Positions—Other	20.0
Fire Stations	6
First-Line Fire Apparatus	
Pumpers	1
Aerial Trucks	1
Quints	4
Squads	0
Rescue	1
Other	2
Fire Department Responses	18,598
Responses for Fires	327
Structural Fires Reported	72
Inspections Completed for Maintenance, Construction, and Reinspections	3,287
Fire Code Violations Reported	4,147
Estimated Fire Loss (millions)	$1.77
Amount of Property Protected in Service Area (billions)	$7.5
Number of Fire Education Programs or Events	254

Full Cost Profile

Cost Breakdown by Percentage

Personal Services	64.9%
Operating Costs	20.1%
Capital Costs	15.0%
TOTAL	100.0%

Cost Breakdown in Dollars

Personal Services	$12,648,017
Operating Costs	$3,924,422
Capital Costs	$2,914,309
TOTAL	$19,486,748

Greenville

Fire Services

Resource Measures

Fire Services Costs per Capita

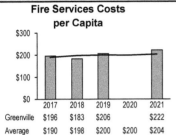

	2017	2018	2019	2020	2021
Greenville	$196	$183	$206		$222
Average	$190	$198	$200	$200	$204

Fire Services Total FTEs per 10,000 Population

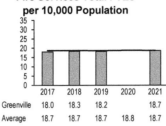

	2017	2018	2019	2020	2021
Greenville	18.0	18.3	18.2		18.7
Average	18.7	18.7	18.7	18.8	18.7

Fire Services Cost per Thousand Dollars of Property Protected

	2017	2018	2019	2020	2021
Greenville	$2.86	$2.46	$2.82		$2.60
Average	$2.00	$1.98	$1.98	$1.83	$1.83

Workload Measures

Actual Fires per 1,000 Population

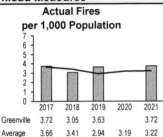

	2017	2018	2019	2020	2021
Greenville	3.72	3.05	3.63		3.72
Average	3.66	3.41	2.94	3.19	3.22

Fire Department Responses per 1,000 Population

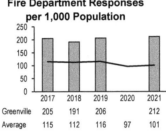

	2017	2018	2019	2020	2021
Greenville	205	191	206		212
Average	115	112	116	97	101

Fire Inspections Completed per 1,000 Population

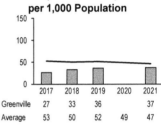

	2017	2018	2019	2020	2021
Greenville	27	33	36		37
Average	53	50	52	49	47

Efficiency Measures

Fire Services Cost per Fire Department Response

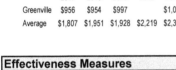

	2017	2018	2019	2020	2021
Greenville	$956	$954	$997		$1,048
Average	$1,807	$1,951	$1,928	$2,219	$2,311

Inspections Completed per Inspector FTE

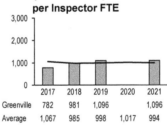

	2017	2018	2019	2020	2021
Greenville	782	981	1,096		1,096
Average	1,067	985	998	1,017	994

Effectiveness Measures

Average Response Time to Priority One Calls in Minutes

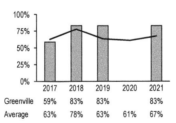

	2017	2018	2019	2020	2021
Greenville	5.8	6.0	5.9		5.9
Average	4.7	4.7	4.7	5.0	5.2

Percentage of Fire Code Violations Cleared within 90 Days

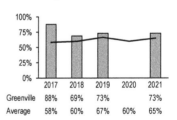

	2017	2018	2019	2020	2021
Greenville	59%	83%	83%		83%
Average	63%	78%	63%	61%	67%

Percentage of Fires Confined to Rooms or Objects Involved on Arrival

	2017	2018	2019	2020	2021
Greenville	88%	69%	73%		73%
Average	58%	60%	67%	60%	65%

Percentage of Fires for Which Cause Was Determined

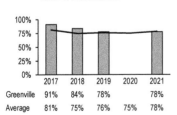

	2017	2018	2019	2020	2021
Greenville	91%	84%	78%		78%
Average	81%	75%	76%	75%	78%

Percentage of Full Response within 8 Minutes Travel Time

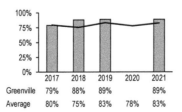

	2017	2018	2019	2020	2021
Greenville	79%	88%	89%		89%
Average	80%	75%	83%	78%	83%

Percentage of Lost Pulse Cases Recovered Pulse at Transfer of Care

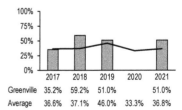

	2017	2018	2019	2020	2021
Greenville	35.2%	59.2%	51.0%		51.0%
Average	36.6%	37.1%	46.0%	33.3%	36.8%

Fiscal Year 2020-21

Explanatory Information

Service Level and Delivery

The goal of the Hickory Fire Department is to provide high-quality emergency services, education, and prevention that protect the community through professional coworkers focused on customer service, compassion, commitment, and innovation. The city provides fire coverage for an area of thirteen square miles beyond city boundaries.

The fire department contains the following divisions: administration, fire and life safety, training, maintenance, and fire suppression.

Fire suppression personnel work a twenty-four-hour shift with forty-eight hours off between shifts. The twenty-four-hour shift begins at 8 a.m.

The city has an ISO rating of 1, as rated in 2020. This is the highest rating possible.

The fire department in Hickory conducted 4,686 fire maintenance, construction, and reinspections during the fiscal year. Fire prevention inspectors are assigned Level I, Level II, and Level III inspections. They also review construction and fire protection plans and inspect the installation of fire protection systems. The inspectors also accompany building inspectors during certificate-of-ccupancy inspections and are responsible for conducting fire investigations, fire hydrant flow tests, occupancy and site visits, and other activities as assigned.

Conditions Affecting Service, Performance, and Costs

Hickory has a fire station staffed at the regional airport, in addition to the six community fire stations.

Municipal Profile

Service Population	48,776
Land Area (Square Miles)	43.42
Persons per Square Mile	1,123

Service Profile

FTE Positions—Firefighters	118.0
FTE Positions—Other	20.5
Fire Stations	7
First-Line Fire Apparatus	
Pumpers	6
Aerial Trucks	2
Quints	0
Squads	1
Rescue	1
Other	6
Fire Department Responses	4,577
Responses for Fires	224
Structural Fires Reported	49
Inspections Completed for Maintenance, Construction, and Reinspections	4,686
Fire Code Violations Reported	3,077
Estimated Fire Loss (millions)	$3.12
Amount of Property Protected in Service Area (billions)	$5.8
Number of Fire Education Programs or Events	159

Full Cost Profile

Cost Breakdown by Percentage	
Personal Services	77.0%
Operating Costs	18.0%
Capital Costs	5.0%
TOTAL	100.0%

Cost Breakdown in Dollars	
Personal Services	$9,496,935
Operating Costs	$2,214,178
Capital Costs	$618,320
TOTAL	$12,329,433

Hickory

Fire Services

Key: Hickory ▓   Benchmarking Average —   Fiscal Years 2017 through 2021

Resource Measures

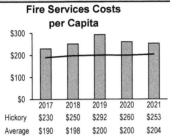

Fire Services Costs per Capita

	2017	2018	2019	2020	2021
Hickory	$230	$250	$292	$260	$253
Average	$190	$198	$200	$200	$204

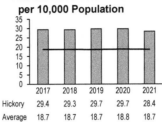

Fire Services Total FTEs per 10,000 Population

	2017	2018	2019	2020	2021
Hickory	29.4	29.3	29.7	29.7	28.4
Average	18.7	18.7	18.7	18.8	18.7

Fire Services Cost per Thousand Dollars of Property Protected

	2017	2018	2019	2020	2021
Hickory	$2.09	$2.22	$2.50	$2.13	$2.12
Average	$2.00	$1.98	$1.98	$1.83	$1.83

Workload Measures

Actual Fires per 1,000 Population

	2017	2018	2019	2020	2021
Hickory	4.61	4.22	3.95	4.66	4.59
Average	3.66	3.41	2.94	3.19	3.22

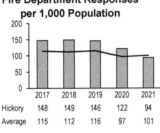

Fire Department Responses per 1,000 Population

	2017	2018	2019	2020	2021
Hickory	148	149	146	122	94
Average	115	112	116	97	101

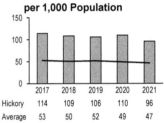

Fire Inspections Completed per 1,000 Population

	2017	2018	2019	2020	2021
Hickory	114	109	106	110	96
Average	53	50	52	49	47

Efficiency Measures

Fire Services Cost per Fire Department Response

	2017	2018	2019	2020	2021
Hickory	$1,555	$1,680	$1,998	$2,133	$2,694
Average	$1,807	$1,951	$1,928	$2,219	$2,311

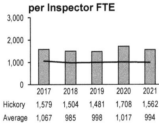

Inspections Completed per Inspector FTE

	2017	2018	2019	2020	2021
Hickory	1,579	1,504	1,481	1,708	1,562
Average	1,067	985	998	1,017	994

Effectiveness Measures

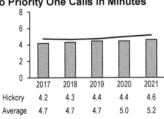

Average Response Time to Priority One Calls in Minutes

	2017	2018	2019	2020	2021
Hickory	4.2	4.3	4.4	4.4	4.6
Average	4.7	4.7	4.7	5.0	5.2

Percentage of Fire Code Violations Cleared within 90 Days

	2017	2018	2019	2020	2021
Hickory	100%	100%	100%		100%
Average	63%	78%	63%	61%	67%

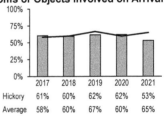

Percentage of Fires Confined to Rooms or Objects Involved on Arrival

	2017	2018	2019	2020	2021
Hickory	61%	60%	62%	62%	53%
Average	58%	60%	67%	60%	65%

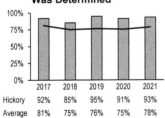

Percentage of Fires for Which Cause Was Determined

	2017	2018	2019	2020	2021
Hickory	92%	85%	95%	91%	93%
Average	81%	75%	76%	75%	78%

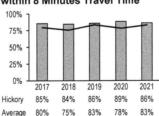

Percentage of Full Response within 8 Minutes Travel Time

	2017	2018	2019	2020	2021
Hickory	85%	84%	86%	89%	86%
Average	80%	75%	83%	78%	83%

Percentage of Lost Pulse Cases Recovered Pulse at Transfer of Care

	2017	2018	2019	2020	2021
Hickory				12.8%	
Average	36.6%	37.1%	46.0%	33.3%	36.8%

Fiscal Year 2020-21

Explanatory Information

Service Level and Delivery
The Raleigh Fire Department provides the following services in carrying out its mission: fire protection, emergency medical first response, extrication, confined space and high-angle rescue, hazardous materials response, fire inspections, and fire education.

The fire department is broken into five primary function areas. The Office of the Fire Chief provides administrative services and oversight; the Office of the Fire Marshal is the enforcement, educational, and informational arm of the department; the Operations Division responds to and manages incidents and special events; the Support Services Division supplies and maintains infrastructure, equipment, clothing, and apparatus; and the Training Division recruits, hires, trains, and manages career development.

The shift schedule for the fire department is a nine-day cycle as follows: five twenty-four-hour days alternating on and off followed by four days off.

The city received an ISO rating of 1 in 2016. This is the highest rating possible.

The fire department in Raleigh conducted 23,209 fire maintenance, construction, and reinspections during the fiscal year. Fire inspections are scheduled by the Office of the Fire Marshal through an automated process based on a priority basis and consistent with section 106 of the NC State Fire Code. Other inspections are scheduled as requested for special events, operational permits, and special requests. Apartment complexes are counted as one inspection per building, and high rises are considered as one inspection with one file.

Conditions Affecting Service, Performance, and Costs
Raleigh currently marks some violations as repaired but not yet completely resolved. This creates more open violations in the system while decisions are made about referrals or penalties before the violation can be cleared.

Municipal Profile

Service Population	468,977
Land Area (Square Miles)	146.47
Persons per Square Mile	3,202

Service Profile

FTE Positions—Firefighters	556.0
FTE Positions—Other	70.0
Fire Stations	28
First-Line Fire Apparatus	
Pumpers	27
Aerial Trucks	9
Quints	0
Squads	2
Rescue	1
Other	12
Fire Department Responses	43,979
Responses for Fires	1,028
Structural Fires Reported	296
Inspections Completed for Maintenance, Construction, and Reinspections	23,209
Fire Code Violations Reported	21,032
Estimated Fire Loss (millions)	$13.69
Amount of Property Protected in Service Area (billions)	$77.4
Number of Fire Education Programs or Events	121

Full Cost Profile

Cost Breakdown by Percentage	
Personal Services	75.1%
Operating Costs	16.3%
Capital Costs	8.6%
TOTAL	100.0%

Cost Breakdown in Dollars	
Personal Services	$58,096,072
Operating Costs	$12,581,317
Capital Costs	$6,631,835
TOTAL	$77,309,224

Raleigh

Fire Services

Key: Raleigh ▦   Benchmarking Average —   Fiscal Years 2017 through 2021

Resource Measures

Fire Services Costs per Capita

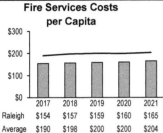

	2017	2018	2019	2020	2021
Raleigh	$154	$157	$159	$160	$165
Average	$190	$198	$200	$200	$204

Fire Services Total FTEs per 10,000 Population

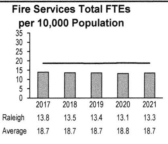

	2017	2018	2019	2020	2021
Raleigh	13.8	13.5	13.4	13.1	13.3
Average	18.7	18.7	18.7	18.8	18.7

Fire Services Cost per Thousand Dollars of Property Protected

	2017	2018	2019	2020	2021
Raleigh	$1.29	$1.22	$1.22	$1.23	$1.00
Average	$2.00	$1.98	$1.98	$1.83	$1.83

Workload Measures

Actual Fires per 1,000 Population

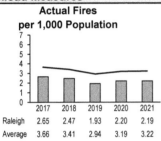

	2017	2018	2019	2020	2021
Raleigh	2.65	2.47	1.93	2.20	2.19
Average	3.66	3.41	2.94	3.19	3.22

Fire Department Responses per 1,000 Population

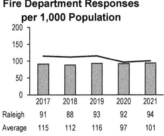

	2017	2018	2019	2020	2021
Raleigh	91	88	93	92	94
Average	115	112	116	97	101

Fire Inspections Completed per 1,000 Population

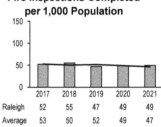

	2017	2018	2019	2020	2021
Raleigh	52	55	47	49	49
Average	53	50	52	49	47

Efficiency Measures

Fire Services Cost per Fire Department Response

	2017	2018	2019	2020	2021
Raleigh	$1,689	$1,779	$1,711	$1,738	$1,758
Average	$1,807	$1,951	$1,928	$2,219	$2,311

Inspections Completed per Inspector FTE

	2017	2018	2019	2020	2021
Raleigh	801	867	871	930	893
Average	1,067	985	998	1,017	994

Effectiveness Measures

Average Response Time to Priority One Calls in Minutes

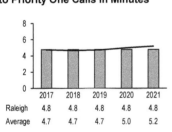

	2017	2018	2019	2020	2021
Raleigh	4.8	4.8	4.8	4.8	4.8
Average	4.7	4.7	4.7	5.0	5.2

Percentage of Fire Code Violations Cleared within 90 Days

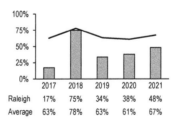

	2017	2018	2019	2020	2021
Raleigh	17%	75%	34%	38%	48%
Average	63%	78%	63%	61%	67%

Percentage of Fires Confined to Rooms or Objects Involved on Arrival

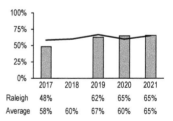

	2017	2018	2019	2020	2021
Raleigh	48%		62%	65%	65%
Average	58%	60%	67%	60%	65%

Percentage of Fires for Which Cause Was Determined

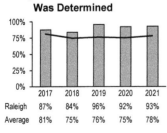

	2017	2018	2019	2020	2021
Raleigh	87%	84%	96%	92%	93%
Average	81%	75%	76%	75%	78%

Percentage of Full Response within 8 Minutes Travel Time

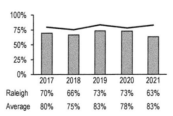

	2017	2018	2019	2020	2021
Raleigh	70%	66%	73%	73%	63%
Average	80%	75%	83%	78%	83%

Percentage of Lost Pulse Cases Recovered Pulse at Transfer of Care

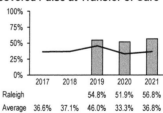

	2017	2018	2019	2020	2021
Raleigh			54.8%	51.9%	56.8%
Average	36.6%	37.1%	46.0%	33.3%	36.8%

Wilson

Fire Services

Fiscal Year 2020-21

Explanatory Information

Service Level and Delivery

Wilson Fire/Rescue Services is a public-safety organization whose mission is to assist the public in the protection of life and property by minimizing the impact of fire, medical emergencies, and potential disasters or events that affect the community and the environment.

Wilson Fire/Rescue Services has two major divisions. Operations handles emergency responses and equipment maintenance. Support Services handles fire prevention and education, facility maintenance, IM/GIS, and budget.

Firefighters work twenty-four hours on and twenty-four hours off. Each work cycle consists of three twenty-four-hour shifts, with a day off between shifts. A four-day break is then provided before the cycle repeats itself.

The city has an ISO rating of 1, as rated in 2018. This is the highest rating that can be achieved. The Wilson Fire Department has been accredited since 2002.

The fire department in Wilson conducted 4,042 fire maintenance, construction, and reinspections during the fiscal year. Fire inspections are conducted by the Fire Prevention Bureau on a daily basis. Each inspector is assigned a district in which he or she handles all inspections. A charge is made on the third reinspection.

Conditions Affecting Service, Performance, and Costs

Municipal Profile

Service Population	47,769
Land Area (Square Miles)	31.02
Persons per Square Mile	1,540

Service Profile

FTE Positions—Firefighters	85.0
FTE Positions—Other	15.0
Fire Stations	5
First-Line Fire Apparatus	
Pumpers	4
Aerial Trucks	1
Quints	1
Squads	0
Rescue	0
Other	0
Fire Department Responses	3,812
Responses for Fires	235
Structural Fires Reported	64
Inspections Completed for Maintenance, Construction, and Reinspections	3,674
Fire Code Violations Reported	4,042
Estimated Fire Loss (millions)	$1.02
Amount of Property Protected in Service Area (billions)	$4.3
Number of Fire Education Programs or Events	18

Full Cost Profile

Cost Breakdown by Percentage

Personal Services	74.5%
Operating Costs	18.4%
Capital Costs	7.1%
TOTAL	100.0%

Cost Breakdown in Dollars

Personal Services	$8,583,263
Operating Costs	$2,123,815
Capital Costs	$816,672
TOTAL	$11,523,750

Wilson

Fire Services

Resource Measures

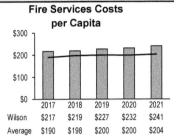

Fire Services Costs per Capita

	2017	2018	2019	2020	2021
Wilson	$217	$219	$227	$232	$241
Average	$190	$198	$200	$200	$204

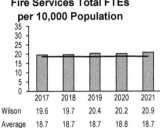

Fire Services Total FTEs per 10,000 Population

	2017	2018	2019	2020	2021
Wilson	19.6	19.7	20.4	20.2	20.9
Average	18.7	18.7	18.7	18.8	18.7

Fire Services Cost per Thousand Dollars of Property Protected

	2017	2018	2019	2020	2021
Wilson	$2.51	$2.66	$2.70	$2.71	$2.65
Average	$2.00	$1.98	$1.98	$1.83	$1.83

Workload Measures

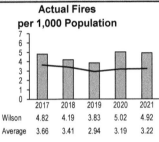

Actual Fires per 1,000 Population

	2017	2018	2019	2020	2021
Wilson	4.82	4.19	3.83	5.02	4.92
Average	3.66	3.41	2.94	3.19	3.22

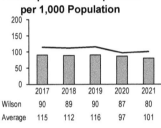

Fire Department Responses per 1,000 Population

	2017	2018	2019	2020	2021
Wilson	90	89	90	87	80
Average	115	112	116	97	101

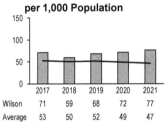

Fire Inspections Completed per 1,000 Population

	2017	2018	2019	2020	2021
Wilson	71	59	68	72	77
Average	53	50	52	49	47

Efficiency Measures

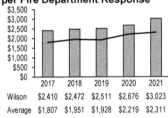

Fire Services Cost per Fire Department Response

	2017	2018	2019	2020	2021
Wilson	$2,410	$2,472	$2,511	$2,676	$3,023
Average	$1,807	$1,951	$1,928	$2,219	$2,311

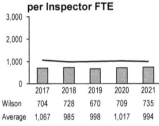

Inspections Completed per Inspector FTE

	2017	2018	2019	2020	2021
Wilson	704	728	670	709	735
Average	1,067	985	998	1,017	994

Effectiveness Measures

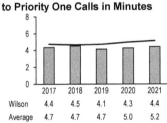

Average Response Time to Priority One Calls in Minutes

	2017	2018	2019	2020	2021
Wilson	4.4	4.5	4.1	4.3	4.4
Average	4.7	4.7	4.7	5.0	5.2

Percentage of Fire Code Violations Cleared within 90 Days

	2017	2018	2019	2020	2021
Wilson	56%	36%	24%	58%	56%
Average	63%	78%	63%	61%	67%

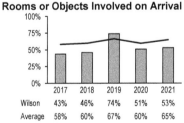

Percentage of Fires Confined to Rooms or Objects Involved on Arrival

	2017	2018	2019	2020	2021
Wilson	43%	46%	74%	51%	53%
Average	58%	60%	67%	60%	65%

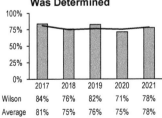

Percentage of Fires for Which Cause Was Determined

	2017	2018	2019	2020	2021
Wilson	84%	76%	82%	71%	78%
Average	81%	75%	76%	75%	78%

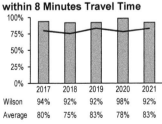

Percentage of Full Response within 8 Minutes Travel Time

	2017	2018	2019	2020	2021
Wilson	94%	92%	92%	98%	92%
Average	80%	75%	83%	78%	83%

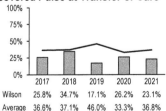

Percentage of Lost Pulse Cases Recovered Pulse at Transfer of Care

	2017	2018	2019	2020	2021
Wilson	25.8%	34.7%	17.1%	26.2%	23.1%
Average	36.6%	37.1%	46.0%	33.3%	36.8%

Fiscal Year 2020-21

Explanatory Information

Service Level and Delivery

The mission of the Winston-Salem Fire Department is to protect the lives and property of all people within Winston-Salem by reducing the occurrence and minimizing the effects of fires.

The Winston-Salem Fire Department contains the following six divisions: fire suppression, vehicle maintenance, planning, community education, fire prevention, and administration.

Fire suppression personnel work a twenty-one-day cycle, with an average of fifty-six hours per week.

The city has an ISO rating of 2, as rated in 2020.

The fire department in Winston-Salem conducted 4,421 fire maintenance, construction, and reinspections during the fiscal year. The fire department inspection program includes inspections that (1) ensure reasonable life safety conditions within a structure, (2) identify fire hazards, and (3) determine the proper installation, operation, and maintenance of fire protection features, systems, and appliances within buildings. The fire department inspection program involves both the Fire Prevention Bureau and the fire engine companies. Similar to the Fire Prevention Bureau, all fire stations have inspection responsibilities and conduct building inspections within their assigned territories. Each business within the city limits is inspected annually and receives as many return visits as necessary for fire code compliance.

Conditions Affecting Service, Performance, and Costs

Winston-Salem has a high number of inspections per inspector full-time equivalent (FTE) when compared to the other jurisdictions due to the fact that many inspections are performed by fire company personnel. The city defines an inspection as a site interior and/or exterior survey of a building, operation, event, condition, and/or activity for the purpose of verifying fire and building code compliance.

Municipal Profile

Service Population	249,986
Land Area (Square Miles)	132.59
Persons per Square Mile	1,885

Service Profile

FTE Positions—Firefighters	336.0
FTE Positions—Other	32.0
Fire Stations	19
First-Line Fire Apparatus	
Pumpers	18
Aerial Trucks	5
Quints	0
Squads	0
Rescue	1
Other	9
Fire Department Responses	16,801
Responses for Fires	738
Structural Fires Reported	200
Inspections Completed for Maintenance, Construction, and Reinspections	4,421
Fire Code Violations Reported	5,899
Estimated Fire Loss (millions)	$5.47
Amount of Property Protected in Service Area (billions)	$23.3
Number of Fire Education Programs or Events	7800

Full Cost Profile

Cost Breakdown by Percentage

Personal Services	78.1%
Operating Costs	14.3%
Capital Costs	7.5%
TOTAL	100.0%

Cost Breakdown in Dollars

Personal Services	$30,172,602
Operating Costs	$5,529,621
Capital Costs	$2,911,458
TOTAL	$38,613,681

Resource Measures

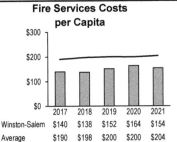

Fire Services Costs per Capita

	2017	2018	2019	2020	2021
Winston-Salem	$140	$138	$152	$164	$154
Average	$190	$198	$200	$200	$204

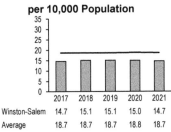

Fire Services Total FTEs per 10,000 Population

	2017	2018	2019	2020	2021
Winston-Salem	14.7	15.1	15.1	15.0	14.7
Average	18.7	18.7	18.7	18.8	18.7

Fire Services Cost per Thousand Dollars of Property Protected

	2017	2018	2019	2020	2021
Winston-Salem	$1.65	$1.53	$1.65	$1.75	$1.66
Average	$2.00	$1.98	$1.98	$1.83	$1.83

Workload Measures

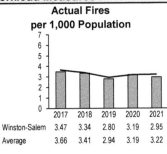

Actual Fires per 1,000 Population

	2017	2018	2019	2020	2021
Winston-Salem	3.47	3.34	2.80	3.19	2.95
Average	3.66	3.41	2.94	3.19	3.22

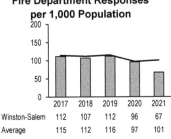

Fire Department Responses per 1,000 Population

	2017	2018	2019	2020	2021
Winston-Salem	112	107	112	96	67
Average	115	112	116	97	101

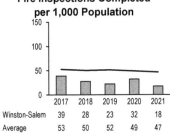

Fire Inspections Completed per 1,000 Population

	2017	2018	2019	2020	2021
Winston-Salem	39	28	23	32	18
Average	53	50	52	49	47

Efficiency Measures

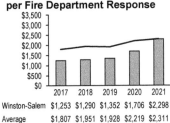

Fire Services Cost per Fire Department Response

	2017	2018	2019	2020	2021
Winston-Salem	$1,253	$1,290	$1,352	$1,706	$2,298
Average	$1,807	$1,951	$1,928	$2,219	$2,311

Inspections Completed per Inspector FTE

	2017	2018	2019	2020	2021
Winston-Salem	2,331	1,688	1,370	1,973	1,105
Average	1,067	985	998	1,017	994

Effectiveness Measures

Average Response Time to Priority One Calls in Minutes

	2017	2018	2019	2020	2021
Winston-Salem	4.7	4.8	4.9	5.5	5.5
Average	4.7	4.7	4.7	5.0	5.2

Percentage of Fire Code Violations Cleared within 90 Days

	2017	2018	2019	2020	2021
Winston-Salem	83%	89%	83%	81%	68%
Average	63%	78%	63%	61%	67%

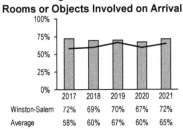

Percentage of Fires Confined to Rooms or Objects Involved on Arrival

	2017	2018	2019	2020	2021
Winston-Salem	72%	69%	70%	67%	72%
Average	58%	60%	67%	60%	65%

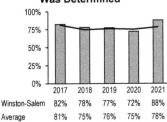

Percentage of Fires for Which Cause Was Determined

	2017	2018	2019	2020	2021
Winston-Salem	82%	78%	77%	72%	88%
Average	81%	75%	76%	75%	78%

Percentage of Full Response within 8 Minutes Travel Time

	2017	2018	2019	2020	2021
Winston-Salem	57%	62%	56%	68%	83%
Average	80%	75%	83%	78%	83%

Percentage of Lost Pulse Cases Recovered Pulse at Transfer of Care

	2017	2018	2019	2020	2021
Winston-Salem	37.7%	27.5%	65.1%	22.5%	14.5%
Average	36.6%	37.1%	46.0%	33.3%	36.8%

Performance and Cost Data

BUILDING INSPECTIONS

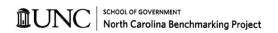

PERFORMANCE MEASURES FOR BUILDING INSPECTIONS

SERVICE DEFINITION

Building Inspections refer to permit issuance and inspections for building, electrical, mechanical (including heating and cooling), and plumbing work on new residential and commercial construction or additions and alterations to enforce the North Carolina State Building Code and related local building regulations. The inspection process includes the receipt of permit applications, review of plans and specifications, issuance of permits, and follow-up field inspections to ensure compliance. Excluded are the enforcement of zoning and subdivision regulations, fire codes, minimum housing codes, erosion and sedimentation control regulations, watershed regulations, historic preservation ordinances, and other development regulations or plans.

NOTES ON PERFORMANCE MEASURES

1. Building Inspections per 1,000 Population

Building inspections are those required by the North Carolina State Building Code for general building, electrical, mechanical (including heating and cooling), and plumbing work associated with construction projects. Inspections include reinspections. They do not include non-building code inspections or consultation visits.

2. Value of Total Building Permits as Percentage of Tax Base of Area Served

When a building permit is issued, the dollar amount of the work specified in the contract(s) authorizing the work is recorded as the value of the building permit. Tax base refers to the taxable valuation used for levying the fiscal year property tax for the area served.

3. Value of Commercial Permits as Percentage of Tax Base of Area Served

Commercial building permits are issued for construction of business, manufacturing, institutional, and other nonresidential buildings or improvements. Tax base as defined above.

4. Cost per Building Inspection and Inspections per Day per Inspector

Building inspections are defined above. Cost is determined using the project's full cost accounting model, including direct, indirect, and capital costs. An inspector full-time equivalent (FTE) is calculated using a work year of 235 days. Inspector FTEs include permanent, temporary, part-time, and full-time inspectors.

5. Value of Building Permits per FTE

Value of building permits as defined above. Inspectors must be certified by the state to enforce the state building code and be able to review plans and conduct inspections to enforce that code. Inspector FTEs exclude supervisors, who may be certified but who spend less than 50 percent of their time performing inspections. Inspector FTEs also exclude support personnel who are not certified.

6. Number of Plan Reviews per Reviewer FTE

The state building code requires that plans and specifications for most commercial and residential construction be reviewed before permits are issued for such construction. Reviewer FTEs are calculated using a 2,080-hour work year, the actual number of plan reviews conducted during the fiscal year, and the number of plan reviewers.

7. Percentage of Inspection Responses within One Working Day of Request

A request for inspection may be made by phone, in person, or in writing. A response refers to at least beginning an inspection, regardless of whether approval of the work occurs. The majority of inspections are completed the same day as initiated. A response to a request within one working day means that the inspection is initiated before the end of the workday following the day on which the request is made.

8. Percentage of Inspections That Are Reinspections

A reinspection occurs when a building inspector must inspect work that has previously been inspected. A reinspection can occur due to problems found in the original inspection or for other reasons.

Building Inspections

Summary of Key Dimensions of Service

City or Town	Area Served (in Square Miles)	Population Growth from 2010 to 2020	Building Inspections by Trade					Number of Plan Reviewers	Building Inspector FTEs	Total Staff FTEs
			Building	Electrical	Mechanical	Plumbing	Total			
Apex	37.6	57.5%	18,756	9,829	6,899	9,190	44,674	4.0	12.0	23.0
Chapel Hill	27.5	8.3%	2,382	2,134	2,216	1,258	7,990	2.0	6.0	15.0
Goldsboro	57.6	-4.2%	1,554	2,149	1,593	970	6,266	1.0	3.0	7.0
Greensboro	134.6	11.2%	19,724	17,616	15,338	11,936	64,614	4.5	16.0	30.5
Greenville	61.8	2.8%	4,810	4,564	4,898	2,831	17,103	1.0	4.0	9.0
Raleigh	181.5	15.5%	25,234	35,721	24,433	17,088	102,476	16.0	43.0	81.0
Wilson	58.5	-2.9%	2,580	2,564	1,973	1,265	8,382	1.0	3.8	7.5
Winston-Salem	396.0	8.8%	16,378	23,238	18,280	13,725	71,621	3.0	18.0	39.0

* Total Inspections for Chapel Hill includes 347 that did not fit into the four major categories.

EXPLANATORY FACTORS
These are factors that the project found affected building inspection performance and cost in one or more of the municipalities:

Rate of growth and development in city
Size and complexity of construction projects
Geographic area served by county building inspections
Inspectors' enforcement of local development regulations
Emphasis given to plan review in each jurisdiction
Inspector specialization
Organization of the building inspection function

Apex

Building Inspections

Fiscal Year 2020-21

Explanatory Information

Service Level and Delivery

The Town of Apex provides building inspection services through the Building Inspections and Permits Department. The department is organized into two major divisions: building inspections and engineering. The department provides inspections for all of Apex and just under thirteen square miles of area in its extraterritorial jurisdiction (ETJ).

All building inspectors in Apex serve each of the major trades. The department enforces the North Carolina State Building Code.

The department has a goal of having all inspectors fully qualified for the technical, administrative, and customer service aspects of their job. Training is accomplished primarily by off-site seminars and conferences offered by state-approved sponsors.

Apex has a standard that all inspection requests recorded by a permit technician or the permit office voicemail by 3 a.m. are to be performed on the next business day. Due to high workload during the latter part of the fiscal year, the city was not able to always meet this standard of service.

Total revenue received from inspection fees amounted to $2,838,149 for the fiscal year.

Conditions Affecting Service, Performance, and Costs

The population served is calculated by adding the population of Apex with the population of the ETJ. The tax base served is calculated by adding the tax base of Apex with the tax base of the ETJ. The population and the tax base of the ETJ are calculated by taking the population and tax base per square mile of Wake County and multiplying them by the square miles of the ETJ.

Apex does not track multifamily as a category of reporting for inspections or plan reviews. Instead, townhomes are included with residential, and condos and apartments are included with commercial.

While Apex has the goal of providing next-day service for building inspections, the large volume of work in the strong-growth community has made this goal difficult to achieve at all times.

Municipal Profile

Population Served	76,678
Land Area Inspected (Square Miles)	37.56
Persons per Square Mile	2,041
Estimated Tax Base in Service Area (billions)	$13.24

Service Profile

FTE Inspectors	
Building	0.0
Electrical	0.0
Mechanical	0.0
Plumbing	0.0
All Trades	12.0
Total Inspectors	12.0
FTE Plan Reviewers	4.0
Other FTE Positions	7.0
Total of All Positions	23.0
Number of Inspections by Type	
Building	18,756
Electrical	9,829
Mechanical	6,899
Plumbing	9,190
TOTAL	44,674
Building Permit Values	
Residential	$312,800,446
Multifamily	included with residential
Commercial	$16,968,128
TOTAL	$329,768,574
Inspection Fee Revenue	$2,838,149

Full Cost Profile

Cost Breakdown by Percentage	
Personal Services	72.0%
Operating Costs	21.6%
Capital Costs	6.4%
TOTAL	100.0%
Cost Breakdown in Dollars	
Personal Services	$2,187,300
Operating Costs	$657,640
Capital Costs	$193,457
TOTAL	$3,038,397

Resource Measures

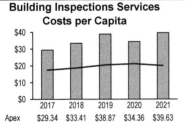

Building Inspections Services Costs per Capita

	2017	2018	2019	2020	2021
Apex	$29.34	$33.41	$38.87	$34.36	$39.63
Average	$17.56	$18.69	$20.51	$21.21	$20.11

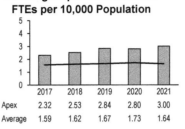

Building Inspections Services FTEs per 10,000 Population

	2017	2018	2019	2020	2021
Apex	2.32	2.53	2.84	2.80	3.00
Average	1.59	1.62	1.67	1.73	1.64

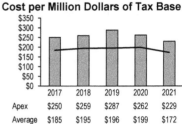

Building Inspections Services Cost per Million Dollars of Tax Base

	2017	2018	2019	2020	2021
Apex	$250	$259	$287	$262	$229
Average	$185	$195	$196	$199	$172

Workload Measures

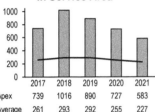

Inspections per 1,000 Population in Service Area

	2017	2018	2019	2020	2021
Apex	739	1016	890	727	583
Average	261	293	292	255	227

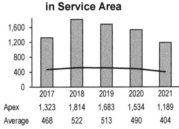

Inspections per Square Mile in Service Area

	2017	2018	2019	2020	2021
Apex	1,323	1,814	1,683	1,534	1,189
Average	468	522	513	490	404

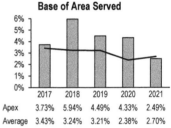

Value of Building Permits as Percentage of Tax Base of Area Served

	2017	2018	2019	2020	2021
Apex	3.73%	5.94%	4.49%	4.33%	2.49%
Average	3.43%	3.24%	3.21%	2.38%	2.70%

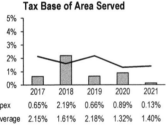

Value of Commercial Permits as Percentage of Tax Base of Area Served

	2017	2018	2019	2020	2021
Apex	0.65%	2.19%	0.66%	0.89%	0.13%
Average	2.15%	1.61%	2.18%	1.32%	1.40%

Value of Building Permits per Inspector FTE in Millions of Dollars

	2017	2018	2019	2020	2021
Apex	$40.6	$57.4	$38.9	$37.3	$27.5
Average	$41.3	$38.4	$37.9	$29.3	$42.5

Efficiency Measures

Building Services Cost per Inspection—All Types

	2017	2018	2019	2020	2021
Apex	$39.71	$32.89	$43.69	$47.25	$68.01
Average	$80.63	$85.51	$90.43	$104.76	$104.66

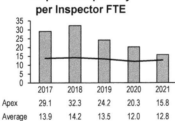

Inspections per Day per Inspector FTE

	2017	2018	2019	2020	2021
Apex	29.1	32.3	24.2	20.3	15.8
Average	13.9	14.2	13.5	12.0	12.8

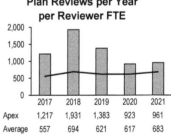

Plan Reviews per Year per Reviewer FTE

	2017	2018	2019	2020	2021
Apex	1,217	1,931	1,383	923	961
Average	557	694	621	617	683

Effectiveness Measures

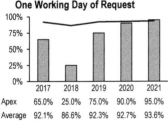

Percentage of Inspection Responses within One Working Day of Request

	2017	2018	2019	2020	2021
Apex	65.0%	25.0%	75.0%	90.0%	95.0%
Average	92.1%	86.6%	92.3%	92.7%	93.6%

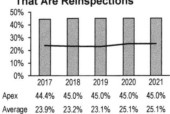

Percentage of Inspections That Are Reinspections

	2017	2018	2019	2020	2021
Apex	44.4%	45.0%	45.0%	45.0%	45.0%
Average	23.9%	23.2%	23.1%	25.1%	25.1%

Fiscal Year 2020-21

Explanatory Information

Service Level and Delivery

The Town of Chapel Hill provides building inspection services within its corporate limits and extra-territorial jurisdiction (ETJ) through its Permits and Inspections Division within the Office of Community Safety. The division is a full-service entity, meeting all requirements mandated by the North Carolina General Statutes.

Inspectors have a main discipline in one of the building trades and usually perform Level 3 inspections, plus they perform inspections in other disciplines when needed. On occasion retired part-time inspectors are brought in to help with overloads and the need for plan review in field inspections.

Total revenue received from inspection fees amounted to $2.05 million for the fiscal year. The fee schedule separates fees for each type of permit, with specific fees depending on a minimum amount, square footage, and other factors. There is a fee for reinspections.

Conditions Affecting Service, Performance, and Costs

Although data for the earlier years are not shown here, Chapel Hill has noted an uptick in permits and construction over prior years. There has particularly been an increase in larger and more complex projects requiring staff attention.

The population served is calculated by adding the population of Chapel Hill with the population of the ETJ. The tax base served is calculated by adding the tax base of Chapel Hill with the tax base of the ETJ. The population and the tax base of the ETJ are calculated by taking the population and tax base per square mile of Orange County and multiplying them by the square miles of the ETJ.

Municipal Profile	
Population Served	64,391
Land Area Inspected (Square Miles)	27.50
Persons per Square Mile	2,341
Estimated Tax Base in Service Area (billions)	$8.74

Service Profile	
FTE Inspectors	
Building	0.0
Electrical	0.0
Mechanical	0.0
Plumbing	0.0
All Trades	6.0
Total Inspectors	6.0
FTE Plan Reviewers	2.0
Other FTE Positions	7.0
Total of All Positions	15.0
Number of Inspections by Type	
Building	2,382
Electrical	2,134
Mechanical	2,216
Plumbing	1,258
TOTAL	7,990
Building Permit Values	
Residential	$149,265,076
Multifamily	included with commercial
Commercial	$77,254,203
TOTAL	$226,519,279
Inspection Fee Revenue	$2,046,768

Full Cost Profile	
Cost Breakdown by Percentage	
Personal Services	69.3%
Operating Costs	27.5%
Capital Costs	3.2%
TOTAL	100.0%
Cost Breakdown in Dollars	
Personal Services	$1,681,704
Operating Costs	$667,446
Capital Costs	$78,786
TOTAL	$2,427,936

Key: Chapel Hill ▨   Benchmarking Average —   Fiscal Years 2017 through 2021

Resource Measures

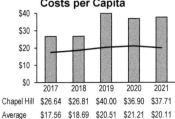

Building Inspections Services Costs per Capita

	2017	2018	2019	2020	2021
Chapel Hill	$26.64	$26.81	$40.00	$36.90	$37.71
Average	$17.56	$18.69	$20.51	$21.21	$20.11

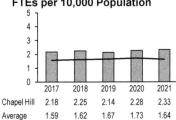

Building Inspections Services FTEs per 10,000 Population

	2017	2018	2019	2020	2021
Chapel Hill	2.18	2.25	2.14	2.28	2.33
Average	1.59	1.62	1.67	1.73	1.64

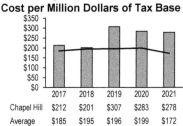

Building Inspections Services Cost per Million Dollars of Tax Base

	2017	2018	2019	2020	2021
Chapel Hill	$212	$201	$307	$283	$278
Average	$185	$195	$196	$199	$172

Workload Measures

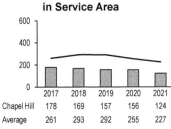

Inspections per 1,000 Population in Service Area

	2017	2018	2019	2020	2021
Chapel Hill	178	169	157	156	124
Average	261	293	292	255	227

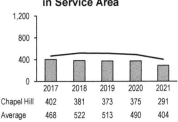

Inspections per Square Mile in Service Area

	2017	2018	2019	2020	2021
Chapel Hill	402	381	373	375	291
Average	468	522	513	490	404

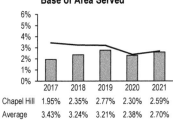

Value of Building Permits as Percentage of Tax Base of Area Served

	2017	2018	2019	2020	2021
Chapel Hill	1.95%	2.35%	2.77%	2.30%	2.59%
Average	3.43%	3.24%	3.21%	2.38%	2.70%

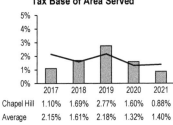

Value of Commercial Permits as Percentage of Tax Base of Area Served

	2017	2018	2019	2020	2021
Chapel Hill	1.10%	1.69%	2.77%	1.60%	0.88%
Average	2.15%	1.61%	2.18%	1.32%	1.40%

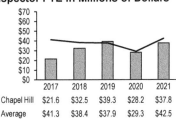

Value of Building Permits per Inspector FTE in Millions of Dollars

	2017	2018	2019	2020	2021
Chapel Hill	$21.6	$32.5	$39.3	$28.2	$37.8
Average	$41.3	$38.4	$37.9	$29.3	$42.5

Efficiency Measures

Building Services Cost per Inspection—All Types

	2017	2018	2019	2020	2021
Chapel Hill	$149.46	$158.76	$255.09	$236.09	$303.87
Average	$80.63	$85.51	$90.43	$104.76	$104.66

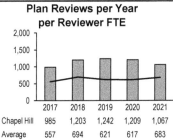

Inspections per Day per Inspector FTE

	2017	2018	2019	2020	2021
Chapel Hill	6.7	7.4	7.3	6.3	5.7
Average	13.9	14.2	13.5	12.0	12.8

Plan Reviews per Year per Reviewer FTE

	2017	2018	2019	2020	2021
Chapel Hill	985	1,203	1,242	1,209	1,067
Average	557	694	621	617	683

Effectiveness Measures

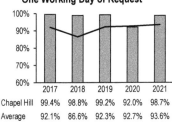

Percentage of Inspection Responses within One Working Day of Request

	2017	2018	2019	2020	2021
Chapel Hill	99.4%	98.8%	99.2%	92.0%	98.7%
Average	92.1%	86.6%	92.3%	92.7%	93.6%

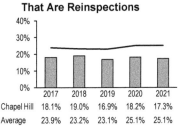

Percentage of Inspections That Are Reinspections

	2017	2018	2019	2020	2021
Chapel Hill	18.1%	19.0%	16.9%	18.2%	17.3%
Average	23.9%	23.2%	23.1%	25.1%	25.1%

Explanatory Information

Service Level and Delivery

Goldsboro Inspections is a separate department that operates independently of the Wayne County inspections function. Goldsboro performs all residential and commercial inspections within the city limits and the extraterritorial jurisdiction areas. The department performs single-phase inspections for commercial and residential properties.

Inspectors for the city are trade-specific. Inspectors are required to take at least six hours of trade specific training each year in addition to thirty hours of state-mandated training.

All requests for inspections have a goal of a response within twenty-four hours. Reinspections are charged $75 for the first time and $125 for each subsequent time.

Conditions Affecting Service, Performance, and Costs

The City of Goldsboro joined the Benchmarking Project in July 2017, with the first year of data showing for FY 2016–17.

Goldsboro combines residential and multifamily when reporting the dollar value of permits.

The City of Goldsboro had a noticeably higher level of residential and building permits for FY 2016–17 due to recovery work following Hurricane Matthew in October 2016.

Municipal Profile

Population Served	40,270
Land Area Inspected (Square Miles)	57.55
Persons per Square Mile	700
Estimated Tax Base in Service Area (billions)	$3.04

Service Profile

FTE Inspectors	
Building	0.0
Electrical	1.0
Mechanical	1.0
Plumbing	1.0
All Trades	0.0
Total Inspectors	3.0
FTE Plan Reviewers	1.0
Other FTE Positions	3.0
Total of All Positions	7.0
Number of Inspections by Type	
Building	1,554
Electrical	2,149
Mechanical	1,593
Plumbing	970
TOTAL	6,266
Building Permit Values	
Residential	$17,600,000
Multifamily	included with residential
Commercial	$65,200,000
TOTAL	$82,800,000
Inspection Fee Revenue	$430,475

Full Cost Profile

Cost Breakdown by Percentage	
Personal Services	94.4%
Operating Costs	5.6%
Capital Costs	0.0%
TOTAL	100.0%
Cost Breakdown in Dollars	
Personal Services	$528,465
Operating Costs	$31,363
Capital Costs	$0
TOTAL	$559,828

Goldsboro

Building Inspections

Key: Goldsboro ▦   Benchmarking Average —   Fiscal Years 2017 through 2021

Resource Measures

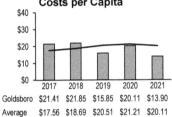

Building Inspections Services Costs per Capita

	2017	2018	2019	2020	2021
Goldsboro	$21.41	$21.85	$15.85	$20.11	$13.90
Average	$17.56	$18.69	$20.51	$21.21	$20.11

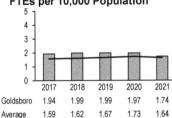

Building Inspections Services FTEs per 10,000 Population

	2017	2018	2019	2020	2021
Goldsboro	1.94	1.99	1.99	1.97	1.74
Average	1.59	1.62	1.67	1.73	1.64

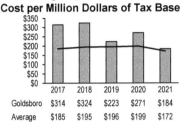

Building Inspections Services Cost per Million Dollars of Tax Base

	2017	2018	2019	2020	2021
Goldsboro	$314	$324	$223	$271	$184
Average	$185	$195	$196	$199	$172

Workload Measures

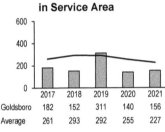

Inspections per 1,000 Population in Service Area

	2017	2018	2019	2020	2021
Goldsboro	182	152	311	140	156
Average	261	293	292	255	227

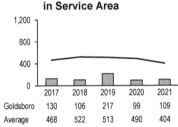

Inspections per Square Mile in Service Area

	2017	2018	2019	2020	2021
Goldsboro	130	106	217	99	109
Average	468	522	513	490	404

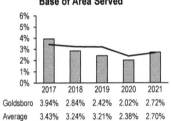

Value of Building Permits as Percentage of Tax Base of Area Served

	2017	2018	2019	2020	2021
Goldsboro	3.94%	2.84%	2.42%	2.02%	2.72%
Average	3.43%	3.24%	3.21%	2.38%	2.70%

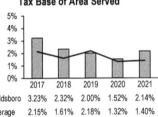

Value of Commercial Permits as Percentage of Tax Base of Area Served

	2017	2018	2019	2020	2021
Goldsboro	3.23%	2.32%	2.00%	1.52%	2.14%
Average	2.15%	1.61%	2.18%	1.32%	1.40%

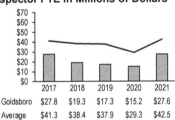

Value of Building Permits per Inspector FTE in Millions of Dollars

	2017	2018	2019	2020	2021
Goldsboro	$27.8	$19.3	$17.3	$15.2	$27.6
Average	$41.3	$38.4	$37.9	$29.3	$42.5

Efficiency Measures

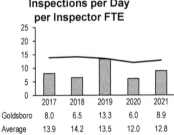

Building Services Cost per Inspection—All Types

	2017	2018	2019	2020	2021
Goldsboro	$117.66	$144.20	$50.92	$143.50	$89.34
Average	$80.63	$85.51	$90.43	$104.76	$104.66

Inspections per Day per Inspector FTE

	2017	2018	2019	2020	2021
Goldsboro	8.0	6.5	13.3	6.0	8.9
Average	13.9	14.2	13.5	12.0	12.8

Plan Reviews per Year per Reviewer FTE

	2017	2018	2019	2020	2021
Goldsboro	249	249	266	306	274
Average	557	694	621	617	683

Effectiveness Measures

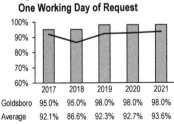

Percentage of Inspection Responses within One Working Day of Request

	2017	2018	2019	2020	2021
Goldsboro	95.0%	95.0%	98.0%	98.0%	98.0%
Average	92.1%	86.6%	92.3%	92.7%	93.6%

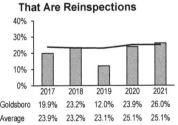

Percentage of Inspections That Are Reinspections

	2017	2018	2019	2020	2021
Goldsboro	19.9%	23.2%	12.0%	23.9%	26.0%
Average	23.9%	23.2%	23.1%	25.1%	25.1%

Explanatory Information

Service Level and Delivery

Inspections is a division of the Engineering and Inspections Department of the City of Greensboro. The inspections division consists of plans review, building inspections, plumbing inspections, mechanical inspections, electrical inspections, and local code enforcement. The city services the incorporated portion of the city but not the extraterritorial jurisdiction areas.

Trade inspectors are required to attain a Level III certification of their primary building trade within two years. Mechanical and plumbing inspectors are required to attain a secondary certification. Local ordinance inspectors are required to attain a Level I certification. All certified inspectors are required to take and pass a law and administrative course.

All requests for inspections are responded to within forty-eight hours or less. Nearly all requests are called into the city's automated system or entered via its website.

Total revenue received from inspection fees amounted to $2.8 million for the fiscal year. If a request for inspection is made and the job is not ready or corrections have not been made, a $45 fee for each reinspection is assessed.

Conditions Affecting Service, Performance, and Costs

Municipal Profile

Population Served	299,556
Land Area Inspected (Square Miles)	134.62
Persons per Square Mile	2,225
Estimated Tax Base in Service Area (billions)	$28.89

Service Profile

FTE Inspectors	
Building	5.0
Electrical	5.0
Mechanical	3.0
Plumbing	3.0
All Trades	0.0
Total Inspectors	16.0
FTE Plan Reviewers	4.5
Other FTE Positions	10.0
Total of All Positions	30.5
Number of Inspections by Type	
Building	19,724
Electrical	17,616
Mechanical	15,338
Plumbing	11,936
TOTAL	64,614
Building Permit Values	
Residential	$166,819,133
Multifamily	$115,235,811
Commercial	$356,328,584
TOTAL	$638,383,528
Inspection Fee Revenue	$2,805,144

Full Cost Profile

Cost Breakdown by Percentage	
Personal Services	84.5%
Operating Costs	15.5%
Capital Costs	0.0%
TOTAL	100.0%
Cost Breakdown in Dollars	
Personal Services	$2,976,720
Operating Costs	$546,694
Capital Costs	$0
TOTAL	$3,523,414

Resource Measures

Building Inspections Services Costs per Capita

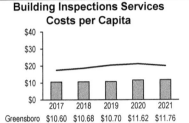

	2017	2018	2019	2020	2021
Greensboro	$10.60	$10.68	$10.70	$11.62	$11.76
Average	$17.56	$18.69	$20.51	$21.21	$20.11

Building Inspections Services FTEs per 10,000 Population

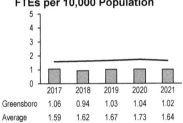

	2017	2018	2019	2020	2021
Greensboro	1.06	0.94	1.03	1.04	1.02
Average	1.59	1.62	1.67	1.73	1.64

Building Inspections Services Cost per Million Dollars of Tax Base

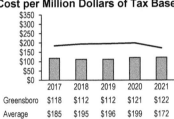

	2017	2018	2019	2020	2021
Greensboro	$118	$112	$112	$121	$122
Average	$185	$195	$196	$199	$172

Workload Measures

Inspections per 1,000 Population in Service Area

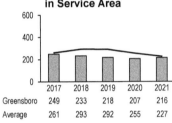

	2017	2018	2019	2020	2021
Greensboro	249	233	218	207	216
Average	261	293	292	255	227

Inspections per Square Mile in Service Area

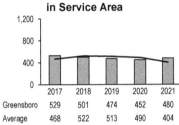

	2017	2018	2019	2020	2021
Greensboro	529	501	474	452	480
Average	468	522	513	490	404

Value of Building Permits as Percentage of Tax Base of Area Served

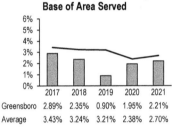

	2017	2018	2019	2020	2021
Greensboro	2.89%	2.35%	0.90%	1.95%	2.21%
Average	3.43%	3.24%	3.21%	2.38%	2.70%

Value of Commercial Permits as Percentage of Tax Base of Area Served

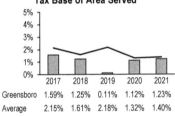

	2017	2018	2019	2020	2021
Greensboro	1.59%	1.25%	0.11%	1.12%	1.23%
Average	2.15%	1.61%	2.18%	1.32%	1.40%

Value of Building Permits per Inspector FTE in Millions of Dollars

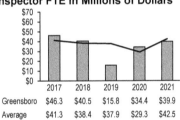

	2017	2018	2019	2020	2021
Greensboro	$46.3	$40.5	$15.8	$34.4	$39.9
Average	$41.3	$38.4	$37.9	$29.3	$42.5

Efficiency Measures

Building Services Cost per Inspection—All Types

	2017	2018	2019	2020	2021
Greensboro	$42.56	$45.90	$49.04	$56.08	$54.53
Average	$80.63	$85.51	$90.43	$104.76	$104.66

Inspections per Day per Inspector FTE

	2017	2018	2019	2020	2021
Greensboro	18.8	17.8	17.0	16.2	17.2
Average	13.9	14.2	13.5	12.0	12.8

Plan Reviews per Year per Reviewer FTE

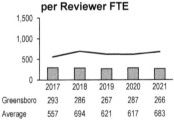

	2017	2018	2019	2020	2021
Greensboro	293	286	267	287	266
Average	557	694	621	617	683

Effectiveness Measures

Percentage of Inspection Responses within One Working Day of Request

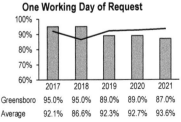

	2017	2018	2019	2020	2021
Greensboro	95.0%	95.0%	89.0%	89.0%	87.0%
Average	92.1%	86.6%	92.3%	92.7%	93.6%

Percentage of Inspections That Are Reinspections

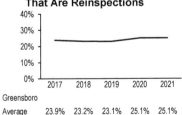

	2017	2018	2019	2020	2021
Greensboro					
Average	23.9%	23.2%	23.1%	25.1%	25.1%

Fiscal Year 2020-21

Explanatory Information

Service Level and Delivery

The City of Greenville provides detailed inspections services within city limits and its extraterritorial jurisdiction (ETJ). The city provides building, plumbing, electrical, and mechanical code enforcement services.

Total revenue received from inspection fees amounted to $1.8 million for the fiscal year. Inspection and permit fees depend on the type of construction or work, value of construction, and other factors.

Conditions Affecting Service, Performance, and Costs

The population served is calculated by adding the population of Greenville with the population of the ETJ. The tax base served is calculated by adding the tax base of Greenville with the tax base of the ETJ. The population and the tax base of the ETJ are calculated by taking the population and tax base per square mile of Pitt County and multiplying them by the square miles of the ETJ.

No data were reported for FY 2019-20 for the city of Greenville.

Municipal Profile

Population Served	93,649
Land Area Inspected (Square Miles)	61.83
Persons per Square Mile	1,515
Estimated Tax Base in Service Area (billions)	$8.01

Service Profile

FTE Inspectors	
Building	0.0
Electrical	0.0
Mechanical	0.0
Plumbing	0.0
All Trades	4.0
Total Inspectors	4.0
FTE Plan Reviewers	1.0
Other FTE Positions	4.0
Total of All Positions	9.0
Number of Inspections by Type	
Building	4,810
Electrical	4,564
Mechanical	4,898
Plumbing	2,831
TOTAL	17,103
Building Permit Values	
Residential	$99,171,694
Multifamily	$36,264,555
Commercial	$210,931,553
TOTAL	$346,367,802
Inspection Fee Revenue	$1,804,467

Full Cost Profile

Cost Breakdown by Percentage	
Personal Services	69.3%
Operating Costs	25.3%
Capital Costs	5.4%
TOTAL	100.0%
Cost Breakdown in Dollars	
Personal Services	$819,887
Operating Costs	$299,412
Capital Costs	$63,364
TOTAL	$1,182,663

Greenville

Building Inspections

Key: Greenville ▓   Benchmarking Average —   Fiscal Years 2017 through 2021

Resource Measures

Building Inspections Services Costs per Capita

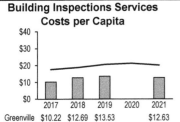

	2017	2018	2019	2020	2021
Greenville	$10.22	$12.69	$13.53		$12.63
Average	$17.56	$18.69	$20.51	$21.21	$20.11

Building Inspections Services FTEs per 10,000 Population

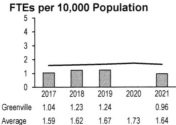

	2017	2018	2019	2020	2021
Greenville	1.04	1.23	1.24		0.96
Average	1.59	1.62	1.67	1.73	1.64

Building Inspections Services Cost per Million Dollars of Tax Base

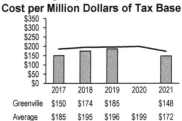

	2017	2018	2019	2020	2021
Greenville	$150	$174	$185		$148
Average	$185	$195	$196	$199	$172

Workload Measures

Inspections per 1,000 Population in Service Area

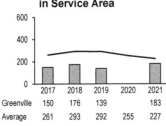

	2017	2018	2019	2020	2021
Greenville	150	176	139		183
Average	261	293	292	255	227

Inspections per Square Mile in Service Area

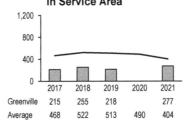

	2017	2018	2019	2020	2021
Greenville	215	255	218		277
Average	468	522	513	490	404

Value of Building Permits as Percentage of Tax Base of Area Served

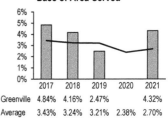

	2017	2018	2019	2020	2021
Greenville	4.84%	4.16%	2.47%		4.32%
Average	3.43%	3.24%	3.21%	2.38%	2.70%

Value of Commercial Permits as Percentage of Tax Base of Area Served

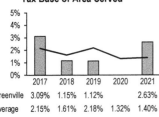

	2017	2018	2019	2020	2021
Greenville	3.09%	1.15%	1.12%		2.63%
Average	2.15%	1.61%	2.18%	1.32%	1.40%

Value of Building Permits per Inspector FTE in Millions of Dollars

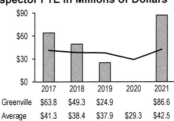

	2017	2018	2019	2020	2021
Greenville	$63.8	$49.3	$24.9		$86.6
Average	$41.3	$38.4	$37.9	$29.3	$42.5

Efficiency Measures

Building Services Cost per Inspection—All Types

	2017	2018	2019	2020	2021
Greenville	$67.94	$72.21	$97.14		$69.15
Average	$80.63	$85.51	$90.43	$104.76	$104.66

Inspections per Day per Inspector FTE

	2017	2018	2019	2020	2021
Greenville	12.3	12.2	8.2		18.2
Average	13.9	14.2	13.5	12.0	12.8

Plan Reviews per Year per Reviewer FTE

	2017	2018	2019	2020	2021
Greenville	593	721	709		1,149
Average	557	694	621	617	683

Effectiveness Measures

Percentage of Inspection Responses within One Working Day of Request

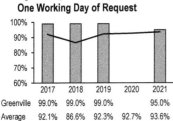

	2017	2018	2019	2020	2021
Greenville	99.0%	99.0%	99.0%		95.0%
Average	92.1%	86.6%	92.3%	92.7%	93.6%

Percentage of Inspections That Are Reinspections

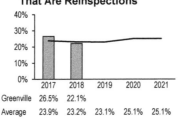

	2017	2018	2019	2020	2021
Greenville	26.5%	22.1%			
Average	23.9%	23.2%	23.1%	25.1%	25.1%

Building Inspections   197

Raleigh

Building Inspections

Fiscal Year 2020-21

Explanatory Information

Service Level and Delivery

The City of Raleigh conducts building inspections through its Building and Safety Division of the Development Services Department. The Development Services Department serves the entire jurisdictional territory of the City of Raleigh.

Inspection services are currently provided by inspectors specializing in each of the major service trades as well as inspectors who cover all trades. A staff of plan reviewers and support specialists further the work in the division.

It is the policy of the inspection work team to respond to an inspection request within twenty-four hours for each type of construction. Most inspections are completed within one day of a request.

Total revenue received from inspection fees was $11.3 million for the fiscal year. Inspection and permit fees depend on the type of construction or work, the value of construction, and other factors. Reinspections are not charged for the first time. Reinspections of the same inspection item that has failed for a second time are subject to a reinspection fee.

Conditions Affecting Service, Performance, and Costs

The permit value of multifamily building projects is included in the totals for commercial projects.

Municipal Profile

Population Served	513,174
Land Area Inspected (Square Miles)	181.50
Persons per Square Mile	2,827
Estimated Tax Base in Service Area (billions)	$84.74

Service Profile

FTE Inspectors	
Building	8.0
Electrical	10.0
Mechanical	7.0
Plumbing	5.0
All Trades	13.0
Total Inspectors	43.0
FTE Plan Reviewers	16.0
Other FTE Positions	22.0
Total of All Positions	81.0
Number of Inspections by Type	
Building	25,234
Electrical	35,721
Mechanical	24,433
Plumbing	17,088
TOTAL	102,476
Building Permit Values	
Residential	$529,555,158
Multifamily	with commercial
Commercial	$1,077,331,681
TOTAL	$1,606,886,839
Inspection Fee Revenue	$11,298,232

Full Cost Profile

Cost Breakdown by Percentage	
Personal Services	76.9%
Operating Costs	15.2%
Capital Costs	7.9%
TOTAL	100.0%
Cost Breakdown in Dollars	
Personal Services	$5,402,299
Operating Costs	$1,067,285
Capital Costs	$558,637
TOTAL	$7,028,221

Key: Raleigh ▪   Benchmarking Average —   Fiscal Years 2017 through 2021

Resource Measures

Building Inspections Services Costs per Capita

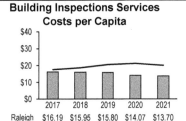

	2017	2018	2019	2020	2021
Raleigh	$16.19	$15.95	$15.80	$14.07	$13.70
Average	$17.56	$18.69	$20.51	$21.21	$20.11

Building Inspections Services FTEs per 10,000 Population

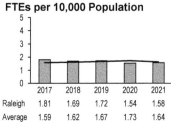

	2017	2018	2019	2020	2021
Raleigh	1.81	1.69	1.72	1.54	1.58
Average	1.59	1.62	1.67	1.73	1.64

Building Inspections Services Cost per Million Dollars of Tax Base

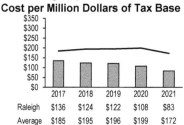

	2017	2018	2019	2020	2021
Raleigh	$136	$124	$122	$108	$83
Average	$185	$195	$196	$199	$172

Workload Measures

Inspections per 1,000 Population in Service Area

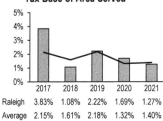

	2017	2018	2019	2020	2021
Raleigh	274	257	257	187	200
Average	261	293	292	255	227

Inspections per Square Mile in Service Area

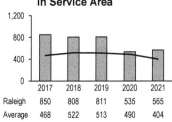

	2017	2018	2019	2020	2021
Raleigh	850	808	811	535	565
Average	468	522	513	490	404

Value of Building Permits as Percentage of Tax Base of Area Served

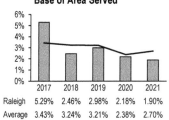

	2017	2018	2019	2020	2021
Raleigh	5.29%	2.46%	2.98%	2.18%	1.90%
Average	3.43%	3.24%	3.21%	2.38%	2.70%

Value of Commercial Permits as Percentage of Tax Base of Area Served

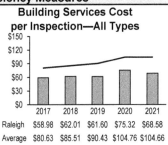

	2017	2018	2019	2020	2021
Raleigh	3.83%	1.08%	2.22%	1.69%	1.27%
Average	2.15%	1.61%	2.18%	1.32%	1.40%

Value of Building Permits per Inspector FTE in Millions of Dollars

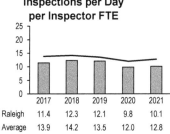

	2017	2018	2019	2020	2021
Raleigh	$61.6	$35.5	$42.8	$35.2	$37.4
Average	$41.3	$38.4	$37.9	$29.3	$42.5

Efficiency Measures

Building Services Cost per Inspection—All Types

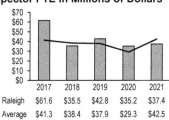

	2017	2018	2019	2020	2021
Raleigh	$58.98	$62.01	$61.60	$75.32	$68.58
Average	$80.63	$85.51	$90.43	$104.76	$104.66

Inspections per Day per Inspector FTE

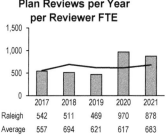

	2017	2018	2019	2020	2021
Raleigh	11.4	12.3	12.1	9.8	10.1
Average	13.9	14.2	13.5	12.0	12.8

Plan Reviews per Year per Reviewer FTE

	2017	2018	2019	2020	2021
Raleigh	542	511	469	970	878
Average	557	694	621	617	683

Effectiveness Measures

Percentage of Inspection Responses within One Working Day of Request

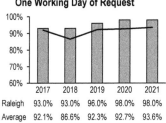

	2017	2018	2019	2020	2021
Raleigh	93.0%	93.0%	96.0%	98.0%	98.0%
Average	92.1%	86.6%	92.3%	92.7%	93.6%

Percentage of Inspections That Are Reinspections

	2017	2018	2019	2020	2021
Raleigh	11.8%	10.3%	15.6%	10.8%	10.3%
Average	23.9%	23.2%	23.1%	25.1%	25.1%

Explanatory Information

Service Level and Delivery

The City of Wilson's inspection team serves the area within the city's incorported boundaries and areas within the city's entire jurisdictional territory .

Inspection services are currently provided by three inspectors, one field supervisor, and the inspections divisions manager. Two permit technicians provide support to this function. For commercial jobs, each inspector is assigned a primary inspection field. For residential jobs, inspectors hold certificates in all trade areas. Fire inspections are typically handled by certified inspectors in the fire department but are occasionally conducted by building inspectors who have fire inspection certification.

It is the policy of the inspection work team to respond to an inspection request on the same working day if the request is made prior to 8:30 a.m. and to respond to an inspection request by the following working day if the request is made after 8:30 a.m. Most inspections are completed on the same day the request is made.

Total revenue received from inspection fees was $330,642 for the fiscal year. Inspection and permit fees depend on the type of construction or work, the value of construction, and other factors. A reinspection fee is assessed when making an inspection for the same trade that had been previously rejected.

Conditions Affecting Service, Performance, and Costs

The broad downturn in the economy reduced building activity and the number of requests for inspections in the earlier years, but since FY 2018–19 activity in commercial buildings has picked up.

Municipal Profile

Population Served	53,375
Land Area Inspected (Square Miles)	58.53
Persons per Square Mile	912
Estimated Tax Base in Service Area (billions)	$4.87

Service Profile

FTE Inspectors	
Building	0.0
Electrical	0.0
Mechanical	0.0
Plumbing	0.0
All Trades	3.8
Total Inspectors	3.8
FTE Plan Reviewers	1.0
Other FTE Positions	2.8
Total of All Positions	7.5
Number of Inspections by Type	
Building	2,370
Electrical	2,564
Mechanical	1,973
Plumbing	1,265
TOTAL	8,382
Building Permit Values	
Residential	$65,152,512
Multifamily	$0
Commercial	$90,003,264
TOTAL	$155,155,776
Inspection Fee Revenue	$330,642

Full Cost Profile

Cost Breakdown by Percentage	
Personal Services	78.1%
Operating Costs	17.3%
Capital Costs	4.6%
TOTAL	100.0%
Cost Breakdown in Dollars	
Personal Services	$805,875
Operating Costs	$178,027
Capital Costs	$47,363
TOTAL	$1,031,265

Wilson

Building Inspections

Key: Wilson ▨ Benchmarking Average — Fiscal Years 2017 through 2021

Resource Measures

Building Inspections Services Costs per Capita

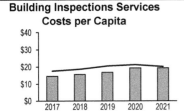

	2017	2018	2019	2020	2021
Wilson	$14.56	$15.53	$16.82	$19.32	$19.32
Average	$17.56	$18.69	$20.51	$21.21	$20.11

Building Inspections Services FTEs per 10,000 Population

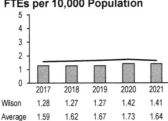

	2017	2018	2019	2020	2021
Wilson	1.28	1.27	1.27	1.42	1.41
Average	1.59	1.62	1.67	1.73	1.64

Building Inspections Services Cost per Million Dollars of Tax Base

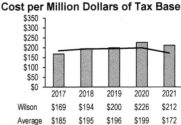

	2017	2018	2019	2020	2021
Wilson	$169	$194	$200	$226	$212
Average	$185	$195	$196	$199	$172

Workload Measures

Inspections per 1,000 Population in Service Area

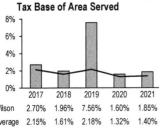

	2017	2018	2019	2020	2021
Wilson	139	157	162	169	157
Average	261	293	292	255	227

Inspections per Square Mile in Service Area

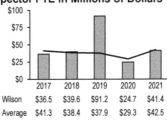

	2017	2018	2019	2020	2021
Wilson	138	148	152	262	143
Average	468	522	513	490	404

Value of Building Permits as Percentage of Tax Base of Area Served

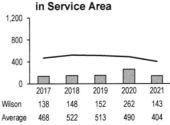

	2017	2018	2019	2020	2021
Wilson	3.10%	3.60%	7.89%	2.34%	3.18%
Average	3.43%	3.24%	3.21%	2.38%	2.70%

Value of Commercial Permits as Percentage of Tax Base of Area Served

	2017	2018	2019	2020	2021
Wilson	2.70%	1.96%	7.56%	1.60%	1.85%
Average	2.15%	1.61%	2.18%	1.32%	1.40%

Value of Building Permits per Inspector FTE in Millions of Dollars

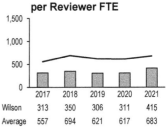

	2017	2018	2019	2020	2021
Wilson	$36.5	$39.6	$91.2	$24.7	$41.4
Average	$41.3	$38.4	$37.9	$29.3	$42.5

Efficiency Measures

Building Services Cost per Inspection—All Types

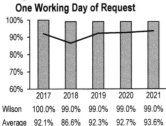

	2017	2018	2019	2020	2021
Wilson	$104.40	$98.95	$103.92	$114.21	$123.03
Average	$80.63	$85.51	$90.43	$104.76	$104.66

Inspections per Day per Inspector FTE

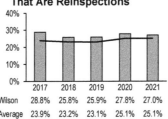

	2017	2018	2019	2020	2021
Wilson	8.1	9.2	9.5	8.9	9.5
Average	13.9	14.2	13.5	12.0	12.8

Plan Reviews per Year per Reviewer FTE

	2017	2018	2019	2020	2021
Wilson	313	350	306	311	415
Average	557	694	621	617	683

Effectiveness Measures

Percentage of Inspection Responses within One Working Day of Request

	2017	2018	2019	2020	2021
Wilson	100.0%	99.0%	99.0%	99.0%	99.0%
Average	92.1%	86.6%	92.3%	92.7%	93.6%

Percentage of Inspections That Are Reinspections

	2017	2018	2019	2020	2021
Wilson	28.8%	25.8%	25.9%	27.8%	27.0%
Average	23.9%	23.2%	23.1%	25.1%	25.1%

Fiscal Year 2020-21

Explanatory Information

Service Level and Delivery

The Inspections Division is a combined program for Winston-Salem and Forsyth County, providing building inspections services for all areas of the county, with the exception of the Town of Kernersville.

Inspectors are certified in one of the following four trades: building, electrical, mechanical, or plumbing. Inspectors drive to and from inspection sites in city-owned vehicles. Besides the North Carolina State Building Code, the Inspections Division enforces zoning codes and soil-and-sedimentation-control regulations. Full-time equivalent positions and costs for these responsibilities are excluded from the project's figures for building inspections.

It is the policy of the Inspections Division to respond to inspection requests within one working day; 90 percent of the time it achieves this goal.

Total revenue received from inspection fees amounted to $5.2 million for the fiscal year. Inspection and permit fees depend on the type of construction or work, value of the construction, and other factors. An extra trip charge of $40 is assessed for each reinspection due to a second and subsequent failed inspection on each permit.

Conditions Affecting Service, Performance, and Costs

Municipal Profile

Population Served	356,777
Land Area Inspected (Square Miles)	396.00
Persons per Square Mile	901
Estimated Tax Base in Service Area (billions)	$35.10

Service Profile

FTE Inspectors	
Building	3.0
Electrical	6.0
Mechanical	6.0
Plumbing	3.0
All Trades	0.0
Total Inspectors	18.0
FTE Plan Reviewers	3.0
Other FTE Positions	18.0
Total of All Positions	39.0
Number of Inspections by Type	
Building	16,378
Electrical	23,238
Mechanical	18,280
Plumbing	13,725
TOTAL	71,621
Building Permit Values	
Residential	$386,428,140
Multifamily	with residential
Commercial	$367,428,140
TOTAL	$753,856,280
Inspection Fee Revenue	$5,249,525

Full Cost Profile

Cost Breakdown by Percentage	
Personal Services	58.6%
Operating Costs	33.7%
Capital Costs	7.6%
TOTAL	100.0%
Cost Breakdown in Dollars	
Personal Services	$2,552,922
Operating Costs	$1,468,946
Capital Costs	$331,791
TOTAL	$4,353,659

Resource Measures

Building Inspections Services Costs per Capita

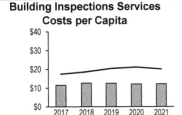

	2017	2018	2019	2020	2021
Winston-Salem	$11.53	$12.62	$12.51	$12.12	$12.20
Average	$17.56	$18.69	$20.51	$21.21	$20.11

Building Inspections Services FTEs per 10,000 Population

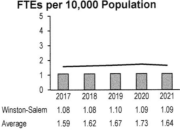

	2017	2018	2019	2020	2021
Winston-Salem	1.08	1.08	1.10	1.09	1.09
Average	1.59	1.62	1.67	1.73	1.64

Building Inspections Services Cost per Million Dollars of Tax Base

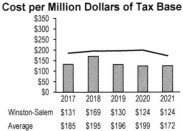

	2017	2018	2019	2020	2021
Winston-Salem	$131	$169	$130	$124	$124
Average	$185	$195	$196	$199	$172

Workload Measures

Inspections per 1,000 Population in Service Area

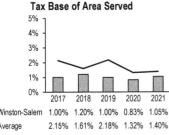

	2017	2018	2019	2020	2021
Winston-Salem	179	182	202	199	201
Average	261	293	292	255	227

Inspections per Square Mile in Service Area

	2017	2018	2019	2020	2021
Winston-Salem	156	161	178	177	181
Average	468	522	513	490	404

Value of Building Permits as Percentage of Tax Base of Area Served

	2017	2018	2019	2020	2021
Winston-Salem	1.73%	2.18%	1.77%	1.57%	2.15%
Average	3.43%	3.24%	3.21%	2.38%	2.70%

Value of Commercial Permits as Percentage of Tax Base of Area Served

	2017	2018	2019	2020	2021
Winston-Salem	1.00%	1.20%	1.00%	0.83%	1.05%
Average	2.15%	1.61%	2.18%	1.32%	1.40%

Value of Building Permits per Inspector FTE in Millions of Dollars

	2017	2018	2019	2020	2021
Winston-Salem	$32.7	$33.4	$33.2	$30.0	$41.9
Average	$41.3	$38.4	$37.9	$29.3	$42.5

Efficiency Measures

Building Services Cost per Inspection—All Types

	2017	2018	2019	2020	2021
Winston-Salem	$64.31	$69.18	$62.07	$60.91	$60.79
Average	$80.63	$85.51	$90.43	$104.76	$104.66

Inspections per Day per Inspector FTE

	2017	2018	2019	2020	2021
Winston-Salem	16.4	15.9	16.7	16.6	16.9
Average	13.9	14.2	13.5	12.0	12.8

Plan Reviews per Year per Reviewer FTE

	2017	2018	2019	2020	2021
Winston-Salem	266	298	324	312	457
Average	557	694	621	617	683

Effectiveness Measures

Percentage of Inspection Responses within One Working Day of Request

	2017	2018	2019	2020	2021
Winston-Salem	90.1%	87.9%	83.3%	82.8%	78.0%
Average	92.1%	86.6%	92.3%	92.7%	93.6%

Percentage of Inspections That Are Reinspections

	2017	2018	2019	2020	2021
Winston-Salem	17.6%	17.1%			
Average	23.9%	23.2%	23.1%	25.1%	25.1%

Performance and Cost Data

FLEET MAINTENANCE

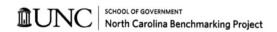

PERFORMANCE MEASURES FOR FLEET MAINTENANCE

SERVICE DEFINITION
Fleet Maintenance represents the scheduled and unscheduled maintenance of rolling stock performed by the central garage and contractual work assigned by the central garage. This includes preventive, predictive, corrective, and breakdown maintenance. Excluded from this definition are rolling stock not maintained by the central garage and the broader activities of fleet services, such as rolling stock replacement and disposal, fuel station operation, and pool vehicle management.

NOTES ON PERFORMANCE MEASURES

1. Number of Vehicle Equivalent Units (VEUs) per Technician FTE
Vehicle Equivalent Units (VEUs) are a weighted measure of the maintenance effort associated with different classes of vehicles. A normal-use car is considered equal to one VEU. Vehicles such as fire trucks or police cars have higher VEUs, reflecting greater expected levels of maintenance effort. The number of VEUs in a municipality is determined by taking the number of rolling stock units in different classes of vehicles and multiplying them by a class weight for that category of vehicle. Vehicle categories include cars; light, medium, and heavy vehicles; trailed equipment; off-road/construction/tractor units; and buses. The number of full-time equivalent (FTE) positions for technicians is the number of employees directly involved in providing the maintenance services for the municipality's rolling stock as approved in the annual operating budget for the fiscal year.

2. Number of Preventive Maintenances Completed In-House per Technician FTE
The number of preventive maintenance jobs (PMs) completed in-house by the municipality's staff is the total number of PMs completed for the fiscal year ending June 30. The number of FTE positions for technicians is the same as defined above.

3. Cost per Work Order
This measure represents the total cost of fleet maintenance and is calculated using the full cost accounting model which captures direct, indirect, and capital costs. Work orders include the total number of work orders produced, including those related to contractual work, for the fiscal year ending June 30.

4. Cost per Vehicle Equivalent Unit (VEU)
This measure represents the total cost of fleet maintenance and is calculated using the full cost accounting model which captures direct, indirect, and capital costs. VEUs are calculated as described above for the fiscal year ending June 30.

5. Hours Billed as a Percentage of Total Hours

The total number of billable hours includes all hours for technicians available for work during the fiscal year. Billable hours are calculated by multiplying 2,080 (hours in a normal working year) by the number of FTE positions for technicians as defined above. However, this number of FTEs is adjusted for vacancies. Hours billed represents actual hours billed during the fiscal year by the central garage to departments, divisions, and programs.

5. Preventive Maintenances (PMs) as a Percentage of All Work Orders

This measure is based on the total number of PMs (done in-house or by outside contractors) completed during the fiscal year divided by the total number of work orders (including contractual work) completed during the fiscal year for that jurisdiction.

7.   Percentage of PMs Completed on Schedule

Based on the total number of PMs as defined above, this measure represents the percentage of PMs completed as scheduled, as defined by the respective jurisdiction's standards.

8.   Percentage of Work Orders Completed within Twenty-Four Hours

Based on the total number of work orders as defined above, this measure represents the percentage of work orders completed during the fiscal year within twenty-four hours of being received.

9.   Percentage of Rolling Stock Available per Day

Based on the total number of rolling stock units as defined above, this measure represents the average percentage of rolling stock available for use per working day of the jurisdiction.

10.   Percentage of Work Orders Requiring Repeat Repair within Thirty Days

Based on the total number of work orders as defined above, this measure represents the percentage of work orders (completed work on a unit of rolling stock) requiring repeat repair for the same problem within thirty days.

Fleet Maintenance

Summary of Key Dimensions of Service

City or Town	Number of Rolling Stock Maintained	Average Age of Rolling Stock (in Years)	Number of Work Orders	Number of Preventive Maintenances	Number of Work Bays	Authorized Technician FTEs	Labor Rate (per Hour)	Fund Type
Apex	510	5.1	1,963	1,112	6	4.0	NA	General Fund
Chapel Hill	356	10.0	1,506	585	10	5.5	$100.00	Internal Service
Concord	1,025	7.4	3,861	1,902	8	8.0	$60.00	General Fund
Goldsboro	560	10.7	3,564	765	11	7.0	$13.50	General Fund
Greensboro	1,731	7.2	11,490	5,127	34	31.0	$65.00	Internal Service
Greenville	732	10.9	6,841	1,928	13	13.0	$60-65	Internal Service
Hickory	569	8.8	4,930	2,353	14	7.0	$60.00	Internal Service
Raleigh	2,730	6.9	22,885	8,271	51	44.0	Heavy, Lead Mech, and Motor Mech - $79; Welder, Auto Specialist, Auto Tire, and PM Tech - $48	Internal Service
Wilson	891	8.4	4,803	1,267	11	11.0	$44.00	General Fund
Winston-Salem	1,872	9.0	9,591	3,949	30	19.0	$50.00	Internal Service

EXPLANATORY FACTORS

These are factors that the project found affected fleet maintenance performance and cost in one or more of the municipalities:

Number of vehicles maintained
Types of vehicles maintained
Fleet replacement plan
Average age of vehicles by type
Average miles driven for each type of vehicle
Preventive maintenance classification system
Preventive maintenance schedule

Apex

Fleet Maintenance

Fiscal Year 2020-21

Explanatory Information

Service Level and Delivery

Fleet Services is a division of the Facility and Fleet Services Department in the Town of Apex. The activities for this operation are accounted for in the general fund.

The town does not charge departments for labor but does track time technicians spend on work orders. There is no charge to departments for parts or sublet work.

The following services were contracted out:

- transmission repairs
- extended repair order work
- major engine repairs
- body work
- EMS ambulance body service work
- electric line truck repairs
- major hydraulic cylinder repairs
- fire truck pump repairs.

Conditions Affecting Service, Performance, and Costs

Vehicle Equivalent Units (VEUs) are a weighted measure of the maintenance effort associated with different classes of vehicles. A normal-use car is considered equal to one VEU. Vehicles such as fire trucks or police cars have higher VEUs, reflecting greater expected levels of maintenance.

The measure "hours billed as a percentage of total hours" is based on a work year of 2,080 hours and only counts those positions that were filled. It should be noted that technicians have responsibilities that do not result in billable hours, and they take normal vacation and sick leave. Therefore, this percentage should not be expected to be near 100 percent.

In Apex the preventive maintenance (PM) completion standard for "percentage of PMs completed as scheduled" is within thirty days of the scheduled date or within mileage parameters.

In addition to rolling stock, Apex's fleet services has maintenance responsibilities for other pieces of equipment, including asphalt rollers, whacker and roller tamps, portable generators, ballfield conditioners, various types of ATVs, weedeaters, lawnmowers, chainsaws, sump pumps, water pumps, snow plows, flail mowers, boat motors, light towers, and stump grinders.

The Apex Fleet Services supervisor provides technician support on an as needed basis.

Municipal Profile

Population (OSBM 2020)	59,368
Land Area (Square Miles)	23.61
Persons per Square Mile	2,514

Service Profile

FTE Positions—Technician	4.0
FTE Positions—Other	1.5
Work Bays	6

Rolling Stock Maintained	No.	Average Age
Cars—Normal Usage	28	9.2 Years
Cars—Severe Usage	109	4.2 Years
Motorcycles	3	8.0 Years
Light Utility Vehicles	14	14.0 Years
Light Vehicles	139	7.4 Years
Medium Vehicles	20	9.5 Years
Heavy—Sanitation	3	8.6 Years
Heavy—Sewer	3	6.6 Years
Heavy—Fire Apparatus	12	11.6 Years
Heavy—Other	27	9.0 Years
Trailed Equipment	84	NA
Off-Road/Construction/Tractors	68	NA
Buses	0	NA
TOTAL	510	

Vehicle Equivalent Units (VEUs)	1,437
Average Rolling Stock Units Available per Day	495
Hours Billed	3,206
Work Orders	1,963
Repeat Repairs within 30 Days	8
Work Orders Completed within 24 hours	1,669
Preventive Maintenance Jobs (PMs)	1,112
PMs Completed as Scheduled	979

Full Cost Profile

Cost Breakdown by Percentage

Personal Services	32.9%
Operating Costs	56.2%
Capital Costs	11.0%
TOTAL	100.0%

Cost Breakdown in Dollars

Personal Services	$406,249
Operating Costs	$693,493
Capital Costs	$135,303
TOTAL	$1,235,045

Apex

Fleet Maintenance

Resource Measures

Fleet Maintenance Services Cost per Capita

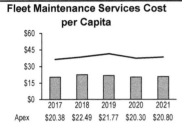

	2017	2018	2019	2020	2021
Apex	$20.38	$22.49	$21.77	$20.30	$20.80
Average	$36.43	$38.60	$41.42	$37.50	$38.57

Fleet Maintenance FTEs per 10,000 Population

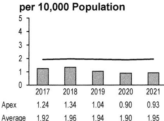

	2017	2018	2019	2020	2021
Apex	1.24	1.34	1.04	0.90	0.93
Average	1.92	1.96	1.94	1.90	1.95

Fleet Maintenance FTEs per 100 Municipal Employees

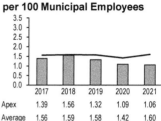

	2017	2018	2019	2020	2021
Apex	1.39	1.56	1.32	1.09	1.06
Average	1.56	1.59	1.58	1.42	1.60

Workload Measures

Number of Vehicle Equivalent Units (VEUs) per Technician FTE

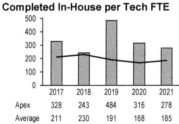

	2017	2018	2019	2020	2021
Apex	277	238	347	354	359
Average	250	262	260	267	261

Preventive Maintenances (PMs) Completed In-House per Tech FTE

	2017	2018	2019	2020	2021
Apex	328	243	484	316	278
Average	211	230	191	168	185

Efficiency Measures

Fleet Maintenance Cost per Work Order

	2017	2018	2019	2020	2021
Apex	$411	$471	$544	$664	$629
Average	$545	$580	$677	$678	$677

Fleet Maintenance Cost per Vehicle Equivalent Unit (VEU)

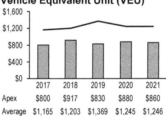

	2017	2018	2019	2020	2021
Apex	$800	$917	$830	$880	$860
Average	$1,165	$1,203	$1,369	$1,245	$1,246

Hours Billed as a Percentage of Total Hours

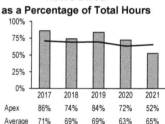

	2017	2018	2019	2020	2021
Apex	86%	74%	84%	72%	52%
Average	71%	69%	69%	63%	65%

Effectiveness Measures

Preventive Maintenances (PMs) as a Percentage of All Work Orders

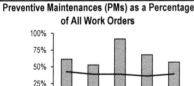

	2017	2018	2019	2020	2021
Apex	61%	52%	91%	68%	57%
Average	43%	39%	39%	36%	39%

Percentage of Preventive Maintenances (PMs) Completed as Scheduled

	2017	2018	2019	2020	2021
Apex	100%	100%	98%	90%	88%
Average	81%	82%	75%	83%	85%

Percentage of Work Orders Completed within 24 Hours

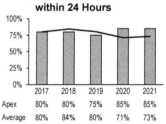

	2017	2018	2019	2020	2021
Apex	80%	80%	75%	85%	85%
Average	80%	84%	80%	71%	73%

Percentage of Rolling Stock Available per Day

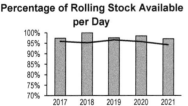

	2017	2018	2019	2020	2021
Apex	97%	100%	97%	98%	97%
Average	96%	95%	97%	96%	94%

Percentage of Work Orders Requiring Repeat Repair within 30 Days

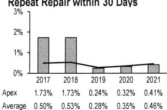

	2017	2018	2019	2020	2021
Apex	1.73%	1.73%	0.24%	0.32%	0.41%
Average	0.50%	0.53%	0.28%	0.35%	0.46%

Explanatory Information

Service Level and Delivery

The Town of Chapel Hill provides fleet maintenance through the Fleet Management Program in the Public Works Department Administration Division. The program is operated as an internal service fund charging departments for services.

A labor rate of $100 per hour is charged for maintenance work. Additionally, a parts markup of 25 percent is applied to the cost of parts, and a 15 percent markup is charged for overseeing sublet work.

The town contracted out some maintenance services during the fiscal year, including towing, body work, lift truck inspections, and parts inventory.

Conditions Affecting Service, Performance, and Costs

Chapel Hill improved its tracking of repeat repairs to more closely follow the benchmarking directions of repairs to the same component, as opposed to repairs to address the same complaint.

Vehicle Equivalent Units (VEUs) are a weighted measure of the maintenance effort associated with different classes of vehicles. A normal-use car is considered equal to one VEU. Vehicles such as fire trucks or police cars have higher VEUs, reflecting greater expected levels of maintenance.

The measure "hours billed as a percentage of total hours" is based on a work year of 2,080 hours and only counts those positions that were filled. It should be noted that technicians have responsibilities that do not result in billable hours, and they take normal vacation and sick leave. Therefore, this percentage should not be expected to be near 100 percent. There was a large degree of turnover in the shop during the prior year, with a full complement only reached at the start of FY 2015–16.

In Chapel Hill the preventive maintenance (PM) completion standard for "percentage of PMs completed as scheduled" includes varying standards depending on the work but must occur within thirty days of the scheduled date, within the scheduled month, or within mileage parameters.

In addition to rolling stock, Chapel Hill's fleet services has maintenance responsibilities for generators, light towers, mowers, weed wackers, leaf blowers, leaf vacuum machines, and sign towers.

Municipal Profile

Population (OSBM 2020)	62,080
Land Area (Square Miles)	21.31
Persons per Square Mile	2,914

Service Profile

FTE Positions—Technician	5.50
FTE Positions—Other	2.25
Work Bays	10

Rolling Stock Maintained	No.	Average Age
Cars—Normal Usage	40	9.9 Years
Cars—Severe Usage	52	8.1 Years
Motorcycles	0	NA
Light Utility Vehicles	10	13.0 Years
Light Vehicles	130	10.2 Years
Medium Vehicles	19	9.6 Years
Heavy—Sanitation	16	6.9 Years
Heavy—Sewer	2	17.9 Years
Heavy—Fire Apparatus	9	10.4 Years
Heavy—Other	10	7.8 Years
Trailed Equipment	51	11.9 Years
Off-Road/Construction/Tractors	17	10.9 Years
Buses	0	NA
TOTAL	356	

Vehicle Equivalent Units (VEUs)	1,092
Average Rolling Stock Units Available per Day	338
Hours Billed	7,121
Work Orders	1,506
Repeat Repairs within 30 Days	6
Work Orders Completed within 24 hours	903
Preventive Maintenance Jobs (PMs)	585
PMs Completed as Scheduled	459

Full Cost Profile

Cost Breakdown by Percentage

Personal Services	35.3%
Operating Costs	55.0%
Capital Costs	9.7%
TOTAL	100.0%

Cost Breakdown in Dollars

Personal Services	$640,266
Operating Costs	$997,469
Capital Costs	$176,173
TOTAL	$1,813,908

Chapel Hill

Fleet Maintenance

Resource Measures

Fleet Maintenance Services Cost per Capita

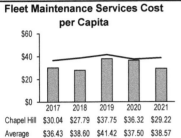

	2017	2018	2019	2020	2021
Chapel Hill	$30.04	$27.79	$37.75	$36.32	$29.22
Average	$36.43	$38.60	$41.42	$37.50	$38.57

Fleet Maintenance FTEs per 10,000 Population

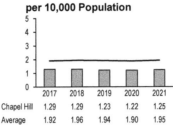

	2017	2018	2019	2020	2021
Chapel Hill	1.29	1.29	1.23	1.22	1.25
Average	1.92	1.96	1.94	1.90	1.95

Fleet Maintenance FTEs per 100 Municipal Employees

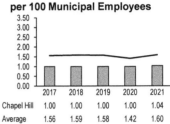

	2017	2018	2019	2020	2021
Chapel Hill	1.00	1.00	1.00	1.00	1.04
Average	1.56	1.59	1.58	1.42	1.60

Workload Measures

Number of Vehicle Equivalent Units (VEUs) per Technician FTE

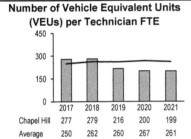

	2017	2018	2019	2020	2021
Chapel Hill	277	279	216	200	199
Average	250	262	260	267	261

Preventive Maintenances (PMs) Completed In-House per Tech FTE

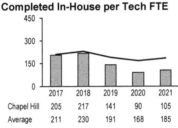

	2017	2018	2019	2020	2021
Chapel Hill	205	217	141	90	105
Average	211	230	191	168	185

Efficiency Measures

Fleet Maintenance Cost per Work Order

	2017	2018	2019	2020	2021
Chapel Hill	$822	$732	$1,356	$1,560	$1,204
Average	$545	$580	$677	$678	$677

Fleet Maintenance Cost per Vehicle Equivalent Unit (VEU)

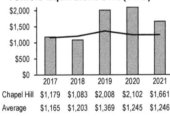

	2017	2018	2019	2020	2021
Chapel Hill	$1,179	$1,083	$2,008	$2,102	$1,661
Average	$1,165	$1,203	$1,369	$1,245	$1,246

Hours Billed as a Percentage of Total Hours

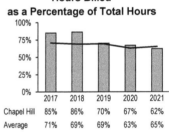

	2017	2018	2019	2020	2021
Chapel Hill	85%	86%	70%	67%	62%
Average	71%	69%	69%	63%	65%

Effectiveness Measures

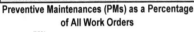

Preventive Maintenances (PMs) as a Percentage of All Work Orders

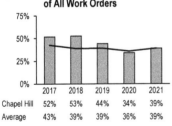

	2017	2018	2019	2020	2021
Chapel Hill	52%	53%	44%	34%	39%
Average	43%	39%	39%	36%	39%

Percentage of Preventive Maintenances (PMs) Completed as Scheduled

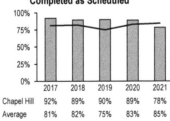

	2017	2018	2019	2020	2021
Chapel Hill	92%	89%	90%	89%	78%
Average	81%	82%	75%	83%	85%

Percentage of Work Orders Completed within 24 Hours

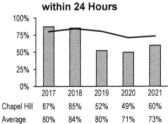

	2017	2018	2019	2020	2021
Chapel Hill	87%	85%	52%	49%	60%
Average	80%	84%	80%	71%	73%

Percentage of Rolling Stock Available per Day

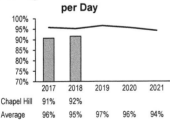

	2017	2018	2019	2020	2021
Chapel Hill	91%	92%			
Average	96%	95%	97%	96%	94%

Percentage of Work Orders Requiring Repeat Repair within 30 Days

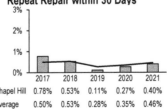

	2017	2018	2019	2020	2021
Chapel Hill	0.78%	0.53%	0.11%	0.27%	0.40%
Average	0.50%	0.53%	0.28%	0.35%	0.46%

Fiscal Year 2020-21

Explanatory Information

Service Level and Delivery

Concord's Fleet Department operates as a separate city department through the general fund, charging other departments for services rendered.

A labor rate of $60 per hour is charged for all maintenance services. There is a 25 percent markup charge for parts and a 10 percent markup on sublet work.

The following services were contracted out:

- body repairs
- aerial device repairs
- front-end alignments.

Conditions Affecting Service, Performance, and Costs

Vehicle Equivalent Units (VEUs) are a weighted measure of the maintenance effort associated with different classes of vehicles. A normal-use car is considered equal to one VEU. Vehicles such as fire trucks or police cars have higher VEUs, reflecting greater expected levels of maintenance.

The measure "hours billed as a percentage of total hours" is based on a work year of 2,080 hours and only counts those positions that were filled. It should be noted that technicians have responsibilities that do not result in billable hours, and they take normal vacation and sick leave. Therefore, this percentage should not be expected to be near 100 percent.

In Concord, the preventive maintenance (PM) completion standard for "percentage of PMs completed as scheduled" is within thirty days of the scheduled date.

In addition to rolling stock, Concord's fleet services has maintenance responsibilities for generators, mowers, weedeaters, chainsaws, chop saws, leaf blowers, tamps, pumps, power washers, and other city equipment.

Municipal Profile

Population (OSBM 2020)	105,936
Land Area (Square Miles)	63.65
Persons per Square Mile	1,664

Service Profile

FTE Positions—Technician	8.00
FTE Positions—Other	6.0
Work Bays	8

Rolling Stock Maintained	No.	Average Age
Cars—Normal Usage	6	4.3 Years
Cars—Severe Usage	199	4.3 Years
Motorcycles	4	2.0 Years
Light Utility Vehicles	64	8.3 Years
Light Vehicles	267	6.1 Years
Medium Vehicles	60	6.1 Years
Heavy—Sanitation	15	6.3 Years
Heavy—Sewer	3	5.1 Years
Heavy—Fire Apparatus	26	9.3 Years
Heavy—Other	68	8.7 Years
Trailed Equipment	183	12.2 Years
Off-Road/Construction/Tractors	119	8.0 Years
Buses	11	7.3 Years
TOTAL	1,025	

Vehicle Equivalent Units (VEUs)	3,140
Average Rolling Stock Units Available per Day	1,012
Hours Billed	10,288
Work Orders	3,861
Repeat Repairs within 30 Days	15
Work Orders Completed within 24 hours	3,812
Preventive Maintenance Jobs (PMs)	1,902
PMs Completed as Scheduled	1,875

Full Cost Profile

Cost Breakdown by Percentage

Personal Services	46.1%
Operating Costs	49.9%
Capital Costs	4.1%
TOTAL	100.0%

Cost Breakdown in Dollars

Personal Services	$1,160,824
Operating Costs	$1,256,094
Capital Costs	$102,581
TOTAL	$2,519,499

Concord
Fleet Maintenance

Key: Concord ■   Benchmarking Average —   Fiscal Years 2017 through 2021

Resource Measures

Fleet Maintenance Services Cost per Capita

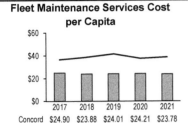

	2017	2018	2019	2020	2021
Concord	$24.90	$23.88	$24.01	$24.21	$23.78
Average	$36.43	$38.60	$41.42	$37.50	$38.57

Fleet Maintenance FTEs per 10,000 Population

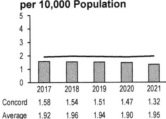

	2017	2018	2019	2020	2021
Concord	1.58	1.54	1.51	1.47	1.32
Average	1.92	1.96	1.94	1.90	1.95

Fleet Maintenance FTEs per 100 Municipal Employees

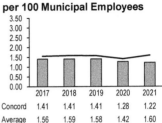

	2017	2018	2019	2020	2021
Concord	1.41	1.41	1.41	1.28	1.22
Average	1.56	1.59	1.58	1.42	1.60

Workload Measures

Number of Vehicle Equivalent Units (VEUs) per Technician FTE

	2017	2018	2019	2020	2021
Concord	348	360	372	381	392
Average	250	262	260	267	261

Preventive Maintenances (PMs) Completed In-House per Tech FTE

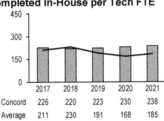

	2017	2018	2019	2020	2021
Concord	226	220	223	230	238
Average	211	230	191	168	185

Efficiency Measures

Fleet Maintenance Cost per Work Order

	2017	2018	2019	2020	2021
Concord	$561	$537	$562	$594	$653
Average	$545	$580	$677	$678	$677

Fleet Maintenance Cost per Vehicle Equivalent Unit (VEU)

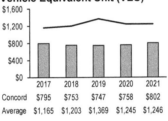

	2017	2018	2019	2020	2021
Concord	$795	$753	$747	$758	$802
Average	$1,165	$1,203	$1,369	$1,245	$1,246

Hours Billed as a Percentage of Total Hours

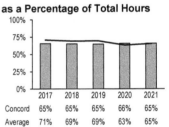

	2017	2018	2019	2020	2021
Concord	65%	65%	65%	66%	65%
Average	71%	69%	69%	63%	65%

Effectiveness Measures

Preventive Maintenances (PMs) as a Percentage of All Work Orders

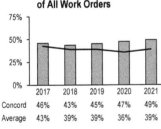

	2017	2018	2019	2020	2021
Concord	46%	43%	45%	47%	49%
Average	43%	39%	39%	36%	39%

Percentage of Preventive Maintenances (PMs) Completed as Scheduled

	2017	2018	2019	2020	2021
Concord	93%	98%	98%		99%
Average	81%	82%	75%	83%	85%

Percentage of Work Orders Completed within 24 Hours

	2017	2018	2019	2020	2021
Concord	98%	99%	99%	99%	99%
Average	80%	84%	80%	71%	73%

Percentage of Rolling Stock Available per Day

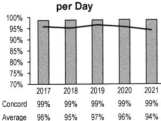

	2017	2018	2019	2020	2021
Concord	99%	99%	99%	99%	99%
Average	96%	95%	97%	96%	94%

Percentage of Work Orders Requiring Repeat Repair within 30 Days

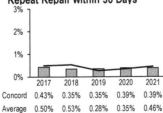

	2017	2018	2019	2020	2021
Concord	0.43%	0.35%	0.35%	0.39%	0.39%
Average	0.50%	0.53%	0.28%	0.35%	0.46%

Goldsboro

Fleet Maintenance

Fiscal Year 2020-21

Explanatory Information

Service Level and Delivery

Goldsboro's fleet maintenance operation is housed within the Garage Division of the Public Works Department. The division is funded out of the city's general fund.

The labor rate for the fiscal year was $13.50 an hour. No markup charges are placed on parts or sublet work performed by the Garage Division.

The following services were contracted out:

- body work
- engine repairs requiring specialized tools
- engine diagnostics
- wheel alignments
- hydraulics.

Conditions Affecting Service, Performance, and Costs

The City of Goldsboro joined the Benchmarking Project in July 2017, with the first year of data showing for FY 2016–17.

Vehicle Equivalent Units (VEUs) are a weighted measure of the maintenance effort associated with different classes of vehicles. A normal-use car is considered equal to one VEU. Vehicles such as fire trucks or police cars have higher VEUs, reflecting greater expected levels of maintenance.

The measure "hours billed as a percentage of total hours" is based on a work year of 2,080 hours and only counts those positions that were filled. It should be noted that technicians have responsibilities that do not result in billable hours, and they take normal vacation and sick leave. Therefore, this percentage should not be expected to be near 100 percent.

In Goldsboro, the preventive maintenance (PM) completion standard for "percentage of PMs completed as scheduled" uses scheduled dates within the calendar month or within thirty days of schedule.

In addition to rolling stock, Goldsboro's Garage Division has maintenance responsibilities for portable generators, mowers, blowers, weed wackers, pressure washers, and other equipment.

Municipal Profile

Population (OSBM 2020)	34,156
Land Area (Square Miles)	29.45
Persons per Square Mile	1,160

Service Profile

FTE Positions—Technician	7.0
FTE Positions—Other	5.0
Work Bays	11

Rolling Stock Maintained	No.	Average Age
Cars—Normal Usage	9	14.6 Years
Cars—Severe Usage	119	7.4 Years
Motorcycles	0	NA
Light Utility Vehicles	156	9.2 Years
Light Vehicles	87	8.9 Years
Medium Vehicles	4	8.0 Years
Heavy—Sanitation	40	14.0 Years
Heavy—Sewer	3	7.0 Years
Heavy—Fire Apparatus	12	26.5 Years
Heavy—Other	23	11.6 Years
Trailed Equipment	67	16.0 Years
Off-Road/Construction/Tractors	38	13.3 Years
Buses	2	3.5 Years
TOTAL	560	

Vehicle Equivalent Units (VEUs)	1,843
Average Rolling Stock Units Available per Day	NA
Hours Billed	4,581
Work Orders	3,564
Repeat Repairs within 30 Days	0
Work Orders Completed within 24 hours	NA
Preventive Maintenance Jobs (PMs)	765
PMs Completed as Scheduled	765

Full Cost Profile

Cost Breakdown by Percentage

Personal Services	36.9%
Operating Costs	63.1%
Capital Costs	0.0%
TOTAL	100.0%

Cost Breakdown in Dollars

Personal Services	$738,658
Operating Costs	$1,260,572
Capital Costs	$0
TOTAL	$1,999,230

Goldsboro   Fleet Maintenance

Resource Measures

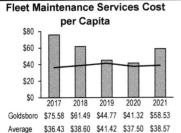

Fleet Maintenance Services Cost per Capita

	2017	2018	2019	2020	2021
Goldsboro	$75.58	$61.49	$44.77	$41.32	$58.53
Average	$36.43	$38.60	$41.42	$37.50	$38.57

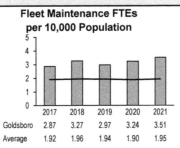

Fleet Maintenance FTEs per 10,000 Population

	2017	2018	2019	2020	2021
Goldsboro	2.87	3.27	2.97	3.24	3.51
Average	1.92	1.96	1.94	1.90	1.95

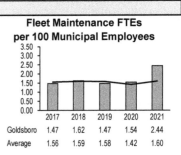

Fleet Maintenance FTEs per 100 Municipal Employees

	2017	2018	2019	2020	2021
Goldsboro	1.47	1.62	1.47	1.54	2.44
Average	1.56	1.59	1.58	1.42	1.60

Workload Measures

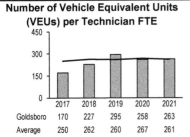

Number of Vehicle Equivalent Units (VEUs) per Technician FTE

	2017	2018	2019	2020	2021
Goldsboro	170	227	295	258	263
Average	250	262	260	267	261

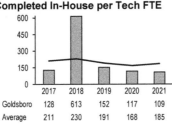

Preventive Maintenances (PMs) Completed In-House per Tech FTE

	2017	2018	2019	2020	2021
Goldsboro	128	613	152	117	109
Average	211	230	191	168	185

Efficiency Measures

Fleet Maintenance Cost per Work Order

	2017	2018	2019	2020	2021
Goldsboro	$689	$526	$396	$414	$561
Average	$545	$580	$677	$678	$677

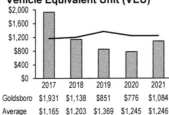

Fleet Maintenance Cost per Vehicle Equivalent Unit (VEU)

	2017	2018	2019	2020	2021
Goldsboro	$1,931	$1,138	$851	$776	$1,084
Average	$1,165	$1,203	$1,369	$1,245	$1,246

Hours Billed as a Percentage of Total Hours

	2017	2018	2019	2020	2021
Goldsboro	27%	26%	34%	30%	31%
Average	71%	69%	69%	63%	65%

Effectiveness Measures

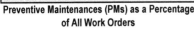

Preventive Maintenances (PMs) as a Percentage of All Work Orders

	2017	2018	2019	2020	2021
Goldsboro	27%		24%	24%	21%
Average	43%	39%	39%	36%	39%

Percentage of Preventive Maintenances (PMs) Completed as Scheduled

	2017	2018	2019	2020	2021
Goldsboro	100%	100%	100%	100%	100%
Average	81%	82%	75%	83%	85%

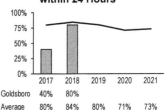

Percentage of Work Orders Completed within 24 Hours

	2017	2018	2019	2020	2021
Goldsboro	40%	80%			
Average	80%	84%	80%	71%	73%

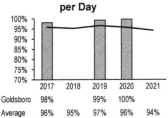

Percentage of Rolling Stock Available per Day

	2017	2018	2019	2020	2021
Goldsboro	98%		99%	100%	
Average	96%	95%	97%	96%	94%

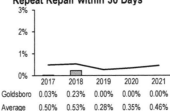

Percentage of Work Orders Requiring Repeat Repair within 30 Days

	2017	2018	2019	2020	2021
Goldsboro	0.03%	0.23%	0.00%	0.00%	0.00%
Average	0.50%	0.53%	0.28%	0.35%	0.46%

Greensboro

Fleet Maintenance

Fiscal Year 2020-21

Explanatory Information

Service Level and Delivery

Greensboro's fleet maintenance operation is housed within the Equipment Services Division of the Finance Department. The division consists of four sections: administration, services, parts, and tires. All activities for this operation are accounted for in an internal service fund, with other departments and programs charged for its maintenance services on a cost recovery basis.

The labor rate for the fiscal year was $65 an hour. Charges included a 25 percent markup for parts sold and a 5 percent markup for sublet work.

The following services were contracted out:

- body work
- glass repair
- upholstery repair
- most automotive and light-duty oil changes
- other repairs when workload exceeded in-house capacity.

Conditions Affecting Service, Performance, and Costs

Vehicle Equivalent Units (VEUs) are a weighted measure of the maintenance effort associated with different classes of vehicles. A normal-use car is considered equal to one VEU. Vehicles such as fire trucks or police cars have higher VEUs, reflecting greater expected levels of maintenance.

The measure "hours billed as a percentage of total hours" is based on a work year of 2,080 hours and only counts those positions that were filled. It should be noted that technicians have responsibilities that do not result in billable hours, and they take normal vacation and sick leave. Therefore, this percentage should not be expected to be near 100 percent.

In Greensboro, the preventive maintenance (PM) completion standard for "percentage of PMs completed as scheduled" uses mileage parameters and scheduled dates within the calendar month or within thirty days of schedule.

In addition to rolling stock, Greensboro's fleet services has maintenance responsibilities for generators, saws, blowers, various police equipment, asphalt pavers, sprayers, hydraulic hammers, a motor mixer, pumps, snow plows, spreaders, and other equipment.

In Greensboro, maintenance on fire vehicles is performed by mechanics in the fire department. The work performed is not counted here.

Municipal Profile

Population (OSBM 2020)	299,556
Land Area (Square Miles)	129.62
Persons per Square Mile	2,311

Service Profile

FTE Positions—Technician	31.0
FTE Positions—Other	17.0
Work Bays	34

Rolling Stock Maintained	No.	Average Age
Cars—Normal Usage	168	7.0 Years
Cars—Severe Usage	394	4.0 Years
Motorcycles	8	1.0 Years
Light Utility Vehicles	40	14.0 Years
Light Vehicles	432	7.0 Years
Medium Vehicles	120	8.0 Years
Heavy—Sanitation	96	6.0 Years
Heavy—Sewer	10	6.0 Years
Heavy—Fire Apparatus	0	NA
Heavy—Other	114	9.0 Years
Trailed Equipment	215	11.0 Years
Off-Road/Construction/Tractors	131	8.0 Years
Buses	3	15.0 Years
TOTAL	1,731	

Vehicle Equivalent Units (VEUs)	5,573
Average Rolling Stock Units Available per Day	1,583
Hours Billed	40,607
Work Orders	11,490
Repeat Repairs within 30 Days	na
Work Orders Completed within 24 hours	10,505
Preventive Maintenance Jobs (PMs)	5,127
PMs Completed as Scheduled	5,127

Full Cost Profile

Cost Breakdown by Percentage
Personal Services	42.4%
Operating Costs	57.6%
Capital Costs	0.0%
TOTAL	100.0%

Cost Breakdown in Dollars
Personal Services	$3,536,375
Operating Costs	$4,799,243
Capital Costs	$0
TOTAL	$8,335,618

Greensboro

Fleet Maintenance

Key: Greensboro ▓   Benchmarking Average —   Fiscal Years 2017 through 2021

Resource Measures

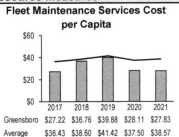

Fleet Maintenance Services Cost per Capita

	2017	2018	2019	2020	2021
Greensboro	$27.22	$36.76	$39.88	$28.11	$27.83
Average	$36.43	$38.60	$41.42	$37.50	$38.57

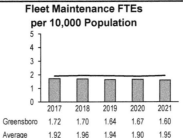

Fleet Maintenance FTEs per 10,000 Population

	2017	2018	2019	2020	2021
Greensboro	1.72	1.70	1.64	1.67	1.60
Average	1.92	1.96	1.94	1.90	1.95

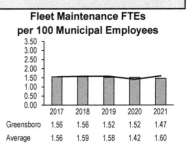

Fleet Maintenance FTEs per 100 Municipal Employees

	2017	2018	2019	2020	2021
Greensboro	1.56	1.56	1.52	1.52	1.47
Average	1.56	1.59	1.58	1.42	1.60

Workload Measures

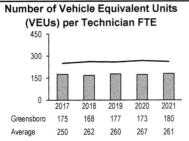

Number of Vehicle Equivalent Units (VEUs) per Technician FTE

	2017	2018	2019	2020	2021
Greensboro	175	168	177	173	180
Average	250	262	260	267	261

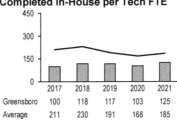

Preventive Maintenances (PMs) Completed In-House per Tech FTE

	2017	2018	2019	2020	2021
Greensboro	100	118	117	103	125
Average	211	230	191	168	185

Efficiency Measures

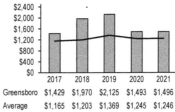

Fleet Maintenance Cost per Work Order

	2017	2018	2019	2020	2021
Greensboro	$648	$832	$955	$733	$725
Average	$545	$580	$677	$678	$677

Fleet Maintenance Cost per Vehicle Equivalent Unit (VEU)

	2017	2018	2019	2020	2021
Greensboro	$1,429	$1,970	$2,125	$1,493	$1,496
Average	$1,165	$1,203	$1,369	$1,245	$1,246

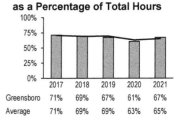

Hours Billed as a Percentage of Total Hours

	2017	2018	2019	2020	2021
Greensboro	71%	69%	67%	61%	67%
Average	71%	69%	69%	63%	65%

Effectiveness Measures

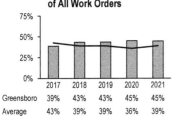

Preventive Maintenances (PMs) as a Percentage of All Work Orders

	2017	2018	2019	2020	2021
Greensboro	39%	43%	43%	45%	45%
Average	43%	39%	39%	36%	39%

Percentage of Preventive Maintenances (PMs) Completed as Scheduled

	2017	2018	2019	2020	2021
Greensboro	100%	100%	100%	100%	100%
Average	81%	82%	75%	83%	85%

Percentage of Work Orders Completed within 24 Hours

	2017	2018	2019	2020	2021
Greensboro	93%	92%	93%	92%	91%
Average	80%	84%	80%	71%	73%

Percentage of Rolling Stock Available per Day

	2017	2018	2019	2020	2021
Greensboro	93%	92%	93%	92%	91%
Average	96%	95%	97%	96%	94%

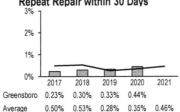

Percentage of Work Orders Requiring Repeat Repair within 30 Days

	2017	2018	2019	2020	2021
Greensboro	0.23%	0.30%	0.33%	0.44%	
Average	0.50%	0.53%	0.28%	0.35%	0.46%

Fiscal Year 2020-21

Explanatory Information

Service Level and Delivery
The Fleet Division is a part of Greenville's Public Works Department. All activities for this operation are accounted for as part of an internal service fund.

The division charges the Transit and Sanitation departments a $6 to $65 per hour labor rate for maintenance services and has a 15 percent markup on parts and a 15 percent markup on sublet work.

The following services were contracted out:

- alignments
- major body and paint repair
- two-way radio installs
- emergency light installs
- exhaust repair
- glass repair or replacement
- transmission overhaul
- major engine repair
- warranty repairs
- towing.

Conditions Affecting Service, Performance, and Costs
Vehicle Equivalent Units (VEUs) are a weighted measure of the maintenance effort associated with different classes of vehicles. A normal-use car is considered equal to one VEU. Vehicles such as fire trucks or police cars have higher VEUs, reflecting greater expected levels of maintenance.

In Greenville, the preventive maintenance (PM) completion standard for "percentage of PMs completed as scheduled" is within thirty days of the scheduled date or mileage parameters.

In addition to rolling stock, Greenville's fleet division has maintenance responsibilities for generators, lawnmowers, blowers, weedeaters, light towers, tampers, chainsaws, golf carts, utility carts, bush hogs, sprayers, fog machines, tractors, salt spreaders, leaf vacuums, concrete saws, an asphalt melter, rollers, a stump grinder, trail mowers, and other equipment.

No data were reported for FY 2019-20 for the city of Greenville.

Municipal Profile

Population (OSBM 2020)	87,428
Land Area (Square Miles)	35.66
Persons per Square Mile	2,452

Service Profile

FTE Positions—Technician	13.0
FTE Positions—Other	5.0
Work Bays	13

Rolling Stock Maintained	No.	Average Age
Cars—Normal Usage	25	8.0 Years
Cars—Severe Usage	190	8.0 Years
Motorcycles	6	6.0 Years
Light Utility Vehicles	11	13.0 Years
Light Vehicles	194	11.0 Years
Medium Vehicles	13	7.0 Years
Heavy—Sanitation	51	9.0 Years
Heavy—Sewer	2	3.0 Years
Heavy—Fire Apparatus	17	12.0 Years
Heavy—Other	16	11.0 Years
Trailed Equipment	79	15.0 Years
Off-Road/Construction/Tractors	110	15.0 Years
Buses	18	10.0 Years
TOTAL	732	

Vehicle Equivalent Units (VEUs)	2,763
Average Rolling Stock Units Available per Day	695
Hours Billed	18,026
Work Orders	6,841
Repeat Repairs within 30 Days	NA
Work Orders Completed within 24 hours	NA
Preventive Maintenance Jobs (PMs)	1,928
PMs Completed as Scheduled	1,779

Full Cost Profile

Cost Breakdown by Percentage

Personal Services	35.1%
Operating Costs	62.4%
Capital Costs	2.5%
TOTAL	100.0%

Cost Breakdown in Dollars

Personal Services	$1,555,697
Operating Costs	$2,766,294
Capital Costs	$109,889
TOTAL	$4,431,880

Key: Greenville ▨   Benchmarking Average —   Fiscal Years 2017 through 2021

Resource Measures

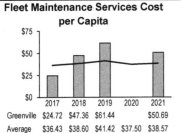

Fleet Maintenance Services Cost per Capita

	2017	2018	2019	2020	2021
Greenville	$24.72	$47.36	$61.44		$50.69
Average	$36.43	$38.60	$41.42	$37.50	$38.57

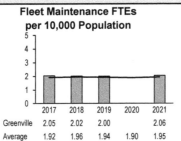

Fleet Maintenance FTEs per 10,000 Population

	2017	2018	2019	2020	2021
Greenville	2.05	2.02	2.00		2.06
Average	1.92	1.96	1.94	1.90	1.95

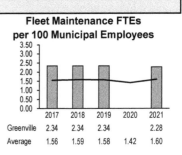

Fleet Maintenance FTEs per 100 Municipal Employees

	2017	2018	2019	2020	2021
Greenville	2.34	2.34	2.34		2.28
Average	1.56	1.59	1.58	1.42	1.60

Workload Measures

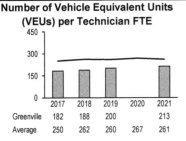

Number of Vehicle Equivalent Units (VEUs) per Technician FTE

	2017	2018	2019	2020	2021
Greenville	182	188	200		213
Average	250	262	260	267	261

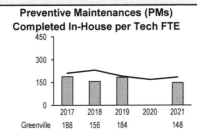

Preventive Maintenances (PMs) Completed In-House per Tech FTE

	2017	2018	2019	2020	2021
Greenville	188	156	184		148
Average	211	230	191	168	185

Efficiency Measures

Fleet Maintenance Cost per Work Order

	2017	2018	2019	2020	2021
Greenville	$364	$735	$952		$648
Average	$545	$580	$677	$678	$677

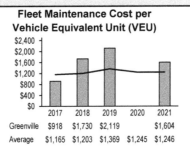

Fleet Maintenance Cost per Vehicle Equivalent Unit (VEU)

	2017	2018	2019	2020	2021
Greenville	$918	$1,730	$2,119		$1,604
Average	$1,165	$1,203	$1,369	$1,245	$1,246

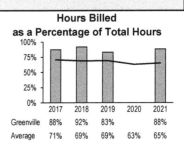

Hours Billed as a Percentage of Total Hours

	2017	2018	2019	2020	2021
Greenville	88%	92%	83%		88%
Average	71%	69%	69%	63%	65%

Effectiveness Measures

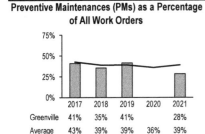

Preventive Maintenances (PMs) as a Percentage of All Work Orders

	2017	2018	2019	2020	2021
Greenville	41%	35%	41%		28%
Average	43%	39%	39%	36%	39%

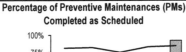

Percentage of Preventive Maintenances (PMs) Completed as Scheduled

	2017	2018	2019	2020	2021
Greenville	0%	0%	0%		92%
Average	81%	82%	75%	83%	85%

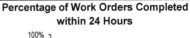
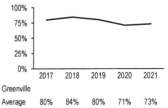

Percentage of Work Orders Completed within 24 Hours

	2017	2018	2019	2020	2021
Greenville					
Average	80%	84%	80%	71%	73%

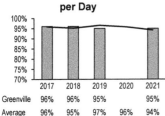

Percentage of Rolling Stock Available per Day

	2017	2018	2019	2020	2021
Greenville	96%	96%	95%		95%
Average	96%	95%	97%	96%	94%

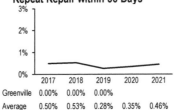

Percentage of Work Orders Requiring Repeat Repair within 30 Days

	2017	2018	2019	2020	2021
Greenville	0.00%	0.00%	0.00%		
Average	0.50%	0.53%	0.28%	0.35%	0.46%

Hickory

Fleet Maintenance

Fiscal Year 2020-21

Explanatory Information

Service Level and Delivery
Fleet Maintenance is a division of Hickory's Public Services Department and consists of a garage office, a parts warehouse, a welding shop, a maintenance shop, a fleet wash station, a fuel station, and a compressed natural gas station. All activities for this operation are accounted for in an internal service fund.

The division charges a $60-per-hour labor rate for maintenance services and a 25 percent markup charge on parts sold. There is no markup charge for sublet work.

The following services were contracted out:

- alignments
- body work
- large wrecker service
- special machine work
- starter/alternator repair
- glass repair or replacement
- transmission repairs.

Conditions Affecting Service, Performance, and Costs
Vehicle Equivalent Units (VEUs) are a weighted measure of the maintenance effort associated with different classes of vehicles. A normal-use car is considered equal to one VEU. Vehicles such as fire trucks or police cars have higher VEUs, reflecting greater expected levels of maintenance.

The measure "hours billed as a percentage of total hours" is based on a work year of 2,080 hours and only counts those positions that were filled. It should be noted that technicians have responsibilities that do not result in billable hours, and they take normal vacation and sick leave. Therefore, this percentage should not be expected to be near 100 percent.

In Hickory, the preventive maintenance (PM) completion standard for "percentage of PMs completed as scheduled" is within thirty days of the scheduled date.

In addition to rolling stock, Hickory's fleet services has maintenance responsibilities for electronic signs, saws, weedeaters, sewer machines, hole piercing tools, boring machines, pumps, mowers, edgers, a sand blaster, pressure washers, blowers, mules, spreaders, generators, tamps, vacuums, airport equipment, grinders, a fleet wash station, a compressed natural gas fuel station, a gasoline and diesel fuel station, and other equipment.

In Hickory, maintenance on fire vehicles is performed by mechanics in the fire department. The work performed is not counted here.

Municipal Profile

Population (OSBM 2020)	43,578
Land Area (Square Miles)	30.50
Persons per Square Mile	1,429

Service Profile

FTE Positions—Technician	7.0
FTE Positions—Other	4.0
Work Bays	14

Rolling Stock Maintained	No.	Average Age
Cars—Normal Usage	23	8.1 Years
Cars—Severe Usage	149	5.9 Years
Motorcycles	0	NA
Light Utility Vehicles	7	12.0 Years
Light Vehicles	108	7.6 Years
Medium Vehicles	38	11.8 Years
Heavy—Sanitation	31	9.3 Years
Heavy—Sewer	6	11.4 Years
Heavy—Fire Apparatus	0	NA
Heavy—Other	19	17.9 Years
Trailed Equipment	69	4.0 Years
Off-Road/Construction/Tractors	119	13.4 Years
Buses	0	NA
TOTAL	569	

Vehicle Equivalent Units (VEUs)	1,936
Average Rolling Stock Units Available per Day	515
Hours Billed	10,678
Work Orders	4,930
Repeat Repairs within 30 Days	29
Work Orders Completed within 24 hours	NA
Preventive Maintenance Jobs (PMs)	2,353
PMs Completed as Scheduled	NA

Full Cost Profile

Cost Breakdown by Percentage

Personal Services	33.4%
Operating Costs	65.2%
Capital Costs	1.4%
TOTAL	100.0%

Cost Breakdown in Dollars

Personal Services	$672,120
Operating Costs	$1,310,448
Capital Costs	$27,163
TOTAL	$2,009,731

Hickory

Fleet Maintenance

Key: Hickory   Benchmarking Average —   Fiscal Years 2017 through 2021

Resource Measures

Fleet Maintenance Services Cost per Capita

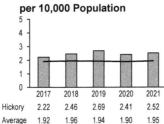

	2017	2018	2019	2020	2021
Hickory	$41.75	$43.90	$49.34	$55.06	$46.12
Average	$36.43	$38.60	$41.42	$37.50	$38.57

Fleet Maintenance FTEs per 10,000 Population

	2017	2018	2019	2020	2021
Hickory	2.22	2.46	2.69	2.41	2.52
Average	1.92	1.96	1.94	1.90	1.95

Fleet Maintenance FTEs per 100 Municipal Employees

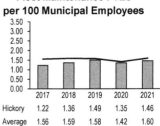

	2017	2018	2019	2020	2021
Hickory	1.22	1.36	1.49	1.35	1.46
Average	1.56	1.59	1.58	1.42	1.60

Workload Measures

Number of Vehicle Equivalent Units (VEUs) per Technician FTE

	2017	2018	2019	2020	2021
Hickory	362	286	238	319	277
Average	250	262	260	267	261

Preventive Maintenances (PMs) Completed In-House per Tech FTE

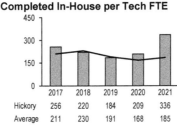

	2017	2018	2019	2020	2021
Hickory	256	220	184	209	336
Average	211	230	191	168	185

Efficiency Measures

Fleet Maintenance Cost per Work Order

	2017	2018	2019	2020	2021
Hickory	$336	$364	$370	$426	$408
Average	$545	$580	$677	$678	$677

Fleet Maintenance Cost per Vehicle Equivalent Unit (VEU)

	2017	2018	2019	2020	2021
Hickory	$932	$1,040	$1,211	$1,190	$1,038
Average	$1,165	$1,203	$1,369	$1,245	$1,246

Hours Billed as a Percentage of Total Hours

	2017	2018	2019	2020	2021
Hickory	84%	84%	85%	84%	79%
Average	71%	69%	69%	63%	65%

Effectiveness Measures

Preventive Maintenances (PMs) as a Percentage of All Work Orders

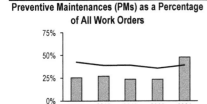

	2017	2018	2019	2020	2021
Hickory	25%	27%	24%	23%	48%
Average	43%	39%	39%	36%	39%

Percentage of Preventive Maintenances (PMs) Completed as Scheduled

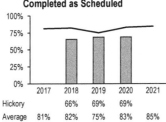

	2017	2018	2019	2020	2021
Hickory		66%	69%	69%	
Average	81%	82%	75%	83%	85%

Percentage of Work Orders Completed within 24 Hours

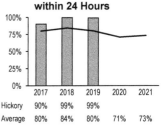

	2017	2018	2019	2020	2021
Hickory	90%	99%	99%		
Average	80%	84%	80%	71%	73%

Percentage of Rolling Stock Available per Day

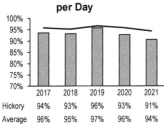

	2017	2018	2019	2020	2021
Hickory	94%	93%	96%	93%	91%
Average	96%	95%	97%	96%	94%

Percentage of Work Orders Requiring Repeat Repair within 30 Days

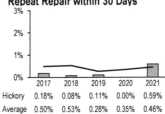

	2017	2018	2019	2020	2021
Hickory	0.18%	0.08%	0.11%	0.00%	0.59%
Average	0.50%	0.53%	0.28%	0.35%	0.46%

Explanatory Information

Service Level and Delivery

The Vehicle Fleet Service Division is under the Engineering Services Department for the City of Raleigh. The division provides maintenance and repair services for all city vehicles and motorized equipment except for Fire Department vehicles and city buses, which are handled by their own department. The city operates three separate locations to service vehicles. The division also handles replacement of new vehicles and equipment, managing fuel operations, and the city motor pool. The division is run as an internal service fund for the city.

Varying labor rates are used for different types of workers ranging from $48 per hour for preventative maintenance technicians up to $79 for heavy equipment mechanics. A markup of 30 percent is added for parts, and a 20 percent markup is added for sublet work.

The following services were contracted out:

- body work
- painting of new vehicles
- transmission work and overhauls
- some engine replacements
- spring work
- natural gas tank inspections
- onsite lubrication services for refuse vehicles
- towing.

Conditions Affecting Service, Performance, and Costs

Vehicle Equivalent Units (VEUs) are a weighted measure of the maintenance effort associated with different classes of vehicles. A normal-use car is considered equal to one VEU. Vehicles such as fire trucks or police cars have higher VEUs, reflecting greater expected levels of maintenance.

In Raleigh, the preventive maintenance (PM) completion standard for "percentage of PMs completed as scheduled" is 45 days and a 30 percent variance for meters, which could be miles or hours.

In addition to maintenance responsibilities for the city's rolling stock, the division also has responsibility for equipment, including pumps, weed eaters, concrete saws, mowers, blowers, compressors, light towers, scissor lifts, vacuums, pipe saws, flashing light arrows, chippers, spray washes, line markers, leaf vacuums, outboard motors, spreaders, generators, paint sprayers, grass trimmers, yard waste handlers, power rodders, golf carts, forklifts, and other city equipment.

Municipal Profile

Population (OSBM 2020)	468,977
Land Area (Square Miles)	146.47
Persons per Square Mile	3,202

Service Profile

FTE Positions—Technician	44.0
FTE Positions—Other	33.0
Work Bays	51

Rolling Stock Maintained	No.	Average Age
Cars—Normal Usage	234	6.0 Years
Cars—Severe Usage	431	5.0 Years
Motorcycles	8	0.4 Years
Light Utility Vehicles	101	6.4 Years
Light Vehicles	900	6.1 Years
Medium Vehicles	156	6.9 Years
Heavy—Sanitation	111	5.8 Years
Heavy—Sewer	28	5.8 Years
Heavy—Fire Apparatus	0	NA
Heavy—Other	152	7.5 Years
Trailed Equipment	365	10.8 Years
Off-Road/Construction/Tractors	226	9.2 Years
Buses	18	10.4 Years
TOTAL	2,730	

Vehicle Equivalent Units (VEUs)	8,077
Average Rolling Stock Units Available per Day	2,601
Hours Billed	53,854
Work Orders	22,885
Repeat Repairs within 30 Days	149
Work Orders Completed within 24 hours	5,247
Preventive Maintenance Jobs (PMs)	8,271
PMs Completed as Scheduled	6,462

Full Cost Profile

Cost Breakdown by Percentage

Personal Services	46.2%
Operating Costs	48.2%
Capital Costs	5.6%
TOTAL	100.0%

Cost Breakdown in Dollars

Personal Services	$5,452,841
Operating Costs	$5,689,336
Capital Costs	$666,423
TOTAL	$11,808,600

Resource Measures

Fleet Maintenance Services Cost per Capita

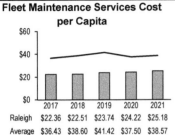

	2017	2018	2019	2020	2021
Raleigh	$22.36	$22.51	$23.74	$24.22	$25.18
Average	$36.43	$38.60	$41.42	$37.50	$38.57

Fleet Maintenance FTEs per 10,000 Population

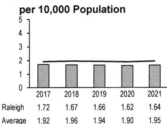

	2017	2018	2019	2020	2021
Raleigh	1.72	1.67	1.66	1.62	1.64
Average	1.92	1.96	1.94	1.90	1.95

Fleet Maintenance FTEs per 100 Municipal Employees

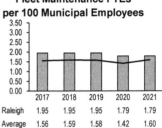

	2017	2018	2019	2020	2021
Raleigh	1.95	1.95	1.95	1.79	1.79
Average	1.56	1.59	1.58	1.42	1.60

Workload Measures

Number of Vehicle Equivalent Units (VEUs) per Technician FTE

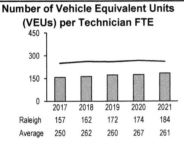

	2017	2018	2019	2020	2021
Raleigh	157	162	172	174	184
Average	250	262	260	267	261

Preventive Maintenances (PMs) Completed In-House per Tech FTE

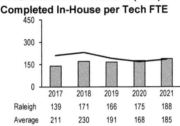

	2017	2018	2019	2020	2021
Raleigh	139	171	166	175	188
Average	211	230	191	168	185

Efficiency Measures

Fleet Maintenance Cost per Work Order

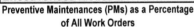

	2017	2018	2019	2020	2021
Raleigh	$459	$522	$481	$491	$516
Average	$545	$580	$677	$678	$677

Fleet Maintenance Cost per Vehicle Equivalent Unit (VEU)

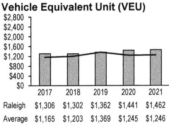

	2017	2018	2019	2020	2021
Raleigh	$1,306	$1,302	$1,362	$1,441	$1,462
Average	$1,165	$1,203	$1,369	$1,245	$1,246

Hours Billed as a Percentage of Total Hours

	2017	2018	2019	2020	2021
Raleigh	59%	56%	65%	65%	70%
Average	71%	69%	69%	63%	65%

Effectiveness Measures

Preventive Maintenances (PMs) as a Percentage of All Work Orders

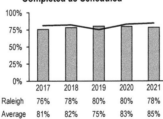

	2017	2018	2019	2020	2021
Raleigh	31%	42%	34%	34%	36%
Average	43%	39%	39%	36%	39%

Percentage of Preventive Maintenances (PMs) Completed as Scheduled

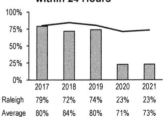

	2017	2018	2019	2020	2021
Raleigh	76%	78%	80%	80%	78%
Average	81%	82%	75%	83%	85%

Percentage of Work Orders Completed within 24 Hours

	2017	2018	2019	2020	2021
Raleigh	79%	72%	74%	23%	23%
Average	80%	84%	80%	71%	73%

Percentage of Rolling Stock Available per Day

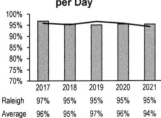

	2017	2018	2019	2020	2021
Raleigh	97%	95%	95%	95%	95%
Average	96%	95%	97%	96%	94%

Percentage of Work Orders Requiring Repeat Repair within 30 Days

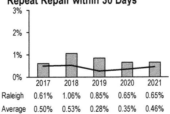

	2017	2018	2019	2020	2021
Raleigh	0.61%	1.06%	0.85%	0.65%	0.65%
Average	0.50%	0.53%	0.28%	0.35%	0.46%

Wilson

Fleet Maintenance

Fiscal Year 2020-21

Explanatory Information

Service Level and Delivery

Wilson's Fleet Maintenance Division is housed within the Department of Public Services. All activities in this operation are accounted for in the general fund.

Charges for maintenance services included a $44-per-hour labor rate, a 25 percent markup charge on parts sold, and a 5 percent markup charge on sublet work.

The following services were contracted out:

- body repairs
- paint work
- wrecker service
- radiator repairs
- alignment
- muffler repairs.

Conditions Affecting Service, Performance, and Costs

Vehicle Equivalent Units (VEUs) are a weighted measure of the maintenance effort associated with different classes of vehicles. A normal-use car is considered equal to one VEU. Vehicles such as fire trucks or police cars have higher VEUs, reflecting greater expected levels of maintenance.

The measure "hours billed as a percentage of total hours" is based on a work year of 2,080 hours and only counts those positions that were filled. It should be noted that technicians have responsibilities that do not result in billable hours, and they take normal vacation and sick leave. Therefore, this percentage should not be expected to be near 100 percent.

In Wilson, the preventive maintenance (PM) completion standard for "percentage of PMs completed as scheduled" varies, including both calendar and mileage standards.

In addition to rolling stock, Wilson's fleet services has maintenance responsibilities for generators, mowers, tamps, leaf machines, water pumps, and other city equipment.

Municipal Profile

Population (OSBM 2020)	47,769
Land Area (Square Miles)	31.02
Persons per Square Mile	1,540

Service Profile

FTE Positions—Technician	11.0
FTE Positions—Other	5.0
Work Bays	11

Rolling Stock Maintained	No.	Average Age
Cars—Normal Usage	40	6.0 Years
Cars—Severe Usage	107	7.0 Years
Motorcycles	3	5.0 Years
Light Utility Vehicles	21	7.0 Years
Light Vehicles	215	9.0 Years
Medium Vehicles	58	14.0 Years
Heavy—Sanitation	33	10.0 Years
Heavy—Sewer	4	7.0 Years
Heavy—Fire Apparatus	10	15.0 Years
Heavy—Other	65	9.0 Years
Trailed Equipment	169	15.0 Years
Off-Road/Construction/Tractors	166	0.0 Years
Buses	0	0.0 Years
TOTAL	891	

Vehicle Equivalent Units (VEUs)	2,877
Average Rolling Stock Units Available per Day	846
Hours Billed	14,144
Work Orders	4,803
Repeat Repairs within 30 Days	48
Work Orders Completed within 24 hours	4,323
Preventive Maintenance Jobs (PMs)	1,267
PMs Completed as Scheduled	1,203

Full Cost Profile

Cost Breakdown by Percentage

Personal Services	33.1%
Operating Costs	61.1%
Capital Costs	5.8%
TOTAL	100.0%

Cost Breakdown in Dollars

Personal Services	$1,244,852
Operating Costs	$2,297,416
Capital Costs	$219,539
TOTAL	$3,761,807

Wilson

Fleet Maintenance

Key: Wilson ▓   Benchmarking Average —   Fiscal Years 2017 through 2021

Resource Measures

Fleet Maintenance Services Cost per Capita

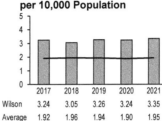

	2017	2018	2019	2020	2021
Wilson	$74.24	$74.80	$88.02	$82.29	$78.75
Average	$36.43	$38.60	$41.42	$37.50	$38.57

Fleet Maintenance FTEs per 10,000 Population

	2017	2018	2019	2020	2021
Wilson	3.24	3.05	3.26	3.24	3.35
Average	1.92	1.96	1.94	1.90	1.95

Fleet Maintenance FTEs per 100 Municipal Employees

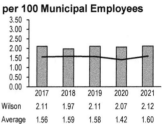

	2017	2018	2019	2020	2021
Wilson	2.11	1.97	2.11	2.07	2.12
Average	1.56	1.59	1.58	1.42	1.60

Workload Measures

Number of Vehicle Equivalent Units (VEUs) per Technician FTE

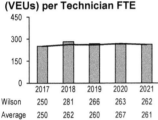

	2017	2018	2019	2020	2021
Wilson	250	281	266	263	262
Average	250	262	260	267	261

Preventive Maintenances (PMs) Completed In-House per Tech FTE

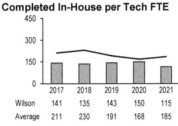

	2017	2018	2019	2020	2021
Wilson	141	135	143	150	115
Average	211	230	191	168	185

Efficiency Measures

Fleet Maintenance Cost per Work Order

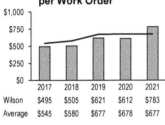

	2017	2018	2019	2020	2021
Wilson	$495	$505	$621	$612	$783
Average	$545	$580	$677	$678	$677

Fleet Maintenance Cost per Vehicle Equivalent Unit (VEU)

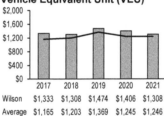

	2017	2018	2019	2020	2021
Wilson	$1,333	$1,308	$1,474	$1,406	$1,308
Average	$1,165	$1,203	$1,369	$1,245	$1,246

Hours Billed as a Percentage of Total Hours

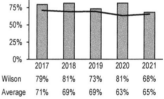

	2017	2018	2019	2020	2021
Wilson	79%	81%	73%	81%	68%
Average	71%	69%	69%	63%	65%

Effectiveness Measures

Preventive Maintenances (PMs) as a Percentage of All Work Orders

	2017	2018	2019	2020	2021
Wilson	21%	19%	23%	25%	26%
Average	43%	39%	39%	36%	39%

Percentage of Preventive Maintenances (PMs) Completed as Scheduled

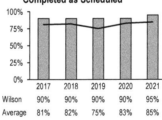

	2017	2018	2019	2020	2021
Wilson	90%	90%	90%	90%	95%
Average	81%	82%	75%	83%	85%

Percentage of Work Orders Completed within 24 Hours

	2017	2018	2019	2020	2021
Wilson	86%	85%	85%	85%	90%
Average	80%	84%	80%	71%	73%

Percentage of Rolling Stock Available per Day

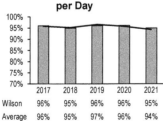

	2017	2018	2019	2020	2021
Wilson	96%	95%	96%	96%	95%
Average	96%	95%	97%	96%	94%

Percentage of Work Orders Requiring Repeat Repair within 30 Days

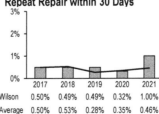

	2017	2018	2019	2020	2021
Wilson	0.50%	0.49%	0.49%	0.32%	1.00%
Average	0.50%	0.53%	0.28%	0.35%	0.46%

Winston-Salem

Fleet Maintenance

Fiscal Year 2020-21

Explanatory Information

Service Level and Delivery

Fleet Services is a division of the Property and Facilities Management Department, consisting of eight units: vehicle maintenance administration, contract monitoring administration, heavy equipment, service station, vehicle leasing, parts, light equipment, and tire shop. All activities in this operation are accounted for in an internal service fund.

Charges for maintenance services included a $50-per-hour labor rate, a 26 percent markup charge for parts sold, and a 13 percent markup charge for sublet work.

The following services were contracted out:

- body work
- welding
- hydraulic cylinder and pump repair
- glass repair
- towing
- transmission repair.

Conditions Affecting Service, Performance, and Costs

Vehicle Equivalent Units (VEUs) are a weighted measure of the maintenance effort associated with different classes of vehicles. A normal-use car is considered equal to one VEU. Vehicles such as fire trucks or police cars have higher VEUs, reflecting greater expected levels of maintenance.

The measure "hours billed as a percentage of total hours" is based on a work year of 2,080 hours and only counts those positions that were filled. It should be noted that technicians have responsibilities that do not result in billable hours, and they take normal vacation and sick leave. Therefore, this percentage should not be expected to be near 100 percent. Winston-Salem indicated that seventeen technician FTEs were actually working during the fiscal year for this calculation.

In addition to rolling stock, Winston-Salem's Fleet Services has maintenance responsibilities for mowers, weedeaters, water pumps, chain saws, whacker tamps, pavement stripers, tractor implements, leaf blowers, power trimmers, salt spreaders, snow plows, and other city equipment.

In Winston-Salem, maintenance on fire vehicles is performed by mechanics in the fire department. Those mechanics and that work performed are not counted here.

Municipal Profile

Population (OSBM 2020)	249,986
Land Area (Square Miles)	132.59
Persons per Square Mile	1,885

Service Profile

FTE Positions—Technician	19.0
FTE Positions—Other	13.0
Work Bays	30

Rolling Stock Maintained	No.	Average Age
Cars—Normal Usage	258	7.5 Years
Cars—Severe Usage	426	6.1 Years
Motorcycles	15	NA
Light Utility Vehicles	12	NA
Light Vehicles	444	10.9 Years
Medium Vehicles	146	12.0 Years
Heavy—Sanitation	58	6.9 Years
Heavy—Sewer	10	3.4 Years
Heavy—Fire Apparatus	0	NA
Heavy—Other	66	7.6 Years
Trailed Equipment	175	13.0 Years
Off-Road/Construction/Tractors	262	10.0 Years
Buses	0	NA
TOTAL	1,872	

Vehicle Equivalent Units (VEUs)	5,413
Average Rolling Stock Units Available per Day	1,701
Hours Billed	27,392
Work Orders	9,591
Repeat Repairs within 30 Days	23
Work Orders Completed within 24 hours	6,277
Preventive Maintenance Jobs (PMs)	3,949
PMs Completed as Scheduled	1,225

Full Cost Profile

Cost Breakdown by Percentage

Personal Services	28.0%
Operating Costs	70.1%
Capital Costs	1.8%
TOTAL	100.0%

Cost Breakdown in Dollars

Personal Services	$1,740,059
Operating Costs	$4,355,462
Capital Costs	$114,087
TOTAL	$6,209,608

Resource Measures

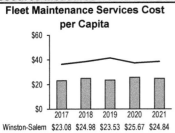

Fleet Maintenance Services Cost per Capita

	2017	2018	2019	2020	2021
Winston-Salem	$23.08	$24.98	$23.53	$25.67	$24.84
Average	$36.43	$38.60	$41.42	$37.50	$38.57

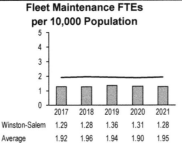

Fleet Maintenance FTEs per 10,000 Population

	2017	2018	2019	2020	2021
Winston-Salem	1.29	1.28	1.36	1.31	1.28
Average	1.92	1.96	1.94	1.90	1.95

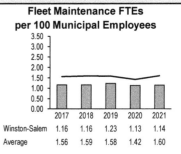

Fleet Maintenance FTEs per 100 Municipal Employees

	2017	2018	2019	2020	2021
Winston-Salem	1.16	1.16	1.23	1.13	1.14
Average	1.56	1.59	1.58	1.42	1.60

Workload Measures

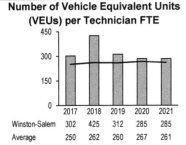

Number of Vehicle Equivalent Units (VEUs) per Technician FTE

	2017	2018	2019	2020	2021
Winston-Salem	302	425	312	285	285
Average	250	262	260	267	261

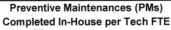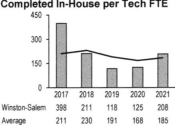

Preventive Maintenances (PMs) Completed In-House per Tech FTE

	2017	2018	2019	2020	2021
Winston-Salem	398	211	118	125	208
Average	211	230	191	168	185

Efficiency Measures

Fleet Maintenance Cost per Work Order

	2017	2018	2019	2020	2021
Winston-Salem	$661	$572	$535	$604	$647
Average	$545	$580	$677	$678	$677

Fleet Maintenance Cost per Vehicle Equivalent Unit (VEU)

	2017	2018	2019	2020	2021
Winston-Salem	$1,022	$793	$966	$1,159	$1,147
Average	$1,165	$1,203	$1,369	$1,245	$1,246

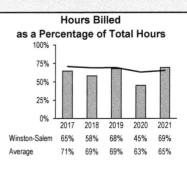

Hours Billed as a Percentage of Total Hours

	2017	2018	2019	2020	2021
Winston-Salem	65%	58%	68%	45%	69%
Average	71%	69%	69%	63%	65%

Effectiveness Measures

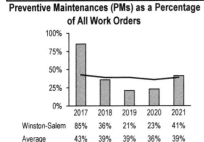

Preventive Maintenances (PMs) as a Percentage of All Work Orders

	2017	2018	2019	2020	2021
Winston-Salem	85%	36%	21%	23%	41%
Average	43%	39%	39%	36%	39%

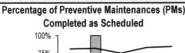

Percentage of Preventive Maintenances (PMs) Completed as Scheduled

	2017	2018	2019	2020	2021
Winston-Salem		100%	28%	48%	31%
Average	81%	82%	75%	83%	85%

Percentage of Work Orders Completed within 24 Hours

	2017	2018	2019	2020	2021
Winston-Salem	67%	68%	66%	66%	65%
Average	80%	84%	80%	71%	73%

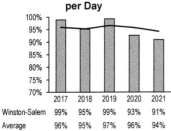

Percentage of Rolling Stock Available per Day

	2017	2018	2019	2020	2021
Winston-Salem	99%	95%	99%	93%	91%
Average	96%	95%	97%	96%	94%

Percentage of Work Orders Requiring Repeat Repair within 30 Days

	2017	2018	2019	2020	2021
Winston-Salem		0.57%		0.78%	0.24%
Average	0.50%	0.53%	0.28%	0.35%	0.46%

Performance and Cost Data

CENTRAL HUMAN RESOURCES

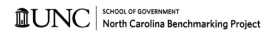

PERFORMANCE MEASURES FOR CENTRAL HUMAN RESOURCES

SERVICE DEFINITION

Central Human Resources represent an internal support service. It is characterized by various functions related to the daily management of human capital or personnel, including compensation analysis; position classification; benefits administration; management of employee training and development; employee relations; position control; employee performance evaluations; recruitment and selection; occupational health, wellness, and safety programs; administration of the Human Resources Information System (HRIS); and general administration of the central human resources office. Excluded from the counts here are staff who may be assisting with certain human resource functions but who are not in the central human resources department, such as employees who might be assigned to individual departments. Also excluded from this service area is risk financing, including general liability insurance and workers' compensation.

NOTES ON PERFORMANCE MEASURES

1. Total Workforce FTEs per 10,000 Population

The number of full-time equivalent (FTE) positions includes all permanent full-time and permanent part-time employees budgeted for the municipality. One FTE equates to 2,080 hours of work per year. Any combination of employees providing 2,080 hours of annual work equals one FTE.

2. Number of Applications Received per 100 Employees

Human resources is responsible for the recruitment and selection of applicants to fill new or vacant positions.

3. Number of Position Requisitions per 100 Employees

Position requisitions are submitted to the human resources office by departments seeking to fill vacant positions.

4. Cost per Employee

This measure represents the total cost of human resources for the fiscal year ending June 30 and is calculated using the project's full cost accounting model, which captures direct, indirect, and capital costs. Cost per employee is the primary measure of cost efficiency for this service area.

5. Ratio of Human Resources Staff to Total Workforce

This is a calculation of human resource FTEs divided by the total number of employees in the permanent municipal workforce, including full- and part-time staff.

6. Probationary Period Completion Rate (New Hires)

Most organizations require that new employees complete a probationary employment period, typically lasting three to eighteen months from the hire date, depending on the job classification. This effectiveness measure is calculated by dividing the total number of employees that completed the probationary period by the number of employees eligible to complete the probationary period during the fiscal year.

7. Employee Total Turnover Rate

The employee turnover rate is calculated by dividing the total number of separated staff during the fiscal year by the total number of authorized positions.

8. Employee Voluntary Turnover Rate

The employee voluntary turnover rate is calculated by dividing the number of voluntarily separated staff during the fiscal year by the total number of authorized positions. Voluntary separations include retirements and resignations.

9. Percentage of Grievances Resolved at the Department Level

Most jurisdictions have a process in place for handling formal grievances filed by employees. This effectiveness measure is calculated by dividing the number of formal grievances that were resolved within the respective department (prior to going to a higher level or third party for resolution) by the total number of grievances filed during the fiscal year.

10. Average Number of Days from Position Post Date to Hire Date

This includes the number of working days from the date a job is posted to the hire date (first day of employment). It includes only recruitments for permanent full-time and part-time positions that were completed during the fiscal year. This measure excludes recruitment of temporary workers.

Central Human Resources

Summary of Key Dimensions of Service

City or Town	Total Number of Authorized Municipal Positions	Average Length of Service (in Years)	Number of Position Requisitions	Number of Employment Applications Processed	Number of Retirees Serviced	Probationary Period	Turnover Rate	Number of HR FTEs
Apex	521	7.4	84	2,184	59	6 & 12 months	8.1%	5.0
Chapel Hill	747	10.0	122	361	50	6 & 12 months	12.4%	6.0
Concord	1,143	9.0	206	5,481	171	6 & 12 months	11.7%	13.0
Goldsboro	491	10.0	288	2,395	18	6 & 12 months	14.5%	5.0
Greensboro	3,274	10.8	460	19,026	45	6 & 12 months	7.9%	35.0
Greenville	790	10.3	141	4,653	120	6 & 12 months	15.8%	11.0
Hickory	753	10.3	99	2,489	104	12 months	16.9%	8.0
Raleigh	4,304	10.6	796	28,178	176	6 & 12 months	9.1%	32.0
Wilson	756	10.0	81	3,849	24	12 months	11.9%	6.0
Winston-Salem	2,803	10.3	522	11,670	1,194	6 & 12 months	9.3%	15.0

NOTES
For municipalities with varying probationary periods, typically fire and/or police personnel have longer probationary periods.

EXPLANATORY FACTORS
These are factors that the project found affected human resources performance and cost in one or more of the municipalities:

Decentralization of HR functions
Personnel policies
External economic climate
Unemployment rate
Extent of contracting out for services
Departmental discretion regarding vacancies
Hiring freezes
State and/or federal mandates

Explanatory Information

Service Level and Delivery

The Human Resources Department for Apex provides a comprehensive assortment of services, including occupational health and wellness, benefits, recruitment and selection, compensation, employee relations, and training and development programs.

One employee compensation study was completed during the fiscal year. The Town of Apex tries to study one-third of the job classifications every three years and uses a consultant to assist in this process.

The town's probationary period for new employees is six months for general employees and twelve months for sworn police, fire, and EMS personnel.

Conditions Affecting Service, Performance, and Costs

Municipal Profile

Population (OSBM 2020)	59,368
Land Area (Square Miles)	23.61
Persons per Square Mile	2,514

Service Profile

Central HR FTE Positions	
Administration	2.0
Generalist/Specialist	2.0
Staff Support/Clerical	1.00
Total Authorized Workforce	521.0
Authorized FTEs	520.2
Average Length of Service (Months)	88.8
Number of Position Requisitions	84
Employment Applications Processed	2,184
Length of Probationary Employment Period	6 & 12 months
Compensation Studies Completed	1
Positions Studied	NA
Employee Turnover	
Voluntary Separations	38
Involuntary Separations	4
TOTAL SEPARATIONS	42
Formal Grievances Filed by Employees	0
Equal Employment Opportunity Commission (EEOC) Complaints Filed	0

Full Cost Profile

Cost Breakdown by Percentage	
Personal Services	55.0%
Operating Costs	44.0%
Capital Costs	1.0%
TOTAL	100.0%
Cost Breakdown in Dollars	
Personal Services	$511,456
Operating Costs	$409,034
Capital Costs	$9,620
TOTAL	$930,110

Apex

Central Human Resources

Resource Measures

Human Resources Services Cost per Capita

	2017	2018	2019	2020	2021
Apex	$11.95	$12.27	$12.43	$11.45	$15.67
Average	$15.02	$15.43	$17.68	$17.62	$19.32

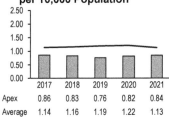

Human Resources FTEs per 10,000 Population

	2017	2018	2019	2020	2021
Apex	0.86	0.83	0.76	0.82	0.84
Average	1.14	1.16	1.19	1.22	1.13

Workload Measures

Total Municipal FTEs per 10,000 Population

	2017	2018	2019	2020	2021
Apex	89	92	88	82	88
Average	122	123	119	122	116

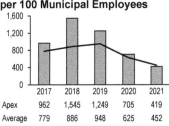

Applications Processed per 100 Municipal Employees

	2017	2018	2019	2020	2021
Apex	962	1,545	1,249	705	419
Average	779	886	948	625	452

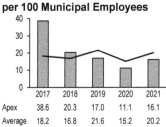

Position Requisitions per 100 Municipal Employees

	2017	2018	2019	2020	2021
Apex	38.6	20.3	17.0	11.1	16.1
Average	18.2	16.8	21.6	15.2	20.2

Efficiency Measures

Human Resources Cost per Municipal Employee

	2017	2018	2019	2020	2021
Apex	$1,338	$1,324	$1,411	$1,393	$1,785
Average	$1,268	$1,271	$1,515	$1,413	$1,674

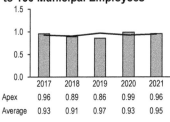

Ratio of Human Resources Staff to 100 Municipal Employees

	2017	2018	2019	2020	2021
Apex	0.96	0.89	0.86	0.99	0.96
Average	0.93	0.91	0.97	0.93	0.95

Effectiveness Measures

Probationary Period Completion Rate (New Hires)

	2017	2018	2019	2020	2021
Apex	89%	97%	92%	96%	100%
Average	84%	87%	84%	82%	87%

Employee Turnover Rate (All Separations)

	2017	2018	2019	2020	2021
Apex	12.2%	11.4%	11.8%	7.1%	8.1%
Average	9.8%	10.6%	10.8%	9.5%	11.8%

Employee Turnover Rate (Voluntary Separations)

	2017	2018	2019	2020	2021
Apex	11.0%	7.3%	10.7%	6.0%	7.3%
Average	8.0%	9.1%	9.4%	8.0%	10.4%

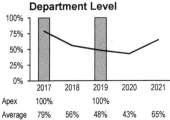

Percentage of Grievances Resolved at Department Level

	2017	2018	2019	2020	2021
Apex	100%		100%		
Average	79%	56%	48%	43%	65%

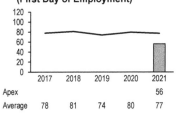

Average Days from Post Date to Hire Date (First Day of Employment)

	2017	2018	2019	2020	2021
Apex					56
Average	78	81	74	80	77

Chapel Hill — Central Human Resources

Fiscal Year 2020-21

Explanatory Information

Service Level and Delivery

The Town of Chapel Hill's Human Resource Development Department is organized into one centralized HR department using a specialist structure with several departmental HR liasons who facilitate communication of the town's processes and procedures, benefits paperwork, and predisciplinary conferences. The department ensures standard operating procedures are followed and coordinates departmental interviews for job openings.

The town provides an employee assistance program at no cost to town staff. Chapel Hill also provides some life insurance coverage and short- and long-term disability at no cost to employees. The town has an on-site wellness clinic staffed with a nurse practitioner and registered nurse. The town also offers a variety of other wellness programs at reduced cost such, as gym membership, nutritionists, and Weight Watchers.

The town's probationary period for most new employees is six months. Department heads and police personnel serve a twelve-month period.

Conditions Affecting Service, Performance, and Costs

Municipal Profile

Population (OSBM 2020)	62,080
Land Area (Square Miles)	21.31
Persons per Square Mile	2,914

Service Profile

Central HR FTE Positions

Administration	2.0
Generalist/Specialist	3.0
Staff Support/Clerical	1.0
Total Authorized Workforce	747.0
Authorized FTEs	743.21
Average Length of Service (Months)	119.58
Number of Position Requisitions	122
Employment Applications Processed	361
Length of Probationary Employment Period	6 & 12 months
Compensation Studies Completed	1
Positions Studied	330

Employee Turnover

Voluntary Separations	89
Involuntary Separations	4
TOTAL SEPARATIONS	93
Formal Grievances Filed by Employees	0
Equal Employment Opportunity Commission (EEOC) Complaints Filed	1

Full Cost Profile

Cost Breakdown by Percentage

Personal Services	33.2%
Operating Costs	66.1%
Capital Costs	0.7%
TOTAL	100.0%

Cost Breakdown in Dollars

Personal Services	$892,755
Operating Costs	$1,777,573
Capital Costs	$17,861
TOTAL	$2,688,189

Key: Chapel Hill ▨   Benchmarking Average —   Fiscal Years 2017 through 2021

Resource Measures

Human Resources Services Cost per Capita

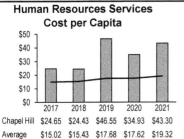

	2017	2018	2019	2020	2021
Chapel Hill	$24.65	$24.43	$46.55	$34.93	$43.30
Average	$15.02	$15.43	$17.68	$17.62	$19.32

Human Resources FTEs per 10,000 Population

	2017	2018	2019	2020	2021
Chapel Hill	1.17	1.34	1.27	1.26	0.97
Average	1.14	1.16	1.19	1.22	1.13

Workload Measures

Total Municipal FTEs per 10,000 Population

	2017	2018	2019	2020	2021
Chapel Hill	128	128	110	121	120
Average	122	123	119	122	116

Applications Processed per 100 Municipal Employees

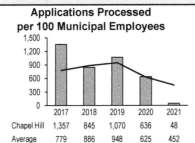

	2017	2018	2019	2020	2021
Chapel Hill	1,357	845	1,070	636	48
Average	779	886	948	625	452

Position Requisitions per 100 Municipal Employees

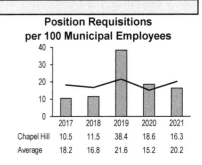

	2017	2018	2019	2020	2021
Chapel Hill	10.5	11.5	38.4	18.6	16.3
Average	18.2	16.8	21.6	15.2	20.2

Efficiency Measures

Human Resources Cost per Municipal Employee

	2017	2018	2019	2020	2021
Chapel Hill	$1,904	$1,894	$4,183	$2,868	$3,599
Average	$1,268	$1,271	$1,515	$1,413	$1,674

Ratio of Human Resources Staff to 100 Municipal Employees

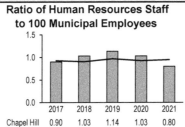

	2017	2018	2019	2020	2021
Chapel Hill	0.90	1.03	1.14	1.03	0.80
Average	0.93	0.91	0.97	0.93	0.95

Effectiveness Measures

Probationary Period Completion Rate (New Hires)

	2017	2018	2019	2020	2021
Chapel Hill	90%	88%	39%	77%	93%
Average	84%	87%	84%	82%	87%

Employee Turnover Rate (All Separations)

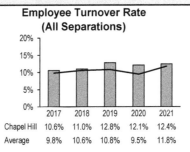

	2017	2018	2019	2020	2021
Chapel Hill	10.6%	11.0%	12.8%	12.1%	12.4%
Average	9.8%	10.6%	10.8%	9.5%	11.8%

Employee Turnover Rate (Voluntary Separations)

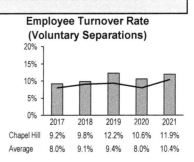

	2017	2018	2019	2020	2021
Chapel Hill	9.2%	9.8%	12.2%	10.6%	11.9%
Average	8.0%	9.1%	9.4%	8.0%	10.4%

Percentage of Grievances Resolved at Department Level

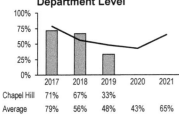

	2017	2018	2019	2020	2021
Chapel Hill	71%	67%	33%		
Average	79%	56%	48%	43%	65%

Average Days from Post Date to Hire Date (First Day of Employment)

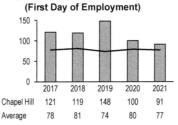

	2017	2018	2019	2020	2021
Chapel Hill	121	119	148	100	91
Average	78	81	74	80	77

Concord

Central Human Resources

Fiscal Year 2020-21

Explanatory Information

Service Level and Delivery
The Human Resources Department for the City of has a full range of responsibilities including policy development and enforcement, employment law compliance, recruitment and selection, employee relations, position classification, competitive compensation, benefit management, employee training, employee development, personnel records management, wellness, safety, and risk management. The city is committed to creating and maintaining a work environment that is safe, inclusive, equitable, and welcoming. Concord values diversity and promises to honor employee experiences, perspective, and unique identity.

The department conducted two compensation studies during the most recent year, covering 145 positions.

The city's probationary period for new employees is six months for non–public safety employees and twelve months for public safety employees.

Conditions Affecting Service, Performance, and Costs

Municipal Profile

Population (OSBM 2020)	105,936
Land Area (Square Miles)	63.65
Persons per Square Mile	1,664

Service Profile

Central HR FTE Positions	
Administration	4.0
Generalist/Specialist	8.0
Staff Support/Clerical	1.0
Total Authorized Workforce	1,143.0
Authorized FTEs	1,077.2
Average Length of Service (Months)	108
Number of Position Requisitions	206
Employment Applications Processed	5,481
Length of Probationary Employment Period	6 & 12 months
Compensation Studies Completed	2
Positions Studied	145
Employee Turnover	
Voluntary Separations	123
Involuntary Separations	11
TOTAL SEPARATIONS	134
Formal Grievances Filed by Employees	11
Equal Employment Opportunity Commission (EEOC) Complaints Filed	3

Full Cost Profile

Cost Breakdown by Percentage	
Personal Services	52.2%
Operating Costs	46.5%
Capital Costs	1.2%
TOTAL	100.0%

Cost Breakdown in Dollars	
Personal Services	$1,108,886
Operating Costs	$988,115
Capital Costs	$26,381
TOTAL	$2,123,382

Concord

Central Human Resources

Resource Measures

Human Resources Services Cost per Capita

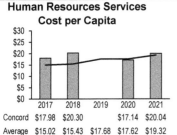

	2017	2018	2019	2020	2021
Concord	$17.98	$20.30		$17.14	$20.04
Average	$15.02	$15.43	$17.68	$17.62	$19.32

Human Resources FTEs per 10,000 Population

	2017	2018	2019	2020	2021
Concord	1.24	1.32		1.36	1.23
Average	1.14	1.16	1.19	1.22	1.13

Workload Measures

Total Municipal FTEs per 10,000 Population

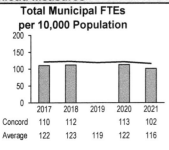

	2017	2018	2019	2020	2021
Concord	110	112		113	102
Average	122	123	119	122	116

Applications Processed per 100 Municipal Employees

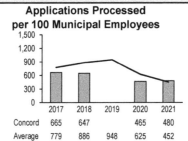

	2017	2018	2019	2020	2021
Concord	665	647		465	480
Average	779	886	948	625	452

Position Requisitions per 100 Municipal Employees

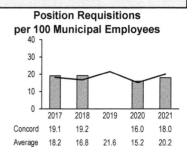

	2017	2018	2019	2020	2021
Concord	19.1	19.2		16.0	18.0
Average	18.2	16.8	21.6	15.2	20.2

Efficiency Measures

Human Resources Cost per Municipal Employee

	2017	2018	2019	2020	2021
Concord	$1,609	$1,785		$1,491	$1,858
Average	$1,268	$1,271	$1,515	$1,413	$1,674

Ratio of Human Resources Staff to 100 Municipal Employees

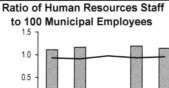
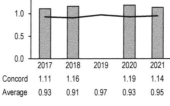

	2017	2018	2019	2020	2021
Concord	1.11	1.16		1.19	1.14
Average	0.93	0.91	0.97	0.93	0.95

Effectiveness Measures

Probationary Period Completion Rate (New Hires)

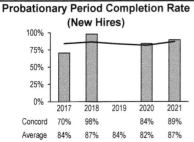

	2017	2018	2019	2020	2021
Concord	70%	98%		84%	89%
Average	84%	87%	84%	82%	87%

Employee Turnover Rate (All Separations)

	2017	2018	2019	2020	2021
Concord	10.4%	14.1%		10.5%	11.7%
Average	9.8%	10.6%	10.8%	9.5%	11.8%

Employee Turnover Rate (Voluntary Separations)

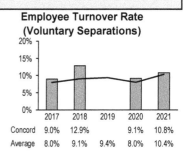

	2017	2018	2019	2020	2021
Concord	9.0%	12.9%		9.1%	10.8%
Average	8.0%	9.1%	9.4%	8.0%	10.4%

Percentage of Grievances Resolved at Department Level

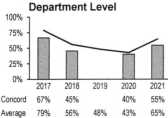

	2017	2018	2019	2020	2021
Concord	67%	45%		40%	55%
Average	79%	56%	48%	43%	65%

Average Days from Post Date to Hire Date (First Day of Employment)

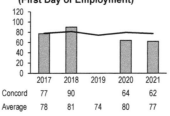

	2017	2018	2019	2020	2021
Concord	77	90		64	62
Average	78	81	74	80	77

Explanatory Information

Service Level and Delivery
The mission of the Human Resources Department for the City of Goldsboro is to provide services that promote a work environment that is characterized by fair treatment of staff, open communications, personal accountability, trust, and mutual respect. The department provides a comprehensive array of services that includes employee selection and recruitment, salary and compensation, benefits, professional development, employee relations, employee health/wellness, and compliance with federal and state safety regulations.

The city's probationary period for new employees is six months for non-public safety employees and twelve months for public safety employees.

During the fiscal year, the city conducted six compensation studies, covering 114 positions.

Conditions Affecting Service, Performance, and Costs
The City of Goldsboro joined the Benchmarking Project in July 2017, with the first year of data showing for FY 2016–17.

The city provides a $20,000 life insurance policy for all active full-time employees.

Municipal Profile

Population (OSBM 2020)	34,156
Land Area (Square Miles)	29.45
Persons per Square Mile	1,160

Service Profile

Central HR FTE Positions	
Administration	1.0
Generalist/Specialist	3.0
Staff Support/Clerical	1.0
Total Authorized Workforce	491.0
Authorized FTEs	485.8
Average Length of Service (Months)	120
Number of Position Requisitions	288
Employment Applications Processed	2,395
Length of Probationary Employment Period	6 & 12 months
Compensation Studies Completed	6
Positions Studied	114
Employee Turnover	
Voluntary Separations	65
Involuntary Separations	6
TOTAL SEPARATIONS	71
Formal Grievances Filed by Employees	3
Equal Employment Opportunity Commission (EEOC) Complaints Filed	2

Full Cost Profile

Cost Breakdown by Percentage	
Personal Services	70.2%
Operating Costs	29.8%
Capital Costs	0.0%
TOTAL	100.0%

Cost Breakdown in Dollars	
Personal Services	$458,572
Operating Costs	$194,954
Capital Costs	$0
TOTAL	$653,526

Goldsboro

Central Human Resources

Key: Goldsboro ▨   Benchmarking Average —   Fiscal Years 2017 through 2021

Resource Measures

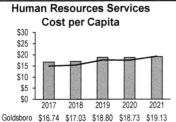

Human Resources Services Cost per Capita

	2017	2018	2019	2020	2021
Goldsboro	$16.74	$17.03	$18.80	$18.73	$19.13
Average	$15.02	$15.43	$17.68	$17.62	$19.32

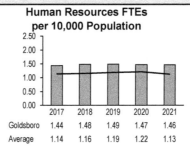

Human Resources FTEs per 10,000 Population

	2017	2018	2019	2020	2021
Goldsboro	1.44	1.48	1.49	1.47	1.46
Average	1.14	1.16	1.19	1.22	1.13

Workload Measures

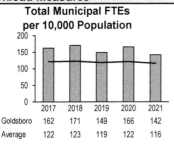

Total Municipal FTEs per 10,000 Population

	2017	2018	2019	2020	2021
Goldsboro	162	171	149	166	142
Average	122	123	119	122	116

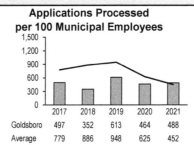

Applications Processed per 100 Municipal Employees

	2017	2018	2019	2020	2021
Goldsboro	497	352	613	464	488
Average	779	886	948	625	452

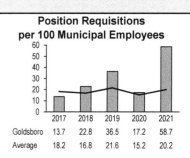

Position Requisitions per 100 Municipal Employees

	2017	2018	2019	2020	2021
Goldsboro	13.7	22.8	36.5	17.2	58.7
Average	18.2	16.8	21.6	15.2	20.2

Efficiency Measures

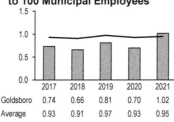

Human Resources Cost per Municipal Employee

	2017	2018	2019	2020	2021
Goldsboro	$857	$759	$1,025	$891	$1,331
Average	$1,268	$1,271	$1,515	$1,413	$1,674

Ratio of Human Resources Staff to 100 Municipal Employees

	2017	2018	2019	2020	2021
Goldsboro	0.74	0.66	0.81	0.70	1.02
Average	0.93	0.91	0.97	0.93	0.95

Effectiveness Measures

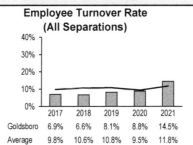

Probationary Period Completion Rate (New Hires)

	2017	2018	2019	2020	2021
Goldsboro	96%	94%	97%	79%	86%
Average	84%	87%	84%	82%	87%

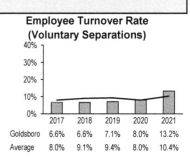

Employee Turnover Rate (All Separations)

	2017	2018	2019	2020	2021
Goldsboro	6.9%	6.6%	8.1%	8.8%	14.5%
Average	9.8%	10.6%	10.8%	9.5%	11.8%

Employee Turnover Rate (Voluntary Separations)

	2017	2018	2019	2020	2021
Goldsboro	6.6%	6.6%	7.1%	8.0%	13.2%
Average	8.0%	9.1%	9.4%	8.0%	10.4%

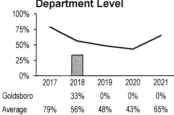

Percentage of Grievances Resolved at Department Level

	2017	2018	2019	2020	2021
Goldsboro		33%	0%	0%	0%
Average	79%	56%	48%	43%	65%

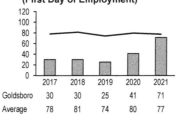

Average Days from Post Date to Hire Date (First Day of Employment)

	2017	2018	2019	2020	2021
Goldsboro	30	30	25	41	71
Average	78	81	74	80	77

Explanatory Information

Service Level and Delivery

The Human Resources Department for the City of Greensboro provides comprehensive personnel services, including recruitment and selection, compensation, benefits, employee relations, safety, and occupational health and wellness. The total number of full-time equivalent (FTE) positions includes staff from the Training Division, which is housed in a separate department from Human Resources. The HR department has a staff attorney who is able to provide legal consultation on a variety of issues confronting the HR department.

The city contracted one compensation study for the year, covering 1,220 positions.

The city's probationary period for new employees is six months for non-public safety employees and twelve months for public safety employees.

Conditions Affecting Service, Performance, and Costs

Municipal Profile

Population (OSBM 2020)	299,556
Land Area (Square Miles)	129.62
Persons per Square Mile	2,311

Service Profile

Central HR FTE Positions	
Administration	3.0
Generalist/Specialist	3.0
Staff Support/Clerical	29.0
Total Authorized Workforce	3,274.0
Authorized FTEs	2,999.0
Average Length of Service (Months)	129.72
Number of Position Requisitions	460
Employment Applications Processed	19,026
Length of Probationary Employment Period	6 & 12 months
Compensation Studies Completed	1
Positions Studied	1,220
Employee Turnover	
Voluntary Separations	226
Involuntary Separations	34
TOTAL SEPARATIONS	260
Formal Grievances Filed by Employees	51
Equal Employment Opportunity Commission (EEOC) Complaints Filed	3

Full Cost Profile

Cost Breakdown by Percentage	
Personal Services	84.4%
Operating Costs	15.6%
Capital Costs	0.0%
TOTAL	100.0%

Cost Breakdown in Dollars	
Personal Services	$2,962,274
Operating Costs	$548,877
Capital Costs	$0
TOTAL	$3,511,151

Greensboro

Central Human Resources

Key: Greensboro ▨   Benchmarking Average —   Fiscal Years 2017 through 2021

Resource Measures

Human Resources Services Cost per Capita

	2017	2018	2019	2020	2021
Greensboro	$12.58	$12.38	$11.68	$12.25	$11.72
Average	$15.02	$15.43	$17.68	$17.62	$19.32

Human Resources FTEs per 10,000 Population

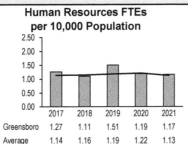

	2017	2018	2019	2020	2021
Greensboro	1.27	1.11	1.51	1.19	1.17
Average	1.14	1.16	1.19	1.22	1.13

Workload Measures

Total Municipal FTEs per 10,000 Population

	2017	2018	2019	2020	2021
Greensboro	110	104	108	103	100
Average	122	123	119	122	116

Applications Processed per 100 Municipal Employees

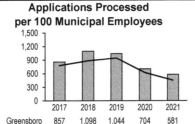

	2017	2018	2019	2020	2021
Greensboro	857	1,098	1,044	704	581
Average	779	886	948	625	452

Position Requisitions per 100 Municipal Employees

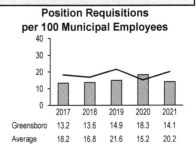

	2017	2018	2019	2020	2021
Greensboro	13.2	13.6	14.9	18.3	14.1
Average	18.2	16.8	21.6	15.2	20.2

Efficiency Measures

Human Resources Cost per Municipal Employee

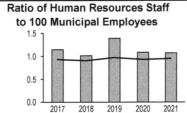

	2017	2018	2019	2020	2021
Greensboro	$1,137	$1,126	$1,078	$1,114	$1,072
Average	$1,268	$1,271	$1,515	$1,413	$1,674

Ratio of Human Resources Staff to 100 Municipal Employees

	2017	2018	2019	2020	2021
Greensboro	1.14	1.01	1.39	1.08	1.07
Average	0.93	0.91	0.97	0.93	0.95

Effectiveness Measures

Probationary Period Completion Rate (New Hires)

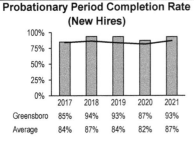

	2017	2018	2019	2020	2021
Greensboro	85%	94%	93%	87%	93%
Average	84%	87%	84%	82%	87%

Employee Turnover Rate (All Separations)

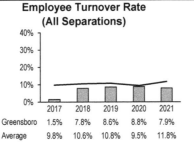

	2017	2018	2019	2020	2021
Greensboro	1.5%	7.8%	8.6%	8.8%	7.9%
Average	9.8%	10.6%	10.8%	9.5%	11.8%

Employee Turnover Rate (Voluntary Separations)

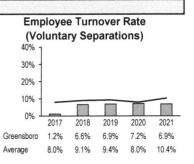

	2017	2018	2019	2020	2021
Greensboro	1.2%	6.6%	6.9%	7.2%	6.9%
Average	8.0%	9.1%	9.4%	8.0%	10.4%

Percentage of Grievances Resolved at Department Level

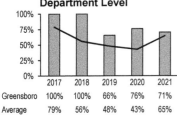

	2017	2018	2019	2020	2021
Greensboro	100%	100%	66%	76%	71%
Average	79%	56%	48%	43%	65%

Average Days from Post Date to Hire Date (First Day of Employment)

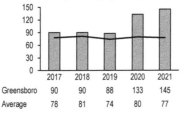

	2017	2018	2019	2020	2021
Greensboro	90	90	88	133	145
Average	78	81	74	80	77

Fiscal Year 2020-21

Explanatory Information

Service Level and Delivery
The Human Resources Department for the City of Greenville is responsible for recruitment and selection, salary and benefits administration, position classification, employee relations, affirmative action and equal employment opportunity, training and development, risk administration, and safety.

The city's probationary period is twelve months for all law enforcement personnel and employees in a trainee status, such as fire/rescue trainees. All other employees serve a six-month probationary period.

Nearly all employment applications are processed online. The Human Resources Department screens applications to ensure that applicants meet the position minimum qualifications. Applications are only accepted for positions that are open for recruitment.

Greenville has a voluntary wellness program focusing on education, fitness, mental health, nutrition, weight management, personal health, and personal safety. A safety specialist provides technical safety and occupational illness and injury prevention training.

A formal grievance by an employee in Greenville requires a written notice appealing a disciplinary action given to a supervisor. The grievance process is an internal one, moving up the chain of command with specific timeframes for responses and appeals to the next level.

Conditions Affecting Service, Performance, and Costs
No data were reported for FY 2019-20 for the city of Greenville.

Municipal Profile

Population (OSBM 2020)	87,428
Land Area (Square Miles)	35.66
Persons per Square Mile	2,452

Service Profile

Central HR FTE Positions	
Administration	4.00
Generalist/Specialist	5.0
Staff Support/Clerical	2.00
Total Authorized Workforce	789.5
Authorized FTEs	789.5
Average Length of Service (Months)	123
Number of Position Requisitions	141
Employment Applications Processed	4,653
Length of Probationary Employment Period	6 & 12 months
Compensation Studies Completed	0
Positions Studied	0
Employee Turnover	
Voluntary Separations	115
Involuntary Separations	10
TOTAL SEPARATIONS	125
Formal Grievances Filed by Employees	3
Equal Employment Opportunity Commission (EEOC) Complaints Filed	0

Full Cost Profile

Cost Breakdown by Percentage	
Personal Services	73.0%
Operating Costs	26.6%
Capital Costs	0.5%
TOTAL	100.0%

Cost Breakdown in Dollars	
Personal Services	$1,044,649
Operating Costs	$380,172
Capital Costs	$7,050
TOTAL	$1,431,871

Key: Greenville ▨   Benchmarking Average —   Fiscal Years 2017 through 2021

Resource Measures

Human Resources Services Cost per Capita

	2017	2018	2019	2020	2021
Greenville	$15.99	$14.78	$14.97		$16.38
Average	$15.02	$15.43	$17.68	$17.62	$19.32

Human Resources FTEs per 10,000 Population

	2017	2018	2019	2020	2021
Greenville	1.02	1.01	1.23		1.26
Average	1.14	1.16	1.19	1.22	1.13

Workload Measures

Total Municipal FTEs per 10,000 Population

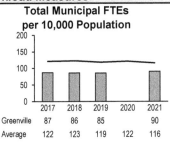

	2017	2018	2019	2020	2021
Greenville	87	86	85		90
Average	122	123	119	122	116

Applications Processed per 100 Municipal Employees

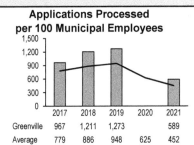

	2017	2018	2019	2020	2021
Greenville	967	1,211	1,273		589
Average	779	886	948	625	452

Position Requisitions per 100 Municipal Employees

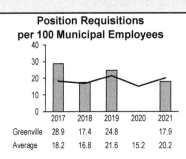

	2017	2018	2019	2020	2021
Greenville	28.9	17.4	24.8		17.9
Average	18.2	16.8	21.6	15.2	20.2

Efficiency Measures

Human Resources Cost per Municipal Employee

	2017	2018	2019	2020	2021
Greenville	$1,830	$1,712	$1,753		$1,814
Average	$1,268	$1,271	$1,515	$1,413	$1,674

Ratio of Human Resources Staff to 100 Municipal Employees

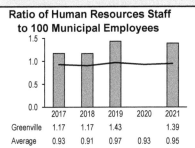

	2017	2018	2019	2020	2021
Greenville	1.17	1.17	1.43		1.39
Average	0.93	0.91	0.97	0.93	0.95

Effectiveness Measures

Probationary Period Completion Rate (New Hires)

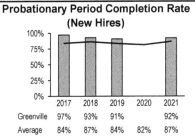

	2017	2018	2019	2020	2021
Greenville	97%	93%	91%		92%
Average	84%	87%	84%	82%	87%

Employee Turnover Rate (All Separations)

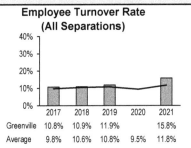

	2017	2018	2019	2020	2021
Greenville	10.8%	10.9%	11.9%		15.8%
Average	9.8%	10.6%	10.8%	9.5%	11.8%

Employee Turnover Rate (Voluntary Separations)

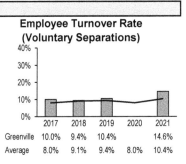

	2017	2018	2019	2020	2021
Greenville	10.0%	9.4%	10.4%		14.6%
Average	8.0%	9.1%	9.4%	8.0%	10.4%

Percentage of Grievances Resolved at Department Level

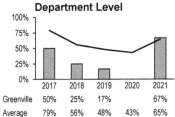

	2017	2018	2019	2020	2021
Greenville	50%	25%	17%		67%
Average	79%	56%	48%	43%	65%

Average Days from Post Date to Hire Date (First Day of Employment)

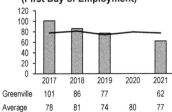

	2017	2018	2019	2020	2021
Greenville	101	86	77		62
Average	78	81	74	80	77

Fiscal Year 2020-21

Explanatory Information

Service Level and Delivery

The human resources function for the City of Hickory contains a director, an organizational development coordinator, a city nurse, two human resources analysts (one oversees benefits administration and the other oversees general employment), and one clerical position. Risk management is a division of the human resources function, which includes a risk manager and a clerical support position.

The city conducted three compensation studies during the fiscal year, covering 300 positions.

The city's probationary period is twelve months for all new city employees.

Conditions Affecting Service, Performance, and Costs

Municipal Profile

Population (OSBM 2020)	43,578
Land Area (Square Miles)	30.50
Persons per Square Mile	1,429

Service Profile

Central HR FTE Positions	
Administration	1.00
Generalist/Specialist	5.0
Staff Support/Clerical	2.00
Total Authorized Workforce	753.0
Authorized FTEs	713.0
Average Length of Service (Months)	123
Number of Position Requisitions	99
Employment Applications Processed	2,489
Length of Probationary Employment Period	12 months
Compensation Studies Completed	3
Positions Studied	300
Employee Turnover	
Voluntary Separations	105
Involuntary Separations	22
TOTAL SEPARATIONS	127
Formal Grievances Filed by Employees	3
Equal Employment Opportunity Commission (EEOC) Complaints Filed	1

Full Cost Profile

Cost Breakdown by Percentage	
Personal Services	68.3%
Operating Costs	30.7%
Capital Costs	1.1%
TOTAL	100.0%

Cost Breakdown in Dollars	
Personal Services	$483,610
Operating Costs	$217,334
Capital Costs	$7,470
TOTAL	$708,414

Hickory

Central Human Resources

Key: Hickory ▓   Benchmarking Average —   Fiscal Years 2017 through 2021

Resource Measures

Human Resources Services Cost per Capita

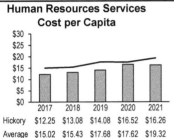

	2017	2018	2019	2020	2021
Hickory	$12.25	$13.08	$14.08	$16.52	$16.26
Average	$15.02	$15.43	$17.68	$17.62	$19.32

Human Resources FTEs per 10,000 Population

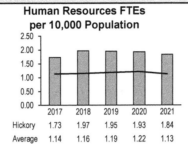

	2017	2018	2019	2020	2021
Hickory	1.73	1.97	1.95	1.93	1.84
Average	1.14	1.16	1.19	1.22	1.13

Workload Measures

Total Municipal FTEs per 10,000 Population

	2017	2018	2019	2020	2021
Hickory	182	181	170	169	164
Average	122	123	119	122	116

Applications Processed per 100 Municipal Employees

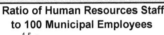
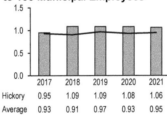

	2017	2018	2019	2020	2021
Hickory	555	593	484	324	331
Average	779	886	948	625	452

Position Requisitions per 100 Municipal Employees

	2017	2018	2019	2020	2021
Hickory	13.9	13.9	9.5	9.5	13.1
Average	18.2	16.8	21.6	15.2	20.2

Efficiency Measures

Human Resources Cost per Municipal Employee

	2017	2018	2019	2020	2021
Hickory	$673	$723	$782	$924	$941
Average	$1,268	$1,271	$1,515	$1,413	$1,674

Ratio of Human Resources Staff to 100 Municipal Employees

	2017	2018	2019	2020	2021
Hickory	0.95	1.09	1.09	1.08	1.06
Average	0.93	0.91	0.97	0.93	0.95

Effectiveness Measures

Probationary Period Completion Rate (New Hires)

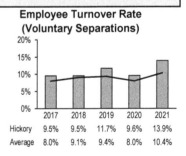

	2017	2018	2019	2020	2021
Hickory	80%	69%	74%	78%	75%
Average	84%	87%	84%	82%	87%

Employee Turnover Rate (All Separations)

	2017	2018	2019	2020	2021
Hickory	10.6%	10.7%	12.9%	11.9%	16.9%
Average	9.8%	10.6%	10.8%	9.5%	11.8%

Employee Turnover Rate (Voluntary Separations)

	2017	2018	2019	2020	2021
Hickory	9.5%	9.5%	11.7%	9.6%	13.9%
Average	8.0%	9.1%	9.4%	8.0%	10.4%

Percentage of Grievances Resolved at Department Level

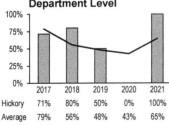

	2017	2018	2019	2020	2021
Hickory	71%	80%	50%	0%	100%
Average	79%	56%	48%	43%	65%

Average Days from Post Date to Hire Date (First Day of Employment)

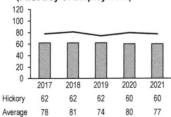

	2017	2018	2019	2020	2021
Hickory	62	62	62	60	60
Average	78	81	74	80	77

Explanatory Information

Service Level and Delivery

The City of Raleigh's Human Resource Department is organized around work units covering benefits and wellness, employee training and organizational development, talent acquisition, classification and compensation, HRIS administration, and health, safety, and worker's compensation. In addition, the department has three business partners who align with the city's assistant city managers and their respective departments.

The city's probationary period for law enforcement officers is twelve months from the date of employment or successful completion of field training. For firefighters, the probationary period is from the date of employment to six months after graduation from the academy. For all other employees, the probation period lasts six months from the date of employment.

Two compensation studies covering 3,311 positions was conducted during the fiscal year. A market review of benchmark jobs was conducted for comparison.

All applications for employment must be completed electronically. HR conducts an initial scan based on minimum qualifications and secondarily by screening questions developed by the hiring manager.

Conditions Affecting Service, Performance, and Costs

Municipal Profile

Population (OSBM 2020)	468,977
Land Area (Square Miles)	146.47
Persons per Square Mile	3,202

Service Profile

Central HR FTE Positions	
Administration	8.0
Generalist/Specialist	20.0
Staff Support/Clerical	4.0
Total Authorized Workforce	4,304.0
Authorized FTEs	4,304.0
Average Length of Service (Months)	127
Number of Position Requisitions	796
Employment Applications Processed	28,178
Length of Probationary Employment Period	6 & 12 months
Compensation Studies Completed	2
Positions Studied	3,311
Employee Turnover	
Voluntary Separations	343
Involuntary Separations	48
TOTAL SEPARATIONS	391
Formal Grievances Filed by Employees	65
Equal Employment Opportunity Commission (EEOC) Complaints Filed	3

Full Cost Profile

Cost Breakdown by Percentage	
Personal Services	78.6%
Operating Costs	20.8%
Capital Costs	0.7%
TOTAL	100.0%

Cost Breakdown in Dollars	
Personal Services	$3,593,069
Operating Costs	$949,600
Capital Costs	$30,398
TOTAL	$4,573,067

Raleigh
Central Human Resources

Key: Raleigh ▓   Benchmarking Average —   Fiscal Years 2017 through 2021

Resource Measures

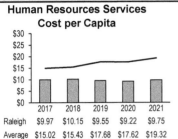

Human Resources Services Cost per Capita

	2017	2018	2019	2020	2021
Raleigh	$9.97	$10.15	$9.55	$9.22	$9.75
Average	$15.02	$15.43	$17.68	$17.62	$19.32

Human Resources FTEs per 10,000 Population

	2017	2018	2019	2020	2021
Raleigh	0.94	0.67	0.69	0.67	0.68
Average	1.14	1.16	1.19	1.22	1.13

Workload Measures

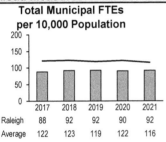

Total Municipal FTEs per 10,000 Population

	2017	2018	2019	2020	2021
Raleigh	88	92	92	90	92
Average	122	123	119	122	116

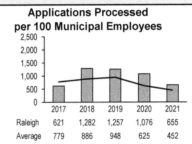

Applications Processed per 100 Municipal Employees

	2017	2018	2019	2020	2021
Raleigh	621	1,282	1,257	1,076	655
Average	779	886	948	625	452

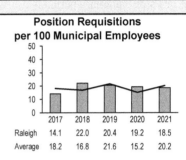

Position Requisitions per 100 Municipal Employees

	2017	2018	2019	2020	2021
Raleigh	14.1	22.0	20.4	19.2	18.5
Average	18.2	16.8	21.6	15.2	20.2

Efficiency Measures

Human Resources Cost per Municipal Employee

	2017	2018	2019	2020	2021
Raleigh	$1,133	$1,108	$1,035	$1,020	$1,063
Average	$1,268	$1,271	$1,515	$1,413	$1,674

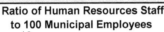
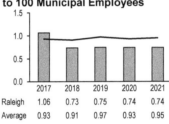

Ratio of Human Resources Staff to 100 Municipal Employees

	2017	2018	2019	2020	2021
Raleigh	1.06	0.73	0.75	0.74	0.74
Average	0.93	0.91	0.97	0.93	0.95

Effectiveness Measures

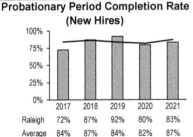

Probationary Period Completion Rate (New Hires)

	2017	2018	2019	2020	2021
Raleigh	72%	87%	92%	80%	83%
Average	84%	87%	84%	82%	87%

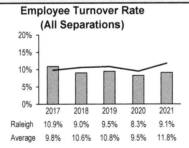

Employee Turnover Rate (All Separations)

	2017	2018	2019	2020	2021
Raleigh	10.9%	9.0%	9.5%	8.3%	9.1%
Average	9.8%	10.6%	10.8%	9.5%	11.8%

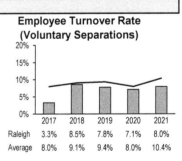

Employee Turnover Rate (Voluntary Separations)

	2017	2018	2019	2020	2021
Raleigh	3.3%	8.5%	7.8%	7.1%	8.0%
Average	8.0%	9.1%	9.4%	8.0%	10.4%

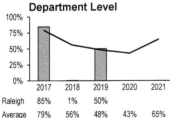

Percentage of Grievances Resolved at Department Level

	2017	2018	2019	2020	2021
Raleigh	85%	1%	50%		
Average	79%	56%	48%	43%	65%

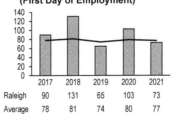

Average Days from Post Date to Hire Date (First Day of Employment)

	2017	2018	2019	2020	2021
Raleigh	90	131	65	103	73
Average	78	81	74	80	77

Explanatory Information

Service Level and Delivery

The City of Wilson has a centralized Human Resources Department that includes policy development and implementation, classification and pay administration, recruitment and selection, benefits administration, and employee relations. The safety and health program is a function of the Risk Management Division under another department. Occupational health needs are met through a contract with the Wilson Medical Center.

The city's probationary period is twelve months for new city employees.

Conditions Affecting Service, Performance, and Costs

Municipal Profile

Population (OSBM 2020)	47,769
Land Area (Square Miles)	31.02
Persons per Square Mile	1,540

Service Profile

Central HR FTE Positions	
Administration	2.0
Generalist/Specialist	2.0
Staff Support/Clerical	2.0
Total Authorized Workforce	756.0
Authorized FTEs	753.0
Average Length of Service (Months)	120
Number of Position Requisitions	81
Employment Applications Processed	3,849
Length of Probationary Employment Period	12 months
Compensation Studies Completed	0
Positions Studied	0
Employee Turnover	
Voluntary Separations	71
Involuntary Separations	19
TOTAL SEPARATIONS	90
Formal Grievances Filed by Employees	4
Equal Employment Opportunity Commission (EEOC) Complaints Filed	1

Full Cost Profile

Cost Breakdown by Percentage	
Personal Services	79.5%
Operating Costs	18.1%
Capital Costs	2.3%
TOTAL	100.0%

Cost Breakdown in Dollars	
Personal Services	$538,549
Operating Costs	$122,633
Capital Costs	$15,850
TOTAL	$677,032

Wilson

Central Human Resources

Resource Measures

Human Resources Services Cost per Capita

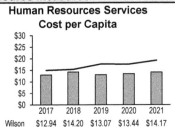

	2017	2018	2019	2020	2021
Wilson	$12.94	$14.20	$13.07	$13.44	$14.17
Average	$15.02	$15.43	$17.68	$17.62	$19.32

Human Resources FTEs per 10,000 Population

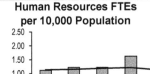
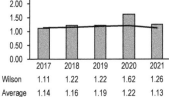

	2017	2018	2019	2020	2021
Wilson	1.11	1.22	1.22	1.62	1.26
Average	1.14	1.16	1.19	1.22	1.13

Workload Measures

Total Municipal FTEs per 10,000 Population

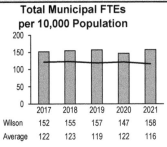

	2017	2018	2019	2020	2021
Wilson	152	155	157	147	158
Average	122	123	119	122	116

Applications Processed per 100 Municipal Employees

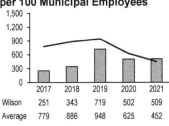

	2017	2018	2019	2020	2021
Wilson	251	343	719	502	509
Average	779	886	948	625	452

Position Requisitions per 100 Municipal Employees

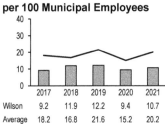

	2017	2018	2019	2020	2021
Wilson	9.2	11.9	12.2	9.4	10.7
Average	18.2	16.8	21.6	15.2	20.2

Efficiency Measures

Human Resources Cost per Municipal Employee

	2017	2018	2019	2020	2021
Wilson	$841	$907	$823	$859	$896
Average	$1,268	$1,271	$1,515	$1,413	$1,674

Ratio of Human Resources Staff to 100 Municipal Employees

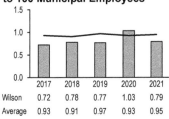

	2017	2018	2019	2020	2021
Wilson	0.72	0.78	0.77	1.03	0.79
Average	0.93	0.91	0.97	0.93	0.95

Effectiveness Measures

Probationary Period Completion Rate (New Hires)

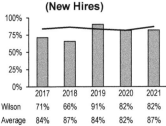

	2017	2018	2019	2020	2021
Wilson	71%	66%	91%	82%	82%
Average	84%	87%	84%	82%	87%

Employee Turnover Rate (All Separations)

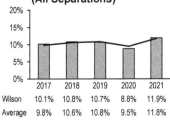

	2017	2018	2019	2020	2021
Wilson	10.1%	10.8%	10.7%	8.8%	11.9%
Average	9.8%	10.6%	10.8%	9.5%	11.8%

Employee Turnover Rate (Voluntary Separations)

	2017	2018	2019	2020	2021
Wilson	8.2%	9.1%	8.2%	7.0%	9.4%
Average	8.0%	9.1%	9.4%	8.0%	10.4%

Percentage of Grievances Resolved at Department Level

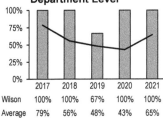

	2017	2018	2019	2020	2021
Wilson	100%	100%	67%	100%	100%
Average	79%	56%	48%	43%	65%

Average Days from Post Date to Hire Date (First Day of Employment)

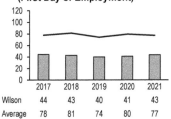

	2017	2018	2019	2020	2021
Wilson	44	43	40	41	43
Average	78	81	74	80	77

Winston-Salem

Central Human Resources

Fiscal Year 2020-21

Explanatory Information

Service Level and Delivery

The human resources function is housed under two separate departments: Human Resources (HR) and Finance. The finance department is responsible for benefits administration and employee safety. The human resources department has three separate sections: general human resources management, employee health, and employee training.

Winston-Salem began having employees go through a probationary period in FY 2015–16 for the first time. The city's probationary period for new general employees is six months and twelve months for police and fire personnel.

Conditions Affecting Service, Performance, and Costs

Winston-Salem now requires all job applications to be submitted online. This process has made it substantially easier to apply for jobs, pushing up the number of applications.

The city has two health insurance plans: a basic plan and the Basic Plus Plan, which has richer benefits and more expensive premiums for employees. The city offers a dental reimbursement plan instead of a dental insurance plan.

The City Attorney's Office handles all Equal Employment Opportunity Commission (EEOC) charges.

Winston-Salem's HR department manually calculates the time from post date to hire by subtracting the "approved for posting date" from the actual hire date as noted in the department's system. Certain current policies can effectively stretch this time period, which accounts for the long time reported in the length of time to hire new employees. For example, graduates from the fire academy may sometimes require five months before all evaluations are completed.

Municipal Profile

Population (OSBM 2020)	249,986
Land Area (Square Miles)	132.59
Persons per Square Mile	1,885

Service Profile

Central HR FTE Positions	
Administration	3.0
Generalist/Specialist	10.0
Staff Support/Clerical	2.0
Total Authorized Workforce	2,803.0
Authorized FTEs	2,614.0
Average Length of Service (Months)	123.37
Number of Position Requisitions	522
Employment Applications Processed	11,670
Length of Probationary Employment Period	6 & 12 months
Compensation Studies Completed	0
Positions Studied	0
Employee Turnover	
Voluntary Separations	221
Involuntary Separations	40
TOTAL SEPARATIONS	261
Formal Grievances Filed by Employees	59
Equal Employment Opportunity Commission (EEOC) Complaints Filed	3

Full Cost Profile

Cost Breakdown by Percentage	
Personal Services	27.7%
Operating Costs	72.3%
Capital Costs	0.1%
TOTAL	100.0%

Cost Breakdown in Dollars	
Personal Services	$1,847,935
Operating Costs	$4,829,903
Capital Costs	$5,320
TOTAL	$6,683,158

Winston-Salem

Central Human Resources

Key: Winston-Salem   Benchmarking Average —   Fiscal Years 2017 through 2021

Resource Measures

Human Resources Services Cost per Capita

	2017	2018	2019	2020	2021
Winston-Salem	$15.17	$15.71	$17.96	$24.93	$26.73
Average	$15.02	$15.43	$17.68	$17.62	$19.32

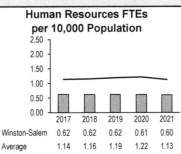

Human Resources FTEs per 10,000 Population

	2017	2018	2019	2020	2021
Winston-Salem	0.62	0.62	0.62	0.61	0.60
Average	1.14	1.16	1.19	1.22	1.13

Workload Measures

Total Municipal FTEs per 10,000 Population

	2017	2018	2019	2020	2021
Winston-Salem	107	108	109	102	105
Average	122	123	119	122	116

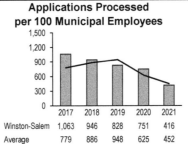

Applications Processed per 100 Municipal Employees

	2017	2018	2019	2020	2021
Winston-Salem	1,063	946	828	751	416
Average	779	886	948	625	452

Position Requisitions per 100 Municipal Employees

	2017	2018	2019	2020	2021
Winston-Salem	21.3	15.7	20.5	17.2	18.6
Average	18.2	16.8	21.6	15.2	20.2

Efficiency Measures

Human Resources Cost per Municipal Employee

	2017	2018	2019	2020	2021
Winston-Salem	$1,364	$1,373	$1,543	$2,152	$2,384
Average	$1,268	$1,271	$1,515	$1,413	$1,674

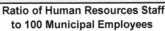

Ratio of Human Resources Staff to 100 Municipal Employees

	2017	2018	2019	2020	2021
Winston-Salem	0.56	0.54	0.53	0.53	0.54
Average	0.93	0.91	0.97	0.93	0.95

Effectiveness Measures

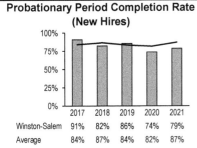

Probationary Period Completion Rate (New Hires)

	2017	2018	2019	2020	2021
Winston-Salem	91%	82%	86%	74%	79%
Average	84%	87%	84%	82%	87%

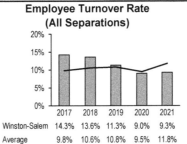

Employee Turnover Rate (All Separations)

	2017	2018	2019	2020	2021
Winston-Salem	14.3%	13.6%	11.3%	9.0%	9.3%
Average	9.8%	10.6%	10.8%	9.5%	11.8%

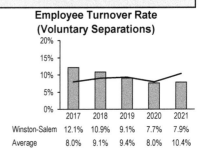

Employee Turnover Rate (Voluntary Separations)

	2017	2018	2019	2020	2021
Winston-Salem	12.1%	10.9%	9.1%	7.7%	7.9%
Average	8.0%	9.1%	9.4%	8.0%	10.4%

Percentage of Grievances Resolved at Department Level

	2017	2018	2019	2020	2021
Winston-Salem	67%	53%	52%	41%	61%
Average	79%	56%	48%	43%	65%

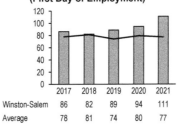

Average Days from Post Date to Hire Date (First Day of Employment)

	2017	2018	2019	2020	2021
Winston-Salem	86	82	89	94	111
Average	78	81	74	80	77

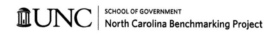

Performance and Cost Data

WATER SERVICES

PERFORMANCE MEASURES FOR WATER SERVICES

SERVICE DEFINITION

Water Services includes the collection, treatment, distribution, and billing related to drinking water services. It includes reservoirs where appropriate, pumping stations, pipes to and from treatment plants, storage tanks, and treatment plants. Activities and costs include the operation, maintenance, and installation of infrastructure. Also included are costs and activities associated with the installation, upkeep, and reading of meters; billing and collection costs for drinking water services; and administrative activities, such as planning, engineering, and testing. Excluded are reclaimed water, sewer collection, and wastewater treatment services.

NOTES ON PERFORMANCE MEASURES

1. Thousands of Gallons Billed Water per Meter

This workload measure captures the amount of water provided per meter in the system. Water that does not make it to customer taps is not included.

2. Miles of Main Line Pipe per Square Mile of Service Area

The amount of pipe per square mile shows the density of the pipe infrastructure to be maintained relative to the geographic size of the area served.

3. Total Cost per Thousand Gallons of Billed Water

This efficiency measure shows the total system cost per 1,000 gallons of water that is actually billed to customers.

4. Million Gallons of Billed Water per All Staff FTEs

Large numbers of staff, including treatment staff, line maintenance staff, meter readers, billing staff, and others, are required to bring drinking water to customer taps. Based on all staff who help support the delivery of drinking water to customers, this efficiency measure shows how much billable water is produced per full-time equivalent (FTE) staff member.

5. Billed Water as a Percentage of Finished Water

Not all water produced at treatment plants makes it to customer meters. Some water is lost through leaks or breaks in the system. Other water is unbilled but authorized for uses such as fighting fires or flushing lines. This efficiency measure shows the percentage of water produced that makes it to customer taps.

6. Percentage of Existing Pipeline Renewed

Replacement or rehabilitation of existing pipeline is needed to ensure that the distribution infrastructure can continue to function. This effectiveness measure shows the percentage of existing water lines that are renewed each year.

7. Percentage of Bills Not Collected

Collection of water bills sent to customers is necessary to ensure revenues for system operation. Adjustments to bills reflecting water-loss adjustments are not included in the amount of billings.

8. Peak Daily Demand as a Percentage of Treatment Capacity

A water system needs sufficient capacity to meet not only average demands, but also peak demands. This measure looks at peak historical demand relative to the water-system-treatment capacity in a day.

9. Breaks and Leaks per Mile of Main Line Pipe

Breaks or leaks in water distribution lines mean the loss of treated water.

10. Customer Complaints about Water Quality per Thousand Meters

Concerns for the adequacy of water are matched with the quality of the water delivered to customers. This effectiveness measure assesses customers' perceptions about their water quality.

Water Services

Summary of Key Dimensions of Service

City or Town	Estimated Residential Population in Service Area	Service Area (in Square Miles)	Average Daily Demand for Water (in MGD)	Operating Treatment Plants	Total Treatment Capacity for Finished Water (in MGD)	Miles of Water Main Lines	Number of Water Meters	Water System FTE Positions
Apex	70,272	25.0	4.4	Shared with Cary	Shared with Cary	325.6	24,505	31.0
Charlotte	1,128,945	546.0	109.7	3	242.0	4,482.0	313,177	477.5
Concord	104,655	142.8	13.4	2	24.0	756.6	44,625	67.0
Goldsboro	34,186	25.0	6.3	1	14.0	270.0	14,744	29.0
Greensboro	318,529	148.0	32.6	2	63.7	1,517.0	108,103	157.5
Hickory	99,530	326.0	11.2	1	32.0	954.1	31,294	55.0
Raleigh	605,000	299.0	51.3	2	106.0	2,377.0	197,720	303.0
Wilson	52,000	40.0	8.9	2	22.0	435.0	22,182	46.5
Winston-Salem	369,282	227.3	35.8	3	91.0	2,348.0	133,161	175.2

NOTES
MGD stands for millions of gallons per day.

EXPLANATORY FACTORS
These are factors that the project found affected water services performance and cost in one or more of the municipalities:

Topography
Water quality of source water
Size of service area
Population density
Age of infrastructure
Growth of population and businesses

Explanatory Information

Service Level and Delivery
The Town of Apex Water Distribution Division is housed within the Department of Public Works. It consists of repairs, preventive maintenance, meter installation and replacement, and testing. The town is co-owner of the Cary/Apex water treatment facility, which draws raw water from Jordan Lake. The Town of Cary provides the operational staff for the treatment plant, but Apex shares in the costs of operation and capital.

Apex bases replacement of water lines on customer complaints, frequency of repairs, street rehabilitation needs, age and material of pipes, and flow concerns.

Currently, nearly all water meters are read by automatic means. Replacement of meters is based on a combination of factors, as is water line replacement.

Conditions Affecting Service, Performance, and Costs
The costs of water services as captured here do not include debt service but do capture depreciation.

Municipal Profile

Estimated Service Population	70,272
Service Land Area (Square Miles)	25.0
Persons per Square Mile	2,811
Topography	Flat; gently rolling
Climate	Temperate; little ice and snow

Service Profile

FTE Staff Positions	
Treatment Plant	0.0
Line Crews	19.0
Meter Readers	5.0
Billing/Collection	4.0
Other	3.0
Total	31.0
Number of Treatment Plants	NA
Total Treatment Capacity	NA
Average Daily Demand	4.4 MGD
Miles of Main Line Pipe	326
Average Age of Main Line Pipe	18 years
Number of Breaks/Leaks	52
Number of Water Meters	24,505
Percent of Meters Read Automatically	97.3%
Total Revenues Collected	$10,182,108

Full Cost Profile

Cost Breakdown by Percentage	
Personal Services	24.7%
Operating Costs	45.6%
Capital Costs	29.7%
TOTAL	100.0%
Cost Breakdown in Dollars	
Personal Services	$2,271,174
Operating Costs	$4,188,567
Capital Costs	$2,730,820
TOTAL	$9,190,561

Apex

Water Services

Key: Apex ▦   Benchmarking Average —   Fiscal Years 2017 through 2021

Resource Measures

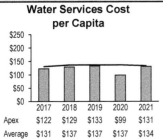

Water Services Cost per Capita

	2017	2018	2019	2020	2021
Apex	$122	$129	$133	$99	$131
Average	$131	$137	$137	$137	$134

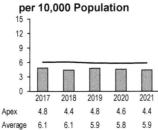

Water Services FTEs per 10,000 Population

	2017	2018	2019	2020	2021
Apex	4.8	4.4	4.8	4.6	4.4
Average	6.1	6.1	5.9	5.8	5.9

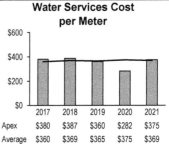

Water Services Cost per Meter

	2017	2018	2019	2020	2021
Apex	$380	$387	$360	$282	$375
Average	$360	$369	$365	$375	$369

Workload Measures

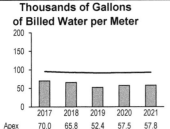

Thousands of Gallons of Billed Water per Meter

	2017	2018	2019	2020	2021
Apex	70.0	65.8	52.4	57.5	57.8
Average	95.5	92.8	91.6	92.2	92.8

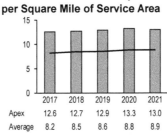

Miles of Main Line Pipe per Square Mile of Service Area

	2017	2018	2019	2020	2021
Apex	12.6	12.7	12.9	13.3	13.0
Average	8.2	8.5	8.6	8.8	8.9

Efficiency Measures

Total Cost per Thousand Gallons of Billed Water

	2017	2018	2019	2020	2021
Apex	$5.43	$5.88	$6.87	$4.91	$6.49
Average	$3.95	$4.15	$4.18	$4.30	$4.18

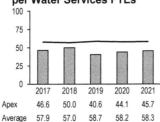

Million Gallons of Billed Water per Water Services FTEs

	2017	2018	2019	2020	2021
Apex	46.6	50.0	40.6	44.1	45.7
Average	57.9	57.0	58.7	58.2	58.3

Billed Water as a Percentage of Finished Water

	2017	2018	2019	2020	2021
Apex	85%	87%	83%	87%	87%
Average	82%	85%	84%	87%	84%

Effectiveness Measures

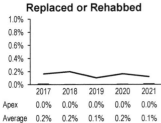

Percentage of Existing Pipeline Replaced or Rehabbed

	2017	2018	2019	2020	2021
Apex	0.0%	0.0%	0.0%	0.0%	0.0%
Average	0.2%	0.2%	0.1%	0.2%	0.1%

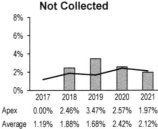

Percentage of Water Bills Not Collected

	2017	2018	2019	2020	2021
Apex	0.00%	2.46%	3.47%	2.57%	1.97%
Average	1.19%	1.88%	1.68%	2.42%	2.12%

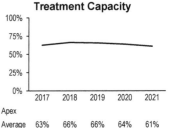

Peak Daily Demand as a Percentage of Treatment Capacity

	2017	2018	2019	2020	2021
Apex					
Average	63%	66%	66%	64%	61%

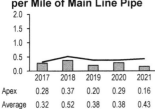

Breaks and Leaks per Mile of Main Line Pipe

	2017	2018	2019	2020	2021
Apex	0.28	0.37	0.20	0.29	0.16
Average	0.32	0.52	0.38	0.38	0.43

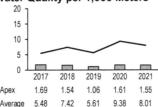

Customer Complaints about Water Quality per 1,000 Meters

	2017	2018	2019	2020	2021
Apex	1.69	1.54	1.06	1.61	1.55
Average	5.48	7.42	5.61	9.38	8.01

Fiscal Year 2020-21

Explanatory Information

Service Level and Delivery

Charlotte Water (CLTWater) is a combined water and sewer utility for Mecklenburg County and the City of Charlotte. The department is run as an official City of Charlotte department. The area served is generally considered to be Mecklenburg County but also includes a small number of metered drinking water interconnections with the City of Concord and the counties of Union in North Carolina and Lancaster and York in South Carolina. The service area covers approximately 546 square miles and serves over one million people.

Source water for the system is drawn from two impounded lakes on the Catawba River, Lake Norman and Mountain Island Lake, which are operated by Duke Energy. The combined estimated safe yield is between 376 and 503 million gallons per day. The system operates three treatment plants with a combined treatment capacity of 242 million gallons per day. The treatment plants are conventional facilities using rapid mix, flocculation, settling, filtration, and chemical application.

The estimated average age of main line pipes in the system is thirty-four years. CMU's replacement policy for pipe is based on flow and quality standards.

All meters are now read automatically. CMU uses a system that allows vans traveling the city to read meters as they drive by. The replacement standard is every fifteen years for water meters.

Conditions Affecting Service, Performance, and Costs

The costs of water services as captured here do not include debt service but do capture depreciation.

The reduction in reported leaks and breaks over time is in large part due to improvements in tracking and data reporting. CMU staff worked on improving how the work order system is used to determine the number of leaks or breaks in the water system.

Municipal Profile	
Estimated Service Population	1,128,945
Service Land Area (Square Miles)	546.0
Persons per Square Mile	2,068
Topography	Flat; gently rolling
Climate	Temperate; little ice and snow

Service Profile	
FTE Staff Positions	
Treatment Plant	53.0
Line Crews	180.0
Meter Readers	4.0
Billing/Collection	12.0
Other	228.5
Total	477.5
Number of Treatment Plants	3
Total Treatment Capacity	242.0 MGD
Average Daily Demand	109.7 MGD
Miles of Main Line Pipe	4,482
Average Age of Main Line Pipe	34 years
Number of Breaks/Leaks	3,045
Number of Water Meters	313,177
Percent of Meters Read Automatically	100.0%
Total Revenues Collected	$175,578,477

Full Cost Profile	
Cost Breakdown by Percentage	
Personal Services	25.2%
Operating Costs	35.6%
Capital Costs	39.3%
TOTAL	100.0%
Cost Breakdown in Dollars	
Personal Services	$32,510,119
Operating Costs	$45,899,741
Capital Costs	$50,662,610
TOTAL	$129,072,470

Charlotte

Water Services

Resource Measures

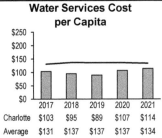

Water Services Cost per Capita

	2017	2018	2019	2020	2021
Charlotte	$103	$95	$89	$107	$114
Average	$131	$137	$137	$137	$134

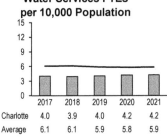

Water Services FTEs per 10,000 Population

	2017	2018	2019	2020	2021
Charlotte	4.0	3.9	4.0	4.2	4.2
Average	6.1	6.1	5.9	5.8	5.9

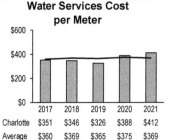

Water Services Cost per Meter

	2017	2018	2019	2020	2021
Charlotte	$351	$346	$326	$388	$412
Average	$360	$369	$365	$375	$369

Workload Measures

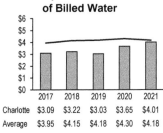

Thousands of Gallons of Billed Water per Meter

	2017	2018	2019	2020	2021
Charlotte	113.7	107.6	107.3	106.3	102.8
Average	95.5	92.8	91.6	92.2	92.8

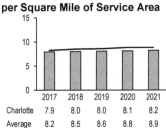

Miles of Main Line Pipe per Square Mile of Service Area

	2017	2018	2019	2020	2021
Charlotte	7.9	8.0	8.0	8.1	8.2
Average	8.2	8.5	8.6	8.8	8.9

Efficiency Measures

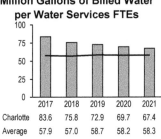

Total Cost per Thousand Gallons of Billed Water

	2017	2018	2019	2020	2021
Charlotte	$3.09	$3.22	$3.03	$3.65	$4.01
Average	$3.95	$4.15	$4.18	$4.30	$4.18

Million Gallons of Billed Water per Water Services FTEs

	2017	2018	2019	2020	2021
Charlotte	83.6	75.8	72.9	69.7	67.4
Average	57.9	57.0	58.7	58.2	58.3

Billed Water as a Percentage of Finished Water

	2017	2018	2019	2020	2021
Charlotte	85%	82%	82%	90%	80%
Average	82%	85%	84%	87%	84%

Effectiveness Measures

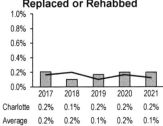

Percentage of Existing Pipeline Replaced or Rehabbed

	2017	2018	2019	2020	2021
Charlotte	0.2%	0.1%	0.2%	0.2%	0.2%
Average	0.2%	0.2%	0.1%	0.2%	0.1%

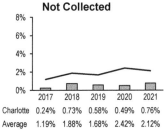

Percentage of Water Bills Not Collected

	2017	2018	2019	2020	2021
Charlotte	0.24%	0.73%	0.58%	0.49%	0.76%
Average	1.19%	1.88%	1.68%	2.42%	2.12%

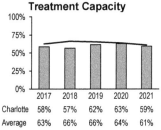

Peak Daily Demand as a Percentage of Treatment Capacity

	2017	2018	2019	2020	2021
Charlotte	58%	57%	62%	63%	59%
Average	63%	66%	66%	64%	61%

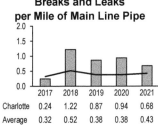

Breaks and Leaks per Mile of Main Line Pipe

	2017	2018	2019	2020	2021
Charlotte	0.24	1.22	0.87	0.94	0.68
Average	0.32	0.52	0.38	0.38	0.43

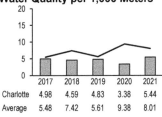

Customer Complaints about Water Quality per 1,000 Meters

	2017	2018	2019	2020	2021
Charlotte	4.98	4.59	4.83	3.38	5.44
Average	5.48	7.42	5.61	9.38	8.01

Fiscal Year 2020-21

Explanatory Information

Service Level and Delivery

The City of Concord Water Resources Department is a water-only utility. The department has three divisions: one for operations and maintenance and one for each of two treatment plants. Meter reading, billing, and collections are handled by the city Finance Department.

Concord's system serves approximately 105,000 people and covers the City of Concord, the Town of Midland, and approximately one-fourth of Cabarrus County. Water sources for the system are Lake Fisher, owned by the city, and Lakes Howell and Concord, reservoirs owned by the Water and Sewer Authority of Cabarrus County. The combined estimated safe yield is 24 million gallons per day.

The city operates two treatment plants with a combined treatment capacity of 24 million gallons per day. Concord has emergency connections with the City of Charlotte and the City of Kannapolis and sells small amounts of water to the Town of Harrisburg and the Town of Midland.

The estimated average age of main line pipes in the system is thirty-seven years. Water meters are read monthly, with all being read using automatic means. The replacement standard for water meters is fifteen years.

Conditions Affecting Service, Performance, and Costs

The costs of water services as captured here do not include debt service but do capture depreciation.

Municipal Profile	
Estimated Service Population	104,655
Service Land Area (Square Miles)	142.8
Persons per Square Mile	733
Topography	Flat; gently rolling
Climate	Temperate; little ice and snow

Service Profile	
FTE Staff Positions	
Treatment Plant	18.0
Line Crews	25.0
Meter Readers	0.0
Billing/Collection	0.0
Other	24.0
Total	67.0
Number of Treatment Plants	2
Total Treatment Capacity	24.0 MGD
Average Daily Demand	13.4 MGD
Miles of Main Line Pipe	757
Average Age of Main Line Pipe	37 years
Number of Breaks/Leaks	224
Number of Water Meters	44,625
Percent of Meters Read Automatically	100.0%
Total Revenues Collected	$25,875,999

Full Cost Profile	
Cost Breakdown by Percentage	
Personal Services	25.9%
Operating Costs	54.6%
Capital Costs	19.5%
TOTAL	100.0%
Cost Breakdown in Dollars	
Personal Services	$6,132,273
Operating Costs	$12,956,531
Capital Costs	$4,627,794
TOTAL	$23,716,598

Concord   Water Services

Key: Concord ▨   Benchmarking Average —   Fiscal Years 2017 through 2021

Resource Measures

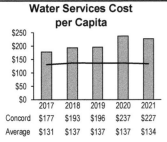

Water Services Cost per Capita

	2017	2018	2019	2020	2021
Concord	$177	$193	$196	$237	$227
Average	$131	$137	$137	$137	$134

Water Services FTEs per 10,000 Population

	2017	2018	2019	2020	2021
Concord	9.0	9.0	6.8	6.8	6.4
Average	6.1	6.1	5.9	5.8	5.9

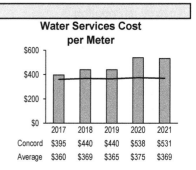

Water Services Cost per Meter

	2017	2018	2019	2020	2021
Concord	$395	$440	$440	$538	$531
Average	$360	$369	$365	$375	$369

Workload Measures

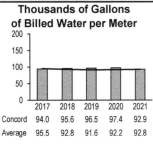

Thousands of Gallons of Billed Water per Meter

	2017	2018	2019	2020	2021
Concord	94.0	95.6	96.5	97.4	92.9
Average	95.5	92.8	91.6	92.2	92.8

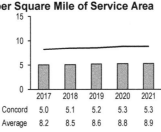

Miles of Main Line Pipe per Square Mile of Service Area

	2017	2018	2019	2020	2021
Concord	5.0	5.1	5.2	5.3	5.3
Average	8.2	8.5	8.6	8.8	8.9

Efficiency Measures

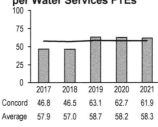

Total Cost per Thousand Gallons of Billed Water

	2017	2018	2019	2020	2021
Concord	$4.21	$4.60	$4.56	$5.53	$5.72
Average	$3.95	$4.15	$4.18	$4.30	$4.18

Million Gallons of Billed Water per Water Services FTEs

	2017	2018	2019	2020	2021
Concord	46.8	46.5	63.1	62.7	61.9
Average	57.9	57.0	58.7	58.2	58.3

Billed Water as a Percentage of Finished Water

	2017	2018	2019	2020	2021
Concord	100%	86%	85%	88%	85%
Average	82%	85%	84%	87%	84%

Effectiveness Measures

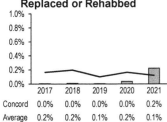

Percentage of Existing Pipeline Replaced or Rehabbed

	2017	2018	2019	2020	2021
Concord	0.0%	0.0%	0.0%	0.0%	0.2%
Average	0.2%	0.2%	0.1%	0.2%	0.1%

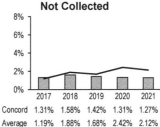

Percentage of Water Bills Not Collected

	2017	2018	2019	2020	2021
Concord	1.31%	1.58%	1.42%	1.31%	1.27%
Average	1.19%	1.88%	1.68%	2.42%	2.12%

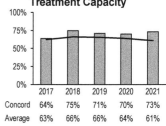

Peak Daily Demand as a Percentage of Treatment Capacity

	2017	2018	2019	2020	2021
Concord	64%	75%	71%	70%	73%
Average	63%	66%	66%	64%	61%

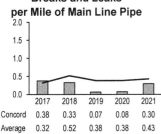

Breaks and Leaks per Mile of Main Line Pipe

	2017	2018	2019	2020	2021
Concord	0.38	0.33	0.07	0.08	0.30
Average	0.32	0.52	0.38	0.38	0.43

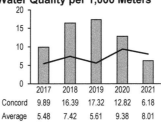

Customer Complaints about Water Quality per 1,000 Meters

	2017	2018	2019	2020	2021
Concord	9.89	16.39	17.32	12.82	6.18
Average	5.48	7.42	5.61	9.38	8.01

Goldsboro

Water Services

Fiscal Year 2020-21

Explanatory Information

Service Level and Delivery

Goldsboro's drinking water services are a joint responsibility between the Public Works and Public Utilities Departments. Both departments are overseen by the Public Works Director. Public Works is responsible for the collection and distribution system lines. Public Utilities is responsible for the operations of the water treatment plant, the water reclamation facility, and pump stations.

The Goldsboro system serves approximately 34,000 people in an area covering twenty-five square miles. Water is collected from the Neuse River. The system also has an emergency option to collect from the Littler River, but this option has not been needed for several years. The estimated safe yield of the system is 6 million gallons per day based on an analysis performed by consultants. The system has emergency connections with Eastern Wayne, Belfast-Patetown, Fork Town, and Southern Wayne Sanitary districts.

The city runs one treatment plant with a capacity of 14 million gallons per day. The plant uses traditional surface-water treatment consisting of coagulation, flocculation, sedimentation, filtration, and disinfection.

Goldsboro handles pipe placement by focusing on breaks in the system.

Conditions Affecting Service, Performance, and Costs

The City of Goldsboro joined the Benchmarking Project in July 2017, with the first year of data showing for FY 2016–17.

The costs of water services as captured here do not include debt service but do capture depreciation.

Hurricane Matthew in October 2016 put stress on the water system due to the extensive flooding.

Municipal Profile

Estimated Service Population	34,186
Service Land Area (Square Miles)	25.0
Persons per Square Mile	1,367
Topography	Flat
Climate	Temperate; little ice and snow

Service Profile

FTE Staff Positions	
Treatment Plant	12.0
Line Crews	5.0
Meter Readers	4.0
Billing/Collection	6.0
Other	2.0
Total	29.0
Number of Treatment Plants	1
Total Treatment Capacity	14.0 MGD
Average Daily Demand	6.3 MGD
Miles of Main Line Pipe	270
Average Age of Main Line Pipe	70 years
Number of Breaks/Leaks	41
Number of Water Meters	14,744
Percent of Meters Read Automatically	100.0%
Total Revenues Collected	$7,516,881

Full Cost Profile

Cost Breakdown by Percentage	
Personal Services	28.4%
Operating Costs	70.7%
Capital Costs	0.9%
TOTAL	100.0%
Cost Breakdown in Dollars	
Personal Services	$721,702
Operating Costs	$1,799,349
Capital Costs	$23,000
TOTAL	$2,544,051

Goldsboro

Water Services

Resource Measures

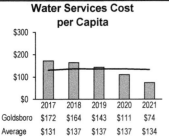

Water Services Cost per Capita

	2017	2018	2019	2020	2021
Goldsboro	$172	$164	$143	$111	$74
Average	$131	$137	$137	$137	$134

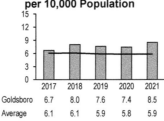

Water Services FTEs per 10,000 Population

	2017	2018	2019	2020	2021
Goldsboro	6.7	8.0	7.6	7.4	8.5
Average	6.1	6.1	5.9	5.8	5.9

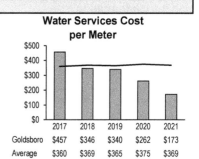

Water Services Cost per Meter

	2017	2018	2019	2020	2021
Goldsboro	$457	$346	$340	$262	$173
Average	$360	$369	$365	$375	$369

Workload Measures

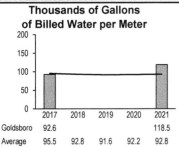

Thousands of Gallons of Billed Water per Meter

	2017	2018	2019	2020	2021
Goldsboro	92.6				118.5
Average	95.5	92.8	91.6	92.2	92.8

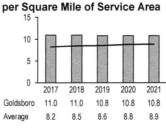

Miles of Main Line Pipe per Square Mile of Service Area

	2017	2018	2019	2020	2021
Goldsboro	11.0	11.0	10.8	10.8	10.8
Average	8.2	8.5	8.6	8.8	8.9

Efficiency Measures

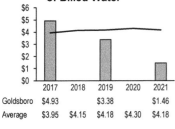

Total Cost per Thousand Gallons of Billed Water

	2017	2018	2019	2020	2021
Goldsboro	$4.93		$3.38		$1.46
Average	$3.95	$4.15	$4.18	$4.30	$4.18

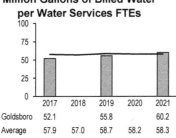

Million Gallons of Billed Water per Water Services FTEs

	2017	2018	2019	2020	2021
Goldsboro	52.1		55.8		60.2
Average	57.9	57.0	58.7	58.2	58.3

Billed Water as a Percentage of Finished Water

	2017	2018	2019	2020	2021
Goldsboro	68%		61%		76%
Average	82%	85%	84%	87%	84%

Effectiveness Measures

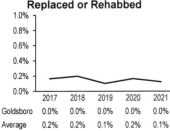

Percentage of Existing Pipeline Replaced or Rehabbed

	2017	2018	2019	2020	2021
Goldsboro	0.0%	0.0%	0.0%	0.0%	0.0%
Average	0.2%	0.2%	0.1%	0.2%	0.1%

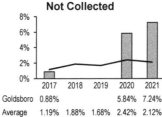

Percentage of Water Bills Not Collected

	2017	2018	2019	2020	2021
Goldsboro	0.88%			5.84%	7.24%
Average	1.19%	1.88%	1.68%	2.42%	2.12%

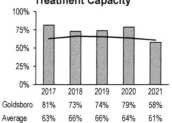

Peak Daily Demand as a Percentage of Treatment Capacity

	2017	2018	2019	2020	2021
Goldsboro	81%	73%	74%	79%	58%
Average	63%	66%	66%	64%	61%

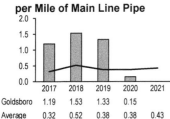

Breaks and Leaks per Mile of Main Line Pipe

	2017	2018	2019	2020	2021
Goldsboro	1.19	1.53	1.33	0.15	
Average	0.32	0.52	0.38	0.38	0.43

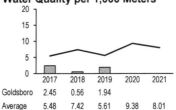

Customer Complaints about Water Quality per 1,000 Meters

	2017	2018	2019	2020	2021
Goldsboro	2.45	0.56	1.94		
Average	5.48	7.42	5.61	9.38	8.01

Greensboro

Water Services

Fiscal Year 2020-21

Explanatory Information

Service Level and Delivery

Greensboro's drinking water is provided by the Water Supply Division, which is part of the Water Resources Department, which also includes wastewater and stormwater services. The water system serves approximately 319,000 people in an area covering about 148 square miles. In addition to City of Greensboro residents, the system serves many addresses in Guilford County in areas adjacent to the city limits.

Water sources for the system are three city-owned reservoirs in the Haw River basin, which is part of the Upper Cape Fear River basin. The estimated safe yield of the system is 36.7 million gallons per day, based on a fifty-year estimate as certified by engineers. The system has emergency interconnections with High Point, Burlington, Reidsville, Winston-Salem, and Piedmont Triad Water Authority.

The city runs two treatment plants with a combined capacity of 63.7 million gallons. Both plants use conventional surface-water treatment.

The estimated average age of main line pipes in the system is forty-two years. Greensboro has begun a spending program on water line rehabilitation and plans to increase funding for this activity for the next several years.

Water meters are read and billed monthly. All meters are read automatically using a radio system.

Conditions Affecting Service, Performance, and Costs

Greensboro has a very high collection rate for water bills. The city has a lien law, so only a small portion of billed amounts goes unpaid. The lien law was changed during FY 2010–11 so that it now only includes owners and not tenants.

Greensboro has a large public-education program to encourage water conservation.

The costs of water services as captured here do not include debt service but do capture depreciation.

Municipal Profile

Estimated Service Population	318,529
Service Land Area (Square Miles)	148.0
Persons per Square Mile	2,152
Topography	Flat; gently rolling
Climate	Temperate; little ice and snow

Service Profile

FTE Staff Positions	
Treatment Plant	54.0
Line Crews	52.0
Meter Readers	18.0
Billing/Collection	7.5
Other	26.0
Total	157.5
Number of Treatment Plants	2
Total Treatment Capacity	63.7 MGD
Average Daily Demand	32.6 MGD
Miles of Main Line Pipe	1,517
Average Age of Main Line Pipe	42 years
Number of Breaks/Leaks	380
Number of Water Meters	108,103
Percent of Meters Read Automatically	100.0%
Total Revenues Collected	$58,857,860

Full Cost Profile

Cost Breakdown by Percentage	
Personal Services	18.0%
Operating Costs	62.9%
Capital Costs	19.1%
TOTAL	100.0%
Cost Breakdown in Dollars	
Personal Services	$7,404,478
Operating Costs	$25,890,537
Capital Costs	$7,870,450
TOTAL	$41,165,465

Resource Measures

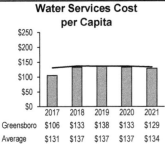

Water Services Cost per Capita

	2017	2018	2019	2020	2021
Greensboro	$106	$133	$138	$133	$129
Average	$131	$137	$137	$137	$134

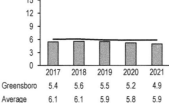

Water Services FTEs per 10,000 Population

	2017	2018	2019	2020	2021
Greensboro	5.4	5.6	5.5	5.2	4.9
Average	6.1	6.1	5.9	5.8	5.9

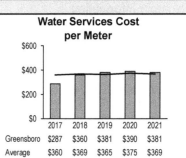

Water Services Cost per Meter

	2017	2018	2019	2020	2021
Greensboro	$287	$360	$381	$390	$381
Average	$360	$369	$365	$375	$369

Workload Measures

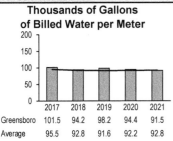

Thousands of Gallons of Billed Water per Meter

	2017	2018	2019	2020	2021
Greensboro	101.5	94.2	98.2	94.4	91.5
Average	95.5	92.8	91.6	92.2	92.8

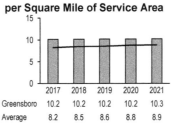

Miles of Main Line Pipe per Square Mile of Service Area

	2017	2018	2019	2020	2021
Greensboro	10.2	10.2	10.2	10.2	10.3
Average	8.2	8.5	8.6	8.8	8.9

Efficiency Measures

Total Cost per Thousand Gallons of Billed Water

	2017	2018	2019	2020	2021
Greensboro	$2.83	$3.82	$3.88	$4.13	$4.16
Average	$3.95	$4.15	$4.18	$4.30	$4.18

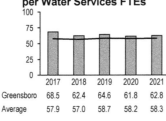

Million Gallons of Billed Water per Water Services FTEs

	2017	2018	2019	2020	2021
Greensboro	68.5	62.4	64.6	61.8	62.8
Average	57.9	57.0	58.7	58.2	58.3

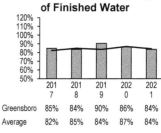

Billed Water as a Percentage of Finished Water

	2017	2018	2019	2020	2021
Greensboro	85%	84%	90%	86%	84%
Average	82%	85%	84%	87%	84%

Effectiveness Measures

Percentage of Existing Pipeline Replaced or Rehabbed

	2017	2018	2019	2020	2021
Greensboro	0.5%	0.3%	0.3%	0.2%	0.0%
Average	0.2%	0.2%	0.1%	0.2%	0.1%

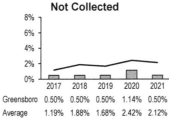

Percentage of Water Bills Not Collected

	2017	2018	2019	2020	2021
Greensboro	0.50%	0.50%	0.50%	1.14%	0.50%
Average	1.19%	1.88%	1.68%	2.42%	2.12%

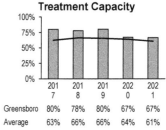

Peak Daily Demand as a Percentage of Treatment Capacity

	2017	2018	2019	2020	2021
Greensboro	80%	78%	80%	67%	67%
Average	63%	66%	66%	64%	61%

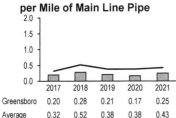

Breaks and Leaks per Mile of Main Line Pipe

	2017	2018	2019	2020	2021
Greensboro	0.20	0.28	0.21	0.17	0.25
Average	0.32	0.52	0.38	0.38	0.43

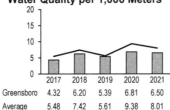

Customer Complaints about Water Quality per 1,000 Meters

	2017	2018	2019	2020	2021
Greensboro	4.32	6.20	5.39	6.81	6.50
Average	5.48	7.42	5.61	9.38	8.01

Explanatory Information

Service Level and Delivery

Water services in Hickory are provided by a combined water distribution division under the Public Services Department. The water system services an area covering roughly 326 square miles and approximately 100,000 people. Water is provided for the City of Hickory and also for the towns of Hildenbran, Brookford, and Catawba; the Sherrill's Ford, Mountain View, and Cooksville communities of Catawba County; and the Bethlehem, Sugarloaf, and Highway 16 communities of Alexander County.

Source water is from the Catawba River basin, with an estimated safe yield of 54 million gallons per day. Hickory sells water to the systems in Conover, Claremont, and Icard Township. The system has one treatment plant, with a capacity of 32 million gallons per day.

Water meters are read monthly. Hickory's replacement standard for water meters is twenty years. About 19 percent of water meters in the system are read by automatic means.

Conditions Affecting Service, Performance, and Costs

The costs of water services as captured here do not include debt service but do capture depreciation.

Municipal Profile

Estimated Service Population	99,530
Service Land Area (Square Miles)	326.0
Persons per Square Mile	305
Topography	Flat; gently rolling
Climate	Temperate; some ice and snow

Service Profile

FTE Staff Positions	
Treatment Plant	13.0
Line Crews	25.0
Meter Readers	6.0
Billing/Collection	5.0
Other	6.0
Total	55.0
Number of Treatment Plants	1
Total Treatment Capacity	32.0 MGD
Average Daily Demand	11.2 MGD
Miles of Main Line Pipe	954
Average Age of Main Line Pipe	40 years
Number of Breaks/Leaks	268
Number of Water Meters	31,294
Percent of Meters Read Automatically	18.9%
Total Revenues Collected	$17,303,090

Full Cost Profile

Cost Breakdown by Percentage	
Personal Services	28.7%
Operating Costs	46.9%
Capital Costs	24.3%
TOTAL	100.0%
Cost Breakdown in Dollars	
Personal Services	$3,024,315
Operating Costs	$4,942,147
Capital Costs	$2,562,067
TOTAL	$10,528,529

Hickory

Key: Hickory ▨   Benchmarking Average —   Fiscal Years 2017 through 2021

Resource Measures

Water Services Cost per Capita

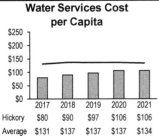

	2017	2018	2019	2020	2021
Hickory	$80	$90	$97	$106	$106
Average	$131	$137	$137	$137	$134

Water Services FTEs per 10,000 Population

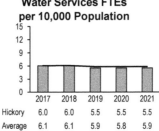

	2017	2018	2019	2020	2021
Hickory	6.0	6.0	5.5	5.5	5.5
Average	6.1	6.1	5.9	5.8	5.9

Water Services Cost per Meter

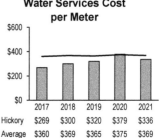

	2017	2018	2019	2020	2021
Hickory	$269	$300	$320	$379	$336
Average	$360	$369	$365	$375	$369

Workload Measures

Thousands of Gallons of Billed Water per Meter

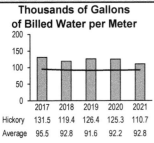

	2017	2018	2019	2020	2021
Hickory	131.5	119.4	126.4	125.3	110.7
Average	95.5	92.8	91.6	92.2	92.8

Miles of Main Line Pipe per Square Mile of Service Area

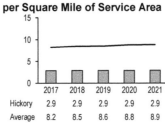

	2017	2018	2019	2020	2021
Hickory	2.9	2.9	2.9	2.9	2.9
Average	8.2	8.5	8.6	8.8	8.9

Efficiency Measures

Total Cost per Thousand Gallons of Billed Water

	2017	2018	2019	2020	2021
Hickory	$2.05	$2.52	$2.53	$3.02	$3.04
Average	$3.95	$4.15	$4.18	$4.30	$4.18

Million Gallons of Billed Water per Water Services FTEs

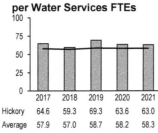

	2017	2018	2019	2020	2021
Hickory	64.6	59.3	69.3	63.6	63.0
Average	57.9	57.0	58.7	58.2	58.3

Billed Water as a Percentage of Finished Water

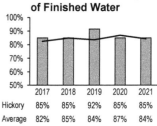

	2017	2018	2019	2020	2021
Hickory	85%	85%	92%	85%	85%
Average	82%	85%	84%	87%	84%

Effectiveness Measures

Percentage of Existing Pipeline Replaced or Rehabbed

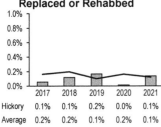

	2017	2018	2019	2020	2021
Hickory	0.1%	0.1%	0.2%	0.0%	0.1%
Average	0.2%	0.2%	0.1%	0.2%	0.1%

Percentage of Water Bills Not Collected

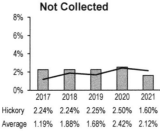

	2017	2018	2019	2020	2021
Hickory	2.24%	2.24%	2.25%	2.50%	1.60%
Average	1.19%	1.88%	1.68%	2.42%	2.12%

Peak Daily Demand as a Percentage of Treatment Capacity

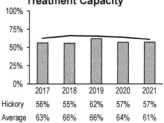

	2017	2018	2019	2020	2021
Hickory	56%	55%	62%	57%	57%
Average	63%	66%	66%	64%	61%

Breaks and Leaks per Mile of Main Line Pipe

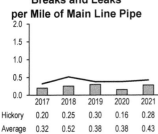

	2017	2018	2019	2020	2021
Hickory	0.20	0.25	0.30	0.16	0.28
Average	0.32	0.52	0.38	0.38	0.43

Customer Complaints about Water Quality per 1,000 Meters

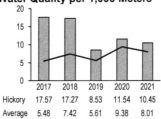

	2017	2018	2019	2020	2021
Hickory	17.57	17.27	8.53	11.54	10.45
Average	5.48	7.42	5.61	9.38	8.01

Explanatory Information

Service Level and Delivery

Public Utilities is a department within the City of Raleigh. It is a combined enterprise system that provides drinking water and sewage treatment services to the City of Raleigh and six merger towns: Garner, Rolesville, Knightdale, Wake Forest, Wendell, and Zebulon. As of FY 2020, approximately 592,000 people live in the contractual service area of 299 square miles. Source water supply is from Falls Lake located in the Neuse River watershed and from Lake Wheeler and Lake Benson, which are in the Swift Creek watershed. During FY 2019, the Utility received a reallocation of its water supply that increased the system's 50-year reliable yield to 98 million gallons per day.

The utility operates two surface-water treatment plants, with a total permitted treatment capacity of 106 million gallons per day. The E.M. Johnson plant provides 86 percent of the potable water using an enhanced coagulation treatment process with the addition of settled water ozone. The Dempsey E. Benton plant also utilizes an enhanced coagulation treatment process using raw water ozone, solids contact sedimentation, a two-stage filter process, and ultraviolet disinfection prior to clearwell storage.

Water meters are read once per month. Currently, nearly all meters are read by automatic means. The standard for meter replacement is fifteen years.

Conditions Affecting Service, Performance, and Costs

The approved reallocation of supply water resources in FY 2019 came with increased costs to maintain and finance the improvement. Due to source water organics, both treatment plants utilize enhanced coagulation with ferric sulfate and chloramine disinfection to control disinfection byproducts. These processes have higher chemical and operating costs than traditional treatment processes. Additionally, Raleigh has a specialized program to manage water age and disinfection byproducts in the distribution system.

The costs of water services as captured here do not include debt service but do capture depreciation.

Municipal Profile

Estimated Service Population	605,000
Service Land Area (Square Miles)	299.0
Persons per Square Mile	2,023
Topography	Flat; gently rolling
Climate	Temperate; little ice and snow

Service Profile

FTE Staff Positions	
Treatment Plant	64.0
Line Crews	82.0
Meter Readers	2.0
Billing/Collection	29.0
Other	126.0
Total	303.0
Number of Treatment Plants	2
Total Treatment Capacity	106.0 MGD
Average Daily Demand	51.3 MGD
Miles of Main Line Pipe	2,377
Average Age of Main Line Pipe	30 years
Number of Breaks/Leaks	476
Number of Water Meters	197,720
Percent of Meters Read Automatically	100.0%
Total Revenues Collected	$123,709,792

Full Cost Profile

Cost Breakdown by Percentage	
Personal Services	36.8%
Operating Costs	43.8%
Capital Costs	19.5%
TOTAL	100.0%
Cost Breakdown in Dollars	
Personal Services	$23,524,932
Operating Costs	$27,975,126
Capital Costs	$12,440,777
TOTAL	$63,940,835

Resource Measures

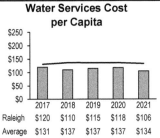

Water Services Cost per Capita

	2017	2018	2019	2020	2021
Raleigh	$120	$110	$115	$118	$106
Average	$131	$137	$137	$137	$134

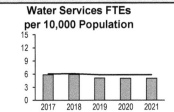

Water Services FTEs per 10,000 Population

	2017	2018	2019	2020	2021
Raleigh	5.8	5.9	5.1	5.0	5.0
Average	6.1	6.1	5.9	5.8	5.9

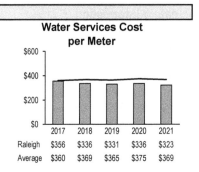

Water Services Cost per Meter

	2017	2018	2019	2020	2021
Raleigh	$356	$336	$331	$336	$323
Average	$360	$369	$365	$375	$369

Workload Measures

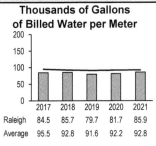

Thousands of Gallons of Billed Water per Meter

	2017	2018	2019	2020	2021
Raleigh	84.5	85.7	79.7	81.7	85.9
Average	95.5	92.8	91.6	92.2	92.8

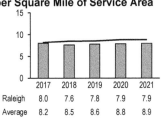

Miles of Main Line Pipe per Square Mile of Service Area

	2017	2018	2019	2020	2021
Raleigh	8.0	7.6	7.8	7.9	7.9
Average	8.2	8.5	8.6	8.8	8.9

Efficiency Measures

Total Cost per Thousand Gallons of Billed Water

	2017	2018	2019	2020	2021
Raleigh	$4.21	$3.92	$4.15	$4.11	$3.77
Average	$3.95	$4.15	$4.18	$4.30	$4.18

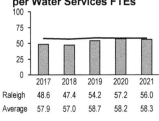

Million Gallons of Billed Water per Water Services FTEs

	2017	2018	2019	2020	2021
Raleigh	48.6	47.4	54.2	57.2	56.0
Average	57.9	57.0	58.7	58.2	58.3

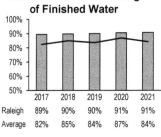

Billed Water as a Percentage of Finished Water

	2017	2018	2019	2020	2021
Raleigh	89%	90%	90%	91%	91%
Average	82%	85%	84%	87%	84%

Effectiveness Measures

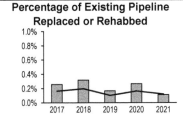

Percentage of Existing Pipeline Replaced or Rehabbed

	2017	2018	2019	2020	2021
Raleigh	0.3%	0.3%	0.2%	0.3%	0.1%
Average	0.2%	0.2%	0.1%	0.2%	0.1%

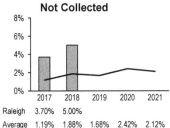

Percentage of Water Bills Not Collected

	2017	2018	2019	2020	2021
Raleigh	3.70%	5.00%			
Average	1.19%	1.88%	1.68%	2.42%	2.12%

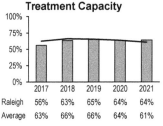

Peak Daily Demand as a Percentage of Treatment Capacity

	2017	2018	2019	2020	2021
Raleigh	56%	63%	65%	64%	64%
Average	63%	66%	66%	64%	61%

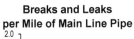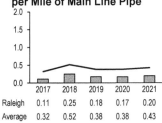

Breaks and Leaks per Mile of Main Line Pipe

	2017	2018	2019	2020	2021
Raleigh	0.11	0.25	0.18	0.17	0.20
Average	0.32	0.52	0.38	0.38	0.43

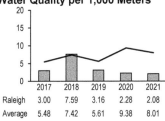

Customer Complaints about Water Quality per 1,000 Meters

	2017	2018	2019	2020	2021
Raleigh	3.00	7.59	3.16	2.28	2.08
Average	5.48	7.42	5.61	9.38	8.01

Service Level and Delivery

Water services in Wilson are handled by a combined water/sewer division under the Department of Public Works. Billing services are handled by the Wilson Finance Department. The water system serves approximately 52,000 people over forty square miles.

Source water for the system comes from four city-owned reservoirs. Water is also pumped from two different reservoirs in the Neuse River basin. The estimated safe yield for the system is 29 million gallons per day.

The system has two treatment plants with a combined treatment capacity of 22 million gallons per day. The plants use conventional surface-water treatment with flocculation, sedimentation, and filtration.

Water meters are read once per month in Wilson. Approximately 90 percent of the water meters in the system are read by automatic remote means using a radio system by Itron.

Conditions Affecting Service, Performance, and Costs

The costs of water services as captured here do not include debt service but do capture depreciation. Large capital improvements are being made to the Buckhorn Lake Dam and Wastewater Projects, which have been required to meet advanced nutrient removal.

The graphed measure for "Breaks and Leaks per Mile of Main Line Pipe" shows a jump for FY2020. This is due to a more complete accounting of breaks and leaks rather than a change in performance. In earlier years, Wilson had only reported the smaller number of breaks in the main lines themselves. This new reporting is more inclusive, as it includes all breaks and leaks for which crews were dispatched.

Municipal Profile

Estimated Service Population	52,000
Service Land Area (Square Miles)	40.0
Persons per Square Mile	1,300
Topography	Flat; gently rolling
Climate	Temperate; little ice and snow

Service Profile

FTE Staff Positions	
Treatment Plant	21.0
Line Crews	20.0
Meter Readers	2.5
Billing/Collection	3.0
Other	0.0
Total	46.5
Number of Treatment Plants	2
Total Treatment Capacity	22.0 MGD
Average Daily Demand	8.9 MGD
Miles of Main Line Pipe	435
Average Age of Main Line Pipe	38 years
Number of Breaks/Leaks	601
Number of Water Meters	22,182
Percent of Meters Read Automatically	90.2%
Total Revenues Collected	$13,797,000

Full Cost Profile

Cost Breakdown by Percentage	
Personal Services	30.3%
Operating Costs	47.3%
Capital Costs	22.4%
TOTAL	100.0%
Cost Breakdown in Dollars	
Personal Services	$3,411,198
Operating Costs	$5,323,175
Capital Costs	$2,526,264
TOTAL	$11,260,637

Wilson

Water Services

Resource Measures

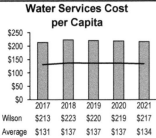

Water Services Cost per Capita

	2017	2018	2019	2020	2021
Wilson	$213	$223	$220	$219	$217
Average	$131	$137	$137	$137	$134

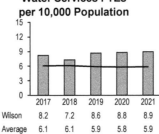

Water Services FTEs per 10,000 Population

	2017	2018	2019	2020	2021
Wilson	8.2	7.2	8.6	8.8	8.9
Average	6.1	6.1	5.9	5.8	5.9

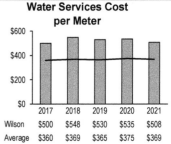

Water Services Cost per Meter

	2017	2018	2019	2020	2021
Wilson	$500	$548	$530	$535	$508
Average	$360	$369	$365	$375	$369

Workload Measures

Thousands of Gallons of Billed Water per Meter

	2017	2018	2019	2020	2021
Wilson	82.2	87.1	85.6	90.8	90.3
Average	95.5	92.8	91.6	92.2	92.8

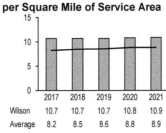

Miles of Main Line Pipe per Square Mile of Service Area

	2017	2018	2019	2020	2021
Wilson	10.7	10.7	10.7	10.8	10.9
Average	8.2	8.5	8.6	8.8	8.9

Efficiency Measures

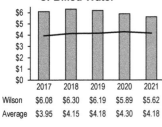

Total Cost per Thousand Gallons of Billed Water

	2017	2018	2019	2020	2021
Wilson	$6.08	$6.30	$6.19	$5.89	$5.62
Average	$3.95	$4.15	$4.18	$4.30	$4.18

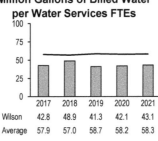

Million Gallons of Billed Water per Water Services FTEs

	2017	2018	2019	2020	2021
Wilson	42.8	48.9	41.3	42.1	43.1
Average	57.9	57.0	58.7	58.2	58.3

Billed Water as a Percentage of Finished Water

	2017	2018	2019	2020	2021
Wilson	58%	80%	83%	85%	84%
Average	82%	85%	84%	87%	84%

Effectiveness Measures

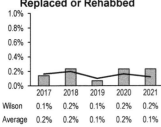

Percentage of Existing Pipeline Replaced or Rehabbed

	2017	2018	2019	2020	2021
Wilson	0.1%	0.2%	0.1%	0.2%	0.2%
Average	0.2%	0.2%	0.1%	0.2%	0.1%

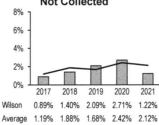

Percentage of Water Bills Not Collected

	2017	2018	2019	2020	2021
Wilson	0.89%	1.40%	2.09%	2.71%	1.22%
Average	1.19%	1.88%	1.68%	2.42%	2.12%

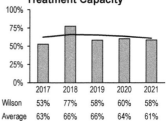

Peak Daily Demand as a Percentage of Treatment Capacity

	2017	2018	2019	2020	2021
Wilson	53%	77%	58%	60%	58%
Average	63%	66%	66%	64%	61%

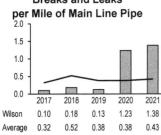

Breaks and Leaks per Mile of Main Line Pipe

	2017	2018	2019	2020	2021
Wilson	0.10	0.18	0.13	1.23	1.38
Average	0.32	0.52	0.38	0.38	0.43

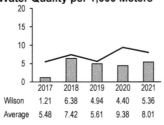

Customer Complaints about Water Quality per 1,000 Meters

	2017	2018	2019	2020	2021
Wilson	1.21	6.38	4.94	4.40	5.36
Average	5.48	7.42	5.61	9.38	8.01

Explanatory Information

Service Level and Delivery

The Winston-Salem and Forsyth County Utilities Division operates a combined water and sewer system that covers the city and most of the remaining population of Forsyth County. Approximately 369,000 people are served in an area covering roughly 227 square miles.

The system has an eleven-member utility commission that was created by an interlocal agreement between the City of Winston-Salem and Forsyth County. The commission sets policy for publicly owned water, wastewater, and solid-waste-disposal facilities. The commission is also charged with the responsibility for long-range planning, authorizing funding for projects, operating and maintaining facilities, and setting policies and rate structures. The commission is not authorized to issue bonds to finance capital improvements.

Water sources for the system are drawn from two separate points on the Yadkin River. The city also uses Salem Lake as a water source. The estimated safe yield for the system is 100 million gallons per day.

The city uses three treatment plants with a daily treatment capacity of 91 million gallons. The plants all use conventional treatment, employing coagulation, flocculation, and sedimentation, followed by rapid sand filtration and then chlorine treatment for disinfection.

The system has 2,348 miles of pipeline. The replacement goal for pipes is seventy-five years.

Water meters are read both monthly and bimonthly depending on the account type. Currently the system has a small number of meters read by automatic means, totaling approximately 13 percent. The replacement standard for water meters is approximately every ten years. The goal is to have completely switched to automatically read meters within ten years.

Conditions Affecting Service, Performance, and Costs

The costs of water services as captured here do not include debt service but do capture depreciation.

Winston-Salem made improvements in their calculation of population served and area covered to improve the accuracy of their data. This had the effect of decreasing the reported population and size of area served from earlier years. The changes seen in FY 2017–18 are due to this improved estimation and not a change in services.

Municipal Profile

Estimated Service Population	369,282
Service Land Area (Square Miles)	227.3
Persons per Square Mile	1,625
Topography	Gently rolling
Climate	Temperate; some ice and snow

Service Profile

FTE Staff Positions	
Treatment Plant	54.0
Line Crews	80.0
Meter Readers	13.0
Billing/Collection	8.2
Other	20.0
Total	175.2
Number of Treatment Plants	3
Total Treatment Capacity	91.0 MGD
Average Daily Demand	35.8 MGD
Miles of Main Line Pipe	2,348
Average Age of Main Line Pipe	75 years
Number of Breaks/Leaks	410
Number of Water Meters	133,161
Percent of Meters Read Automatically	13.5%
Total Revenues Collected	$67,806,289

Full Cost Profile

Cost Breakdown by Percentage	
Personal Services	27.2%
Operating Costs	36.2%
Capital Costs	36.6%
TOTAL	100.0%
Cost Breakdown in Dollars	
Personal Services	$10,202,678
Operating Costs	$13,597,904
Capital Costs	$13,769,147
TOTAL	$37,569,729

Resource Measures

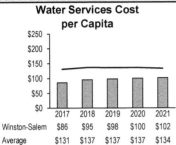

Water Services Cost per Capita

	2017	2018	2019	2020	2021
Winston-Salem	$86	$95	$98	$100	$102
Average	$131	$137	$137	$137	$134

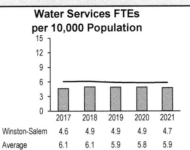

Water Services FTEs per 10,000 Population

	2017	2018	2019	2020	2021
Winston-Salem	4.6	4.9	4.9	4.9	4.7
Average	6.1	6.1	5.9	5.8	5.9

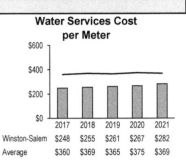

Water Services Cost per Meter

	2017	2018	2019	2020	2021
Winston-Salem	$248	$255	$261	$267	$282
Average	$360	$369	$365	$375	$369

Workload Measures

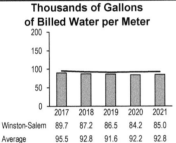

Thousands of Gallons of Billed Water per Meter

	2017	2018	2019	2020	2021
Winston-Salem	89.7	87.2	86.5	84.2	85.0
Average	95.5	92.8	91.6	92.2	92.8

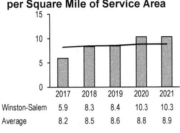

Miles of Main Line Pipe per Square Mile of Service Area

	2017	2018	2019	2020	2021
Winston-Salem	5.9	8.3	8.4	10.3	10.3
Average	8.2	8.5	8.6	8.8	8.9

Efficiency Measures

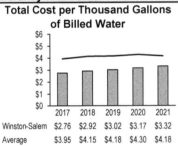

Total Cost per Thousand Gallons of Billed Water

	2017	2018	2019	2020	2021
Winston-Salem	$2.76	$2.92	$3.02	$3.17	$3.32
Average	$3.95	$4.15	$4.18	$4.30	$4.18

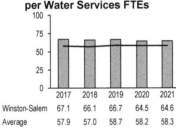

Million Gallons of Billed Water per Water Services FTEs

	2017	2018	2019	2020	2021
Winston-Salem	67.1	66.1	66.7	64.5	64.6
Average	57.9	57.0	58.7	58.2	58.3

Billed Water as a Percentage of Finished Water

	2017	2018	2019	2020	2021
Winston-Salem	87%	86%	86%	84%	87%
Average	82%	85%	84%	87%	84%

Effectiveness Measures

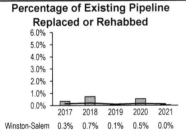

Percentage of Existing Pipeline Replaced or Rehabbed

	2017	2018	2019	2020	2021
Winston-Salem	0.3%	0.7%	0.1%	0.5%	0.0%
Average	0.2%	0.2%	0.1%	0.2%	0.1%

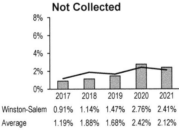

Percentage of Water Bills Not Collected

	2017	2018	2019	2020	2021
Winston-Salem	0.91%	1.14%	1.47%	2.76%	2.41%
Average	1.19%	1.88%	1.68%	2.42%	2.12%

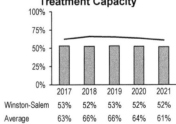

Peak Daily Demand as a Percentage of Treatment Capacity

	2017	2018	2019	2020	2021
Winston-Salem	53%	52%	53%	52%	52%
Average	63%	66%	66%	64%	61%

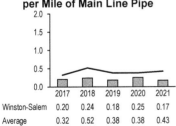

Breaks and Leaks per Mile of Main Line Pipe

	2017	2018	2019	2020	2021
Winston-Salem	0.20	0.24	0.18	0.25	0.17
Average	0.32	0.52	0.38	0.38	0.43

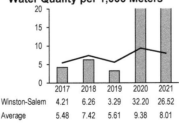

Customer Complaints about Water Quality per 1,000 Meters

	2017	2018	2019	2020	2021
Winston-Salem	4.21	6.26	3.29	32.20	26.52
Average	5.48	7.42	5.61	9.38	8.01

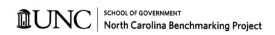

Performance and Cost Data

WASTEWATER SERVICES

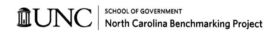

PERFORMANCE MEASURES FOR WASTEWATER SERVICES

SERVICE DEFINITION
Wastewater Services include the collection, treatment, wastewater discharge, solids disposal, and billing related to sewer services. This service area includes the collection system after leaving the customer's outlet, lift stations, pretreatment, and treatment plants. Activities and costs include the operation, maintenance, and installation of infrastructure. Also included are costs and activities associated with billing and collection for sewer services and administrative activities, such as planning, engineering, and testing. This includes wastewater treated for reuse at the plant site and for other purposes. Excluded are potable water systems and stormwater systems.

NOTES ON PERFORMANCE MEASURES

1. Volume of Sewage per Account
This workload measure captures the amount of wastewater generated and received at the treatment plant relative to the number of customers.

2. Miles of Sewer Main Line Pipe per Square Mile of Service Area
The amount of sewer main line pipe per square mile shows the density of the pipe infrastructure to be maintained relative to the geographic size of the area served.

3. Number of Lift Stations per Thousand Accounts
This workload measure provides some idea of the amount of reliance on pumping in a system to supplement gravity-fed delivery. Lift stations also generate additional maintenance workload.

4. Cost per Thousand Gallons of Collected and Treated Wastewater
This efficiency measure shows total system costs relative to the volume of wastewater reaching treatment plants. Some wastewater does not make it to treatment plants.

5. Wastewater Volume in Millions of Gallons per FTE
This efficiency measure captures the number of workers the system is using relative to the volume of wastewater treated.

6. Customer Accounts per FTE
The number of customer accounts relative to the number of workers is another efficiency measure showing how many customers are being served per worker.

7. Percentage of Bills Collected

Collection of wastewater bills sent to customers is necessary to ensure revenues for system operation. Bills not collected reflect potential lost revenue to the system, but some loss is unavoidable.

8. Average Daily Treatment as a Percent of Permitted Capacity

A wastewater system needs sufficient capacity to meet not only average demands, but also peak demands. This measure looks at average daily demand relative to the wastewater system treatment capacity in a day. Some excess capacity is needed to allow for daily service variations and to plan for future expansion needs.

9. Percent of Existing Main Line Pipe Rehabilitated or Replaced

As the wastewater systems age, pipe needs to be replaced to ensure that service will not be interrupted. This effectiveness measure captures the amount of current stock being replaced or rehabilitated during a given year.

10. Overflows Per 100 Miles of Main Line Pipe

Sanitary system overflows may be due to blockages or breaks in pipe. Keeping these breaks to a low level is an important measure of the effectiveness of preventive maintenance and system upkeep. Overflows, if large enough, may also represent a public-health concern.

11. Sewer Backups per 100 Miles of Main Line Pipe

Backups in sewer pipes are another measure of potential maintenance concerns and potential public health concerns. Backups may also be a sign of insufficient maintenance.

12. Billed Sewer Effluents as a Percent of Treated Effluent

The volume of wastewater that is billed relative to the volume received at the treatment plant is an effectiveness measure that points to potential losses in the collection system. Some loss is inevitable in sewer systems, and not all drinking water billed for is used in such a way that it should make it back to the wastewater treatment plant. But comparisons may reveal excessive infiltration or leakage.

Wastewater Services

Summary of Key Dimensions of Service

City or Town	Estimated Residential Population in Service Area	Service Area (in Square Miles)	Operating Treatment Plants	Average Daily Flow of Wastewater at Plants (in MGD)	Total Treatment Capacity for Wastewater (in MGD)	Miles of Gravity and Forced Main Lines	Number of Wastewater Accounts	Sewer System FTE Positions
Apex	70,272	25.0	1 + 1 jointly operated with Cary	4.7	9.7	311.2	22,143	24.0
Charlotte	1,128,945	546.0	7	87.2	123.2	4,476.0	276,499	541.5
Concord	94,443	105.7	0	na	na	599.6	39,331	33.0
Goldsboro	33,906	25.0	1	12.7	14.2	244.0	11,568	39.0
Greensboro	318,529	148.0	1	35.4	56.0	1,527.0	99,658	168.5
Hickory	37,478	65.0	3	6.2	16.5	544.0	17,426	44.0
Raleigh	605,000	299.0	3	52.7	80.2	2,557.0	183,622	351.0
Wilson	53,000	42.0	1	11.1	14.0	364.4	20,253	64.5
Winston-Salem	329,156	148.5	2	38.1	51.0	1,772.0	102,921	174.2

NOTES
MGD stands for millions of gallons per day.

EXPLANATORY FACTORS
These are factors that the project found affected wastewater services performance and cost in one or more of the municipalities:

Topography
Size of service area
Population density
Age of infrastructure
Growth of population and businesses

Apex

Wastewater Services

Fiscal Year 2020-21

Explanatory Information

Service Level and Delivery

Wastewater services for the Town of Apex are managed by the Water Reclamation and Wastewater Collections Division under the Department of Water Resources. The system covers the area within the municipal limits.

Apex has one treatment plant, which uses bar screens, grit removal, biological nutrient removal (BNR), oxidation ditches, secondary clarifiers, sand filters, ultraviolet disinfection, aerobic sludge digestion, and rotary-drum-sludge dewatering as part of its treatment process. The Apex wastewater system has nutrient limits in place that restrict what can be discharged from the plant to protect water quality. Apex uses land application for biosolids resulting from treatment and also dries some biosolids as fertilizer pellets. Apex also pays for one-third of the operation of a separate treatment plant, which is jointly owned with the Town of Cary.

The town's system reported no regulatory violation for the treatment portion of the system nor the collection system during the fiscal year.

Conditions Affecting Service, Performance, and Costs

The costs of wastewater or sewer services as captured here do not include debt service but do capture depreciation of capital.

Municipal Profile

Estimated Service Population	70,272
Service Land Area (Square Miles)	25.0
Persons per Square Mile	2,811
Topography	Flat; gently rolling
Climate	Temperate; little ice and snow

Service Profile

Total FTE Staff Positions	24.0
Treatment Plant	8.0
Line Crews	12.0
Billing/Collection	2.0
Other	2.0
Number of Treatment Plants	2
Total Treatment Capacity	9.7 MGD
Average Daily Flow	4.7 MGD
River Basin into Which System Discharges	Neuse
Miles of Gravity Main Line Pipe	273
Miles of Forced Main Line Pipe	38
Average Age of Main Line Pipe	17 years
Blocks in Sewer Mains	52
Number of System Breaks	25
Sanitary System Overflows	2
Number of Customer Accounts	22,143
Total Revenues Collected	$14,343,766

Full Cost Profile

Cost Breakdown by Percentage	
Personal Services	20.5%
Operating Costs	44.3%
Capital Costs	35.1%
TOTAL	100.0%

Cost Breakdown in Dollars	
Personal Services	$2,366,581
Operating Costs	$5,105,098
Capital Costs	$4,049,049
TOTAL	$11,520,728

Apex

Wastewater Services

Key: Apex　　　　Benchmarking Average —　　　　Fiscal Years 2017 through 2021

Resource Measures

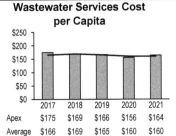

Wastewater Services Cost per Capita

	2017	2018	2019	2020	2021
Apex	$175	$169	$166	$156	$164
Average	$166	$169	$165	$160	$160

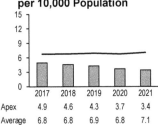

Wastewater Services FTEs per 10,000 Population

	2017	2018	2019	2020	2021
Apex	4.9	4.6	4.3	3.7	3.4
Average	6.8	6.8	6.9	6.8	7.1

Wastewater Services Cost per Customer Account

	2017	2018	2019	2020	2021
Apex	$527	$499	$494	$471	$520
Average	$494	$490	$473	$471	$471

Workload Measures

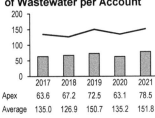

Thousands of Gallons of Wastewater per Account

	2017	2018	2019	2020	2021
Apex	63.6	67.2	72.5	63.1	78.5
Average	135.0	126.9	150.7	135.2	151.8

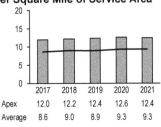

Miles of Sewer Main Line Pipe per Square Mile of Service Area

	2017	2018	2019	2020	2021
Apex	12.0	12.2	12.4	12.6	12.4
Average	8.6	9.0	8.9	9.3	9.3

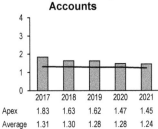

Number of Lift Stations per 1,000 Accounts

	2017	2018	2019	2020	2021
Apex	1.83	1.63	1.62	1.47	1.45
Average	1.31	1.30	1.28	1.28	1.24

Efficiency Measures

Total Cost per 1,000 Gallons of Treated Wastewater

	2017	2018	2019	2020	2021
Apex	$8.29	$7.43	$6.81	$7.46	$6.63
Average	$4.07	$4.21	$3.59	$4.08	$3.92

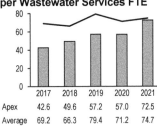

Million Gallons of Wastewater per Wastewater Services FTE

	2017	2018	2019	2020	2021
Apex	42.6	49.6	57.2	57.0	72.5
Average	69.2	66.3	79.4	71.2	74.7

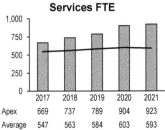

Customer Accounts per Wastewater Services FTE

	2017	2018	2019	2020	2021
Apex	669	737	789	904	923
Average	547	563	584	603	593

Effectiveness Measures

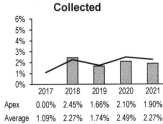

Percentage of Wastewater Bills Not Collected

	2017	2018	2019	2020	2021
Apex	0.00%	2.45%	1.66%	2.10%	1.90%
Average	1.09%	2.27%	1.74%	2.49%	2.27%

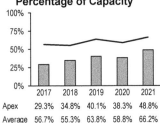

Average Daily Treatment as a Percentage of Capacity

	2017	2018	2019	2020	2021
Apex	29.3%	34.8%	40.1%	38.3%	48.8%
Average	56.7%	55.3%	63.8%	58.8%	66.2%

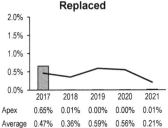

Percent of Main Line Rehabbed or Replaced

	2017	2018	2019	2020	2021
Apex	0.65%	0.01%	0.00%	0.00%	0.01%
Average	0.47%	0.36%	0.59%	0.56%	0.21%

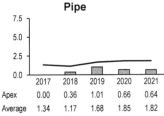

Overflows per 100 Miles of Main Line Pipe

	2017	2018	2019	2020	2021
Apex	0.00	0.36	1.01	0.66	0.64
Average	1.34	1.17	1.68	1.85	1.82

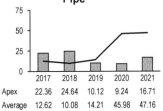

Backups per 100 Miles of Main Line Pipe

	2017	2018	2019	2020	2021
Apex	22.36	24.64	10.12	9.24	16.71
Average	12.62	10.08	14.21	45.98	47.16

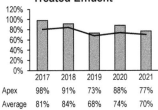

Billed Wastewater as a Percent of Treated Effluent

	2017	2018	2019	2020	2021
Apex	98%	91%	73%	88%	77%
Average	81%	84%	68%	74%	70%

Charlotte

Wastewater Services

Fiscal Year 2020-21

Explanatory Information

Service Level and Delivery
Wastewater collection and treatment are handled by Charlotte Water (CLTWater). This is a combined water and sewer utility for Mecklenburg County and the City of Charlotte. The department is run as an official City of Charlotte department. The service area corresponds roughly to the boundaries of Mecklenburg County.

There are seven wastewater treatment plants owned and operated by Charlotte Water. Each of CLTWater's treatment plants applies primary, secondary, and advanced treatment to the waste stream. The system does have regulatory limits in place on nutrient loads, which can be discharged in order to protect water quality. In addition to the treatment of wastewater, the system handles biosolids, most of which are applied to land (unless non-conforming) and then taken to the landfill.

The system had one regulatory violation connected to treatment issues and six regulatory violations connected to the collection portion of the system during the year.

Conditions Affecting Service, Performance, and Costs
The costs of wastewater or sewer services as captured here do not include debt service but do capture depreciation of capital.

Municipal Profile

Estimated Service Population	1,128,945
Service Land Area (Square Miles)	546
Persons per Square Mile	2,068
Topography	Flat; gently rolling
Climate	Temperate; little ice and snow

Service Profile

Total FTE Staff Positions	541.5
Treatment Plant	121.0
Line Crews	180.0
Billing/Collection	12.0
Other	228.5
Number of Treatment Plants	7
Total Treatment Capacity	123.2 MGD
Average Daily Flow	87.2 MGD
River Basin into Which System Discharges	Catawba and Yadkin
Miles of Gravity Main Line Pipe	4,341
Miles of Forced Main Line Pipe	135
Average Age of Main Line Pipe	34 years
Blocks in Sewer Mains	102
Number of System Breaks	646
Sanitary System Overflows	152
Number of Customer Accounts	276,499
Total Revenues Collected	$286,608,768

Full Cost Profile
Cost Breakdown by Percentage

Personal Services	18.5%
Operating Costs	32.6%
Capital Costs	49.0%
TOTAL	100.0%

Cost Breakdown in Dollars

Personal Services	$37,453,080
Operating Costs	$66,065,859
Capital Costs	$99,305,132
TOTAL	$202,824,071

Charlotte
Wastewater Services

Resource Measures

Wastewater Services Cost per Capita

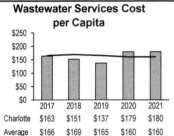

	2017	2018	2019	2020	2021
Charlotte	$163	$151	$137	$179	$180
Average	$166	$169	$165	$160	$160

Wastewater Services FTEs per 10,000 Population

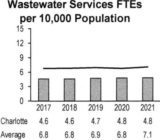

	2017	2018	2019	2020	2021
Charlotte	4.6	4.6	4.7	4.8	4.8
Average	6.8	6.8	6.9	6.8	7.1

Wastewater Services Cost per Customer Account

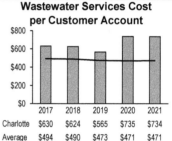

	2017	2018	2019	2020	2021
Charlotte	$630	$624	$565	$735	$734
Average	$494	$490	$473	$471	$471

Workload Measures

Thousands of Gallons of Wastewater per Account

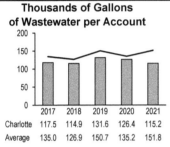

	2017	2018	2019	2020	2021
Charlotte	117.5	114.9	131.6	126.4	115.2
Average	135.0	126.9	150.7	135.2	151.8

Miles of Sewer Main Line Pipe per Square Mile of Service Area

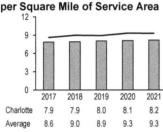

	2017	2018	2019	2020	2021
Charlotte	7.9	7.9	8.0	8.1	8.2
Average	8.6	9.0	8.9	9.3	9.3

Number of Lift Stations per 1,000 Accounts

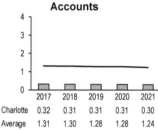

	2017	2018	2019	2020	2021
Charlotte	0.32	0.31	0.31	0.31	0.30
Average	1.31	1.30	1.28	1.28	1.24

Efficiency Measures

Total Cost per 1,000 Gallons of Treated Wastewater

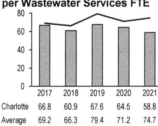

	2017	2018	2019	2020	2021
Charlotte	$5.36	$5.43	$4.29	$5.81	$6.37
Average	$4.07	$4.21	$3.59	$4.08	$3.92

Million Gallons of Wastewater per Wastewater Services FTE

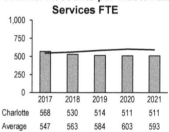

	2017	2018	2019	2020	2021
Charlotte	66.8	60.9	67.6	64.5	58.8
Average	69.2	66.3	79.4	71.2	74.7

Customer Accounts per Wastewater Services FTE

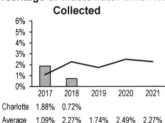

	2017	2018	2019	2020	2021
Charlotte	568	530	514	511	511
Average	547	563	584	603	593

Effectiveness Measures

Percentage of Wastewater Bills Not Collected

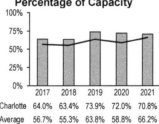

	2017	2018	2019	2020	2021
Charlotte	1.88%	0.72%			
Average	1.09%	2.27%	1.74%	2.49%	2.27%

Average Daily Treatment as a Percentage of Capacity

	2017	2018	2019	2020	2021
Charlotte	64.0%	63.4%	73.9%	72.0%	70.8%
Average	56.7%	55.3%	63.8%	58.8%	66.2%

Percent of Main Line Rehabbed or Replaced

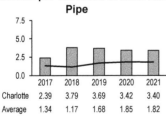

	2017	2018	2019	2020	2021
Charlotte	0.37%	0.36%	0.49%	0.30%	0.25%
Average	0.47%	0.36%	0.59%	0.56%	0.21%

Overflows per 100 Miles of Main Line Pipe

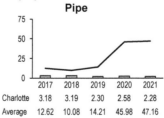

	2017	2018	2019	2020	2021
Charlotte	2.39	3.79	3.69	3.42	3.40
Average	1.34	1.17	1.68	1.85	1.82

Backups per 100 Miles of Main Line Pipe

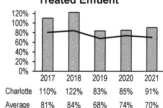

	2017	2018	2019	2020	2021
Charlotte	3.18	3.19	2.30	2.58	2.28
Average	12.62	10.08	14.21	45.98	47.16

Billed Wastewater as a Percent of Treated Effluent

	2017	2018	2019	2020	2021
Charlotte	110%	122%	83%	85%	91%
Average	81%	84%	68%	74%	70%

Concord

Wastewater Services

Fiscal Year 2020-21

Explanatory Information

Service Level and Delivery

The City of Concord has a wastewater department that focuses on the inspection, maintenance, and repair of the wastewater collection system. Concord does not have its own treatment plant, making it unique among the benchmarking partner cities. Instead, treatment is handled by the Water and Sewer Authority of Cabarrus County, a regional system. All treatment and disposal of wastewater and biosolids are handled by the regional authority using two treatment plants.

The Concord wastewater collection system had three violations on the collection portion of the system involving sanitary system overflows.

Conditions Affecting Service, Performance, and Costs

The costs of wastewater or sewer services as captured here do not include debt service but do capture depreciation of capital.

Municipal Profile

Estimated Service Population	94,443
Service Land Area (Square Miles)	105.7
Persons per Square Mile	894
Topography	Flat; gently rolling
Climate	Temperate; little ice and snow

Service Profile

Total FTE Staff Positions	33.0
Treatment Plant	NA
Line Crews	27.0
Billing/Collection	0.0
Other	6.0
Number of Treatment Plants	0
Total Treatment Capacity	NA
Average Daily Flow	NA
River Basin into Which System Discharges	Yadkin and Pee-Dee
Miles of Gravity Main Line Pipe	587
Miles of Forced Main Line Pipe	13
Average Age of Main Line Pipe	42 years
Blocks in Sewer Mains	3
Number of System Breaks	0
Sanitary System Overflows	6
Number of Customer Accounts	39,331
Total Revenues Collected	$18,106,601

Full Cost Profile

Cost Breakdown by Percentage

Personal Services	25.4%
Operating Costs	54.2%
Capital Costs	20.4%
TOTAL	100.0%

Cost Breakdown in Dollars

Personal Services	$4,587,204
Operating Costs	$9,769,426
Capital Costs	$3,671,361
TOTAL	$18,027,991

Concord

Wastewater Services

Resource Measures

Wastewater Services Cost per Capita

	2017	2018	2019	2020	2021
Concord	$155	$151	$168	$162	$191
Average	$166	$169	$165	$160	$160

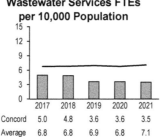

Wastewater Services FTEs per 10,000 Population

	2017	2018	2019	2020	2021
Concord	5.0	4.8	3.6	3.6	3.5
Average	6.8	6.8	6.9	6.8	7.1

Wastewater Services Cost per Customer Account

	2017	2018	2019	2020	2021
Concord	$395	$381	$420	$389	$458
Average	$494	$490	$473	$471	$471

Workload Measures

Thousands of Gallons of Wastewater per Account

	2017	2018	2019	2020	2021
Concord	96.3	84.7	105.6	82.0	84.3
Average	135.0	126.9	150.7	135.2	151.8

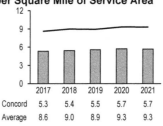

Miles of Sewer Main Line Pipe per Square Mile of Service Area

	2017	2018	2019	2020	2021
Concord	5.3	5.4	5.5	5.7	5.7
Average	8.6	9.0	8.9	9.3	9.3

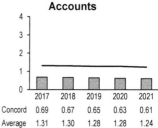

Number of Lift Stations per 1,000 Accounts

	2017	2018	2019	2020	2021
Concord	0.69	0.67	0.65	0.63	0.61
Average	1.31	1.30	1.28	1.28	1.24

Efficiency Measures

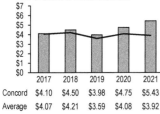

Total Cost per 1,000 Gallons of Treated Wastewater

	2017	2018	2019	2020	2021
Concord	$4.10	$4.50	$3.98	$4.75	$5.43
Average	$4.07	$4.21	$3.59	$4.08	$3.92

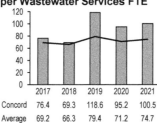

Million Gallons of Wastewater per Wastewater Services FTE

	2017	2018	2019	2020	2021
Concord	76.4	69.3	118.6	95.2	100.5
Average	69.2	66.3	79.4	71.2	74.7

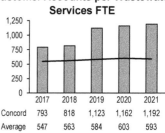

Customer Accounts per Wastewater Services FTE

	2017	2018	2019	2020	2021
Concord	793	818	1,123	1,162	1,192
Average	547	563	584	603	593

Effectiveness Measures

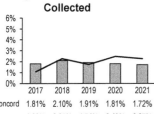

Percentage of Wastewater Bills Not Collected

	2017	2018	2019	2020	2021
Concord	1.81%	2.10%	1.91%	1.81%	1.72%
Average	1.09%	2.27%	1.74%	2.49%	2.27%

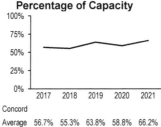

Average Daily Treatment as a Percentage of Capacity

	2017	2018	2019	2020	2021
Concord					
Average	56.7%	55.3%	63.8%	58.8%	66.2%

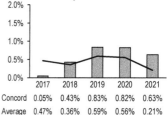

Percent of Main Line Rehabbed or Replaced

	2017	2018	2019	2020	2021
Concord	0.05%	0.43%	0.83%	0.82%	0.63%
Average	0.47%	0.36%	0.59%	0.56%	0.21%

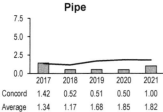

Overflows per 100 Miles of Main Line Pipe

	2017	2018	2019	2020	2021
Concord	1.42	0.52	0.51	0.50	1.00
Average	1.34	1.17	1.68	1.85	1.82

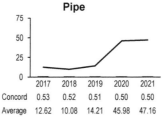

Backups per 100 Miles of Main Line Pipe

	2017	2018	2019	2020	2021
Concord	0.53	0.52	0.51	0.50	0.50
Average	12.62	10.08	14.21	45.98	47.16

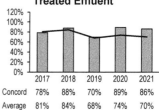

Billed Wastewater as a Percent of Treated Effluent

	2017	2018	2019	2020	2021
Concord	78%	88%	70%	89%	86%
Average	81%	84%	68%	74%	70%

Explanatory Information

Service Level and Delivery

Wastewater treatment in Goldsboro is a joint responsibility between the Public Works and Public Utilities Departments. The Public Works Director oversees both departments. The Public Works Department is responsible for the collection and distribution system lines. The Public Utilities Department is responsible for the operation of the water treatment plant, the water reclamation facility, and pump stations.

The sewer system covers the city of Goldsboro and receives wastewater from neighboring systems in Wayne County. Wastewater treatment is done by one plant, with a total treatment capacity of 14.2 million gallons per day. The plant uses advanced biological processes to remove pollutants from the water. Besides removing oxygen-consuming wastes, the facility is able to remove nutrients such as nitrogen and phosphorus to very low levels. The system has nutrient regulatory limits in place that restrict what can be discharged in order to protect water quality. All biosolids produced by the Goldsboro treatment plant are dewatered and then composted.

During the fiscal year, the system had four regulatory violations with the treatment portion of the system but no violations for the collection portion of the system.

Conditions Affecting Service, Performance, and Costs

The City of Goldsboro joined the Benchmarking Project in July 2017, with the first year of data showing for FY 2016–17.

The costs of wastewater or sewer services as captured here do not include debt service but do capture depreciation of capital.

Hurricane Matthew in October 2016 put stress on the wastewater system in Goldsboro due to the extensive flooding.

Goldsboro has improved its tracking system for a number of data items, which reflects greater accuracy in the most recent year.

Municipal Profile

Estimated Service Population	33,906
Service Land Area (Square Miles)	25
Persons per Square Mile	1,356
Topography	Flat; gently rolling
Climate	Temperate; little ice and snow

Service Profile

Total FTE Staff Positions	39.0
Treatment Plant	19.0
Line Crews	5.0
Billing/Collection	6.0
Other	9.0
Number of Treatment Plants	1
Total Treatment Capacity	14.2 MGD
Average Daily Flow	12.7 MGD
River Basin into Which System Discharges	Neuse
Miles of Gravity Main Line Pipe	227
Miles of Forced Main Line Pipe	17
Average Age of Main Line Pipe	75 years
Blocks in Sewer Mains	7
Number of System Breaks	18
Sanitary System Overflows	2
Number of Customer Accounts	11,568
Total Revenues Collected	$9,350,082

Full Cost Profile

Cost Breakdown by Percentage	
Personal Services	42.7%
Operating Costs	56.5%
Capital Costs	0.8%
TOTAL	100.0%

Cost Breakdown in Dollars	
Personal Services	$1,292,317
Operating Costs	$1,711,130
Capital Costs	$23,621
TOTAL	$3,027,068

Goldsboro

Wastewater Services

Resource Measures

Wastewater Services Cost per Capita

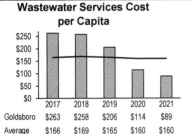

	2017	2018	2019	2020	2021
Goldsboro	$263	$258	$206	$114	$89
Average	$166	$169	$165	$160	$160

Wastewater Services FTEs per 10,000 Population

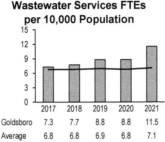

	2017	2018	2019	2020	2021
Goldsboro	7.3	7.7	8.8	8.8	11.5
Average	6.8	6.8	6.9	6.8	7.1

Wastewater Services Cost per Customer Account

	2017	2018	2019	2020	2021
Goldsboro	$810	$746	$565	$344	$262
Average	$494	$490	$473	$471	$471

Workload Measures

Thousands of Gallons of Wastewater per Account

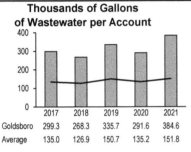

	2017	2018	2019	2020	2021
Goldsboro	299.3	268.3	335.7	291.6	384.6
Average	135.0	126.9	150.7	135.2	151.8

Miles of Sewer Main Line Pipe per Square Mile of Service Area

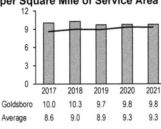

	2017	2018	2019	2020	2021
Goldsboro	10.0	10.3	9.7	9.8	9.8
Average	8.6	9.0	8.9	9.3	9.3

Number of Lift Stations per 1,000 Accounts

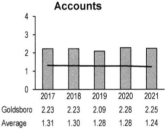

	2017	2018	2019	2020	2021
Goldsboro	2.23	2.23	2.09	2.28	2.25
Average	1.31	1.30	1.28	1.28	1.24

Efficiency Measures

Total Cost per 1,000 Gallons of Treated Wastewater

	2017	2018	2019	2020	2021
Goldsboro	$2.70	$2.78	$1.68	$1.18	$0.68
Average	$4.07	$4.21	$3.59	$4.08	$3.92

Million Gallons of Wastewater per Wastewater Services FTE

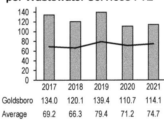

	2017	2018	2019	2020	2021
Goldsboro	134.0	120.1	139.4	110.7	114.1
Average	69.2	66.3	79.4	71.2	74.7

Customer Accounts per Wastewater Services FTE

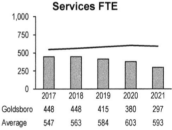

	2017	2018	2019	2020	2021
Goldsboro	448	448	415	380	297
Average	547	563	584	603	593

Effectiveness Measures

Percentage of Wastewater Bills Not Collected

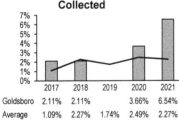

	2017	2018	2019	2020	2021
Goldsboro	2.11%	2.11%		3.66%	6.54%
Average	1.09%	2.27%	1.74%	2.49%	2.27%

Average Daily Treatment as a Percentage of Capacity

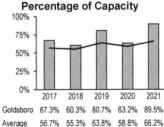

	2017	2018	2019	2020	2021
Goldsboro	67.3%	60.3%	80.7%	63.2%	89.5%
Average	56.7%	55.3%	63.8%	58.8%	66.2%

Percent of Main Line Rehabbed or Replaced

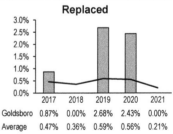

	2017	2018	2019	2020	2021
Goldsboro	0.87%	0.00%	2.68%	2.43%	0.00%
Average	0.47%	0.36%	0.59%	0.56%	0.21%

Overflows per 100 Miles of Main Line Pipe

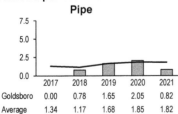

	2017	2018	2019	2020	2021
Goldsboro	0.00	0.78	1.65	2.05	0.82
Average	1.34	1.17	1.68	1.85	1.82

Backups per 100 Miles of Main Line Pipe

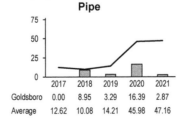

	2017	2018	2019	2020	2021
Goldsboro	0.00	8.95	3.29	16.39	2.87
Average	12.62	10.08	14.21	45.98	47.16

Billed Wastewater as a Percent of Treated Effluent

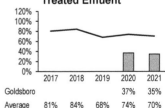

	2017	2018	2019	2020	2021
Goldsboro				37%	35%
Average	81%	84%	68%	74%	70%

Greensboro

Wastewater Services

Fiscal Year 2020-21

Explanatory Information

Service Level and Delivery
Wastewater treatment in Greensboro is handled by the Water Reclamation Division. This is part of the Water Resources Department, which also includes stormwater and drinking water services. The director of water resources reports to the city manager. Services are provided to most of the City of Greensboro and to some addresses outside city limits within Guilford County.

Wastewater treatment in Greensboro is now handled by one treatment plant. In October 2017 one plant was decommissioned, with the effective capacity transferred to the remaining plant through a large construction upgrade. This plant uses advanced tertiary treatment. The system has nutrient regulatory limits in place that restrict what can be discharged in order to protect water quality. All biosolids produced by the Greensboro treatment plant are incinerated.

During the fiscal year, the system had nineteen regulatory violations connected to the treatment portion of the system. No violations connected to the collection portion of the system were reported.

Conditions Affecting Service, Performance, and Costs
The costs of wastewater or sewer services as captured here do not include debt service but do capture depreciation of capital.

The full implementation of a new asset management system designed for utilities took place in FY 2016–17. Work orders are now assigned and tracked by more specific types of duties, which has resulted in an increase in certain metrics over prior years.

Municipal Profile

Estimated Service Population	318,529
Service Land Area (Square Miles)	148
Persons per Square Mile	2,152
Topography	Flat; gently rolling
Climate	Temperate; little ice and snow

Service Profile

Total FTE Staff Positions	168.5
Treatment Plant	51.0
Line Crews	84.0
Billing/Collection	7.5
Other	26.0
Number of Treatment Plants	1
Total Treatment Capacity	56.0 MGD
Average Daily Flow	35.4 MGD
River Basin into Which System Discharges	Cape Fear
Miles of Gravity Main Line Pipe	1,452
Miles of Forced Main Line Pipe	75
Average Age of Main Line Pipe	40 years
Blocks in Sewer Mains	3,036
Number of System Breaks	2,056
Sanitary System Overflows	36
Number of Customer Accounts	99,658
Total Revenues Collected	$64,421,253

Full Cost Profile
Cost Breakdown by Percentage

Personal Services	18.2%
Operating Costs	53.7%
Capital Costs	28.1%
TOTAL	100.0%

Cost Breakdown in Dollars

Personal Services	$7,800,202
Operating Costs	$23,049,076
Capital Costs	$12,040,058
TOTAL	$42,889,336

Greensboro

Wastewater Services

Resource Measures

Wastewater Services Cost per Capita

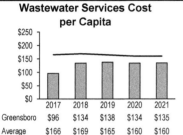

	2017	2018	2019	2020	2021
Greensboro	$96	$134	$138	$134	$135
Average	$166	$169	$165	$160	$160

Wastewater Services FTEs per 10,000 Population

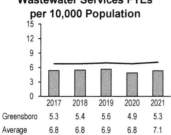

	2017	2018	2019	2020	2021
Greensboro	5.3	5.4	5.6	4.9	5.3
Average	6.8	6.8	6.9	6.8	7.1

Wastewater Services Cost per Customer Account

	2017	2018	2019	2020	2021
Greensboro	$268	$375	$395	$399	$430
Average	$494	$490	$473	$471	$471

Workload Measures

Thousands of Gallons of Wastewater per Account

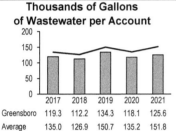

	2017	2018	2019	2020	2021
Greensboro	119.3	112.2	134.3	118.1	125.6
Average	135.0	126.9	150.7	135.2	151.8

Miles of Sewer Main Line Pipe per Square Mile of Service Area

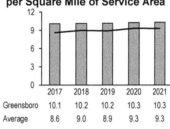

	2017	2018	2019	2020	2021
Greensboro	10.1	10.2	10.2	10.3	10.3
Average	8.6	9.0	8.9	9.3	9.3

Number of Lift Stations per 1,000 Accounts

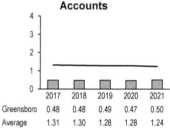

	2017	2018	2019	2020	2021
Greensboro	0.48	0.48	0.49	0.47	0.50
Average	1.31	1.30	1.28	1.28	1.24

Efficiency Measures

Total Cost per 1,000 Gallons of Treated Wastewater

	2017	2018	2019	2020	2021
Greensboro	$2.25	$3.34	$2.94	$3.38	$3.43
Average	$4.07	$4.21	$3.59	$4.08	$3.92

Million Gallons of Wastewater per Wastewater Services FTE

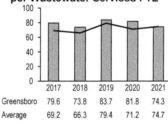

	2017	2018	2019	2020	2021
Greensboro	79.6	73.8	83.7	81.8	74.3
Average	69.2	66.3	79.4	71.2	74.7

Customer Accounts per Wastewater Services FTE

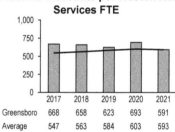

	2017	2018	2019	2020	2021
Greensboro	668	658	623	693	591
Average	547	563	584	603	593

Effectiveness Measures

Percentage of Wastewater Bills Not Collected

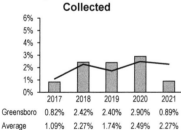

	2017	2018	2019	2020	2021
Greensboro	0.82%	2.42%	2.40%	2.90%	0.89%
Average	1.09%	2.27%	1.74%	2.49%	2.27%

Average Daily Treatment as a Percentage of Capacity

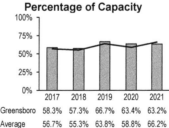

	2017	2018	2019	2020	2021
Greensboro	58.3%	57.3%	66.7%	63.4%	63.2%
Average	56.7%	55.3%	63.8%	58.8%	66.2%

Percent of Main Line Rehabbed or Replaced

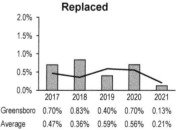

	2017	2018	2019	2020	2021
Greensboro	0.70%	0.83%	0.40%	0.70%	0.13%
Average	0.47%	0.36%	0.59%	0.56%	0.21%

Overflows per 100 Miles of Main Line Pipe

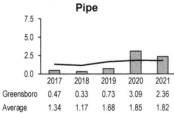

	2017	2018	2019	2020	2021
Greensboro	0.47	0.33	0.73	3.09	2.36
Average	1.34	1.17	1.68	1.85	1.82

Backups per 100 Miles of Main Line Pipe

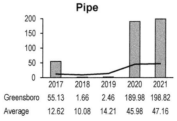

	2017	2018	2019	2020	2021
Greensboro	55.13	1.66	2.46	189.98	198.82
Average	12.62	10.08	14.21	45.98	47.16

Billed Wastewater as a Percent of Treated Effluent

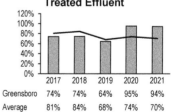

	2017	2018	2019	2020	2021
Greensboro	74%	74%	64%	95%	94%
Average	81%	84%	68%	74%	70%

Fiscal Year 2020-21

Explanatory Information

Service Level and Delivery

Wastewater is handled by the City of Hickory's Collection Division, which is part of Public Utilities under the Public Services Department. The service area covers the City of Hickory and several adjoining areas in Catawba County.

The system relies on three treatment plants to handle wastewater. One plant uses activated-sludge biological nutrient removal (BNR), the second uses oxidation-ditch-activated-sludge BNR, and the third uses conventional activated sludge. The entire system does not have nutrient limits in place at this time. Biosolids generated are handled as Class A compost.

The system in Hickory had four regulatory violations connected to the treatment portion of the system and eight violations connected to the collection portion of the system during the fiscal year.

Conditions Affecting Service, Performance, and Costs

The costs of wastewater or sewer services as captured here do not include debt service but do capture depreciation of capital.

Municipal Profile

Estimated Service Population	37,478
Service Land Area (Square Miles)	65.0
Persons per Square Mile	577
Topography	Gently rolling
Climate	Temperate; some ice and snow

Service Profile

Total FTE Staff Positions	44.0
Treatment Plant	29.0
Line Crews	10.0
Billing/Collection	2.5
Other	2.5
Number of Treatment Plants	3
Total Treatment Capacity	16.5 MGD
Average Daily Flow	6.2 MGD
River Basin into Which System Discharges	Catawba
Miles of Gravity Main Line Pipe	501
Miles of Forced Main Line Pipe	43
Average Age of Main Line Pipe	49 years
Blocks in Sewer Mains	83
Number of System Breaks	12
Sanitary System Overflows	8
Number of Customer Accounts	17,426
Total Revenues Collected	$11,766,249

Full Cost Profile

Cost Breakdown by Percentage

Personal Services	37.3%
Operating Costs	46.1%
Capital Costs	16.6%
TOTAL	100.0%

Cost Breakdown in Dollars

Personal Services	$3,030,602
Operating Costs	$3,753,531
Capital Costs	$1,349,615
TOTAL	$8,133,748

Resource Measures

Wastewater Services Cost per Capita

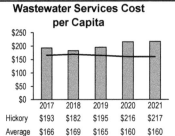

	2017	2018	2019	2020	2021
Hickory	$193	$182	$195	$216	$217
Average	$166	$169	$165	$160	$160

Wastewater Services FTEs per 10,000 Population

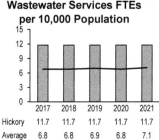

	2017	2018	2019	2020	2021
Hickory	11.7	11.7	11.7	11.7	11.7
Average	6.8	6.8	6.9	6.8	7.1

Wastewater Services Cost per Customer Account

	2017	2018	2019	2020	2021
Hickory	$465	$435	$459	$501	$467
Average	$494	$490	$473	$471	$471

Workload Measures

Thousands of Gallons of Wastewater per Account

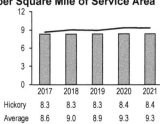

	2017	2018	2019	2020	2021
Hickory	131.0	138.7	156.6	142.3	139.5
Average	135.0	126.9	150.7	135.2	151.8

Miles of Sewer Main Line Pipe per Square Mile of Service Area

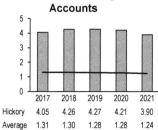

	2017	2018	2019	2020	2021
Hickory	8.3	8.3	8.3	8.4	8.4
Average	8.6	9.0	8.9	9.3	9.3

Number of Lift Stations per 1,000 Accounts

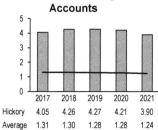

	2017	2018	2019	2020	2021
Hickory	4.05	4.26	4.27	4.21	3.90
Average	1.31	1.30	1.28	1.28	1.24

Efficiency Measures

Total Cost per 1,000 Gallons of Treated Wastewater

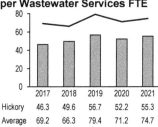

	2017	2018	2019	2020	2021
Hickory	$3.55	$3.13	$2.93	$3.52	$3.35
Average	$4.07	$4.21	$3.59	$4.08	$3.92

Million Gallons of Wastewater per Wastewater Services FTE

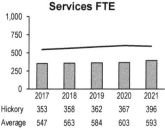

	2017	2018	2019	2020	2021
Hickory	46.3	49.6	56.7	52.2	55.3
Average	69.2	66.3	79.4	71.2	74.7

Customer Accounts per Wastewater Services FTE

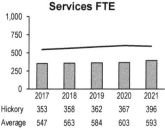

	2017	2018	2019	2020	2021
Hickory	353	358	362	367	396
Average	547	563	584	603	593

Effectiveness Measures

Percentage of Wastewater Bills Not Collected

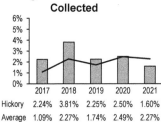

	2017	2018	2019	2020	2021
Hickory	2.24%	3.81%	2.25%	2.50%	1.60%
Average	1.09%	2.27%	1.74%	2.49%	2.27%

Average Daily Treatment as a Percentage of Capacity

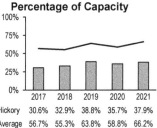

	2017	2018	2019	2020	2021
Hickory	30.6%	32.9%	38.8%	35.7%	37.9%
Average	56.7%	55.3%	63.8%	58.8%	66.2%

Percent of Main Line Rehabbed or Replaced

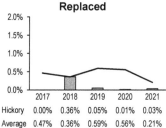

	2017	2018	2019	2020	2021
Hickory	0.00%	0.36%	0.05%	0.01%	0.03%
Average	0.47%	0.36%	0.59%	0.56%	0.21%

Overflows per 100 Miles of Main Line Pipe

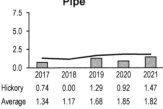

	2017	2018	2019	2020	2021
Hickory	0.74	0.00	1.29	0.92	1.47
Average	1.34	1.17	1.68	1.85	1.82

Backups per 100 Miles of Main Line Pipe

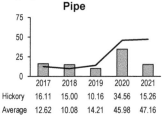

	2017	2018	2019	2020	2021
Hickory	16.11	15.00	10.16	34.56	15.26
Average	12.62	10.08	14.21	45.98	47.16

Billed Wastewater as a Percent of Treated Effluent

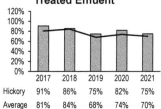

	2017	2018	2019	2020	2021
Hickory	91%	86%	75%	82%	75%
Average	81%	84%	68%	74%	70%

Explanatory Information

Service Level and Delivery

Public Utilities is a department within the City of Raleigh. It is a combined enterprise system that provides drinking water and sewage treatment services to the City of Raleigh and six merger towns: Garner, Rolesville, Knightdale, Wake Forest, Wendell, and Zebulon. The City of Raleigh also provides wastewater treatment for the Towns of Middlesex and Clayton. As of FY 2021, approximately 605,000 people live in the contractual service area of 299 square miles.

Wastewater is treated at three plants. The total combined treatment capacity at the three plants is 80.2 million gallons per day. The plants use primary treatment, a nutrient removal process for secondary treatment, and tertiary treatment, along with biosolids treatment and land application. A portion of the treated effluent is distributed as reclaimed water. The system had no wastewater treatment violations.

The system had no reported regulatory violations for the treatment system, but four violations for the collection portion of the system during the fiscal year.

Conditions Affecting Service, Performance, and Costs

The Utility has a full-functioning farm with a dedicated Land Management program consisting of 15 FTEs. The farm uses a portion of the biosolids produced at the plant as fertilizer to grow soybeans, corn, and hay.

The costs of wastewater or sewer services as captured here do not include debt service but do capture depreciation of capital.

Municipal Profile

Estimated Service Population	605,000
Service Land Area (Square Miles)	299.0
Persons per Square Mile	2,023
Topography	Flat; gently rolling
Climate	Temperate; little ice and snow

Service Profile

Total FTE Staff Positions	351.0
Treatment Plant	47.0
Line Crews	141.0
Billing/Collection	36.0
Other	127.0
Number of Treatment Plants	3
Total Treatment Capacity	80.2 MGD
Average Daily Flow	52.7 MGD
River Basin into Which System Discharges	Neuse
Miles of Gravity Main Line Pipe	2,426
Miles of Forced Main Line Pipe	131
Average Age of Main Line Pipe	34 years
Blocks in Sewer Mains	na
Number of System Breaks	227
Sanitary System Overflows	30
Number of Customer Accounts	183,622
Total Revenues Collected	$156,317,001

Full Cost Profile

Cost Breakdown by Percentage	
Personal Services	38.2%
Operating Costs	43.0%
Capital Costs	18.9%
TOTAL	100.0%

Cost Breakdown in Dollars	
Personal Services	$25,224,711
Operating Costs	$28,425,262
Capital Costs	$12,462,549
TOTAL	$66,112,522

Resource Measures

Wastewater Services Cost per Capita

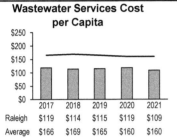

	2017	2018	2019	2020	2021
Raleigh	$119	$114	$115	$119	$109
Average	$166	$169	$165	$160	$160

Wastewater Services FTEs per 10,000 Population

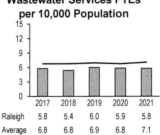

	2017	2018	2019	2020	2021
Raleigh	5.8	5.4	6.0	5.9	5.8
Average	6.8	6.8	6.9	6.8	7.1

Wastewater Services Cost per Customer Account

	2017	2018	2019	2020	2021
Raleigh	$391	$353	$360	$391	$360
Average	$494	$490	$473	$471	$471

Workload Measures

Thousands of Gallons of Wastewater per Account

	2017	2018	2019	2020	2021
Raleigh	107.3	93.2	103.4	102.4	104.7
Average	135.0	126.9	150.7	135.2	151.8

Miles of Sewer Main Line Pipe per Square Mile of Service Area

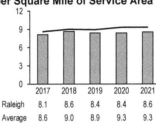

	2017	2018	2019	2020	2021
Raleigh	8.1	8.6	8.4	8.4	8.6
Average	8.6	9.0	8.9	9.3	9.3

Number of Lift Stations per 1,000 Accounts

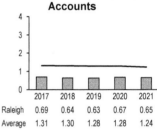

	2017	2018	2019	2020	2021
Raleigh	0.69	0.64	0.63	0.67	0.65
Average	1.31	1.30	1.28	1.28	1.24

Efficiency Measures

Total Cost per 1,000 Gallons of Treated Wastewater

	2017	2018	2019	2020	2021
Raleigh	$3.65	$3.78	$3.49	$3.82	$3.44
Average	$4.07	$4.21	$3.59	$4.08	$3.92

Million Gallons of Wastewater per Wastewater Services FTE

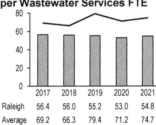

	2017	2018	2019	2020	2021
Raleigh	56.4	56.0	55.2	53.0	54.8
Average	69.2	66.3	79.4	71.2	74.7

Customer Accounts per Wastewater Services FTE

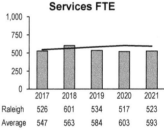

	2017	2018	2019	2020	2021
Raleigh	526	601	534	517	523
Average	547	563	584	603	593

Effectiveness Measures

Percentage of Wastewater Bills Not Collected

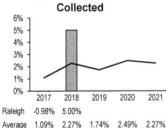

	2017	2018	2019	2020	2021
Raleigh	-0.98%	5.00%			
Average	1.09%	2.27%	1.74%	2.49%	2.27%

Average Daily Treatment as a Percentage of Capacity

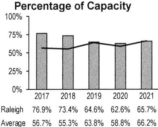

	2017	2018	2019	2020	2021
Raleigh	76.9%	73.4%	64.6%	62.6%	65.7%
Average	56.7%	55.3%	63.8%	58.8%	66.2%

Percent of Main Line Rehabbed or Replaced

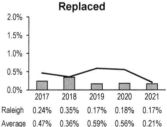

	2017	2018	2019	2020	2021
Raleigh	0.24%	0.35%	0.17%	0.18%	0.17%
Average	0.47%	0.36%	0.59%	0.56%	0.21%

Overflows per 100 Miles of Main Line Pipe

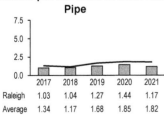

	2017	2018	2019	2020	2021
Raleigh	1.03	1.04	1.27	1.44	1.17
Average	1.34	1.17	1.68	1.85	1.82

Backups per 100 Miles of Main Line Pipe

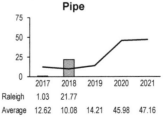

	2017	2018	2019	2020	2021
Raleigh	1.03	21.77			
Average	12.62	10.08	14.21	45.98	47.16

Billed Wastewater as a Percent of Treated Effluent

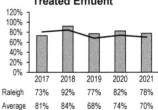

	2017	2018	2019	2020	2021
Raleigh	73%	92%	77%	82%	78%
Average	81%	84%	68%	74%	70%

Wilson

Wastewater Services

Fiscal Year 2020-21

Explanatory Information

Service Level and Delivery

Wastewater in Wilson is handled by the Water Reclamation and Wastewater Collection Division, which is part of Water Resources in the Public Services Department. Billing for large customers is handled by Water Resources, but residential customer billing is handled by the Customer Services Division in the Finance Department. The system covers the City of Wilson and several small adjoining areas outside the city in Wilson County.

Wastewater treatment is handled by one plant. The treatment plant uses advanced five-stage biological nutrient removal with deep-bed filters with methanol and biological and chemical phosphorous reduction. The system had very stringent nutrient limits in place to protect water quality in the Neuse River basin. The system produced Class A and B biosolids, with most of this solid waste being composted. A small portion is applied on city land or other permitted farmland.

The system had one reported regulatory violation for the treatment system and five violations for the collection portion of the system during the fiscal year.

Conditions Affecting Service, Performance, and Costs

The costs of wastewater or sewer services as captured here do not include debt service but do capture depreciation of capital.

Large capital improvements are being made to the Buckhorn Lake Dam and Wastewater Projects, which have been required to meet advanced nutrient removal standards.

Municipal Profile

Estimated Service Population	53,000
Service Land Area (Square Miles)	42
Persons per Square Mile	1,262
Topography	Flat
Climate	Temperate; little ice and snow

Service Profile

Total FTE Staff Positions	64.5
Treatment Plant	31.0
Line Crews	28.0
Billing/Collection	5.5
Other	0.0
Number of Treatment Plants	1
Total Treatment Capacity	14.0 MGD
Average Daily Flow	11.1 MGD
River Basin into Which System Discharges	Neuse
Miles of Gravity Main Line Pipe	335
Miles of Forced Main Line Pipe	30
Average Age of Main Line Pipe	39 years
Blocks in Sewer Mains	485
Number of System Breaks	1
Sanitary System Overflows	5
Number of Customer Accounts	20,253
Total Revenues Collected	$14,334,000

Full Cost Profile

Cost Breakdown by Percentage

Personal Services	37.1%
Operating Costs	39.6%
Capital Costs	23.3%
TOTAL	100.0%

Cost Breakdown in Dollars

Personal Services	$4,651,351
Operating Costs	$4,963,341
Capital Costs	$2,921,141
TOTAL	$12,535,833

Wilson

Wastewater Services

Resource Measures

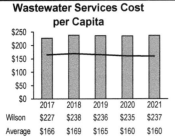

Wastewater Services Cost per Capita

	2017	2018	2019	2020	2021
Wilson	$227	$238	$236	$235	$237
Average	$166	$169	$165	$160	$160

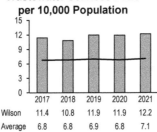

Wastewater Services FTEs per 10,000 Population

	2017	2018	2019	2020	2021
Wilson	11.4	10.8	11.9	11.9	12.2
Average	6.8	6.8	6.9	6.8	7.1

Wastewater Services Cost per Customer Account

	2017	2018	2019	2020	2021
Wilson	$596	$620	$622	$632	$619
Average	$494	$490	$473	$471	$471

Workload Measures

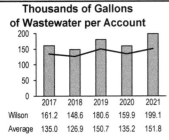

Thousands of Gallons of Wastewater per Account

	2017	2018	2019	2020	2021
Wilson	161.2	148.6	180.6	159.9	199.1
Average	135.0	126.9	150.7	135.2	151.8

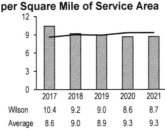

Miles of Sewer Main Line Pipe per Square Mile of Service Area

	2017	2018	2019	2020	2021
Wilson	10.4	9.2	9.0	8.6	8.7
Average	8.6	9.0	8.9	9.3	9.3

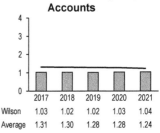

Number of Lift Stations per 1,000 Accounts

	2017	2018	2019	2020	2021
Wilson	1.03	1.02	1.02	1.03	1.04
Average	1.31	1.30	1.28	1.28	1.24

Efficiency Measures

Total Cost per 1,000 Gallons of Treated Wastewater

	2017	2018	2019	2020	2021
Wilson	$3.70	$4.17	$3.44	$3.95	$3.11
Average	$4.07	$4.21	$3.59	$4.08	$3.92

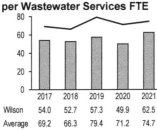

Million Gallons of Wastewater per Wastewater Services FTE

	2017	2018	2019	2020	2021
Wilson	54.0	52.7	57.3	49.9	62.5
Average	69.2	66.3	79.4	71.2	74.7

Customer Accounts per Wastewater Services FTE

	2017	2018	2019	2020	2021
Wilson	335	355	318	312	314
Average	547	563	584	603	593

Effectiveness Measures

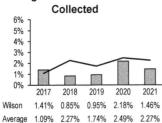

Percentage of Wastewater Bills Not Collected

	2017	2018	2019	2020	2021
Wilson	1.41%	0.85%	0.95%	2.18%	1.46%
Average	1.09%	2.27%	1.74%	2.49%	2.27%

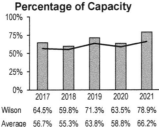

Average Daily Treatment as a Percentage of Capacity

	2017	2018	2019	2020	2021
Wilson	64.5%	59.8%	71.3%	63.5%	78.9%
Average	56.7%	55.3%	63.8%	58.8%	66.2%

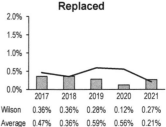

Percent of Main Line Rehabbed or Replaced

	2017	2018	2019	2020	2021
Wilson	0.36%	0.36%	0.28%	0.12%	0.27%
Average	0.47%	0.36%	0.59%	0.56%	0.21%

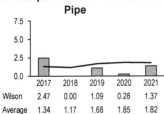

Overflows per 100 Miles of Main Line Pipe

	2017	2018	2019	2020	2021
Wilson	2.47	0.00	1.09	0.28	1.37
Average	1.34	1.17	1.68	1.85	1.82

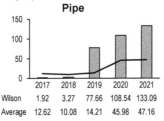

Backups per 100 Miles of Main Line Pipe

	2017	2018	2019	2020	2021
Wilson	1.92	3.27	77.66	108.54	133.09
Average	12.62	10.08	14.21	45.98	47.16

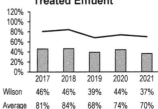

Billed Wastewater as a Percent of Treated Effluent

	2017	2018	2019	2020	2021
Wilson	46%	46%	39%	44%	37%
Average	81%	84%	68%	74%	70%

Fiscal Year 2020-21

Explanatory Information

Service Level and Delivery

The Winston-Salem and Forsyth County Utilities Division operates a combined water and sewer system that covers the city and most of the remaining population of Forsyth County. The system also serves several adjoining areas in Davie and Davidson counties. Beyond water and wastewater, the Utilities Division also handles solid-waste disposal. Operations are divided among several divisions by function.

The system has two separate treatment plants. The plants use conventional activated sludge with anaerobic digestion for treatment. The system currently does not have regulatory nutrient limits in place. Biosolids produced are disposed after first using thermal drying, with subsequent reuse as a soil amendment.

During the fiscal year, the system had one regulatory violation connected to the treatment portion of the system and twenty-three reported violations for the collection portion of the system connected to sanitary system overflows.

Conditions Affecting Service, Performance, and Costs

The costs of wastewater or sewer services as captured here do not include debt service but do capture depreciation of capital.

The city has used improvements in its GIS mapping systems and incident records to change the process by which the division ranks and proactively cleans pipes. This process is expected to lower the number of breaks and overflows.

Winston-Salem made improvements in their calculation of population served and area covered to improve the accuracy of their data. This had the effect of decreasing the reported population and size of the area served from earlier years. The changes seen in the data in FY 2017–18 are due to this improved estimation and not a change in services.

Municipal Profile

Estimated Service Population	329,156
Service Land Area (Square Miles)	148
Persons per Square Mile	2,217
Topography	Gently rolling
Climate	Temperate; some ice and snow

Service Profile

Total FTE Staff Positions	174.2
Treatment Plant	87.0
Line Crews	59.0
Billing/Collection	8.2
Other	20.0
Number of Treatment Plants	2
Total Treatment Capacity	51.0 MGD
Average Daily Flow	38.1 MGD
River Basin into Which System Discharges	Yadkin
Miles of Gravity Main Line Pipe	1,734
Miles of Forced Main Line Pipe	38
Average Age of Main Line Pipe	75 years
Blocks in Sewer Mains	138
Number of System Breaks	156
Sanitary System Overflows	74
Number of Customer Accounts	102,921
Total Revenues Collected	$69,158,962

Full Cost Profile

Cost Breakdown by Percentage

Personal Services	25.0%
Operating Costs	34.0%
Capital Costs	40.9%
TOTAL	100.0%

Cost Breakdown in Dollars

Personal Services	$9,998,561
Operating Costs	$13,596,874
Capital Costs	$16,344,762
TOTAL	$39,940,197

Winston-Salem

Wastewater Services

Key: Winston-Salem   Benchmarking Average —   Fiscal Years 2017 through 2021

Resource Measures

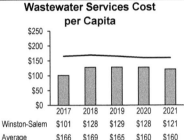

Wastewater Services Cost per Capita

	2017	2018	2019	2020	2021
Winston-Salem	$101	$128	$129	$128	$121
Average	$166	$169	$165	$160	$160

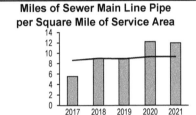

Wastewater Services FTEs per 10,000 Population

	2017	2018	2019	2020	2021
Winston-Salem	5.0	6.0	5.9	5.8	5.3
Average	6.8	6.8	6.9	6.8	7.1

Wastewater Services Cost per Customer Account

	2017	2018	2019	2020	2021
Winston-Salem	$362	$376	$377	$376	$388
Average	$494	$490	$473	$471	$471

Workload Measures

Thousands of Gallons of Wastewater per Account

	2017	2018	2019	2020	2021
Winston-Salem	119.1	114.0	135.8	131.4	135.0
Average	135.0	126.9	150.7	135.2	151.8

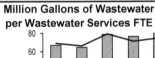

Miles of Sewer Main Line Pipe per Square Mile of Service Area

	2017	2018	2019	2020	2021
Winston-Salem	5.5	9.0	9.0	12.2	11.9
Average	8.6	9.0	8.9	9.3	9.3

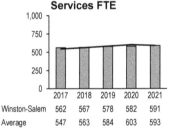

Number of Lift Stations per 1,000 Accounts

	2017	2018	2019	2020	2021
Winston-Salem	0.51	0.50	0.48	0.46	0.46
Average	1.31	1.30	1.28	1.28	1.24

Efficiency Measures

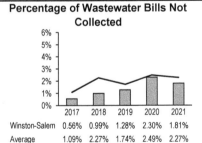

Total Cost per 1,000 Gallons of Treated Wastewater

	2017	2018	2019	2020	2021
Winston-Salem	$3.04	$3.30	$2.78	$2.86	$2.88
Average	$4.07	$4.21	$3.59	$4.08	$3.92

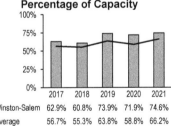

Million Gallons of Wastewater per Wastewater Services FTE

	2017	2018	2019	2020	2021
Winston-Salem	66.9	64.6	78.6	76.4	79.7
Average	69.2	66.3	79.4	71.2	74.7

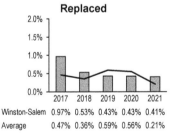

Customer Accounts per Wastewater Services FTE

	2017	2018	2019	2020	2021
Winston-Salem	562	567	578	582	591
Average	547	563	584	603	593

Effectiveness Measures

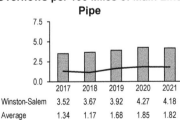

Percentage of Wastewater Bills Not Collected

	2017	2018	2019	2020	2021
Winston-Salem	0.56%	0.99%	1.28%	2.30%	1.81%
Average	1.09%	2.27%	1.74%	2.49%	2.27%

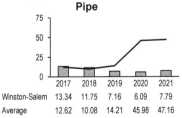

Average Daily Treatment as a Percentage of Capacity

	2017	2018	2019	2020	2021
Winston-Salem	62.9%	60.8%	73.9%	71.9%	74.6%
Average	56.7%	55.3%	63.8%	58.8%	66.2%

Percent of Main Line Rehabbed or Replaced

	2017	2018	2019	2020	2021
Winston-Salem	0.97%	0.53%	0.43%	0.43%	0.41%
Average	0.47%	0.36%	0.59%	0.56%	0.21%

Overflows per 100 Miles of Main Line Pipe

	2017	2018	2019	2020	2021
Winston-Salem	3.52	3.67	3.92	4.27	4.18
Average	1.34	1.17	1.68	1.85	1.82

Backups per 100 Miles of Main Line Pipe

	2017	2018	2019	2020	2021
Winston-Salem	13.34	11.75	7.16	6.09	7.79
Average	12.62	10.08	14.21	45.98	47.16

Billed Wastewater as a Percent of Treated Effluent

	2017	2018	2019	2020	2021
Winston-Salem	75%	77%	63%	63%	61%
Average	81%	84%	68%	74%	70%

Wastewater Services   303

Performance and Cost Data

CORE PARKS AND RECREATION

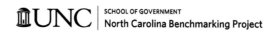

PERFORMANCE MEASURES FOR CORE PARKS AND RECREATION

SERVICE DEFINITION

Parks and Recreation include both passive and active recreation opportunities maintained and operated by a local government. For the purposes of this benchmarking effort, this service area includes core operational functions, such as parks, multipurpose recreation facilities, athletic facilities, greenways, and trails. This also includes programs and events.

However, parks and recreation departments frequently may include a variety of other activities and facilities. To support reasonable comparisons, this service benchmarking excludes these secondary recreational activities, including performance venues, museums, historic sites, golf courses, marinas/boat ramps, and professional stadiums. Also excluded are other non-recreational activities sometimes performed by parks and recreation departments, such as care of cemeteries; maintenance of rights-of-way along city streets; maintenance of facilities owned by a municipality but not parks-related; and maintenance of city lots. The dollars and people associated with these secondary and non-park activities are excluded.

Parks and recreation does offer an important difference from many of the other services provided by local governments. Much of the objective of this service area is to provide facilities for use by citizens. Use of many of these facilities is not easily tracked. Many of the measures shown for this service area are accordingly measures of facility availability rather than the traditional workload type of measures seen in other service areas.

NOTES ON PERFORMANCE MEASURES

1. Land Acres of All Municipal Parks per 10,000 Population

This resource measure captures the amount of park land that is available relative to the population in the communities.

2. Recreation Centers per 10,000 Population

Recreation centers provide space for a variety of indoor recreational activities. This measure shows the number of centers relative to the population.

3. Swimming Pools per 10,000 Population

Indoor and outdoor pools are desirable recreational facilities. This resource measure captures the number of pools relative to the population.

4. Athletic Fields per 10,000 Population

Outdoor athletic fields are used for organized and informal recreation. This measure counts the number of formal athletic fields, including rectangular fields, such as those for football and soccer; diamond fields for baseball, and nondesignated fields that can be used for multiple activities. The count includes both natural grass and artificial-surface fields, where available.

5. Playgrounds per 10,000 Population

Formal playgrounds include a variety of fixed equipment, such as swings, jungle gyms, slides, and other apparatus. This measure captures these playgrounds relative to the population.

6. Miles of Trails per 10,000 Population

Outdoor trails of all types represent an important type of active recreation. This measure captures the total miles of trails in a community relative to the population. The miles total includes paved and unpaved trails and covers various types of trails, such as those for walking, bike riding, and equestrian riding.

7. Total Core Parks and Recreation Costs

This efficiency measure represents the level of spending relative to the park acreage in a community. Although funds may be spent on facilities and activities, this measure provides some comparison of the intensity of spending.

8. Acres of Park Maintained per Maintenance Full-Time Equivalent (FTE)

This efficiency measure compares the amount of acres in the park system relative to the number of FTEs used by a jurisdiction to provide maintenance.

9. Volunteer Hours in FTEs as a Percent of Paid Staff FTEs

Volunteers represent an important resource to help support parks and recreation activities. This efficiency measure compares the estimated amount of volunteer labor relative to the paid staff in order to provide a measure of the benefit these volunteers bring to a community.

10. Revenue Gained as a Percent of Total Core Parks and Recreation Costs

Parks and recreation is a service that is primarily supported by general funding from a local government budget. But gaining additional revenues in the form of user fees, grants, donations, and sponsorships helps to leverage spending and provide services. This effectiveness measure shows how much revenue has been raised from these other sources relative to the total costs reported.

11. Acts of Vandalism per 10,000 Population

Vandalism damages parks and recreation facilities, making them unavailable or less useful to citizens. This effectiveness measure compares the number of acts of vandalism relative to the population to indicate the extent of this problem.

Core Parks and Recreation

Summary of Key Dimensions of Service

City or Town	Municipal Population as of July 2020	Core Parks and Recreation FTEs	Number of Parks	Park Land Acreage	Number of Recreation and Senior Centers	Number of Playgrounds	Number of Athletic Fields	Miles of Trails
Apex	59,368	41.8	13	618.3	2	12	27	23.0
Chapel Hill	62,080	47.5	31	1,114.0	2	11	16	15.5
Concord	105,936	35.0	13	400.3	4	13	34	17.1
Goldsboro	34,156	49.5	14	233.0	4	10	23	4.5
Greensboro	299,556	137.5	512	7,449.0	12	105	75	101.8
Greenville	87,428	154.5	28	1,833.6	8	18	24	13.0
Hickory	43,578	49.8	27	558.0	7	40	23	16.0
Raleigh	468,977	759.4	200	6,209.0	41	106	100	108.0
Wilson	47,769	75.5	28	400.0	4	26	26	7.5
Winston-Salem	249,986	213.0	84	4,279.2	17	46	97	33.0

EXPLANATORY FACTORS

These are some factors that the project found affected core parks and recreation services performance and cost in one or more of the municipalities:

Youth Population
Total Acreage
Miles of Trails
Number of Facilities

Explanatory Information

Service Level and Delivery
The Town of Apex provides recreation services through the separate Parks, Recreation, and Cultural Resources Department. The city has priority-use agreements with the Wake County School System in exchange for maintenance of areas used by the town.

The town has thirteen separate parks and sites. These parks cover 618 land acres; most of this area is currently developed. The city has twenty-three miles of trails.

In addition to the core parks and recreational facilities, Apex has a performing arts center. The operation of this other facility is not included in the Core Parks and Recreation comparisons reported here. This facility is not included here in dollars or staff as part of core parks and recreation facilities and activities.

Conditions Affecting Service, Performance, and Costs

Municipal Profile

Population (OSBM 2020)	59,368
Land Area (Square Miles)	23.61
Persons per Square Mile	2,514
Topography	Flat; gently rolling
Climate	Temperate; little ice and snow

Service Profile

Parks and Recreation Staff
Administrative Position FTEs	5.0
Maintenance Staff FTEs	25.5
Program and Facility FTEs	11.3
Other Staff FTEs	0.0
TOTAL	41.8

Number of Parks and Sites	13
Total Land Acreage in Parks	618.3
Miles of Trails in Parks	23.0

Recreational Facilities
Indoor and Outdoor Pools	0
Recreation Centers	2
Outdoor Basketball Courts	15.5
Outdoor Tennis Courts	15
Playgrounds	12
Diamond Fields	13
Rectangular Fields	12
Other Athletic Fields	2
Picnic Shelters	11

Parks and Recreation Revenues
User Fees	$718,875
Grants	$0
Sponsorships	$0
Donations	$0

Full Cost Profile

Cost Breakdown by Percentage
Personal Services	50.4%
Operating Costs	40.4%
Capital Costs	9.2%
TOTAL	100.0%

Cost Breakdown in Dollars
Personal Services	$2,815,524
Operating Costs	$2,255,033
Capital Costs	$510,732
TOTAL	$5,581,289

Apex

Core Parks and Recreation

Key: Apex ▦   Benchmarking Average —   Fiscal Years 2017 through 2021

Resource Measures

Core Parks and Recreation Services per Capita

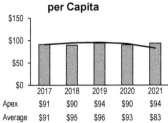

	2017	2018	2019	2020	2021
Apex	$91	$90	$94	$90	$94
Average	$91	$95	$96	$93	$83

Core Parks and Recreation Staff per 10,000 Population

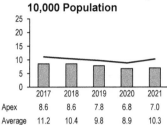

	2017	2018	2019	2020	2021
Apex	8.6	8.6	7.8	6.8	7.0
Average	11.2	10.4	9.8	8.9	10.3

Facilities Measures

Land Acres of Parks per 10,000 Population

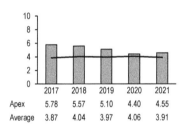

	2017	2018	2019	2020	2021
Apex	119.52	115.12	116.86	100.83	104.14
Average	143.50	143.92	137.34	125.84	136.33

Recreation Centers per 10,000 Population

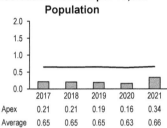

	2017	2018	2019	2020	2021
Apex	0.21	0.21	0.19	0.16	0.34
Average	0.65	0.65	0.65	0.63	0.66

Swimming Pools per 10,000 Population

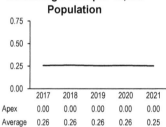

	2017	2018	2019	2020	2021
Apex	0.00	0.00	0.00	0.00	0.00
Average	0.26	0.26	0.26	0.26	0.25

Athletic Fields per 10,000 Population

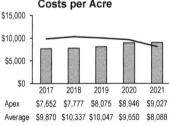

	2017	2018	2019	2020	2021
Apex	5.78	5.57	5.10	4.40	4.55
Average	3.87	4.04	3.97	4.06	3.91

Playgrounds per 10,000 Population

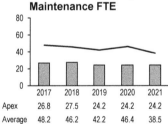

	2017	2018	2019	2020	2021
Apex	2.36	2.48	2.27	1.96	2.02
Average	4.11	4.16	3.33	3.40	3.22

Miles of Land Trails per 10,000 Population

	2017	2018	2019	2020	2021
Apex	3.00	4.02	3.92	3.56	3.87
Average	2.37	2.37	2.30	2.45	2.30

Efficiency Measures

Total Core Parks and Recreation Costs per Acre

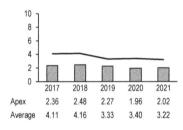

	2017	2018	2019	2020	2021
Apex	$7,652	$7,777	$8,075	$8,946	$9,027
Average	$9,870	$10,337	$10,047	$9,650	$8,088

Acres of Park Maintained per Maintenance FTE

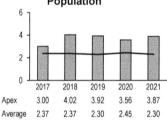

	2017	2018	2019	2020	2021
Apex	26.8	27.5	24.2	24.2	24.2
Average	48.2	46.2	42.2	46.4	38.5

Volunteer Hours in FTEs as a Percent of Paid Staff FTEs

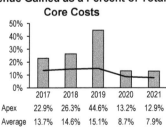

	2017	2018	2019	2020	2021
Apex	7.2%	7.0%	7.0%	7.0%	8.1%
Average	18.9%	19.7%	21.9%	6.1%	6.7%

Effectiveness Measures

Revenue Gained as a Percent of Total Core Costs

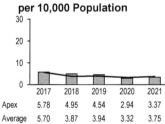

	2017	2018	2019	2020	2021
Apex	22.9%	26.3%	44.6%	13.2%	12.9%
Average	13.7%	14.6%	15.1%	8.7%	7.9%

Acts of Vandalism at Parks Facilities per 10,000 Population

	2017	2018	2019	2020	2021
Apex	5.78	4.95	4.54	2.94	3.37
Average	5.70	3.87	3.94	3.32	3.75

Explanatory Information

Service Level and Delivery

The Town of Chapel Hill provides recreation services through the separate Parks and Recreation Department. The town has agreements with Orange County for use of the senior center and county resident participation in other programs. The town also has agreements with the Town of Carrboro, the Street Scene Teen Center, Holmes Childcare Center, and Chapel Hill-Carrboro City Schools.

The town has thirty-one separate parks and sites. These parks cover 1,114 land acres, much of which is currently undeveloped. The town has about sixteen miles of trails.

Conditions Affecting Service, Performance, and Costs

Municipal Profile

Population (OSBM 2020)	62,080
Land Area (Square Miles)	21.31
Persons per Square Mile	2,914
Topography	Flat; gently rolling
Climate	Temperate; little ice and snow

Service Profile

Parks and Recreation Staff	
Administrative Position FTEs	7.0
Maintenance Staff FTEs	21.5
Program and Facility FTEs	19.0
Other Staff FTEs	0.0
TOTAL	47.5

Number of Parks and Sites	31
Total Land Acreage in Parks	1,114.0
Miles of Trails in Parks	15.5

Recreational Facilities	
Indoor and Outdoor Pools	3
Recreation Centers	2
Outdoor Basketball Courts	7
Outdoor Tennis Courts	18
Playgrounds	11
Diamond Fields	7
Rectangular Fields	9
Other Athletic Fields	0
Picnic Shelters	8

Parks and Recreation Revenues	
User Fees	$636,714
Grants	$0
Sponsorships	$1,600
Donations	$11,040

Full Cost Profile

Cost Breakdown by Percentage	
Personal Services	50.3%
Operating Costs	40.6%
Capital Costs	9.2%
TOTAL	100.0%

Cost Breakdown in Dollars	
Personal Services	$3,225,378
Operating Costs	$2,602,901
Capital Costs	$588,388
TOTAL	$6,416,667

Key: Chapel Hill   Benchmarking Average — Fiscal Years 2017 through 2021

Resource Measures

Core Parks and Recreation Services per Capita

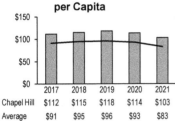

	2017	2018	2019	2020	2021
Chapel Hill	$112	$115	$118	$114	$103
Average	$91	$95	$96	$93	$83

Core Parks and Recreation Staff per 10,000 Population

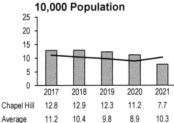

	2017	2018	2019	2020	2021
Chapel Hill	12.8	12.9	12.3	11.2	7.7
Average	11.2	10.4	9.8	8.9	10.3

Facilities Measures

Land Acres of Parks per 10,000 Population

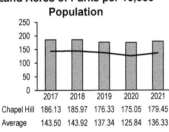

	2017	2018	2019	2020	2021
Chapel Hill	186.13	185.97	176.33	175.05	179.45
Average	143.50	143.92	137.34	125.84	136.33

Recreation Centers per 10,000 Population

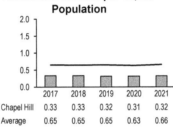

	2017	2018	2019	2020	2021
Chapel Hill	0.33	0.33	0.32	0.31	0.32
Average	0.65	0.65	0.65	0.63	0.66

Swimming Pools per 10,000 Population

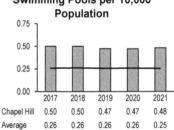

	2017	2018	2019	2020	2021
Chapel Hill	0.50	0.50	0.47	0.47	0.48
Average	0.26	0.26	0.26	0.26	0.25

Athletic Fields per 10,000 Population

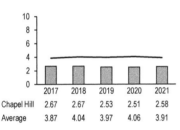

	2017	2018	2019	2020	2021
Chapel Hill	2.67	2.67	2.53	2.51	2.58
Average	3.87	4.04	3.97	4.06	3.91

Playgrounds per 10,000 Population

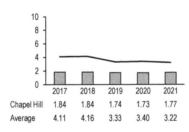

	2017	2018	2019	2020	2021
Chapel Hill	1.84	1.84	1.74	1.73	1.77
Average	4.11	4.16	3.33	3.40	3.22

Miles of Land Trails per 10,000 Population

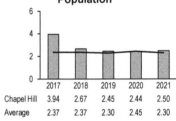

	2017	2018	2019	2020	2021
Chapel Hill	3.94	2.67	2.45	2.44	2.50
Average	2.37	2.37	2.30	2.45	2.30

Efficiency Measures

Total Core Parks and Recreation Costs per Acre

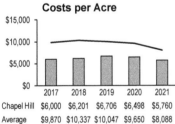

	2017	2018	2019	2020	2021
Chapel Hill	$6,000	$6,201	$6,706	$6,498	$5,760
Average	$9,870	$10,337	$10,047	$9,650	$8,088

Acres of Park Maintained per Maintenance FTE

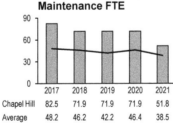

	2017	2018	2019	2020	2021
Chapel Hill	82.5	71.9	71.9	71.9	51.8
Average	48.2	46.2	42.2	46.4	38.5

Volunteer Hours in FTEs as a Percent of Paid Staff FTEs

	2017	2018	2019	2020	2021
Chapel Hill	17.4%	13.2%	10.8%	5.6%	3.1%
Average	18.9%	19.7%	21.9%	6.1%	6.7%

Effectiveness Measures

Revenue Gained as a Percent of Total Core Costs

	2017	2018	2019	2020	2021
Chapel Hill	17.3%	20.8%	19.3%	13.4%	10.1%
Average	13.7%	14.6%	15.1%	8.7%	7.9%

Acts of Vandalism at Parks Facilities per 10,000 Population

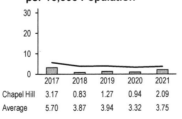

	2017	2018	2019	2020	2021
Chapel Hill	3.17	0.83	1.27	0.94	2.09
Average	5.70	3.87	3.94	3.32	3.75

Explanatory Information

Service Level and Delivery
The City of Concord provides recreation services through the separate Parks and Recreation Department. The city provides an array of facilities and activities for recreation.

The city has thirteen separate parks and sites. These parks cover 400 land acres. The city has seventeen miles of recreational trails, most of them paved.

In addition to the core parks and recreational facilities, Concord has two small amphitheaters and one boat ramp.

Conditions Affecting Service, Performance, and Costs

Municipal Profile

Population (OSBM 2020)	105,936
Land Area (Square Miles)	63.65
Persons per Square Mile	1,664
Topography	Flat; gently rolling
Climate	Temperate; little ice and snow

Service Profile

Parks and Recreation Staff
Administrative Position FTEs	7.0
Maintenance Staff FTEs	0.0
Program and Facility FTEs	28.0
Other Staff FTEs	0.0
TOTAL	35.0

Number of Parks and Sites	13
Total Land Acreage in Parks	400.3
Miles of Trails in Parks	17.1

Recreational Facilities
Indoor and Outdoor Pools	1
Recreation Centers	4
Outdoor Basketball Courts	5
Outdoor Tennis Courts	14
Playgrounds	13
Diamond Fields	20
Rectangular Fields	11
Other Athletic Fields	3
Picnic Shelters	15

Parks and Recreation Revenues
User Fees	$220,670
Grants	$0
Sponsorships	$12,375
Donations	$0

Full Cost Profile

Cost Breakdown by Percentage
Personal Services	24.9%
Operating Costs	68.1%
Capital Costs	7.0%
TOTAL	100.0%

Cost Breakdown in Dollars
Personal Services	$1,740,517
Operating Costs	$4,759,722
Capital Costs	$489,856
TOTAL	$6,990,095

Concord — Core Parks and Recreation

Key: Concord ■ Benchmarking Average — Fiscal Years 2017 through 2021

Resource Measures

Core Parks and Recreation Services per Capita

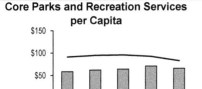

	2017	2018	2019	2020	2021
Concord	$59	$62	$64	$71	$66
Average	$91	$95	$96	$93	$83

Core Parks and Recreation Staff per 10,000 Population

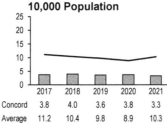

	2017	2018	2019	2020	2021
Concord	3.8	4.0	3.6	3.8	3.3
Average	11.2	10.4	9.8	8.9	10.3

Facilities Measures

Land Acres of Parks per 10,000 Population

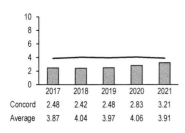

	2017	2018	2019	2020	2021
Concord	25.45	24.88	24.41	40.19	37.78
Average	143.50	143.92	137.34	125.84	136.33

Recreation Centers per 10,000 Population

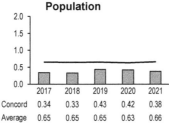

	2017	2018	2019	2020	2021
Concord	0.34	0.33	0.43	0.42	0.38
Average	0.65	0.65	0.65	0.63	0.66

Swimming Pools per 10,000 Population

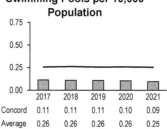

	2017	2018	2019	2020	2021
Concord	0.11	0.11	0.11	0.10	0.09
Average	0.26	0.26	0.26	0.26	0.25

Athletic Fields per 10,000 Population

	2017	2018	2019	2020	2021
Concord	2.48	2.42	2.48	2.83	3.21
Average	3.87	4.04	3.97	4.06	3.91

Playgrounds per 10,000 Population

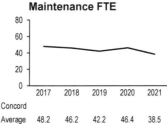

	2017	2018	2019	2020	2021
Concord	1.58	1.54	1.40	1.36	1.23
Average	4.11	4.16	3.33	3.40	3.22

Miles of Land Trails per 10,000 Population

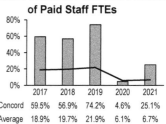

	2017	2018	2019	2020	2021
Concord	1.20	1.71	1.32	1.66	1.61
Average	2.37	2.37	2.30	2.45	2.30

Efficiency Measures

Total Core Parks and Recreation Costs per Acre

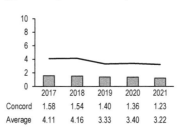

	2017	2018	2019	2020	2021
Concord	$23,056	$24,913	$26,303	$17,683	$17,464
Average	$9,870	$10,337	$10,047	$9,650	$8,088

Acres of Park Maintained per Maintenance FTE

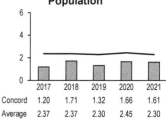

	2017	2018	2019	2020	2021
Concord					
Average	48.2	46.2	42.2	46.4	38.5

Volunteer Hours in FTEs as a Percent of Paid Staff FTEs

	2017	2018	2019	2020	2021
Concord	59.5%	56.9%	74.2%	4.6%	25.1%
Average	18.9%	19.7%	21.9%	6.1%	6.7%

Effectiveness Measures

Revenue Gained as a Percent of Total Core Costs

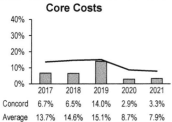

	2017	2018	2019	2020	2021
Concord	6.7%	6.5%	14.0%	2.9%	3.3%
Average	13.7%	14.6%	15.1%	8.7%	7.9%

Acts of Vandalism at Parks Facilities per 10,000 Population

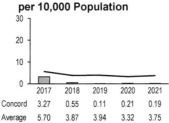

	2017	2018	2019	2020	2021
Concord	3.27	0.55	0.11	0.21	0.19
Average	5.70	3.87	3.94	3.32	3.75

Core Parks and Recreation 315

Fiscal Year 2020-21

Explanatory Information

Service Level and Delivery

The City of Goldsboro provides recreation services through the separate Parks and Recreation Department. The department aims to serve the community through programs in youth athletics, adult athletics, seniors, and special populations both adult and youth. The city has a cooperative agreement with the public school system. The city has also formalized an agreement with the U.S. Air Force Base Seymour Johnson for the use of certain base facilities. County residents from outside the city are also users of the Goldsboro city system facilities and programmed activities.

The city has fourteen separate parks, covering 233 acres. There are about five miles of trails, two outdoor pools, greenways, and a number of school indoor and outdoor facilities.

In addition to the core parks and recreational facilities, Goldsboro has a historic property it manages. The city also runs a municipal golf course. The operation of this course is not included here in dollars or staff as part of core parks and recreation facilities and activities.

Conditions Affecting Service, Performance, and Costs

The City of Goldsboro joined the Benchmarking Project in July 2017, with the first year of data showing for FY 2016–17.

There are no extra fees charged for non-resident users of Goldsboro's facilities. Goldsboro is one of just two municipalities in Wayne County that has a Parks and Recreation Department. Wayne County does not have a Parks and Recreation Department as one of its services offered. Goldsboro Parks and Recreation has teamed up with the Travel and Tourism Department to bring sports tournaments to Goldsboro. This helps expose more people to the city's offering of services and facilities.

Municipal Profile	
Population (OSBM 2020)	34,156
Land Area (Square Miles)	29.45
Persons per Square Mile	1,160
Topography	Flat
Climate	Temperate; little ice and snow

Service Profile	
Parks and Recreation Staff	
Administrative Position FTEs	5.0
Maintenance Staff FTEs	26.0
Program and Facility FTEs	11.0
Other Staff FTEs	7.5
TOTAL	49.5
Number of Parks and Sites	14
Total Land Acreage in Parks	233.0
Miles of Trails in Parks	4.5
Recreational Facilities	
Indoor and Outdoor Pools	2
Recreation Centers	4
Outdoor Basketball Courts	11
Outdoor Tennis Courts	18
Playgrounds	10
Diamond Fields	4
Rectangular Fields	13
Other Athletic Fields	6
Picnic Shelters	13
Parks and Recreation Revenues	
User Fees	$102,723
Grants	$19,388
Sponsorships	$55,000
Donations	$0

Full Cost Profile	
Cost Breakdown by Percentage	
Personal Services	77.6%
Operating Costs	22.4%
Capital Costs	0.0%
TOTAL	100.0%
Cost Breakdown in Dollars	
Personal Services	$2,241,997
Operating Costs	$645,544
Capital Costs	$0
TOTAL	$2,887,541

Key: Goldsboro ▨   Benchmarking Average —   Fiscal Years 2017 through 2021

Resource Measures

Core Parks and Recreation Services per Capita

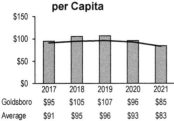

	2017	2018	2019	2020	2021
Goldsboro	$95	$105	$107	$96	$85
Average	$91	$95	$96	$93	$83

Core Parks and Recreation Staff per 10,000 Population

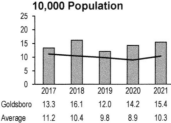

	2017	2018	2019	2020	2021
Goldsboro	13.3	16.1	12.0	14.2	15.4
Average	11.2	10.4	9.8	8.9	10.3

Facilities Measures

Land Acres of Parks per 10,000 Population

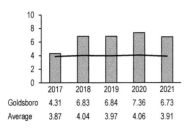

	2017	2018	2019	2020	2021
Goldsboro	48.51	50.47	69.27	68.59	68.22
Average	143.50	143.92	137.34	125.84	136.33

Recreation Centers per 10,000 Population

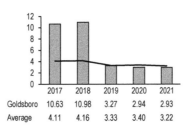

	2017	2018	2019	2020	2021
Goldsboro	0.57	0.59	0.59	0.88	0.88
Average	0.65	0.65	0.65	0.63	0.66

Swimming Pools per 10,000 Population

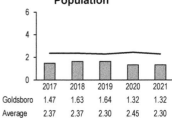

	2017	2018	2019	2020	2021
Goldsboro	0.57	0.59	0.59	0.59	0.59
Average	0.26	0.26	0.26	0.26	0.25

Athletic Fields per 10,000 Population

	2017	2018	2019	2020	2021
Goldsboro	4.31	6.83	6.84	7.36	6.73
Average	3.87	4.04	3.97	4.06	3.91

Playgrounds per 10,000 Population

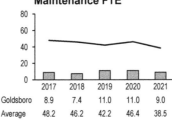

	2017	2018	2019	2020	2021
Goldsboro	10.63	10.98	3.27	2.94	2.93
Average	4.11	4.16	3.33	3.40	3.22

Miles of Land Trails per 10,000 Population

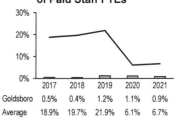

	2017	2018	2019	2020	2021
Goldsboro	1.47	1.63	1.64	1.32	1.32
Average	2.37	2.37	2.30	2.45	2.30

Efficiency Measures

Total Core Parks and Recreation Costs per Acre

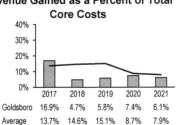

	2017	2018	2019	2020	2021
Goldsboro	$19,567	$20,815	$15,420	$13,998	$12,393
Average	$9,870	$10,337	$10,047	$9,650	$8,088

Acres of Park Maintained per Maintenance FTE

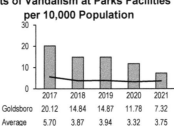

	2017	2018	2019	2020	2021
Goldsboro	8.9	7.4	11.0	11.0	9.0
Average	48.2	46.2	42.2	46.4	38.5

Volunteer Hours in FTEs as a Percent of Paid Staff FTEs

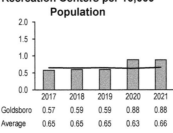

	2017	2018	2019	2020	2021
Goldsboro	0.5%	0.4%	1.2%	1.1%	0.9%
Average	18.9%	19.7%	21.9%	6.1%	6.7%

Effectiveness Measures

Revenue Gained as a Percent of Total Core Costs

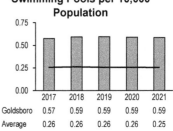

	2017	2018	2019	2020	2021
Goldsboro	16.9%	4.7%	5.8%	7.4%	6.1%
Average	13.7%	14.6%	15.1%	8.7%	7.9%

Acts of Vandalism at Parks Facilities per 10,000 Population

	2017	2018	2019	2020	2021
Goldsboro	20.12	14.84	14.87	11.78	7.32
Average	5.70	3.87	3.94	3.32	3.75

Greensboro

Core Parks and Recreation

Fiscal Year 2020-21

Explanatory Information

Service Level and Delivery

The City of Greensboro provides recreation services through the separate Parks and Recreation Department. The city has several cooperative agreements with the local schools and some nonprofits for the provision of services or use of facilities. The city provides a full array of recreational facilities and activities.

The city has 512 separate parks and sites. These parks cover 7,449 land acres; most of them are developed and include dedicated drainageway and open spaces. In addition, the city has a number of acres in water space as part of the parks system. The city has about 102 miles of trails.

In addition to the core parks and recreational facilities, Greensboro has a large outdoor-performance-event site, a historic property, a famers market, a boat ramp and marina, and operates two municipal golf courses, four municipal cemetaries, and four botanical gardens. The operation of these other facilities is not included in the Core Parks and Recreation comparisons reported here. These facilities are not included here in dollars or staff as part of core parks and recreation facilities and activities.

Conditions Affecting Service, Performance, and Costs

Greensboro has been updating its lists of properties, including a number of drainageway and open-space properties that were dedicated to the city but never accepted. These parcels have been added to the inventory of parks, which has increased the number of parks reported.

Municipal Profile

Population (OSBM 2020)	299,556
Land Area (Square Miles)	129.62
Persons per Square Mile	2,311
Topography	Flat
Climate	Temperate; little ice and snow

Service Profile

Parks and Recreation Staff

Administrative Position FTEs	17.0
Maintenance Staff FTEs	79.5
Program and Facility FTEs	41.0
Other Staff FTEs	0.0
TOTAL	137.5

Number of Parks and Sites	512
Total Land Acreage in Parks	7,449.0
Miles of Trails in Parks	101.8

Recreational Facilities

Indoor and Outdoor Pools	5
Recreation Centers	12
Outdoor Basketball Courts	46
Outdoor Tennis Courts	75
Playgrounds	105
Diamond Fields	39
Rectangular Fields	36
Other Athletic Fields	0
Picnic Shelters	124

Parks and Recreation Revenues

User Fees	$618,675
Grants	$35,610
Sponsorships	$2,000
Donations	$17,269

Full Cost Profile

Cost Breakdown by Percentage

Personal Services	61.0%
Operating Costs	39.0%
Capital Costs	0.0%
TOTAL	100.0%

Cost Breakdown in Dollars

Personal Services	$9,851,807
Operating Costs	$6,311,099
Capital Costs	$0
TOTAL	$16,162,906

Key: Greensboro ▨   Benchmarking Average —   Fiscal Years 2017 through 2021

Resource Measures

Core Parks and Recreation Services per Capita

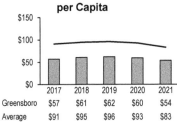

	2017	2018	2019	2020	2021
Greensboro	$57	$61	$62	$60	$54
Average	$91	$95	$96	$93	$83

Core Parks and Recreation Staff per 10,000 Population

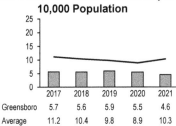

	2017	2018	2019	2020	2021
Greensboro	5.7	5.6	5.9	5.5	4.6
Average	11.2	10.4	9.8	8.9	10.3

Facilities Measures

Land Acres of Parks per 10,000 Population

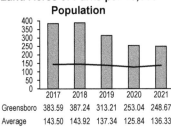

	2017	2018	2019	2020	2021
Greensboro	383.59	387.24	313.21	253.04	248.67
Average	143.50	143.92	137.34	125.84	136.33

Recreation Centers per 10,000 Population

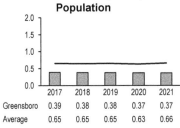

	2017	2018	2019	2020	2021
Greensboro	0.39	0.38	0.38	0.37	0.37
Average	0.65	0.65	0.65	0.63	0.66

Swimming Pools per 10,000 Population

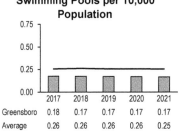

	2017	2018	2019	2020	2021
Greensboro	0.18	0.17	0.17	0.17	0.17
Average	0.26	0.26	0.26	0.26	0.25

Athletic Fields per 10,000 Population

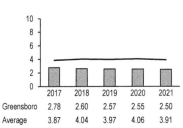

	2017	2018	2019	2020	2021
Greensboro	2.78	2.60	2.57	2.55	2.50
Average	3.87	4.04	3.97	4.06	3.91

Playgrounds per 10,000 Population

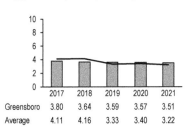

	2017	2018	2019	2020	2021
Greensboro	3.80	3.64	3.59	3.57	3.51
Average	4.11	4.16	3.33	3.40	3.22

Miles of Land Trails per 10,000 Population

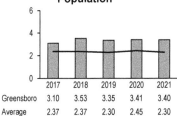

	2017	2018	2019	2020	2021
Greensboro	3.10	3.53	3.35	3.41	3.40
Average	2.37	2.37	2.30	2.45	2.30

Efficiency Measures

Total Core Parks and Recreation Costs per Acre

	2017	2018	2019	2020	2021
Greensboro	$1,493	$1,570	$1,991	$2,358	$2,170
Average	$9,870	$10,337	$10,047	$9,650	$8,088

Acres of Park Maintained per Maintenance FTE

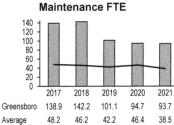

	2017	2018	2019	2020	2021
Greensboro	138.9	142.2	101.1	94.7	93.7
Average	48.2	46.2	42.2	46.4	38.5

Volunteer Hours in FTEs as a Percent of Paid Staff FTEs

	2017	2018	2019	2020	2021
Greensboro	16.3%	13.1%	8.2%	9.5%	2.4%
Average	18.9%	19.7%	21.9%	6.1%	6.7%

Effectiveness Measures

Revenue Gained as a Percent of Total Core Costs

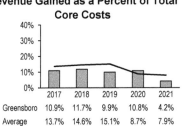

	2017	2018	2019	2020	2021
Greensboro	10.9%	11.7%	9.9%	10.8%	4.2%
Average	13.7%	14.6%	15.1%	8.7%	7.9%

Acts of Vandalism at Parks Facilities per 10,000 Population

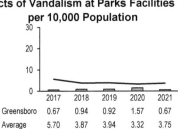

	2017	2018	2019	2020	2021
Greensboro	0.67	0.94	0.92	1.57	0.67
Average	5.70	3.87	3.94	3.32	3.75

Fiscal Year 2020-21

Explanatory Information		Municipal Profile	

Service Level and Delivery

The City of Greenville provides recreation services through the separate Recreation and Parks Department. The city has a number of ad hoc or handshake agreements with other organizations but is moving to more formal agreements. Partner groups include Pitt County, local sports organizations, and concert entertainment groups.

The city has twenty-eight separate parks and sites. These parks cover 1,834 acres; about two-thirds of them are developed. The city has thirteen miles of trails.

In addition to the core parks and recreational facilities, Greenville has a large outdoor-performance-event site, a historic property, a boat ramp, a museum, and an eighteen-hole golf course. The operation of these other facilities is not included in the Core Parks and Recreation comparisons reported here. These facilities are not included here in dollars or staff as part of core parks and recreation facilities and activities.

Conditions Affecting Service, Performance, and Costs

No data were reported for FY 2019-20 for the city of Greenville.

Municipal Profile

Population (OSBM 2020)	87,428
Land Area (Square Miles)	35.66
Persons per Square Mile	2,452
Topography	Flat
Climate	Temperate; little ice and snow

Service Profile

Parks and Recreation Staff	
Administrative Position FTEs	7.0
Maintenance Staff FTEs	71.0
Program and Facility FTEs	71.0
Other Staff FTEs	5.5
TOTAL	154.5

Number of Parks and Sites	28
Total Land Acreage in Parks	1833.6
Miles of Trails in Parks	13.0

Recreational Facilities	
Indoor and Outdoor Pools	2
Recreation Centers	8
Outdoor Basketball Courts	1
Outdoor Tennis Courts	18
Playgrounds	18
Diamond Fields	16
Rectangular Fields	5
Other Athletic Fields	3
Picnic Shelters	24

Parks and Recreation Revenues	
User Fees	$428,670
Grants	$24,383
Sponsorships	$0
Donations	$4,839

Full Cost Profile

Cost Breakdown by Percentage	
Personal Services	58.0%
Operating Costs	34.3%
Capital Costs	7.7%
TOTAL	100.0%

Cost Breakdown in Dollars	
Personal Services	$4,552,545
Operating Costs	$2,695,543
Capital Costs	$604,717
TOTAL	$7,852,805

Resource Measures

Core Parks and Recreation Services per Capita

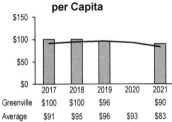

	2017	2018	2019	2020	2021
Greenville	$100	$100	$96		$90
Average	$91	$95	$96	$93	$83

Core Parks and Recreation Staff per 10,000 Population

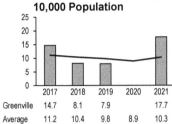

	2017	2018	2019	2020	2021
Greenville	14.7	8.1	7.9		17.7
Average	11.2	10.4	9.8	8.9	10.3

Facilities Measures

Land Acres of Parks per 10,000 Population

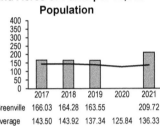

	2017	2018	2019	2020	2021
Greenville	166.03	164.28	163.55		209.72
Average	143.50	143.92	137.34	125.84	136.33

Recreation Centers per 10,000 Population

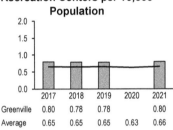

	2017	2018	2019	2020	2021
Greenville	0.80	0.78	0.78		0.80
Average	0.65	0.65	0.65	0.63	0.66

Swimming Pools per 10,000 Population

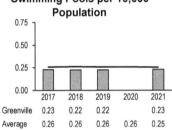

	2017	2018	2019	2020	2021
Greenville	0.23	0.22	0.22		0.23
Average	0.26	0.26	0.26	0.26	0.25

Athletic Fields per 10,000 Population

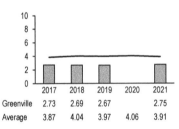

	2017	2018	2019	2020	2021
Greenville	2.73	2.69	2.67		2.75
Average	3.87	4.04	3.97	4.06	3.91

Playgrounds per 10,000 Population

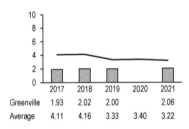

	2017	2018	2019	2020	2021
Greenville	1.93	2.02	2.00		2.06
Average	4.11	4.16	3.33	3.40	3.22

Miles of Land Trails per 10,000 Population

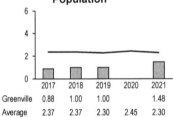

	2017	2018	2019	2020	2021
Greenville	0.88	1.00	1.00		1.48
Average	2.37	2.37	2.30	2.45	2.30

Efficiency Measures

Total Core Parks and Recreation Costs per Acre

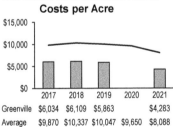

	2017	2018	2019	2020	2021
Greenville	$6,034	$6,109	$5,863		$4,283
Average	$9,870	$10,337	$10,047	$9,650	$8,088

Acres of Park Maintained per Maintenance FTE

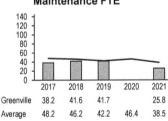

	2017	2018	2019	2020	2021
Greenville	38.2	41.6	41.7		25.8
Average	48.2	46.2	42.2	46.4	38.5

Volunteer Hours in FTEs as a Percent of Paid Staff FTEs

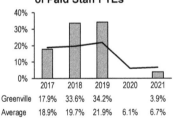

	2017	2018	2019	2020	2021
Greenville	17.9%	33.6%	34.2%		3.9%
Average	18.9%	19.7%	21.9%	6.1%	6.7%

Effectiveness Measures

Revenue Gained as a Percent of Total Core Costs

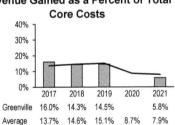

	2017	2018	2019	2020	2021
Greenville	16.0%	14.3%	14.5%		5.8%
Average	13.7%	14.6%	15.1%	8.7%	7.9%

Acts of Vandalism at Parks Facilities per 10,000 Population

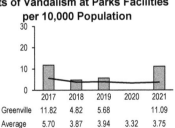

	2017	2018	2019	2020	2021
Greenville	11.82	4.82	5.68		11.09
Average	5.70	3.87	3.94	3.32	3.75

Explanatory Information

Service Level and Delivery

The City of Hickory Parks and Recreation Department is a separate department under the city organization. The city has partnerships with other organizations to provide recreational services, including a priority-use agreement with local schools for use of facilities over other non-school users and a priority-use agreement with Catawba Valley Youth Soccer for use of city soccer fields.

The city has twenty-seven separate parks and sites. This includes 558 acres of park acreage, mostly developed. The city has sixteen miles of trails.

In addition to the core parks and recreational facilities, Hickory has one historic property, one professional sports facility, one boat ramp, one museum, two community gardens, and a tower ropes course. The operation of these other facilities is not included in the Core Parks and Recreation comparisons reported here. These facilities are not included here in dollars or staff as part of core parks and recreation facilities and activities.

Conditions Affecting Service, Performance, and Costs

Municipal Profile

Population (OSBM 2020)	43,578
Land Area (Square Miles)	30.50
Persons per Square Mile	1,429
Topography	Gently rolling
Climate	Temperate; some ice and snow

Service Profile

Parks and Recreation Staff

Administrative Position FTEs	5.0
Maintenance Staff FTEs	26.5
Program and Facility FTEs	18.3
Other Staff FTEs	0.0
TOTAL	49.8

Number of Parks and Sites	27
Total Land Acreage in Parks	558.0
Miles of Trails in Parks	16.0

Recreational Facilities

Indoor and Outdoor Pools	0
Recreation Centers	7
Outdoor Basketball Courts	17
Outdoor Tennis Courts	16
Playgrounds	40
Diamond Fields	11
Rectangular Fields	12
Other Athletic Fields	0
Picnic Shelters	13

Parks and Recreation Revenues

User Fees	$112,384
Grants	$50,000
Sponsorships	$0
Donations	$15,000

Full Cost Profile

Cost Breakdown by Percentage

Personal Services	34.3%
Operating Costs	42.0%
Capital Costs	23.7%
TOTAL	100.0%

Cost Breakdown in Dollars

Personal Services	$943,314
Operating Costs	$1,154,982
Capital Costs	$650,200
TOTAL	$2,748,496

Key: Hickory ▧   Benchmarking Average —   Fiscal Years 2017 through 2021

Resource Measures

Core Parks and Recreation Services per Capita

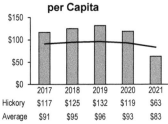

	2017	2018	2019	2020	2021
Hickory	$117	$125	$132	$119	$63
Average	$91	$95	$96	$93	$83

Core Parks and Recreation Staff per 10,000 Population

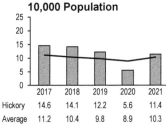

	2017	2018	2019	2020	2021
Hickory	14.6	14.1	12.2	5.6	11.4
Average	11.2	10.4	9.8	8.9	10.3

Facilities Measures

Land Acres of Parks per 10,000 Population

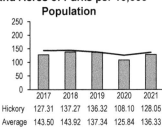

	2017	2018	2019	2020	2021
Hickory	127.31	137.27	136.32	108.10	128.05
Average	143.50	143.92	137.34	125.84	136.33

Recreation Centers per 10,000 Population

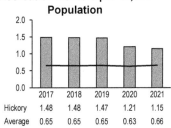

	2017	2018	2019	2020	2021
Hickory	1.48	1.48	1.47	1.21	1.15
Average	0.65	0.65	0.65	0.63	0.66

Swimming Pools per 10,000 Population

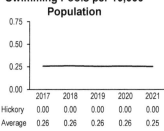

	2017	2018	2019	2020	2021
Hickory	0.00	0.00	0.00	0.00	0.00
Average	0.26	0.26	0.26	0.26	0.25

Athletic Fields per 10,000 Population

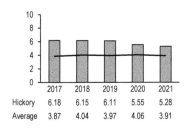

	2017	2018	2019	2020	2021
Hickory	6.18	6.15	6.11	5.55	5.28
Average	3.87	4.04	3.97	4.06	3.91

Playgrounds per 10,000 Population

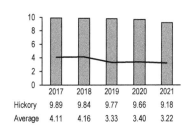

	2017	2018	2019	2020	2021
Hickory	9.89	9.84	9.77	9.66	9.18
Average	4.11	4.16	3.33	3.40	3.22

Miles of Land Trails per 10,000 Population

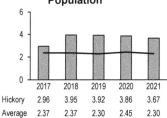

	2017	2018	2019	2020	2021
Hickory	2.96	3.95	3.92	3.86	3.67
Average	2.37	2.37	2.30	2.45	2.30

Efficiency Measures

Total Core Parks and Recreation Costs per Acre

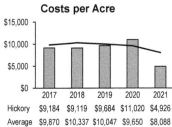

	2017	2018	2019	2020	2021
Hickory	$9,184	$9,119	$9,684	$11,020	$4,926
Average	$9,870	$10,337	$10,047	$9,650	$8,088

Acres of Park Maintained per Maintenance FTE

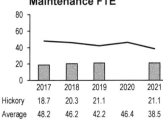

	2017	2018	2019	2020	2021
Hickory	18.7	20.3	21.1		21.1
Average	48.2	46.2	42.2	46.4	38.5

Volunteer Hours in FTEs as a Percent of Paid Staff FTEs

	2017	2018	2019	2020	2021
Hickory	47.7%	48.6%	60.4%		
Average	18.9%	19.7%	21.9%	6.1%	6.7%

Effectiveness Measures

Revenue Gained as a Percent of Total Core Costs

	2017	2018	2019	2020	2021
Hickory	7.8%	6.4%	5.3%	4.0%	6.5%
Average	13.7%	14.6%	15.1%	8.7%	7.9%

Acts of Vandalism at Parks Facilities per 10,000 Population

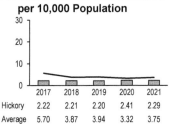

	2017	2018	2019	2020	2021
Hickory	2.22	2.21	2.20	2.41	2.29
Average	5.70	3.87	3.94	3.32	3.75

Explanatory Information

Service Level and Delivery

The City of Raleigh Parks, Recreation, and Cultural Resources Department is a stand-alone unit within the city. The department is comprised of five divisions: Business Process Management, Park Development and Communications, Parks, Recreation, and Resources.

The department has a public/private partnership with the Dix Park Conservancy to provide funding for master planning and programming at Dorothea Dix Park. The city also has joint-use agreements and memorandums of understanding with other entities, including Wake County, the Wake County Public School System, NC State University, and local nonprofit organizations.

Raleigh has a full array of recreational facilities available. The department plays a leading role in determining the quality of life and character of the Capital City. With over 6,200 acres of parkland, 108 miles of greenway trails, and over 1.3 million square feet of facilities, the department provides a wide range of creative programming opportunities that promote the social, cultural, mental, and physical well-being of citizens. The city's vision for its parks, recreation, and cultural resources system is "bringing people to parks and parks to people."

In addition to traditional recreational facilities, Raleigh has a large outdoor-performance-event site, historic properties, a performing arts center, boats ramps, and city museums. These facilities are not included here in dollars or staff as part of core parks and recreation facilities and activities.

Conditions Affecting Service, Performance, and Costs

Municipal Profile

Population (OSBM 2020)	468,977
Land Area (Square Miles)	146.47
Persons per Square Mile	3,202
Topography	Flat; gently rolling
Climate	Temperate; little ice and snow

Service Profile

Parks and Recreation Staff

Administrative Position FTEs	20.9
Maintenance Staff FTEs	182.0
Program and Facility FTEs	523.5
Other Staff FTEs	33.0
TOTAL	759.4

Number of Parks and Sites	200
Total Land Acreage in Parks	6,209.0
Miles of Trails in Parks	108.0

Recreational Facilities

Indoor and Outdoor Pools	8
Recreation Centers	41
Outdoor Basketball Courts	64
Outdoor Tennis Courts	110
Playgrounds	106
Diamond Fields	59
Rectangular Fields	0
Other Athletic Fields	41
Picnic Shelters	90

Parks and Recreation Revenues

User Fees	$4,980,117
Grants	$2,916,500
Sponsorships	$0
Donations	$21,088

Full Cost Profile

Cost Breakdown by Percentage

Personal Services	61.6%
Operating Costs	33.3%
Capital Costs	5.1%
TOTAL	100.0%

Cost Breakdown in Dollars

Personal Services	$32,630,770
Operating Costs	$17,610,798
Capital Costs	$2,711,322
TOTAL	$52,952,890

Raleigh

Core Parks and Recreation

Resource Measures

Core Parks and Recreation Services per Capita

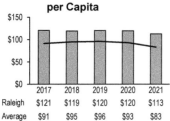

	2017	2018	2019	2020	2021
Raleigh	$121	$119	$120	$120	$113
Average	$91	$95	$96	$93	$83

Core Parks and Recreation Staff per 10,000 Population

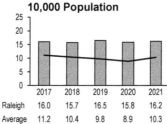

	2017	2018	2019	2020	2021
Raleigh	16.0	15.7	16.5	15.8	16.2
Average	11.2	10.4	9.8	8.9	10.3

Facilities Measures

Land Acres of Parks per 10,000 Population

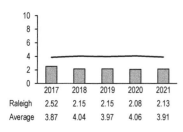

	2017	2018	2019	2020	2021
Raleigh	137.38	133.92	131.92	130.87	132.39
Average	143.50	143.92	137.34	125.84	136.33

Recreation Centers per 10,000 Population

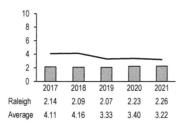

	2017	2018	2019	2020	2021
Raleigh	0.87	0.85	0.84	0.82	0.83
Average	0.65	0.65	0.65	0.63	0.66

Swimming Pools per 10,000 Population

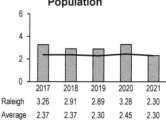

	2017	2018	2019	2020	2021
Raleigh	0.20	0.20	0.17	0.17	0.17
Average	0.26	0.26	0.26	0.26	0.25

Athletic Fields per 10,000 Population

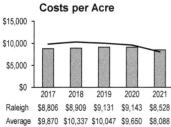

	2017	2018	2019	2020	2021
Raleigh	2.52	2.15	2.15	2.08	2.13
Average	3.87	4.04	3.97	4.06	3.91

Playgrounds per 10,000 Population

	2017	2018	2019	2020	2021
Raleigh	2.14	2.09	2.07	2.23	2.26
Average	4.11	4.16	3.33	3.40	3.22

Miles of Land Trails per 10,000 Population

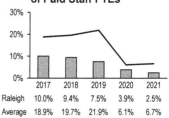

	2017	2018	2019	2020	2021
Raleigh	3.26	2.91	2.89	3.28	2.30
Average	2.37	2.37	2.30	2.45	2.30

Efficiency Measures

Total Core Parks and Recreation Costs per Acre

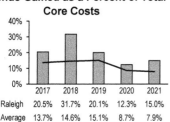

	2017	2018	2019	2020	2021
Raleigh	$8,806	$8,909	$9,131	$9,143	$8,528
Average	$9,870	$10,337	$10,047	$9,650	$8,088

Acres of Park Maintained per Maintenance FTE

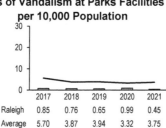

	2017	2018	2019	2020	2021
Raleigh	35.7	31.3	35.1	34.8	34.1
Average	48.2	46.2	42.2	46.4	38.5

Volunteer Hours in FTEs as a Percent of Paid Staff FTEs

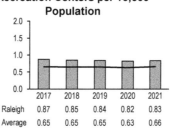

	2017	2018	2019	2020	2021
Raleigh	10.0%	9.4%	7.5%	3.9%	2.5%
Average	18.9%	19.7%	21.9%	6.1%	6.7%

Effectiveness Measures

Revenue Gained as a Percent of Total Core Costs

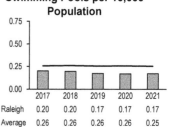

	2017	2018	2019	2020	2021
Raleigh	20.5%	31.7%	20.1%	12.3%	15.0%
Average	13.7%	14.6%	15.1%	8.7%	7.9%

Acts of Vandalism at Parks Facilities per 10,000 Population

	2017	2018	2019	2020	2021
Raleigh	0.85	0.76	0.65	0.99	0.45
Average	5.70	3.87	3.94	3.32	3.75

Wilson

Core Parks and Recreation

Fiscal Year 2020-21

Explanatory Information

Service Level and Delivery

The City of Wilson Parks and Recreation Department is a separate department under the city organization. The city has partnerships with other organizations to provide recreational services, including the Wilson County Schools, the Wilson Youth Soccer Association, Wilson City Little League, Special Olympics, Youth Soccer Association, the Senior Games of North Carolina, and the Wilson Arts Council.

The city has twenty-eight separate parks and sites. These parks cover 400 acres, most currently undeveloped. The city has seven-and-half miles of trails.

In addition to the core parks and recreational facilities, Wilson has three boat ramps and one museum. The city also runs a municipal eighteen-hole golf course. The operation of these other facilities is not included in the Core Parks and Recreation comparisons reported here. These facilities are not included here in dollars or staff as part of core parks and recreation facilities and activities.

Conditions Affecting Service, Performance, and Costs

Municipal Profile

Population (OSBM 2020)	47,769
Land Area (Square Miles)	31.02
Persons per Square Mile	1,540
Topography	Flat
Climate	Temperate; little ice and snow

Service Profile

Parks and Recreation Staff

Administrative Position FTEs	6.5
Maintenance Staff FTEs	17.0
Program and Facility FTEs	28.0
Other Staff FTEs	4.0
TOTAL	55.5

Number of Parks and Sites	28
Total Land Acreage in Parks	400.0
Miles of Trails in Parks	7.5

Recreational Facilities

Indoor and Outdoor Pools	2
Recreation Centers	4
Outdoor Basketball Courts	7
Outdoor Tennis Courts	16
Playgrounds	26
Diamond Fields	11
Rectangular Fields	14
Other Athletic Fields	1
Picnic Shelters	19

Parks and Recreation Revenues

User Fees	$485,000
Grants	$8,000
Sponsorships	$65,000
Donations	$0

Full Cost Profile

Cost Breakdown by Percentage

Personal Services	59.4%
Operating Costs	32.1%
Capital Costs	8.4%
TOTAL	100.0%

Cost Breakdown in Dollars

Personal Services	$3,110,969
Operating Costs	$1,682,330
Capital Costs	$441,195
TOTAL	$5,234,494

Wilson

Core Parks and Recreation

Resource Measures

Core Parks and Recreation Services per Capita

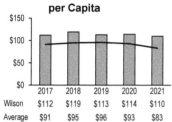

	2017	2018	2019	2020	2021
Wilson	$112	$119	$113	$114	$110
Average	$91	$95	$96	$93	$83

Core Parks and Recreation Staff per 10,000 Population

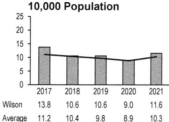

	2017	2018	2019	2020	2021
Wilson	13.8	10.6	10.6	9.0	11.6
Average	11.2	10.4	9.8	8.9	10.3

Facilities Measures

Land Acres of Parks per 10,000 Population

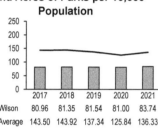

	2017	2018	2019	2020	2021
Wilson	80.96	81.35	81.54	81.00	83.74
Average	143.50	143.92	137.34	125.84	136.33

Recreation Centers per 10,000 Population

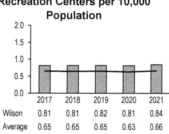

	2017	2018	2019	2020	2021
Wilson	0.81	0.81	0.82	0.81	0.84
Average	0.65	0.65	0.65	0.63	0.66

Swimming Pools per 10,000 Population

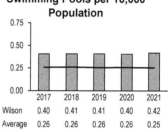

	2017	2018	2019	2020	2021
Wilson	0.40	0.41	0.41	0.40	0.42
Average	0.26	0.26	0.26	0.26	0.25

Athletic Fields per 10,000 Population

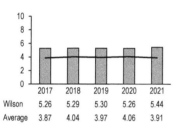

	2017	2018	2019	2020	2021
Wilson	5.26	5.29	5.30	5.26	5.44
Average	3.87	4.04	3.97	4.06	3.91

Playgrounds per 10,000 Population

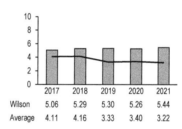

	2017	2018	2019	2020	2021
Wilson	5.06	5.29	5.30	5.26	5.44
Average	4.11	4.16	3.33	3.40	3.22

Miles of Land Trails per 10,000 Population

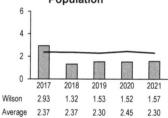

	2017	2018	2019	2020	2021
Wilson	2.93	1.32	1.53	1.52	1.57
Average	2.37	2.37	2.30	2.45	2.30

Efficiency Measures

Total Core Parks and Recreation Costs per Acre

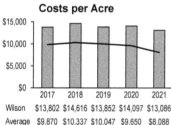

	2017	2018	2019	2020	2021
Wilson	$13,802	$14,616	$13,852	$14,097	$13,086
Average	$9,870	$10,337	$10,047	$9,650	$8,088

Acres of Park Maintained per Maintenance FTE

	2017	2018	2019	2020	2021
Wilson	30.8	25.0	25.0	25.0	23.5
Average	48.2	46.2	42.2	46.4	38.5

Volunteer Hours in FTEs as a Percent of Paid Staff FTEs

	2017	2018	2019	2020	2021
Wilson	8.6%	12.0%	12.9%	15.1%	12.1%
Average	18.9%	19.7%	21.9%	6.1%	6.7%

Effectiveness Measures

Revenue Gained as a Percent of Total Core Costs

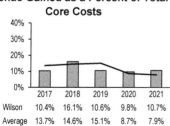

	2017	2018	2019	2020	2021
Wilson	10.4%	16.1%	10.6%	9.8%	10.7%
Average	13.7%	14.6%	15.1%	8.7%	7.9%

Acts of Vandalism at Parks Facilities per 10,000 Population

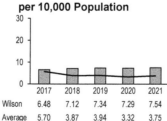

	2017	2018	2019	2020	2021
Wilson	6.48	7.12	7.34	7.29	7.54
Average	5.70	3.87	3.94	3.32	3.75

Fiscal Year 2020-21

Explanatory Information

Service Level and Delivery

The City of Winston-Salem Recreation and Parks Department is a separate department under the city organization. The department is overseen by the advisory Parks and Recreation Commission, which has eleven members appointed by the mayor and approved by the city council. The city has formal cooperative arrangements with Forsyth County and various public-private partnerships with other organizations to provide recreational services.

The city has eighty-four separate parks and sites. This includes 4,279 acres of parkland, most of which is developed. The city has thirty-three miles of trails, about two-thirds of which are paved.

In addition to the core parks and recreational facilities, Winston-Salem has two large outdoor-performance-event sites, a historic property, one boat ramp, and one museum. The city also runs two municipal eighteen-hole golf courses. The operation of these other facilities is not included in the Core Parks and Recreation comparisons reported here. These facilities are not included here in dollars or staff as part of core parks and recreation facilities and activities.

Conditions Affecting Service, Performance, and Costs

Many Forsyth County residents make use of the city's parks and recreational facilities. Most of the city's facilities were built in the 1960s to 1980s and are aging. Several support services are in other departments to improve efficiency and reduce costs, including property maintenance and vegetation management.

Municipal Profile

Population (OSBM 2020)	249,986
Land Area (Square Miles)	132.59
Persons per Square Mile	1,885
Topography	Gently rolling
Climate	Temperate; some ice and snow

Service Profile

Parks and Recreation Staff	
Administrative Position FTEs	31.3
Maintenance Staff FTEs	67.8
Program and Facility FTEs	111.9
Other Staff FTEs	2.0
TOTAL	213.0

Number of Parks and Sites	84
Total Land Acreage in Parks	4,279.2
Miles of Trails in Parks	33.0

Recreational Facilities	
Indoor and Outdoor Pools	10
Recreation Centers	17
Outdoor Basketball Courts	23
Outdoor Tennis Courts	106
Playgrounds	46
Diamond Fields	47
Rectangular Fields	50
Other Athletic Fields	0
Picnic Shelters	51

Parks and Recreation Revenues	
User Fees	$526,945
Grants	$123,250
Sponsorships	$0
Donations	$1,735

Full Cost Profile

Cost Breakdown by Percentage	
Personal Services	51.2%
Operating Costs	33.7%
Capital Costs	15.1%
TOTAL	100.0%

Cost Breakdown in Dollars	
Personal Services	$7,113,984
Operating Costs	$4,676,905
Capital Costs	$2,090,317
TOTAL	$13,881,206

Winston-Salem   # Core Parks and Recreation

Key: Winston-Salem ▦   Benchmarking Average —   Fiscal Years 2017 through 2021

Resource Measures

Core Parks and Recreation Services per Capita

	2017	2018	2019	2020	2021
Winston-Salem	$50	$53	$55	$54	$56
Average	$91	$95	$96	$93	$83

Core Parks and Recreation Staff per 10,000 Population

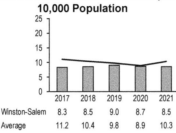

	2017	2018	2019	2020	2021
Winston-Salem	8.3	8.5	9.0	8.7	8.5
Average	11.2	10.4	9.8	8.9	10.3

Facilities Measures

Land Acres of Parks per 10,000 Population

	2017	2018	2019	2020	2021
Winston-Salem	160.10	158.66	159.99	174.85	171.18
Average	143.50	143.92	137.34	125.84	136.33

Recreation Centers per 10,000 Population

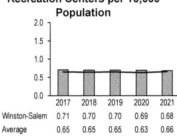

	2017	2018	2019	2020	2021
Winston-Salem	0.71	0.70	0.70	0.69	0.68
Average	0.65	0.65	0.65	0.63	0.66

Swimming Pools per 10,000 Population

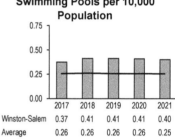

	2017	2018	2019	2020	2021
Winston-Salem	0.37	0.41	0.41	0.41	0.40
Average	0.26	0.26	0.26	0.26	0.25

Athletic Fields per 10,000 Population

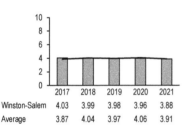

	2017	2018	2019	2020	2021
Winston-Salem	4.03	3.99	3.98	3.96	3.88
Average	3.87	4.04	3.97	4.06	3.91

Playgrounds per 10,000 Population

	2017	2018	2019	2020	2021
Winston-Salem	1.87	1.85	1.89	1.88	1.84
Average	4.11	4.16	3.33	3.40	3.22

Miles of Land Trails per 10,000 Population

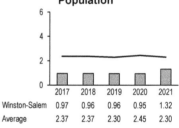

	2017	2018	2019	2020	2021
Winston-Salem	0.97	0.96	0.96	0.95	1.32
Average	2.37	2.37	2.30	2.45	2.30

Efficiency Measures

Total Core Parks and Recreation Costs per Acre

	2017	2018	2019	2020	2021
Winston-Salem	$3,104	$3,344	$3,444	$3,107	$3,244
Average	$9,870	$10,337	$10,047	$9,650	$8,088

Acres of Park Maintained per Maintenance FTE

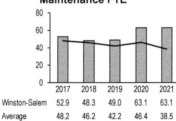

	2017	2018	2019	2020	2021
Winston-Salem	52.9	48.3	49.0	63.1	63.1
Average	48.2	46.2	42.2	46.4	38.5

Volunteer Hours in FTEs as a Percent of Paid Staff FTEs

	2017	2018	2019	2020	2021
Winston-Salem	3.5%	2.5%	2.7%	2.0%	2.0%
Average	18.9%	19.7%	21.9%	6.1%	6.7%

Effectiveness Measures

Revenue Gained as a Percent of Total Core Costs

	2017	2018	2019	2020	2021
Winston-Salem	7.5%	7.8%	7.2%	4.7%	4.7%
Average	13.7%	14.6%	15.1%	8.7%	7.9%

Acts of Vandalism at Parks Facilities per 10,000 Population

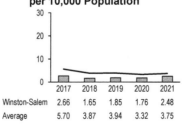

	2017	2018	2019	2020	2021
Winston-Salem	2.66	1.65	1.85	1.76	2.48
Average	5.70	3.87	3.94	3.32	3.75

CPSIA information can be obtained
at www.ICGtesting.com
Printed in the USA
LVHW050002150422
716233LV00007B/319